The Nineteenth-Century History
of English Studies

For my family

The
Nineteenth-Century
History of
English Studies

Edited by
ALAN BACON

Ashgate

Aldershot • Brookfield USA • Singapore • Sydney

Published by
Ashgate Publishing Limited
Gower House
Croft Road
Aldershot
Hants GU11 3HR
England

Ashgate Publishing Company
Old Post Road
Brookfield
Vermont 05036–9704
USA

British Library Cataloguing-in-Publication data

Bacon, Alan
   The nineteenth-century history of English studies. – (The nineteenth century series)
   1. English literature—19th century—History and criticism
   2. English literature—Study and teaching—History—19th century
   3. English language—Study and teaching—History—19th century
   I. Title
   820.9'008

Library of Congress Cataloguing-in-Publication Data

Bacon, Alan.
   The nineteenth-century history of English studies / Alan Bacon.
      p.   cm. – (Nineteenth century series)
   Includes index.
   1. English philology—Study and teaching—Great Britain—History—19th century—Sources.   I. Title.   II. Series: Nineteenth century (Aldershot, England)
   PE68.G5B33   1998
   420'.7'04109034—dc21

98–8700
CIP

ISBN 1 84014 278 2

Typeset in 10 point Palatino by Ponting–Green Publishing Services, 36 Bois Moor Rd, Chesham, Buckinghamshire, HP5 1SN and printed in on acid-free paper by MPG Books Ltd, Bodmin

Contents

CONTENTS

CONTENTS

The Nineteenth Century

General Editors' Preface

The aim of this series is to reflect, develop and extend the great burgeoning of interest in the nineteenth century that has been an inevitable feature of recent decades, as that former epoch has come more sharply into focus as a locus for our understanding, not only of the past but of the contours of our modernity. Though it is dedicated principally to the publication of original monographs and symposia in literature, history, cultural analysis, and associated fields, there will be a salient role for reprints of significant texts from, or about, the period. Our overarching policy is to address the spectrum of nineteenth-century studies without exception, achieving the widest scope in chronology, approach and range of concern. This, we believe, distinguishes our project from comparable ones, and means, for example, that in the relevant areas of scholarship we both recognize and cut innovatively across such parameters as those suggested by the designations 'Romantic' and 'Victorian'. We welcome new ideas, while valuing tradition. It is hoped that the world which predates yet so forcibly predicts and engages our own will emerge in parts, as a whole, and in the lively currents of debate and change that are so manifest an aspect of its intellectual, artistic and social landscape.

Vincent Newey
Joanne Shattock

University of Leicester

Acknowledgements

I acknowledge with much appreciation the advice and encouragement which I have received from Alan Bellringer while preparing this collection.

I am grateful to the Librarian of University College, London for permission to reproduce extracts from the report of the Committee of the Senate on the candidates for the Chair of English Language and Literature, November 1865. This manuscript document is held in University College Library (College Correspondence AM105).

Editor's Note

In supplying footnotes, I have borne in mind John Churton Collins's condemnation of what he considered the over-extensive notes in the Clarendon Press edition of Milton, 'They serve no end; they satisfy no need.' I hope that I have avoided this danger, while providing explication and information which will be helpful to readers.

I have indicated authors' original notes with a # to distinguish them from my own notes. Where I have added to an original note, the additional matter is shown in square brackets.

Introduction

In recent years there has been an awakening of interest in the history of English studies, with a number of books and articles dealing with the subject. This interest has arisen in parallel with the rise to prominence of critical theory. Awareness of alternative critical methods of studying literary texts, structuralist, post-structuralist, feminist, new historicist and so on, has led scholars to examine the critical assumptions of the past and the institutionalizing of these assumptions in educational establishments. Cultural studies, in particular, have provided both impetus and methodology for an analysis of how and why this academic discipline became established.

It is the purpose of this collection of material to provide anyone interested in this history with some of its important texts, most of which were ephemeral and have been long out of print. As long ago as 1921, in an English Association pamphlet about the teaching of English language and literature, R.B. McKerrow wrote that, for advanced students of English, an important part of the course should be 'a sketch of the historical development of the study of our language and literature, and this not as a means of commemorating those who have been before us but for the purpose of criticizing their methods, and evaluating their statements.'[1] More recently, in 1982, in an essay entitled 'The Hidden History of English Studies,' Brian Doyle concluded, 'I want to urge the necessity of including under any "English" rubric a course which retrieves the hidden history which I have outlined.'[2] The obstacle which has always stood in the way of anyone seeking to discover this history, however, let alone to plan a course, is that the raw material, the primary texts, has not been readily available.

Any collection of writing dealing with a particular subject has to begin and end somewhere. The title of this book limits this collection to the nineteenth century, since that century not only saw the introduction of English in a form which is immediately recognizable to us, but also saw much debate about what the subject should be. It would obviously have been possible to begin earlier, but this would have been pre-history. It would certainly have been possible to have continued into the twentieth century, but many of the important texts are already in print, so there is less justification for reproducing them here. An exception to the nineteenth-century rule is made in respect of just two texts: a lecture from Hugh Blair's *Lectures on Rhetoric and Belles Lettres* (1783) and a chapter from the government report, *The Teaching of English in England* (1921). The former represents a very influential text, which remained in print throughout the first half of the nineteenth century, but against which some of the writers collected here reacted strongly. *The Teaching of English in England* has been included because it marks in its most extreme form the hopes that had, by the early twentieth century, become attached to English as an agent of culture and healer of class division, ideas which are prominent in the nineteenth-century texts collected here. Neither of these texts from outside the nineteenth century is currently in print.

A collection is also bound to be a selection; some texts are left out, and which ones are included depends on the editor's personal assessment of their relative significance. The following brief introduction to the history of English studies in the nineteenth century is intended to alert readers to some of this editor's conceptions concerning the development which took place.

It is a commonplace that English is a modern subject; indeed, popular belief places the genesis of English even later in time than the facts will allow, ascribing prime responsibility to Matthew Arnold. In fact, as this collection evidences, there was much discussion concerning its desirability as a subject and its possible content, and some institutions were actually teaching it, before Arnold's contributions to the ongoing debate. What is more, English did not suddenly appear where there was nothing before. It was born containing elements of educational subjects which had gone before: pupils had been taught to read and write using vernacular literature, and they had been taught rhetoric, long before the advent of anything recognizable as English. Then, when English did appear on the stage, notions and methods connected with the eighteenth-century reading and spelling books and with the ancient subject of rhetoric were transferred to this new subject.

Rhetoric, the art of using language for persuasion, was considered of supreme importance in ancient Greece and Rome; major textbooks on the subject were written by Aristotle, Quintilian and Cicero. In the Middle Ages it was one of the seven liberal arts, grouped with grammar and logic to form the *trivium*. It retained its position after the Middle Ages, achieving its highest modern status in the sixteenth, seventeenth and early eighteenth centuries. It was, however, attacked as being dangerous by John Locke in his *Essay Concerning Human Understanding* (1690), on the grounds that it impeded the pursuit of real truth and knowledge, and this attack perhaps marked the beginning of a very gradual decline in its position and influence. During the eighteenth century it continued to be widely taught and textbooks were published, but a gradual change took place. The emphasis came to be less on composition, and more attention was given to the study of literature. Furthermore, the literature used ceased to be wholly classical, and modern literature was introduced alongside Latin and Greek. This was especially the case in the so-called Dissenters' Academies, set up in response to the Act of Uniformity (1662) and the Five Mile Act (1665), which barred all non-Anglicans from teaching in schools and universities. Many anthologies of English literature for use in schools were published, particularly between 1770 and 1800.

A work by the French rhetorician, Charles Rollin, *The Method of Teaching and Studying the Belles Lettres*, was very influential in the eighteenth century. This was published first in France between 1726 and 1728, and the first English translation appeared in 1734. Its popularity in England is demonstrated by the fact that it went into its final, eleventh edition as late as 1810. The phrase 'belles lettres' used in Rollin's title became increasingly common in England, and for that matter in Scotland.

Between 1748 and 1751 Adam Smith delivered a course of lectures on rhetoric and belles lettres at Edinburgh University, in which he used extracts from English literature as illustrations of rhetorical techniques. These lectures influenced in their turn those by Hugh Blair, appointed in 1762 to a new professorship of Rhetoric and Belles Lettres at Edinburgh, and whose book, *Lectures on Rhetoric and Belles Lettres* (1783), proved as popular as had Rollin's half a century earlier.

The creeping changes in the teaching of rhetoric signalled by the common addition of the phrase 'belles lettres' and characterized by attention to standards of taste did not, however, prevent its decline, and De Quincey in 1828 wrote that 'the age of Rhetoric, like that of Chivalry, has passed amongst forgotten things.'[3] He was perhaps writing somewhat prematurely here, since the final edition of Blair's *Rhetoric* was not published until 1845, and a new textbook by Richard Whately, *Elements of Rhetoric*, came out in 1828, the very year when De Quincey was declaring rhetoric, not only dead and buried, but forgotten too. Nevertheless, rhetoric certainly was in decline, and in some respects English replaced it. In some of its manifestations English represented a very conscious break with rhetoric, but on the other hand links with rhetoric helped in certain circumstances to make English acceptable. It gave the new subject a connection with something which was at least as old as Aristotle, and it could also be used to help emphasize the practical, instrumental aspects of English, the composition and elocution. Rhetoric was therefore an inescapable element in the genetic make-up of English.

For much of its history in England rhetoric had formed part of the classical curriculum, and rhetoric was not the only element in this curriculum to influence English studies. Classics more generally provided a reference point for the new subject. In the eighteenth century, classics had been the main subject, sometimes the only subject, in most public schools and grammar schools. At Oxford, too, the main part of the undergraduate curriculum was Latin and Greek grammar and literature, rhetoric, logic and scholastic philosophy, though at Cambridge there was more emphasis on mathematics from mid-century on.

Very many pupils did not continue their studies long enough to derive much benefit from the classical literature. Like Tom Tulliver with his private tutor in *The Mill on the Floss*, they did not advance much further than rather barren language-learning, and when they left school they quickly forgot all that they had learnt. Even amongst those who had gone on to university, the situation was often little better. This very negative aspect of classics helped to provide some of the impetus for English studies, which, it was argued, would at least ensure a greater exposure to literature for the majority of the boys who were then being driven through the classical curriculum.

On the other hand, although English was in some senses a response to the failings of classics, it still borrowed a number of features from the older subject. The language-learning aspect of classics could be regarded in a positive light. It gave the subject weight, difficulty and therefore academic respectability, and this respectability was desperately needed by the newcomer. Anglo-Saxon and Middle English could provide the ballast which would otherwise be lacking. The techniques of analysing classical texts could also be replicated with English texts, students being required to construe passages, study the etymology of particular words, and so on.

Moreover, the teaching of classics was not entirely monolithic and unchanging. At the end of the eighteenth century and in the early nineteenth century there had grown up in Germany a movement for what was known as *Altertumswissenschaft*, a study of the ancient world in all its aspects, rather than simply its language and literature, and this enthusiasm in some measure spread to England. The concept of attempting to recapture the whole spirit of the age being studied, essentially an interdisciplinary study, inspired an approach to English literature in which it was very closely tied to English history.

The influence of rhetoric on the early history of English studies may be seen very clearly in the case of University College, London,[4] where Thomas Dale was appointed to a Chair of English Language and Literature in 1828. Although this was a landmark in the history of English studies, in that this was the first time that English literature had been included in the title of a professorship, Dale's work was not far removed from that of a teacher of rhetoric. He taught two courses: the main one was the principles and practice of composition, and the other, entitled

'English literature,' was modelled very closely on a traditional study of genres, such as had been common in rhetoric courses. The stress on the instrumental value of English in the form of composition helped to make it acceptable in the utilitarian ethos of the new college. Dale did not stay long at University College, resigning in 1830 after just two years in his post. In 1835, however, he became the first Professor of English Literature and History at King's College, London,[5] where he seems to have taken up again the teaching of rhetoric during the five years that he remained there.

Thomas Dale's successor at King's College was F.D. Maurice, who broke determinedly with the rhetoric and belles lettres tradition, and set a very different and influential agenda for English studies. Maurice wanted to move from vague generalizations about literature to close textual study, and here his own classical education played a part in shaping his conception of what English might be. His tutor at Cambridge had been Julius Hare, who was one of the most prominent English enthusiasts for *Altertumswissenschaft*, and this had been reflected in his teaching. At the time when Maurice was setting out on his career as a professor of English literature and history, he wrote to Hare, discussing his plans. He wanted to treat English books with the same accuracy as if they had been in a foreign language, but at the same time to use literary texts to shed light upon the life of the times in which they were written. Chaucer was particularly useful to him, in that the language represented a difficulty, and therefore it would be necessary to pay strict attention to the words, and even to 'construe.'[6] Thus, what Maurice considered the best of classics, as he had experienced it at Cambridge, could be recreated through the English syllabus.

Maurice's thought concerning English studies illustrates at least four other main strands in the history of the development of the subject, all of which are also represented in other writers' work in this collection. One is its role as a weapon in the anti-utilitarian armoury. At University College it had been possible to present it as a subject with utilitarian credentials, but at King's College, which was itself a response to what was seen as the other college's Godless utilitarianism, its purpose was quite different. H.J. Rose, the first Principal of King's College, had preached a sermon in Cambridge in 1826, the year of the opening of University College, which is usually seen as having opened the campaign which led eventually to the founding of King's College. Rose argued that the 'tendency' then prevalent in the world was the pursuit of 'knowledge of the material Universe, as tending most directly to add to the conveniences and comforts of life, and to bestow immediate reward on those whose sagacity leads them to discovery themselves, or to profit by the discoveries of others.'[7] By contrast, Rose's view of education, which was very close to Coleridge's, was that 'by a mighty process of cultivation in a world of sense, the most wonderful and noble powers should be educed.'[8]

Maurice, in his introductory lecture at King's College, placed his view of English very firmly in this anti-utilitarian tradition. He reminded his listeners that English, together with theology, classics and mathematics, was not primarily concerned with teaching information. Still less was it concerned with providing students with the means to advance in the world, a view which Dale had seemed to put forward in his inaugural lecture at University College, and for which he had been roundly condemned in Maurice's *Athenaeum*.[9] Rather, English should enable its students to rise 'above what is apparent and transitory to what is real and permanent.' They should learn a reverence for English words, and there is a latent anti-commercialism in the line, 'They are living words. They have their roots deep in our soil; they have been growing for generations. These English words are not mere words to buy and sell with.'

Underlying all Maurice's other ideas is a providentialist conception of England's history and literature which was common in the thought of nineteenth-century Liberal Anglicans, often known as the Broad Church. God was working through history, and this could be studied particularly clearly in a nation's history, most importantly in England's history and the literature produced at different points throughout this history. At a later date, when Maurice had already left King's College, he wrote of the lectures which he had delivered there, 'They were formed upon the belief that all history and all literature exhibit God's education of mankind; that the history and literature of England exhibit the education of our people and of ourselves.'

This providentialist basis of Maurice's thought introduces the second important strand in the history of the subject which is illustrated by his work. He saw his two subjects of English literature and English history in a specifically national light; they were intimately connected for him with a consciousness of nationality, a wish to cultivate a national spirit. There is thus a ready link with the thought of other figures associated with the Liberal Anglican tradition. J.R. Seeley, the historian, for example, enthusiastically adopted the idea, deriving from Coleridge, of a National Church, in which Church and State would be identified as closely as possible. In the extract included here, he suggests English literature as a national Bible, through which the whole people could make contact with its past. Nationalism was not, of course, created by the Broad Church. English studies and Broad Church theology both grew out of the same soil, in which middle-class nationalism was already a powerful force. In the eighteenth century a rich and powerful aristocracy signalled its difference from the rest of English society by ostentatiously adopting a cosmopolitan, heavily French-influenced life style and culture. The middle classes were unable to compete effectively; indeed they were not intended to be able to compete. Instead, they reacted by elevating and embracing the local and national. In education, classics was a quintessentially cosmopolitan curriculum, and as such was general at the public schools. In the more middle-class grammar schools, also, classics was dominant, but there were exceptions, and there were also the Dissenters' Academies already mentioned. By the early nineteenth century, when the London colleges, University College and King's College, were founded very consciously as middle-class institutions, a place for the national, as epitomized by English studies, was demanded. Maurice and other Broad Church thinkers, including Charles Kingsley, helped to give this national study a religious basis.

It is the place of English as a middle-class subject which represents the third influential element in Maurice's thinking on English studies. In *Has the Church, or the State, the Power to Educate the Nation?*, published in 1839, the year before his appointment at King's College, Maurice suggested that the middle class had, or at least ought to have, a peculiarly national character, and that England owed its identity to its middle class. England's knights were supranational, fighting for Christendom as warriors of the cross. There was a role for these aristocrats, and they should be educated for this role by training them, along with professional men, in Latin and Greek, 'the two most Catholic languages.' The middle classes, by contrast, contributed a specifically English identity, not using a common Christendom language, but a native tongue.Their education should reflect and nurture this English identity. In his inaugural lecture the following year, Maurice developed this idea, using the example of Chaucer, with whom he intended to begin his course of lectures. Chaucer, he argued, belonged to the age when the middle class first started to appear in England, the age when the language first became established and English literature began. *The Canterbury Tales* are cited as proof that English literature had no grand and stately origin, but was essentially middle-class from the beginning. English literature was a middle-class literature suitable for study by middle-class students. In the making of the English middle class we begin to see the construction of English literature, too.

Identification of the subject with a particular social class also had political implications, which Maurice was not slow to draw out. In *Has the Church, or the State, the Power to Educate the Nation?*, he drew attention to its potential as a socially stabilizing influence in what was a time of Chartist unrest. If a boy from the middle classes had been educated in the 'national' way which Maurice advocated, he would be filled with a lasting sense of belonging to England, and would be inoculated against the propaganda of political agitators. The effect should extend well beyond the middle class, because this class had the capacity to unite the nation, to bridge the chasm between the lower and upper classes, and to lessen feelings of alienation and estrangement of one class from another.

The political role of English studies has been a theme of a number of modern historians of the subject, but the tendency, using mainly evidence from a later period, is to see English as having been designed to render the working class passive and quiescent. In F.D. Maurice, however, we find a particularly clear example of how in the early years of English studies the shaping conception was of a subject for the middle class. What is more, this remained the dominant conception throughout the nineteenth century. Nevertheless, the idea of extending English down the social scale grew gradually, and by 1921, the year of publication of the report, *The Teaching of English in England*, English was seen as the central element in an education system for the whole nation.

The fourth important element in Maurice's concern for English studies was his vision of it as an appropriate subject for women, for pre-eminently a women's subject is what it duly became. The report of the Taunton Commission (1868) into the state of middle-class education contains this revealing dialogue between Lord Taunton and the famous Miss Frances Buss, Principal of the North London Collegiate School for Girls: '"I suppose you teach English literature. Do you teach mathematics at all?" – "No; we have no pupils sufficiently advanced."'[10] English literature could be taken for granted in a girls' school, whereas mathematics turned out not to be taught at all in one of the leading girls' schools of the time. English studies had become established, at least in the area of female education.

Maurice had espoused the cause of female education in an article in the *Metropolitan Quarterly Magazine* as early as 1826, long before his involvement with King's College, and English studies were part of the agenda which he set then. One of the first things necessary was to change the books used to teach criticism, and in particular to consign Blair's *Rhetoric* to oblivion. Girls' schools were, in Maurice's view, particularly likely to be using what he considered an outmoded book and therefore outmoded approaches to literature. The rhetoric and belles lettres tradition seemed almost designed to stifle imagination, an aim which made it very attractive to many of those who directed the education of girls. The imagination, he believed, was 'a terrible object of the dread, the hatred, and the hostility of the mistress of establishments, and the governesses of young ladies,' whereas he followed Coleridge in prizing above all else the 'shaping spirit of Imagination.' Maurice suggested that Shakespeare, Milton and Wordsworth would be the most suitable authors to study, with Wordsworth, though a lesser figure than the other two, being particularly well suited for women.[11]

Maurice was unable to put his ideas about female education into practice until 1848, many years after his *Metropolitan Quarterly Magazine* article, when he became the first Principal of Queen's College, a college set up in London specifically for the training of governesses. In his inaugural lecture there as Principal he outlined the subjects to be taught, and both English language and literature figured prominently, with Charles Kingsley being appointed the Professor.

The first London university colleges, University College and King's College, have a particularly important place in the history of English studies, as the first institutions of higher education in England to give room to the new subject. This support from the London colleges led in turn to the eventual inclusion of English in the list of subjects for degrees offered by the examining body, the University of London. This did not happen until 1859, but it marked another significant step in English's advance, not least because the London degrees came to be taken by students in the many new colleges and universities which were being established in the mid- and late-nineteenth century, both in Britain and in the Empire. English needed the status of being examinable, as other subjects were, if it were to survive in the academic world, and the London degrees gave it this status. At a lower level, matriculation examinations and also the place given to English in the Army and India Civil Service examinations gave a boost to its study in schools. The sort of questions asked in these latter examinations did, however, have the unfortunate effect of establishing English in many people's minds as a subject which required no real understanding but just a great deal of 'cramming.' This association of English with crammers did little to enhance its prestige and was ammunition which could be used against it by its opponents.

Nevertheless, the mid-century saw English advancing steadily in schools, particularly those schools which catered primarily for middle-class pupils, the schools investigated by the Taunton Commission. In addition to the evidence given to this commission, a number of articles were published at this time which recommended English, pointed out its advantages, especially when compared with classics, and in some instances discussed the sorts of syllabus which were possible. In almost all cases this meant both language and literature, including in the term 'literature' not only the work of poets and dramatists, but also of philosophers and historians. Novelists, of course, were mostly excluded, though this hardly needed to be stated explicitly.

At this point, some brief explanation should perhaps be offered for the inclusion of so little of Matthew Arnold's writing in this collection, and for including nothing from the well-known essays. After all, Arnold is often considered almost the only begetter of English studies, and there is no doubt that *Culture and Anarchy*, 'The Function of Criticism at the Present Time' and others of his writings had an immense influence on thinking about English. For Arnold undoubtedly helped to popularize the notion that literature and literary criticism, in fact all that could be included under the umbrella of 'culture,' had social importance, and could even help stave off social anarchy. Nevertheless, Arnold's main concern in these essays was not with English; indeed, he was often disparaging about English literature and English criticism, and always encouraged a European sensibility based first and foremost on the classics, but also including Goethe, Dante and other foreign-language writers. In fact, far from being an acknowledged leader of a campaign for English, Arnold is criticized in one of the articles collected here from the *Museum and English Journal of Education* for his negative attitude towards English. The extracts included here from Arnold's reports as a Her Majesty's Inspector of Schools show a greater interest in English as an instrument of education and cultivation than might ever have been guessed at from his essays. However, he was here writing about children whose only chance of being cultivated lay in the learning by heart of a hundred or two hundred lines of poetry, which was what English literature, one of the optional subjects available in elementary schools at the time, amounted to. For pupil teachers more was obviously possible, but even so, effective foreign language learning, whether of ancient or modern languages, was usually closed to them because of the limitations of time. Instead, they could be elevated, humanized, cultivated, moralized (all these terms are employed) by the study of English authors and by composition. In his professional work, which is what these reports represent, Arnold was forced to deal with present realities and practical means by which such realities could be improved. In his essays, on the other hand, he was free to give full scope to an inclination to withdraw from the search for practical remedies to immediate problems, and to think in terms of a cultivated "remnant" whose job it was to keep the flame of culture alive in preparation for the distant day when they would be able to reshape the world.

One of the highest hurdles which had to be jumped before English could be said to have arrived as a fully respectable academic subject was to find acceptance at the ancient universities of Oxford and Cambridge. The subject had become established in schools and in the new universities and colleges, but was very slow to make any impression on what were still commonly referred to as 'the Universities.' At

Oxford, there were during the nineteenth century various modifications to the School of *Literae Humaniores*, so that it eventually included more than simply classics, and it allowed for ancient writers to be compared with modern ones. This did not mean, however, any teaching of English. There were also Chairs of Anglo-Saxon and of Comparative Philology, both of which dealt with aspects of the history of the English language, but there was little provision for English literature until 1894 and no separate Chair of English Literature until 1904. At Cambridge, English was not given a tripos of its own until 1917, although it had found a mainly grammatical and philological place there as a small province of Modern Languages since 1883.

It was in connection with Oxford that the case for English studies came to be widely debated in 1886 and 1887.[12] In 1885, mainly in response to external pressure, it had been decided to endow a Chair of English Language and Literature, a title which was a compromise and which left plenty of room for further squabbling. The appointment of A.S. Napier, an Anglo-Saxon specialist, brought howls of protest from some quarters that Oxford was trying to substitute philology for literature. The university then compounded the felony by proposing to introduce an Honours School of Modern Languages at Oxford, a school which would have been basically philological, giving no place to the literary study of literature. One of those who had, rather over-optimistically, applied for the Merton Chair was John Churton Collins, an Oxford graduate in classics who had been teaching English through the University Extension Movement. It was Collins who led the campaign to force Oxford to do more for English, he who wrote the most vociferous articles, and he who, with the help of W.T. Stead, editor of the *Pall Mall Gazette*, canvassed the views of many eminent people of the day. The campaign was a success to the extent that the proposal for the School of Modern Languages was defeated in Congregation in November 1887, but Oxford remained without an Honours School of English Literature.

The term 'philology' features very prominently in the texts relating to this debate, and requires some elucidation, since its use underwent subtle changes during the course of the nineteenth century. In the eighteenth century, it commonly meant the study of classics, embodying a focus on language, since this was the approach to classics then current. Early in the nineteenth century, however, the usage tended to develop in two completely divergent ways. On the one hand, philology meant the new, broader classical studies suggested by the German word *Altertumswissenschaft*, already discussed. On the other hand, it came to mean comparative philology, effectively a new study which traced developments within families of languages. This comparative philology, drawing its inspiration from the German Romantic Movement, just as

Altertumswissenschaft did, attributed to language many of the Romantic virtues. Language, particularly when considered in terms of words, could be represented as the antithesis of whatever was materialistic, utilitarian and commercial. The vogue for comparative philology, which began in Germany and Scandinavia, first spread to England in the 1820s, with Friedrich Rosen at University College and Benjamin Thorpe at Cambridge. University College rapidly became a centre for this study in England, and the Philological Society was founded there.

Despite its origins in the Romantic Movement, comparative philology was rarely, in practice, a very inspiring subject. Formulating rules to explain the ways in which languages changed turned out to be a far less certain enterprise, and far more difficult, than it had seemed in the pioneering days. R.W. Chambers, reminiscing about his own time as a student at University College, wrote of Professor Postgate, who held the Chair of Comparative Philology there from 1880 to 1910, 'there was so little enthusiasm for the subject that I am afraid Postgate, eminent scholar and fine teacher as he was, sometimes found great difficulties in forming a class… . One year I constituted Professor Postgate's class.'[13]

In the context of the Oxford debate over English, 'philology' became a blanket term of abuse for an emphasis on the study of language, rather than on what were considered literary matters. It thus included the study of Anglo-Saxon, which had received a boost from the appointment of Napier to the Merton Chair. Philology was the cuckoo in the nest, cheating English of its rightful inheritance.

On the whole, John Churton Collins was successful in finding a majority in favour of what he wanted: increased attention to English literature at Oxford, less concentration on language, and an indissoluble link between the study of classics and the study of English. Most of those whose opinions Collins sought had themselves received a classical education and had been successful in it. A number of them were involved in some way with the teaching of classics. They tended to see in English, as presented by Collins, something that might help preserve the spirit of an education system in which they had a vested interest. They saw it as an additional weapon in the armoury of culture to use in the battle to halt the advancing forces of science in education. On the other hand, the cause of English literature was also espoused by the opposing party, the party of science, which believed that classics had failed as an educational instrument. The science party shared with its opponents the belief that the curriculum should embody morally educative subjects, but unlike its opponents, believed that classics had little or no part to play. English literature, together with other modern European literatures, was an obvious replacement, and English had the advantage over French, German and Italian, because of its ready accessibility to English speakers.

One argument which the supporters of English were now able to deploy was that the subject of English already existed. Schools, teacher training colleges and new universities at home, together with countless institutions throughout the Empire, all taught English. It was, therefore, the duty of 'the Universities' to regulate these studies. Until Oxford and Cambridge took up English seriously, there could be no guarantee that it would be studied properly anywhere, for there would be no certainty that the teachers had been properly taught.

There was also opposition, however, to any idea of introducing an Honours School of English Literature at Oxford, opposition from within the university which ensured that no such school was established at this time, but also opposition from without. Until this point, English had invaded more and more educational institutions without any large-scale opposition manifesting itself. Part of the reason for this had undoubtedly been the chameleon nature of the subject. It was able to appear in the guise of rhetoric, belles lettres, composition, comparative philology, literary history or whatever; it could be a utilitarian subject at University College or anti-utilitarian at King's College. At University College it even went through a number of very different fashions over a period of time. There had, however, been a unifying feature, which was the role of English as a predominantly middle-class subject. At Oxford the case was different. As one of 'the Universities,' it had always catered for the Establishment, and here this most middle-class of subjects was not universally welcomed. What had been good enough for elsewhere was not necessarily good enough for Oxford. Some saw English as more of a threat than a support to classics; many were concerned about the association of English with 'cramming,' and feared that English would never escape being labelled an easy School. Others saw in the proposals an attempt to institute a School of 'Taste,' a subject which could not be properly taught or examined.

One of the tensions in late-nineteenth-century universities which had a bearing on the Oxford debate was between the idea of universities as teaching institutions and the idea of universities as primarily orientated towards research and learning. John Churton Collins, a University Extension lecturer, regarded English as an agent of culture, potentially more effective than the traditional agents of Greek and Latin classics. The Oxford University establishment, on the other hand, in so far as it was willing to do anything in the matter at all, wished to support philology, which Collins claimed had 'been allowed to fill a place in education altogether disproportionate to its insignificance as an instrument of culture,' but which could be more easily represented as a scholarly subject.

In the event, it was the twentieth century before English studies became firmly established at Oxford and Cambridge, and it was also in the twentieth century, not until after the First World War, that English reached its high water mark in terms of the confidence placed in it. This was the report of a government departmental committee appointed by the President of the Board of Education to inquire into the position of English in the educational system. Entitled *The Teaching of English in England*, but commonly known as the Newbolt Report from the name of its chairman, Sir Henry Newbolt, an extract from this work stands as a twentieth-century epilogue to this nineteenth-century history.

The Newbolt Report includes a lengthy retrospect of the development of English studies, and may itself be seen as a culmination of the tradition of regarding English primarily as an instrument of culture. In the nineteenth century, the main concern to be found in writers on English studies was with culturing the middle class, but by 1921 the perceived need and possibility was to do something for the whole nation, and in particular the working class. The image used for English studies in the introductory chapter of the report is that of a stone which builders have previously rejected as useless; the committee is seen as an architect; national education as presently existing is an arch in need of repair. The architect has been called in to advise on what work is required on the arch, and he believes that the stone could be put to very good use. However, it cannot simply be used to hold the arch together; rather, the arch needs complete reconstruction, using the stone of English studies as the keystone. This image recalls Psalm 119, a psalm of praise, with its lines:

> The stone which the builders refused is become the head stone of the corner.
> This is the Lord's doing; it is marvellous in our eyes.

The quasi-religious mission of English, a recurring theme in a number of the writers anthologized here, surfaces once again. English is God's gift to the nation to hold the education system together and thereby to unite the nation. It has, however, been hitherto rejected, its merits left unrecognized. There is significance in the change from the corner-stone of a building to the keystone of an arch. The arch image suggests magnificence, while emphasizing the danger of collapse, and the keystone is not only the crowning glory but also locks together the whole structure, a structure which includes all the classes.

Notes

1. R.B. McKerrow, *A Note on the Teaching of 'English Language and Literature,'* English Association Pamphlet No. 49 (London:1921), p.31.
2. Brian Doyle, 'The Hidden History of English Studies,' in *Re-Reading English*, ed. Peter Widdowson (London:1982), p.28.
3. Thomas De Quincey, 'Rhetoric,' *Collected Writings*, ed. David Masson (London: 1890), X, 97.
4. For a full discussion of the place of University College in the history of English studies, see Alan Bacon, 'The Changing Fashions in English Studies at University College, London,' *Durham University Journal*, 85 (1993), 45–6.
5. See Alan Bacon, 'English Literature Becomes a University Subject: King's College, London as Pioneer,' *Victorian Studies*, 29 (1986), 591–612.
6. Frederick Maurice, *The Life of Frederick Denison Maurice* (London:1884), I, 290.
7. Hugh James Rose, *Eight Sermons Preached before the University of Cambridge* (London:1833), p.228.
8. *ibid*, p.229.
9. 'Mr. Dale's Introductory Lecture,' *Athenaeum*, No. 54 (1828), 858.
10. Schools Inquiry Commission, *Report of the Commissioners* (London:1868), V, 253.
11. F.D. Maurice, 'Female Education,' *Metropolitan Quarterly Magazine*, 2 (1826), 273.
12. See Alan Bacon, 'Attempts to Introduce a School of English Literature at Oxford: the National Debate of 1886 and 1887,' *History of Education*, 9 (1980), 303–13.
13. R.W. Chambers, *Philologists at University College, London* (1927), pp.28–9.

CHAPTER ONE

Hugh Blair

Hugh Blair (1718–1800)) was born in Edinburgh. He became Minister to the High Church, Edinburgh, in 1758. In 1759 he began to give lectures on composition in the university, and in 1760 became Professor of Rhetoric. On 7 April 1762 a Regius Professorship of Rhetoric and Belles Lettres was founded, to which Blair was appointed. Blair confessed that in his lectures he had borrowed some ideas from Adam Smith's lectures on rhetoric and belles lettres, which had been delivered in Edinburgh between 1748 and 1751.

Blair's *Lectures on Rhetoric and Belles Lettres* was first published in London and Edinburgh in 1783, and went through many editions in England and America, continuing to be published throughout most of the nineteenth century. There were abridgements, translations into French, Italian and Spanish, and text-book versions which included questions for the student to work through. It was a popular text book for many years; we know, for example, that Alexander Blair used it as the basis for his courses at University College, London, when he was appointed Professor of English Language and Literature there in 1831. Thomas Dale, who had been Alexander Blair's predecessor at University College, prepared a new edition for the press as late as 1845.

However, Hugh Blair's work was roundly condemned by F.D. Maurice and Charles Kingsley, who saw their own teaching of English language and literature as marking a complete break with Blair's exaltation of 'taste' and what they regarded as a low estimate of the importance of imagination. In time, the teaching of literature through genres, a characteristic of the approach adopted in rhetoric text books and classes was superseded by other approaches.

The extracts here are from the introductory lecture, which is in the nature of an *apologia* for the study of rhetoric and belles lettres. There was a long tradition, dating back to Plato, of condemning rhetoric as spurious and deceitful, closely allied to flattery, and leading to the perversion of justice and integrity. Blair attempts to meet such charges and justify the study of eloquence and composition, not only for would-be practitioners of these skills but for everyone, enabling people to judge what they read and hear. This text is taken from the 1817 edition.

Introduction to *Lectures on Rhetoric and Belles Lettres*

One of the most distinguished privileges which Providence has conferred upon mankind, is the power of communicating their thoughts to one another. Destitute of this power, reason would be a solitary, and, in some measure, an unavailing principle. Speech is the great instrument by which man becomes beneficial to man: and it is to the intercourse and transmission of thought, by means of speech, that we are chiefly indebted for the improvement of thought itself. Small are the advances which a single unassisted individual can make towards perfecting any of his powers. What we call human reason, is not the effort or ability of one, so much as it is the result of the reason of many, arising from lights mutually communicated, in consequence of discourse and writing.

It is obvious, then, that writing and discourse are objects entitled to the highest attention. Whether the influence of the speaker, or the entertainment of the hearer, be consulted; whether utility or pleasure be the principal aim in view, we are prompted, by the strongest motives, to study how we may communicate our thoughts to one another with most advantage. Accordingly, we find, that in almost every nation, as soon as language had extended itself beyond that scanty communication which was requisite for the supply of men's necessities, the improvement of discourse began to attract regard. In the language even of rude, uncultivated tribes, we can trace some attention to the grace and force of those expressions which they used, when they sought to persuade or to affect. They were early sensible of a beauty in discourse, and endeavoured to give it certain decorations, which experience had taught them it was capable of receiving, long before the study of those decorations was formed into a regular art.

But, among nations in a civilized state, no art has been cultivated with more care, than that of language, style, and composition. The attention paid to it may, indeed, be assumed as one mark of the progress of society towards its most improved period. For, according as society improves and flourishes, men acquire more influence over one another by means of reasoning and discourse; and in proportion as that influence is felt to enlarge, it must follow, as a natural consequence, that they will bestow more care upon the methods of expressing their conceptions with propriety and eloquence. Hence we find, that in all the polished nations of Europe, this study has been treated as highly important, and has possessed a considerable place in every plan of liberal education.

Indeed, when the arts of speech and writing are mentioned, I am sensible that prejudices against them are apt to rise in the minds of many. A sort of art is immediately thought of, that is ostentatious and deceitful; the minute and trifling study of words alone; the pomp of expression; the studied fallacies of rhetoric; ornament substituted in the room of use. We need not wonder, that, under such imputations, all study of discourse, as an art, should have suffered in the opinion of men of understanding; and I am far from denying, that rhetoric and criticism have sometimes been so managed as to tend to the corruption, rather than to the improvement, of good taste and true eloquence. But sure it is equally possible to apply the principles of reason and good sense to this art, as to any other that is cultivated among men... .

* * *

Of those who peruse the following Lectures, some, in consequence either of their profession, or of their prevailing inclination, may have the view of being employed in composition, or in public speaking; others, without any prospect of this kind, may wish only to improve their taste with respect to writing and discourse, and to acquire principles which will enable them to judge for themselves in that part of literature called the Belles Lettres.

With respect to the former, such as may have occasion to communicate their sentiments to the public, it is abundantly clear that some preparation of study is requisite for the end which they have in view. To speak or to write perspicuously and agreeably, with purity, with grace and strength, are attainments of the utmost consequence to all who propose, either by speech or writing, to address the public. For without being master of these attainments, no man can do justice to his own conceptions; but how rich soever he may be in knowledge and in good sense, will be able to avail himself less of those treasures, than such as possess not half his store, but who can display what they possess with more propriety. Neither are these attainments of that kind for which we are indebted to nature merely. Nature has, indeed, conferred upon some a very favourable distinction in this respect beyond others. But in these, as in most other talents she bestows, she has left much to be wrought out by every man's own industry. So conspicuous have been the effects of study and improvement in every part of eloquence; such remarkable examples have appeared of persons surmounting, by their diligence, the disadvantages of the most untoward nature; that, among the learned, it has long been a contested, and remains still an undecided point, whether nature or art confer most towards excelling in writing and discourse.

* * *

All that regards the study of eloquence and composition, merits the higher attention upon this account, that it is intimately connected with the improvement of our intellectual powers. For I must be allowed to say, that when we are employed after a proper manner in the study of composition, we are cultivating reason itself. True rhetoric and sound logic are very nearly allied. The study of arranging and expressing our thoughts with propriety, teaches to think, as well as to speak accurately. By putting our sentiments into words, we always conceive them more distinctly. Every one who has the slightest acquaintance with composition knows, that when he expresses himself ill on any subject, when his arrangement is loose, and his sentences become feeble, the defects of his style can, almost on every occasion, be traced back to his indistinct conception of the subject; so close is the connection between thoughts and the words in which they are clothed.

* * *

In an age when works of genius and literature are so frequently the subjects of discourse, when every one erects himself into a judge, and when we can hardly mingle in polite society without bearing some share in such discussions, studies of this kind, it is not to be doubted, will appear to derive part of their importance from the use to which they may be applied in furnishing materials for those fashionable topics of discourse, and thereby enabling us to support a proper rank in social life.

But I should be sorry if we could not rest the merit of such studies on somewhat of solid and intrinsical use, independent of appearance and show. The exercise of taste and of sound criticism is, in truth, one of the most improving employments of the understanding. To apply the principles of good sense to composition and discourse; to examine what is beautiful, and why it is so; to employ ourselves in distinguishing accurately between the specious and the solid, between affected and natural ornament, must certainly improve us not a little in the most valuable part of all philosophy, the philosophy of human nature. For such disquisitions are very intimately connected with the knowledge of ourselves. They necessarily lead us to reflect on the operations of the imagination, and the movements of the heart; and increase our acquaintance with some of the most refined feelings which belong to our frame.

Logical and ethical disquisitions move in a higher sphere, and are conversant with objects of a more severe kind; the progress of the understanding in its search after knowledge, and the direction of the will in the proper pursuit of good. They point out to man the improvement of his nature as an intelligent being, and his duties as the subject of moral obligation. Belles Lettres and criticism chiefly consider him as a being endowed with those powers of taste and imagination, which were intended to embellish his mind, and to supply him with rational and useful entertainment. They open a field of investigation peculiar to themselves. All that relates to beauty, harmony, grandeur, and elegance; all that can soothe the mind, gratify the fancy, or move the affections, belongs to their province. They present human nature under a different aspect from that which it assumes when viewed by other sciences. They bring to light various springs of action, which, without their aid, might have passed unobserved; and which, though of a delicate nature, frequently exert a powerful influence on several departments of human life.

Such studies have also this peculiar advantage, that they exercise our reason without fatiguing it. They lead to inquiries acute, but not painful; profound, but not dry nor abstruse. They strew flowers in the path of science; and while they keep the mind bent in some degree, and active, they relieve it, at the same time, from that more toilsome labour to which it must submit in the acquisition of necessary erudition, or the investigation of abstract truth.

The cultivation of taste is farther recommended by the happy effects which it naturally tends to produce on human life. The most busy man, in the most active sphere, cannot be always occupied by business. Men of serious professions, cannot always be on the stretch of serious thought. Neither can the most gay and flourishing situations of fortune afford any man the power of filling all his hours with pleasure. Life must always languish in the hands of the idle. It will frequently languish even in the hands of the busy, if they have not some employment subsidiary to that which forms their main pursuit. How then shall all these vacant spaces, those unemployed intervals, which, more or less, occur in the life of every one, be filled up? How can we contrive to dispose of them in any way that shall be more agreeable in itself, or more consonant to the dignity of the human mind, than in the entertainments of taste, and the study of polite literature? He who is so happy as to have acquired a relish for these, has always at hand an innocent and irreproachable amusement for his leisure hours, to save him from the danger of many a pernicious passion. He is not in hazard of being a burden to himself. He is not obliged to fly to low company, or to court the riot of loose pleasures, in order to cure the tediousness of existence.

Providence seems plainly to have pointed out this useful purpose to which the pleasures of taste may be applied, by interposing them in a middle station between the pleasures of sense and those of pure intellect. We were not designed to grovel always among objects so low as the former; nor are we capable of dwelling constantly in so high a region as the latter. The pleasures of taste refresh the mind after the toils of the intellect, and the labours of abstract study; and they gradually raise it above the attachments of sense, and prepare it for the enjoyments of virtue.

*
*　*

I will not go so far as to say that the improvement of taste and of virtue is the same; or that they may always be expected to co-exist in an equal degree. More powerful correctives than taste can apply, are necessary for reforming the corrupt propensities which too frequently prevail among mankind. Elegant speculations are sometimes found to float on the surface of the mind, while bad passions possess the interior regions of the heart. At the same time this cannot but be admitted, that the exercise of taste is, in its native tendency, moral and purifying. From reading the most admired productions of genius, whether in poetry or prose, almost every one rises with some good impressions left on his mind: and though these may not always be durable, they are at least to be ranked among the means of disposing the heart to virtue. One thing is certain, and I shall hereafter have occasion to illustrate it more fully, that without possessing the virtuous affections in a strong degree, no man can attain eminence in the sublime parts of eloquence. He must feel what a good man feels, if he expects greatly to move, or to interest mankind. They are the ardent sentiments of honour, virtue, magnanimity, and public spirit, that only can kindle that fire of genius, and call up into the mind those high ideas, which attract the admiration of ages; and if this spirit be necessary to produce the most distinguished efforts of eloquence, it must be necessary also to our relishing them with proper taste and feeling.

*
*　*

CHAPTER TWO

Thomas Campbell

Thomas Campbell (1777–1844) was a Scottish poet and graduate of Glasgow University. During the 1820s he was living in London, and apparently mooted the idea of a university in London as early as 1821. However, it was in the second half of 1824 that he began to give serious consideration to putting the scheme into effect. On 9 February 1825 *The Times* published an open letter from Campbell to Lord Brougham in which he outlined his plan for the institution which was to become University College.

University College tends to be thought of as a child of Utilitarianism. However, the Utilitarians were but one of the forces active in its founding. They were important, because they strongly disapproved of the traditional, mainly classical and mathematical education offered by Oxford and Cambridge, and therefore saw the chance of promoting useful knowledge in a new university in London. Also important, however, were Dissenters, Jews and Roman Catholics, who were barred from entry to the ancient universities, because they could not subscribe to the Thirty-Nine Articles of the Church of England. Then, in addition to these groups, there were those who were interested in the new university because they believed it would provide the opportunity of a higher education to young men of the metropolis whose parents could not afford the expense of sending them to Oxford or Cambridge. It is into this last category that Campbell, the prime mover of the campaign to set up University College, comes.

Comparatively early in the planning for University College, Campbell withdrew from the business arrangements and played little further part. Nevertheless, he remained a member of college committees, including the Education Committee, and this involvement with the new college may well have helped to secure a place for English literature in the list of subjects to be taught. In a two-part article published in 1825, he argued that there was a ready market for the new university among the mercantile classes and that the study of English literature there would be both popular and valuable.

This short extract is taken from the second part of Campbell's article, 'Suggestions Respecting the Plan of a College in London' in *New Monthly Magazine and Literary Journal*, 14 (1825).

'Suggestions respecting the Plan of a College in London'

*
* *

It has been objected to our scheme, that it would tend to increase the number of candidates in the learned professions, which are already over-stocked. I beg to give this point a patient discussion; and to inquire, first of all, on what grounds it is assumed that a new college would over-increase competition in law, physic, and divinity. It could only do so by increasing the diffusion of knowledge. But those who object to a college on this account are acting inconsistently, if they have not been opposers of every improvement in education which has taken place in our own times. If improvement is to be stopped, because it may injure particular callings, the Bell and Lancaster system of teaching[1] ought never to have been adopted; for surely the business of the poor amanuensis and bank-er's clerk must be now sadly impoverished by overstocked competition, when every pauper can be instructed in writing and cyphering. Is not the monopoly of horn-book erudition, once enjoyed by the village school-mistress, also encroached upon by the establishment of national schools on the new system of tuition, which the aged dame has great difficulty to learn, whilst every urchin of ten years old is becoming her rival in learn-ing? Now if education is to be discountenanced for the protection of this or that vocation against over-competition, society owes its protecting interference quite as much to the humble school-keeper or copyist, as to the lawyer, and priest, and physician.

But the evil of particular professions being overstocked, is one which has a natural tendency to cure itself; and the more education is diffused, and the great body of the people enlightened, the more readily will com-mon sense direct men to abandon overstocked professions, and, laying their pride and prejudices aside, to embrace industrious vocations where the competition is less intense. There was a time when proud families, though very poor, thought themselves degraded by their sons entering into trade. Better notions now prevail, and, as long as England is a coun-try, trade and commerce will be the main highway for the bulk of her middling classes to enter into wealth and competence. The profession of the law, nevertheless, receives a great many superfluous pupils, who prefer it solely from an aristocratic liking for its gentility. Many men enter on the profession, who, prone as men are to overrate their own abilities, know themselves quite well enough, to be conscious that their prospects of rising to legal honours and emoluments is a forlorn hope. Yet they prefer this forlorn hope to businesses which bring humbler associations to the mind with regard to precedence in society. This is, at least, one great cause of the profession of the law being overstocked; and connected with this aristocratic predilection, there may be also a more pardonable pride, in a young man choosing a profession that may lead him, more than an unlearned vocation, into intellectual companionship and society. But if a college is to favour the general diffusion of knowledge, it will certainly tend to emancipate men's minds from a great deal of the false pride which prevails on the score of professional dignity. Looking at much of its business, the law is one of the meanest and most servile vocations that a man can follow – a vocation of hireable zeal – of eloquence to let, for the purposes of justice and chicanery – a profession tending to give apathy, sophistry, and contractedness to the human mind. On the other hand, the increase of commerce, and of the intercourse of civilized nations, must continue to give new importance every day to the mercantile character; and in proportion as manufactures flourish, the successful manufacturer will cease to be a plodding and mechanical speculator, and will derive his success from scientific improvements and inventions. Perhaps the knowledge either becoming or requisite in a finished mercantile man is really more liberal, though less technical, than what goes to constitute a mere lawyer. The knowledge of foreign languages – of domestic and foreign statistics – and of political economy, ought to enter fully into the education of a British merchant of superior grade; and the manufactures of England have been the most important springs of national glory in the arts and sciences. As to the literature of taste and imagination, there is no reason why a merchant or manufacturer should not have as much time and leisure to addict himself to it, as the lawyer or any other professional man; and, in fact, there may be seen in that part of our community which lives by trade, a general fondness for polite literature, distinctly marked by the books which fill their libraries, and by the literary institutions which they support. The establishment of a college would promote the literary and scientific character of all that portion of the community – it would raise their respectability – it would occasion the young man, who is choosing his vocation for life, to anticipate no illiterate companionship, if he should go from his college to a counting-house – it would dissipate many prejudices about the comparative *gentility* of professions; and, instead of tending to overstock the profession of the law, would rather tend to diminish the number of its candidates.

* * *

Notes

1. The monitorial system of education created by Andrew Bell and Joseph Lancaster, and widely used by the rival British and National schools established in the early nineteenth century.

CHAPTER THREE

Edward Copleston

Edward Copleston (1776–1849) was a classical scholar, Professor
of Poetry at Oxford from 1802 to 1812, Provost of Oriel College,
Oxford from 1814 to 1828, then Bishop of Llandaff and Dean of St
Paul's from 1827. During his time at Oxford, one of Copleston's
main concerns was with the promotion of classical studies. In 1810
he had published anonymously a pamphlet entitled *A Reply to the
Calumnies of the Edinburgh Review against Oxford*, in which he had
argued that the study of Greek and Latin literature 'enriches and
ennobles all'.

In 1825, Copleston reviewed together Campbell's *Letter to Mr.
Brougham on the Subject of a London University* and 'Suggestions respecting the Plan of a College in London. He did not completely
oppose Campbell's ideas for the teaching of English literature, but
he dealt with them grudgingly to say the least, suggesting that they
were romantic and unrealistic. Campbell had marked out the sons
of the middle classes as the likely clientele for University College,
but Copleston saw a danger of breeding amongst these young men
'an ardent love of literature', and perhaps 'unsettling the minds of
many, who cannot aspire to live by it'. He admitted that the study
of English literature might not necessarily have the effect of unfit-
ting men for commerce, but he expressed the reservation that
prolonged and systematic study was unnecessary. He thereby hinted
at what became one of the major objections to the academic study
of English in later debates, as for example at Oxford in 1886 and
1887, that as a subject it was not sufficiently rigorous.

The following brief extract is taken from Copleston's review
which was published in the *Quarterly Review*, 33 (December 1825).

Review of Thomas Campbell's Plans for a College in London

* *
*

... the difficulty here lies in the supply of adequate motives for regular
and effective attendance; even supposing, (what is at first perhaps not
improbable) that a considerable number of persons in the middling
departments of trade will consent to grant their sons three or four years

of the prime of life, to be spent in studies that have no bearing upon their future occupation; and, what is more important, in studies which are not unlikely to breed a disgust in many minds for the less liberal employments to which they are in after-life destined.

The provision made against this difficulty by Mr. Campbell is to be found in the prospect held out of honours and rewards. 'I would advise,' says he, 'an annual distribution of prizes; and such an august spectacle in a London University would light up a generous emulation in every youthful breast, and stamp an improved character on the rising generation.' This is not so well said as it might have been, and partakes a little of the style of rhodomontade, from which the pamphlet is in general tolerably free. The distribution of prizes is doubtless a powerful incentive to those who expect by means of them to promote their interests in life, or to recommend themselves to employment, or, if placed beyond the necessity of employment, to acquire a reputation and an influence in the higher departments of society. They are of great utility also in schools, because a school is a world within itself; it constitutes the entire horizon, and is itself the sole business or profession of each boy while he belongs to it. But to be detained several years from entering upon active life in order to struggle for a prize by means of studies which have no connexion with the calling that awaits them, and when it is manifest that not one in fifty can actually succeed, is rather incongruous with the spirit of sober calculation by which trade prospers, and must cause many an industrious and unambitious parent to hesitate, before he barters the solid advantages of gain for the contingency of 'empty praise.'

If, on the other hand, the excitement be such as to breed an ardent love of literature, the danger undoubtedly is not to be overlooked of unsettling the minds of many, who cannot aspire to live by it, nor hope to obtain situations in virtue of this qualification. We are not starting vulgar and unphilosophical objections when we say this. They are such at least as occurred to the mind of one, whose zeal for the advancement of learning was only equalled by the enlarged view he also took of the moral, social, and political interests of mankind. 'Concerning the advancement of learning,' says Lord Bacon,

> I do subscribe to the opinion of one of the wisest and greatest men of your kingdom: That for grammar-schools there are already too many, and therefore no providence to add where there is excess: for the great number of schools which are in your highness's realm doth cause a want, and doth cause likewise an overflow; both of them inconvenient, and one of them dangerous. For by means thereof they find want in the country and towns, both of servants for husbandry, and apprentices for trade: and on the other side, there being more scholars

bred than the state can prefer and employ, and the active part of that life not bearing a proportion to the preparative, it must needs fall out, that many persons will be bred unfit for other vocations, and unprofitable for that in which they are brought up: which fills the realm full of indigent, idle, and wanton people, which are but *materia rerum novarum*.[1]

Still we are ready to admit that the lapse of two centuries has materially altered the case, especially in this country. We are become a nation of readers, as well as a commercial and an industrious nation. The enjoyment of English literature at least, is within the reach of every tradesman's family, as it actually forms the recreation of many of them in large towns; and it certainly has not come within our knowledge that such families are less attentive to their interests or less successful in business than others. But the education requisite to qualify men for this pleasure is not of the lengthened or systematic kind here contemplated. Authors, as well as readers, are to be the production of this nursery: and of those individuals who aim at distinction the majority must naturally incline to the profession of letters.

All these considerations, although they do not outweigh the arguments for affording greater facilities for instruction to the youth of the metropolis, yet ought to check the romantic hopes which seem to be entertained of a new character about to be impressed upon the population of London by this institution. Our object is not to suggest difficulties which may obstruct the undertaking, but to caution its friends against attempting too much, and by this error exciting a prejudice inimical to the whole design. Let that design be submitted to the judgment of the country, in its true lineaments, with no rhetorical ornament, and no exaggerated anticipations. Let it consist of a provision for instructing in certain branches of science and literature, those young men whose parents can spare two or three years for that purpose, previous to the life of business on which they must soon enter, but who cannot afford to support them at a distance from home as the associates of a class destined to fill the higher ranks and the more liberal employments of life.

*   *
*

Notes

1. #*Advice to the King touching Mr Sutton's Estate*. [This letter is included in *The Letters and the Life of Francis Bacon*, ed. James Spedding (1868), IV, 252–253.] *Materia rerum novarum*: an occasion for revolution.

CHAPTER FOUR

Thomas Babington Macaulay

Thomas Babington Macaulay (1800–1859) had a varied career as barrister, MP, Member of the Supreme Council of India, essayist and historian. In at least two of these roles he lent support to English studies.

As an essayist writing in the *Edinburgh Review* in 1826, he attacked the vested interests which were opposing the new college in London proposed by Thomas Campbell. Macaulay believed that Oxford and Cambridge had become ossified; the world had moved on, but they had not, and competition would be good for them. Among the subjects which the new college should teach were, Macaulay believed, English history, literature and language.

Then, as Member of the Supreme Council of India, he again urged the importance of English studies, this time for potential servants of the East India Company. Later, in 1854, he was chairman of a committee for laying down the rules for examination of candidates for employment in India, and as a result of the work of this committee, English studies became one of the most important subjects. Its inclusion in these examinations provided English with a huge impetus, although it is also true to say that the emphasis on being able to learn and reproduce large numbers of facts helped to establish the subject in many minds as a crammer's delight.

This extract is taken from Macaulay's 1826 article for the *Edinburgh Review*, 'Thoughts on the Advancement of Academical Education in England.' It shows his low regard for Latin, both the language and literature, his high regard for Greek, but also a sense that the cost of learning Greek was very high in terms of the neglect of much else. Modern continental languages were neglected, and even worse, so was English literature.

It is interesting to find the customary absence of classics in female education being used as an argument for omitting it from boys' education as well. A conversation with an accomplished woman ought to give the lie to any idea that a knowledge of Latin is essential to purity of English diction. Later, in the context of the Schools Inquiry Commission, we find the excellence of women novelists being cited in a similar way by the Earl of Harrowby as evidence against the absolute importance of classics in education.

'Thoughts on the Advancement of Academical Education in England'

* *
*

… We feel the warmest admiration for the great remains of antiquity. We gratefully acknowledge the benefits which mankind has owed to them. But we would no more suffer a pernicious system to be protected by the reverence which is due to them, than we would show our reverence for a saint by erecting his shrine into a sanctuary for criminals.

An eloquent scholar has said, that ancient literature was the ark in which all the civilization of the world was preserved during the deluge of barbarism. We confess it. But we do not read that Noah thought himself bound to live in the ark after the deluge had subsided. When our ancestors first began to consider the study of the classics as the principal part of education, little or nothing worth reading was to be found in any modern language. Circumstances have confessedly changed. Is it not possible that a change of system may be desirable?

Our opinion of the Latin tongue will, we fear, be considered heretical. We cannot but think that its vocabulary is miserably poor, and its mechanism deficient both in power and precision. The want of a definite article, and of a distinction between the preterite and the aorist tenses, are two defects which are alone sufficient to place it below any other language with which we are acquainted. In its most flourishing era it was reproached with poverty of expression. Cicero, indeed, was induced, by his patriotic feelings, to deny the charge. But the perpetual recurrence of Greek words in his most hurried and familiar letters, and the frequent use which he is compelled to make of them, in spite of all his exertions to avoid them, in his philosophical works, fully prove that even this great master of the Latin tongue felt the evil which he laboured to conceal from others.

We do not think much better of the writers, as a body, than of the language. The literature of Rome was born old. All the signs of decrepitude were on it in the cradle. We look in vain for the sweet lisp and the graceful wildness of an infant dialect. We look in vain for a single great creative mind, – for a Homer or a Dante, a Shakespeare or a Cervantes. In their place we have a crowd of fourth-rate and fifth-rate authors, translators, and imitators without end. The rich heritage of Grecian philosophy and poetry was fatal to the Romans. They would have acquired more wealth, if they had succeeded to less. Instead of accumulating fresh intellectual treasures, they contented themselves with enjoying, disposing in new forms, or impairing by an injudicious management, those which they took by descent. Hence, in most of their works, there is scarcely any thing spontaneous and racy, scarcely any originality in the thoughts, scarcely any idiom in the style. Their poetry tastes of the hot-house. It is transplanted from Greece, with the earth of Pindus clinging round its roots. It is nursed in careful seclusion from the Italian air. The gardeners are often skilful; but the fruit is almost always sickly. One hardy and prickly shrub, of genuine Latin growth, must indeed be excepted. Satire was the only indigenous produce of Roman talent; and, in our judgment, by far the best.

We are often told the Latin language is more strictly grammatical than the English; and that it is, therefore, necessary to study it, in order to speak English with elegance and accuracy. This is one of those remarks, which are repeated till they pass into axioms, only because they have so little meaning, that no body thinks it worth while to refute them at their first appearance. If those who say that the Latin language is more strictly grammatical than the English, mean only that it is more regular, that there are fewer exceptions to its general laws of derivation, inflection, and construction, we grant it. This is, at least for the purposes of the orator and the poet, rather a defect than a merit; but be it merit or defect, it can in no possible way facilitate the acquisition of any other language. It would be about as reasonable to say, that the simplicity of the Code Napoleon renders the study of the laws of England easier than formerly. If it be meant, that the Latin language is formed in more strict accordance with the general principles of grammar than the English, that is to say, that the relations which words bear to each other are more strictly analogous to the relations between the ideas which they represent in Latin than in English, we venture to doubt the fact.... A man who thinks the knowledge of Latin essential to the purity of English diction, either has never conversed with an accomplished woman, or does not deserve to have conversed with her. We are sure, that all persons who are in the habit of hearing public speaking must have observed, that the orators who are fondest of quoting Latin, are by no means the most scrupulous about marring their native tongue. We could mention several Members of Parliament, who never fail to usher in their scraps of Horace and Juvenal with half a dozen false concords.

The Latin language is principally valuable as an introduction to the Greek, the insignificant portico of a most chaste and majestic fabric. On this subject, our Confession of Faith will, we trust, be approved by the most orthodox scholar. We cannot refuse our admiration to that most wonderful and perfect machine of human thought, to the flexibility, the harmony, the gigantic power, the exquisite delicacy, the infinite wealth of words, the incomparable felicity of expression, in which are united the energy of the English, the neatness of the French, the sweet and infantine simplicity of the Tuscan. Of all dialects, it is the best fitted for

31

the purposes both of science and of elegant literature. The philosophical vocabularies of ancient Rome, and of modern Europe, have been derived from that of Athens. Yet none of the imitations has ever approached the richness and precision of the original... .

* *
*

But though we are sensible that great advantages may be derived from the study of the Greek language, we think that they may be purchased at too high a price: And we think that seven or eight years of the life of a man who is to enter into active life at two or three-and-twenty, is too high a price. Those are bad economists who look only to the excellence of the article for which they are bargaining, and never ask about the cost. The cost, in the present instance, is too often the whole of that invaluable portion of time during which a fund of intellectual pleasure is to be stored up, and the foundations of wisdom and usefulness laid. No person doubts that much knowledge may be obtained from the Classics. It is equally certain that much gold may be found in Spain. But it by no means necessarily follows, that it is wise to work the Spanish mines, or to learn the ancient languages. Before the voyage of Columbus, Spain supplied all Europe with the precious metals. The discovery of America changed the state of things. New mines were found, from which gold could be procured in greater plenty, and with less labour. The old works were therefore abandoned – it being manifest those who persisted in laying out capital on them would be undersold and ruined. A new world of literature and science has also been discovered. New veins of intellectual wealth have been laid open. But a monstrous system of bounties and prohibitions compels us still to go on delving for a few glittering grains in the dark and laborious shaft of antiquity, instead of penetrating a district which would reward a less painful search with a more lucrative return. If, after the conquest of Peru, Spain had enacted that, in order to enable the old mines to maintain a competition against the new, a hundred pistoles should be given to every person who should extract an ounce of gold from them, the parallel would be complete.

* *
*

No man, we allow, can be said to have received a complete and liberal education, unless he have acquired a knowledge of the ancient languages. But not one gentleman in fifty can possibly receive what we should call a complete and liberal education. That term includes not only the ancient languages, but those of France, Italy, Germany, and Spain. It includes mathematics, the experimental sciences, and moral philosophy. An intimate acquaintance with the profound and polite parts of English literature is indispensable. Few of those who are intended for professional or commercial life can find time for all these studies. It necessarily follows, that some portion of them must be given up: And the question is, what portion? We say, provide for the mind as you provide for the body, – first necessaries, – then conveniences, – lastly luxuries. Under which of those heads do the Greek and Latin languages come? Surely under the last. Of all the pursuits which we have mentioned, they require the greatest sacrifice of time. He who can afford time for them, and for the others also, is perfectly right in acquiring them. He who cannot, will, if he is wise, be content to go without them. If a man is able to continue his studies till his twenty-eighth or thirtieth year, by all means let him learn Latin and Greek. If he must terminate them at one-and-twenty, we should in general advise him to be satisfied with the modern languages. If he is forced to enter into active life at fifteen or sixteen, we should think it best that he should confine himself almost entirely to his native tongue, and thoroughly imbue his mind with the spirit of its best writers. But no! The artificial restraints and encouragements which our academic system has introduced have altogether *reversed* this natural and salutary order of things. We deny ourselves what is indispensable, that we may procure what is superfluous. We act like a day-labourer who should stint himself in bread, that he might now and then treat himself with a pottle of January strawberries. Cicero tells us, in the *Offices*, a whimsical anecdote of Cato the Censor. Somebody asked him what was the best mode of employing capital. He said, To farm good pasture land. What the next? To farm middling pasture land. What next? To farm bad pasture land. Now the notions which prevail in England respecting classical learning seem to us very much to resemble those which the old Roman entertained with regard to his favourite method of cultivation. Is a young man able to spare the time necessary for passing through the University? Make him a good classical scholar! But a second, instead of residing at the University, must go into business when he leaves school. Make him then a tolerable classical scholar! A third has still less time for snatching up knowledge, and is destined for active employment while still a boy. Make him a bad classical scholar! If he does not become a Flaminius or a Buchanan, he may learn to write nonsense verses. If he does not get on to Horace, he may read the first book of Caesar. If there is not time even for such a degree of improvement, he may at least be flogged through that immemorial vestibule of learning. 'Quis docet? Who teacheth? Magister docet. The master teacheth.' Would to heaven that he taught something better worth knowing!

* * *

CHAPTER FIVE

Thomas Dale

Thomas Dale (1797–1870) was educated at Christ's Hospital and Corpus Christi College, Cambridge. He published his first collection of poetry while still a student, and went on to publish several more, as well as a verse translation of the tragedies of Sophocles. After Cambridge, he was for a short time a very successful private tutor, before being ordained in 1822 and becoming a popular evangelical preacher, holding incumbencies in a number of different parishes in and around London. In 1828, he was appointed Professor of English Language and Literature at the newly-founded University College, London (then known as 'the University of London'), thereby holding the first chair of English in England. His time at University College was not altogether happy, and he resigned in 1830. However, in 1836, he went on to become the first Professor of English Literature and History at University College's rival in London, King's College, staying there until 1839. Thereafter, Dale made his career mainly in the Church, finishing his life as Dean of Rochester.

The text printed here is from Dale's introductory lecture at University College. Although the title of the Chair includes both language and literature, the title of the course for which this is the introduction is 'Principles and Practice of English Composition.' He did also teach a literature course, but this was run as an evening class, designed for anyone who wanted to attend, whether full-time University College students or not. In this introductory lecture to his main course, Dale's enthusiasm for English literature is clear, but its study figures here only in connection with language and composition. Students will learn to write or speak good English only if they study English authors. The course, and therefore this lecture, is mainly concerned with the history and 'philosophy' of the language, leading up to its use and application, or composition. Finally, he stresses his intention of being a moral as well as mental instructor, an aim for which he has probably been most remembered. All his lectures, but particularly those dealing with literature, will aim to teach moral lessons.

THOMAS DALE

'Introductory Lecture' at University College, London, 1828

* * *

... In the formation of my plan, I have been guided solely by a view to the general benefit; it is the offspring of much serious and patient deliberation – and I have at least brought to my task one qualification for judging of its probable efficiency. I am not destitute of experience in the ordinary acquirements of those young men who may be expected to constitute the larger proportion of my future audience, and whose benefit therefore I have especially consulted – those, I mean, who having completed their scholastic education, are now, as it were, preparing their weapons and polishing their armour, that they may enter fully equipped into the arena of public or professional life. I am aware that young men of this description, however conversant with studies that are strictly classical, are sometimes comparatively unpractised in English composition, and often wholly unacquainted with the principles of the English language, whenever it differs – as it does in many and important particulars – from the Latin and the Greek. Nor can I have any hesitation in stating explicitly, to what cause this deficiency may be ascribed. 'Youths,' it is erroneously argued, 'must learn the ancient or foreign languages from tutors, while an acquaintance with their own is spontaneously and inevitably attained; – in this they require neither instruction nor assistance – reading and observation will be found of themselves sufficient to accomplish all.'

The fallacy of this argument will sufficiently appear, when we arrive at the consideration of the study of the English language, as detached and distinguished from the study of English literature: the observations which I am *now* about to offer, relate to the connection of each with the other – perhaps it would be better to say, the union of both. You will, I think, Gentlemen, readily admit, that in order to form a correct estimate of the value and utility of any particular study, it requires to be contemplated not merely in an independent and exclusive aspect, but in its general relation to the entire system and primary object of a liberal education; – just as we should calculate the dimensions of a mountain, not by its elevation above the valley, but by the comparative altitude of other hills with which it is surrounded. Now the system of a liberal education may be modelled on the principle of comprehending all useful knowledge, which is called general education; or of preparing the pupils more immediately for some specific occupation or pursuit, which is termed professional education. The object of both, however, must be identical; namely, that the student may hereafter occupy a respectable, if not an eminent, position in society. And, as an unavoidable inference, we should attach the highest importance to those studies, by which that desirable object may be most effectually promoted.

Regarding the main trunk of education, therefore, as dividing itself into two great branches, – general and professional education, – you will naturally inquire, what relation the study of the English language, connected with that of English literature, sustains to each of these? To this I reply, that for professional education it is expedient – to general education it is essential. Happily, in proof of the former of these positions, there is no need that I should lead you far, or detain you long. I have only to bring to your remembrance the opening Lecture which was delivered within the walls of this University by the Professor of Physiology,[1] at which some of you, I doubt not, had the gratification to be present. It becomes not me to speak of that gentleman's distinguished rank in his peculiar profession, which has long been (as it ever must be) decided by the unerring suffrage of the public voice: but I may with propriety advert to that combined perspicuity, copiousness, and elegance of diction, which rendered the communication of science from his lips as delightful as it was instructive. I may cite him as an illustrious example of the advantages which redound to a professional man, from an intimate and practical acquaintance with the beauties and peculiarities of his own language; for if – you will bear me witness – if the scientific information which he imparted on that occasion excited the interest of many, the chaste and expressive language in which it was conveyed commanded the approbation of all. – One such example has more influence than a thousand arguments.

Having thus confirmed by example (the most convincing of all evidence) the truth of our first position, – that the study of the English language and literature is expedient for professional education, – I am now to establish the second; that it is an essential part of general education. This point, however, may be promptly decided by the answer to a very simple question, Why do we educate our children? To this enquiry a judicious and reflecting parent will reply, 'to promote in the first instance their individual benefit; then to furnish them with the means of contributing to the benefit of others.' Now if the former of these objects is best ensured by correctness of thought, the latter demands in an equal degree accuracy of expression. For though our conceptions may be clear, our sentiments just, our imagination lively, our information varied and extensive; unless we also possess the power of expressing our thoughts in appropriate and adequate terms, all these advantages, great as they are, will contribute little to the enjoyment or improvement of those with whom we may be connected. While therefore the youthful mind, as its powers gradually expand, is copiously stored with materials for future reflection, derived from the oral instructions of sensible and experienced teachers, or from the inexhaustible treasures of ancient and modern literature, the work of education is yet far from complete. Not only should the student be trained to receive and to retain the ideas of others; he must be taught to arrange, to combine, and above all, to express his own; and in so doing, to identify the language of the lips and of the pen with the language of the mind; to acquire, as far as practicable, powers of expression progressively commensurate with the growing capacity of thought. This point, however, notwithstanding its evident importance, is seldom sufficiently regarded in systems of instruction, and consequently the means of attaining it are proportionably neglected. Yet to what other cause, than the want of early attention to the perusal of English authors and the practice of English composition, can we attibute the familiar fact – that the classical student, when summoned to sustain his part in the active intercourse of society, is so often found to speak in his own language with hesitation, and to write with difficulty? Wherefore is he thus embarrassed and perplexed, – but because he feels that his powers of expression are altogether inadequate to embody in a suitable form, the conceptions of his mind; and that unless he will hoard his intellectual stores, like the gold of a miser, for his own selfish and solitary gratification, his only alternative is to occupy a much lower place in public estimation, than that to which he is justly entitled?

To point out how this error might be obviated in a system of education which should commence with the opening dawn of the intellectual powers, would be no difficult task: but it will be a much more arduous undertaking to apply the remedy where the evil has been of long continuance; and, above all, to combine the delicacy which the feelings of such students demand, with that familiarity and minuteness of explanation, which are indispensable to learners of less advanced age, and of inferior attainments. Fully alive to the importance of this part of my duty, I yet hope that I shall be enabled to accomplish it; and I shall feel peculiar pleasure in affording to gentlemen who may favour me with a private interview, any information which they may require on the subjects of the different lectures, and in directing them to such a course of English reading, as may be calculated to supply their conscious deficiency, while at the same time it is congenial with a classical taste, and gratifying to a cultivated mind. They will not be long in discovering, that regard and admiration are far from being exclusively due to the great masters of antiquity; that their own literature can boast of writers equally eminent in almost every department of composition; and that, if the claims of a language on our attention are to be decided by the number, variety, and excellence of the authors who have employed it, the English language may fear-lessly challenge comparison with any other, living or dead.

* * *

Here then I dismiss all further reference to the study of English lit-erature, as connected with that of the language; – not, I confess, with-out reluctance; for it is a theme on which I could expatiate with almost enthusiastic delight, – a theme which is far better calculated to awaken general interest, than the less attractive, but not less important subject, to which I must now direct your exclusive consideration, – the expedi-ency and usefulness of the distinct study of the English language. Your own good sense, Gentlemen, will spare me the necessity of demon-strating a proposition, the truth of which is so obvious, that it may be accounted nearly equivalent to an axiom; – That of all languages to which the attention of the student can be directed, *that* is first entitled to consideration, which will be called into most frequent exercise in active life; and of his proficiency in which almost every individual, with whom he may in future chance to be associated, will be competent to form an opinion. As at Athens the refined ear of a common herb-woman could detect a trivial inaccuracy in the dialect of an accomplished phi-losopher, so in the present improved condition of society, many per-sons of the lowest rank, especially in this metropolis, are often no contemptible judges of propriety and purity of diction, and will natu-rally estimate the acquirements of an individual by the only criterion which they are able to apply. Consequently, if to excel in other lan-guages be creditable, to be deficient in this is both injurious and dis-graceful; nor can the English student be too earnestly recommended to cultivate a critical acquaintance with his native tongue. According to the judicious observations of an eminent living author,[2] who has con-tributed greatly to facilitate the study of the English language, by re-storing that simplicity of structure which is among its principal recommendations: 'It is an egregious error to imagine, that a perfect knowledge of Greek and Latin precludes the necessity of studying the principles of English Grammar. The structure of the ancient and that of the modern languages are very dissimilar. Nay, the peculiar idioms of any language, how like soever in its general principles to any other, must be learned by study, and an attentive perusal of the best writers in that language. Nor can any imputation be more reproachful to the pro-ficient in Classical literature, than with a critical knowledge of Greek and Latin, which are now dead languages, to be superficially acquainted with his native tongue, in which he must think, and speak, and write.'

The distinguished author to whom I am indebted for this seasonable quotation, has combined in its concluding sentence the three great constituents of a perfect English scholar. He should be able to think, to speak, and to write in his own language: to think with freedom and correctness; to speak with promptitude and propriety; to write with ease and perspicuity. The first of these qualifications, as we have already seen, is more immediately connected with, and dependent on, the study of literature in general, and specifically of English literature, as yielding to no other branch of the majestic and ever-expanding tree of knowledge in the luxuriance of its foliage and the flavour of its fruit; – the second and third involve the study of Grammar. The object of Grammar is to convey the knowledge of a language; and it is quite an error to imagine that grammatical information can only be attained by a mere mechanical process, – by the exertion of the memory apart from the exercise of the intellect. 'Grammar, in its general principles,' observes the author of that invaluable work, *The Philosophy of Rhetoric*, 'has a close connection with the understanding.'[3] Nor is this assertion more true of Grammar in general, than of English Grammar in particular. Accordingly, I can enumerate many ways in which the intellectual powers are agreeably and profitably exercised in this study, as it may be pursued by students of not very immature age; such, for example, as inquiring into the formation of alphabets, investigating the etymology of words, tracing cognate terms through various languages, observing the gradual influx of new words and phrases, comparing the diversified modes of expression by which the same meaning may be conveyed, examining the structure of the several languages which are derived from one parent stock, and many others: but we must not forget that the plan of the Lectures on the English Language still remains to be indicated; and I will therefore confine myself to one further benefit resulting from the study of English Grammar, the value of which, Gentlemen, you can all appreciate: – I mean, the acquisition of a copious stock of words, coupled with judgment to select the most appropriate.

Words are defined by grammarians to be the signs of things or of ideas. Obviously, therefore, those words are to be preferred, both in speaking and in writing, which most correctly represent the thing or idea intended, and which not only convey the desired impression to the hearer or reader, but convey no impression of an opposite or different character. But how can the student expect to attain the faculty of thus discriminating his words, without a previous initiation into the mysteries of the language; without having traced terms backward to their original signification, and followed them onward to the meaning which is now assigned to them by the unappealable law of custom.[4] For the observation of Horace respecting the Latin is equally applicable to the English tongue, – that many words, in the lapse of time, have widely deviated from their primitive signification; some have become diametrically opposed to it; many terms which were employed by the early writers are now wholly discarded; and not a few are introduced by authors of the present day, which deserve, and in all probability will hereafter experience, a similar fate. If therefore the English student is anxious to unite in his own speech and writing the three distinguishing features of a chaste and perspicuous style: – first, that his words be pure English, free from the rust of obsoleteness on the one hand, and the tinsel of novelty on the other; next, that the construction and arrangement of his sentences be in the English idiom, unalloyed by those solecisms which may pass undiscovered in speech, but will infallibly be detected in writing; and lastly, that his words and phrases be employed to express the precise meaning which custom has affixed to them, – so that obscurity and ambiguity may be altogether banished from both, these useful ends can only be attained by combining a careful perusal of the great English masters in every species of composition, with a close examination of their diction, and an accurate investigation of their style. He must not only compute the dimensions and ascertain the exact proportions of the building, but inspect the quality and substance of the materials of which it is composed.

Permit me now, Gentlemen, to direct your attention to the projected plan and arrangement of the Lectures on the Principles and Practice of English Composition, to which the present is introductory.

My plan for the critical study of the English language, as adapted to young men who have previously received the rudiments of a classical education, embraces three great divisions.

I. THE HISTORY OF THE LANGUAGE, comprehending a view of its origin, formation, progress, and perfection. – I use the term perfection in a relative sense (for absolute perfection can be predicated of no language whatever); but assuming that a language to whose stock of words no material addition has been made for upwards of two centuries, may now be accounted *stationary*, or perfect in proportion to its capacity.

II. THE PHILOSOPHY OF THE LANGUAGE; under which head I include the classification and analysis of its constituent parts, or sorts of words; their relation to, and dependence on, each other; the principles of pronunciation and orthography; the etymologies of words; the construction of sentences; the force and harmony of periods: in short, all that relates to the genius and structure of the language.

III. THE USE AND APPLICATION OF THE LANGUAGE in the various kinds of speaking and composition; commencing with the plain and perspicuous, and proceeding upward to the elevated and majestic style.

On each of these divisions it will be expedient, and I hope not tedious, to offer a few observations.

An inquiry into the origin, formation, and progress of the English language, may be compared to a voyage up the channel of a magnificent and hitherto unexplored river. In ascending the stream, as you pass the confluence of one tributary after another with the parent flood, the width may be observed continually to diminish, and the depth gradually to decrease; – at length all further progress is impeded by some natural barrier; and though the river has now dwindled to a rill, the fountain whence it issues cannot be precisely ascertained; for it divides itself into innumerable branches, or escapes among impassable rocks. Thus in tracing the stream of our language backward to its remoter sources, when we have ascended beyond the derivatives which successively flowed into it from the Latin, Greek, and French, and arrived at the scanty dialect of our Saxon forefathers, – henceforth all is obscurity and conjecture… .

*
 * *

From the HISTORY we pass, by an obvious and easy transition, to the PHILOSOPHY of the Language, a term which I have adopted rather from regard to comprehensiveness of arrangement, than to its primary and peculiar signification. Did I not fear to be suspected of invading the department of my medical colleagues, I should almost prefer to entitle it the ANATOMY OF THE LANGUAGE. It involves, in fact, a species of dissection in which I possess one great advantage over those gentlemen; there is here no deficiency of subjects, and they may be procured without any difficulty. In this division of the Lectures, my first step will be to exhibit a series of alphabets derived in succession from each other:[5] the Ionic Greek, the Roman, the Gothic, the Anglo-Saxon, and the English. This will naturally lead to a comparative view of the English Alphabet with others, both ancient and modern; an inquiry into its deficiencies and redundancies; an examination of the various sounds which it produces, and the combinations of letters by which they are produced. This is called the science of ORTHÖEPY, or the just utterance of words. ORTHOGRAPHY, in the proper sense, is the expression of words by suitable characters or letters: and here I shall content myself with laying down a few rules to be applied in doubtful cases; since to enter into detail would be tedious, and in most instances unnecessary. Much time and attention, on the other hand, will be devoted to a subject, which I account of peculiar interest; viz. the ETYMOLOGY OF

41

THE LANGUAGE. Admitting the position first adduced, and, I think, established by Mr Tooke, that there are in English, properly speaking, but two essential parts of speech, Noun and Verb; I shall yet develope in succession the nature, properties, and use of all the parts of speech as they are generally enumerated by grammarians, and for the common appellatives of which I know of no others that could be substituted with advantage... .

Reverting now to our former comparison between the acquisition of a language and the erection of a building, we may presume that by this time the foundation will have been excavated, the materials prepared, the effect of their judicious combination and the proportion of their respective parts fully ascertained, and every thing in preparation for the production of a solid and substantial, but not an ornamental structure. In other words, we may now suppose the student to be fully provided with every knowledge of the language, which is requisite for composing with precision and perspicuity. But how shall we ensure that he *will* be thus provided? For it must be obvious to all of you, Gentlemen, that the mere exposition of the theory of a language in lectures, however lucid or interesting those lectures may be at the time of their delivery, can be of little permanent advantage, unless the information thus conveyed be deeply imprinted on the memory, and fully apprehended by the understanding. To ensure the former of these objects, therefore, I shall make it my particular request, that at the close of each lecture, every student will deliver to me an epitome in writing of the subjects which have been discussed, to which purpose a sufficient interval shall be appropriated. I shall then dictate a series of questions on the lecture immediately preceding, and as the answers are presented to me, an opportunity will be afforded of offering such observations on the epitome as may seem expedient. Thus will also be ensured the advantage of the teacher coming into personal communication with every individual in his class, and ascertaining their respective proficiency by oral as well as written examinations. And let me here express my full persuasion, that for the preservation of order on this and on all occasions, I shall have a sufficient guarantee in that propriety of demeanour and delicacy of feeling which are always conspicuous in young men of liberal education, especially when they see in their instructor – what I trust I may venture to promise them – a lively solicitude for their welfare, and unwearied endeavours for their improvement.

Having thus provided, during the previous portion of the course, for those important points, – the recollection and understanding of the principles of the language, – I purpose to proceed, Gentlemen, to the third great division, THE USE AND APPLICATION OF THESE PRINCIPLES, in various styles of composition. The students will here commence their written exercises with themes or essays on given subjects in a plain and perspicuous style, from which every species of ornament will be in the first instance studiously excluded. For to speak and to write with correctness are the first considerations; elegant and graceful decoration, however desirable, are yet of secondary import. A very effective oration may be delivered, a very interesting letter written, a very ingenious essay composed, without a single ornament from the commencement to the close. Assuming therefore that propriety of costume is indispensable to the advantageous display of ornament, I shall attempt to secure in the first instance that purity and propriety of diction, unaccompanied by which, figurative language must be always inconsistent and not seldom ridiculous. This being attained, I shall no longer defer the description and explanation of the various figures of speech, commencing with that first-born of fancy, Simile, and proceeding next to others of the same class, Metaphor, Personification, Allegory, and the rest; constantly illustrating the misemployment, as well as the proper and legitimate use of each, by appropriate examples, selected as far as practicable from writers of established reputation. For I consider it an object of far greater moment to preclude the admission of inappropriate or unnatural metaphor, than even to supply directions for its judicious and tasteful management: remembering, that while prose composition of almost every description may interest and even attract, without any decoration whatever, an unseasonable ornament is a blemish which cannot fail in written composition to offend the eye, and seldom even in speaking to grate upon the ear. Never do these *'purpurei panni'*[6] appear to so little advantage, as when they differ in colour or in texture from the garment which they are intended to adorn.

I propose to conclude the course with a few lectures on style, delineating the character, analysing the constituents, and exemplifying the employment of various styles, which I will not now detain you by enumerating. Nor yet will I stop to particularize some other subjects, which could not consistently enter into the order of the course, but may be profitably considered in a single lecture; such for example as an investigation of the causes of Ambiguity of expression and of the means by which it may be avoided. I will only express my hope, that those students who may have pursued the course throughout, will be enabled at its termination to speak their own language with accuracy, and to write it with perspicuity, if not to speak with fluency, and to compose with elegance.

Such then are the duties which I consider to be connected with my office, and such are the means by which I trust and purpose to discharge them. But, Gentlemen, I cannot enter upon the arduous and important task which awaits me in this University, without reminding you – and I would do so with that seriousness and solemnity which become my office here and my profession everywhere – that mere intellectual improvement is not, or should not be, the exclusive or even the primary object of education. Moral and religious principles are infinitely more momentous to the character and interests of the future man, than the cultivation of the mind alone, whether we look to the individual himself, or to the influence which he will hereafter exercise upon society. The talented and accomplished scholar may shine in public and social life; may astonish by the depth of his erudition, or charm by the graces of his eloquence, or dazzle by the coruscations of his wit; – but the MAN OF PRINCIPLE ONLY is the centre round which domestic felicity revolves; he ONLY contibutes to the real and enduring benefit of his near and dear connections. Contemplated in this aspect – and few I think will refuse thus to contemplate it – the morality which may be learned from ANY system of religious opinions that professes to take the Bible for its basis, deserves to be estimated far more highly than the most extensive acquirements and even the most splendid abilities, if uncontrolled by those motives and principles of action, which alone can direct them to the production of solid and abiding advantage. Devoid of these principles, they have been almost invariably found – like sharp and polished weapons in the hands of a lunatic – to inflict a mortal wound on their possessor, and strike deep at the best interests of society. In the history of our literature, more particularly of the drama, it will be my painful duty to point out too many names which exemplify this assertion; – too many, whose wreath of imperishable laurel is interwoven with bitter and deadly herbs, which, like the envenomed diadem that encircled the brow of the Christian virgin in the days of fiery persecution, insinuate a subtle poison into the veins, and convey it even to the heart!

Gentlemen, I do not offer these observations from any apprehension that the course which I purpose to take in this respect can require apology. – I believe that the absence of such considerations on such an occasion would do violence to your feelings, – I am sure it would be a dereliction of my duty. I owe it to the Council of the University, in whose benevolent and enlightened views I most heartily concur, and in the purity of whose motives I most implicitly confide; I owe it to those parents, who may entrust the education of their sons to this rising Institution, and who, whatever be their religious tenets, are fully aware that no intellectual attainment could compensate to their children for the absence of sound and salutary moral principle; I owe it to my own character, as a member and minister of the National Church, to avow openly and unreservedly, that both in these Lectures – and in the other course which it will be my duty to deliver, I shall invariably aim to be a moral as well as mental instructor. Indeed, I know not how to separate these characters: it has been the business of my life to combine them; and were the union incompatible with my office in this University, I should not address you now. But in all my lectures, more particularly when treating upon that glorious and inexhaustible subject, the LIT-ERATURE of our country – I shall esteem it my duty – and I trust shall find it my delight, – to inculcate lessons of virtue, through the medium of the masters of our language. Nor to those parents who are acquainted with the earlier productions of English Literature, will such a declaration appear superfluous or misplaced. *They* know, that the gems with which it is so copiously adorned, sometimes require to be extracted and exhibited with a careful hand, lest they should convey pollution with the foul mass of daring profaneness or disgusting wantonness in which they are too often incrusted. *They* at least, therefore, will appreciate my motive, when I delare, that never, in tracking the course of those brilliant luminaries that sparkle in the firmament of our literature, – never will I suffer the eye of unexperienced youth to be dazzled by the brilliancy of genius, when its broad lustre obscures the deformity of vice; never will I affect to stifle the expression of a just indignation, when wit, taste and talent, have been designedly prostituted by their unworthy possessors to the excitement of unholy passions, the palliation of guilty indulgences, the ridicule of virtue, or the disparagement of religion. All extracts which I may present from successive authors in exemplification of the progress of our language; all specimens which I may exhibit as models of composition, shall be selected with a scrupulous regard to their scope and tendency: nor will I, however apt or pertinent the illustration which might thus be afforded, cite any passage which insinuates an immoral sentiment, or implies, however obliquely, an impure idea. And I reiterate my full conviction, that in thus combining the moral instruction with the mental improvement of the students, I shall act in accordance with the great principle which influences the directors and supporters of this noble establishment. Their object is indeed to accelerate the 'march of intellect,' – a phrase now scarcely preserved by its expressiveness from degenerating into mere cant, and for which I would prefer to substitute the progress of knowledge. But they know that the march of intellect, or the progress of knowledge, call it which you may, will never be retarded, because virtue and religion accompany her on either side. They see that knowledge and virtue derive a lustre from Religion, which she cannot derive from them; for if knowledge be excellent, and virtue admirable – RELIGION IS DIVINE.

Gentlemen, in thus introducing the sacred name of RELIGION to an assemblage like the present, where various and perhaps conflicting

45

opinions are entertained by many on this most important of all subjects, I feel that I have ventured upon difficult ground. Let me not however be suspected of affixing an exclusive meaning to the word. Firmly attached, from examination and reflection, to that form of Christianity which is the established religion of the state, I yet disclaim from my heart the most distant intention of interfering with the sacred right of private judgment, or of compromising in any degree the leading principle of this truly liberal Institution, – that scientific and literary pursuits have no connection whatever with the religious persuasion of any individual. While therefore I announce with unfeigned gratification, that the munificence of noble and distinguished individuals connected with the University has provided the means of religious instruction for students of the Church of England – a means which it shall be my care to make effectual, – not to such alone will the moral lessons, which may incidentally be conveyed in these lectures be adapted. There I shall make no distinction, for there will I know no difference; and if there are any to whose peculiar opinions violence will be offered, those only are the persons who discard from their system, whatever it be, the PRACTICAL INFLUENCE OF MORAL PRINCIPLES, and who, in the cultivation of the intellect, the most valuable endowment of our nature, have no higher or nobler aim than to advance their sordid interest, and minister to their sensual enjoyment; regardless alike of the happiness of their connections, the welfare of society, their own true dignity, or the honour of their God. Never, never may this seat of learning be desecrated by the intermixture of such persons with its train of youthful and ingenuous students; or if any such enter its walls, may they retire from hence, living instances of the truth of that approved saying, 'THAT THE CULTIVATION OF THE MIND IS THE SUREST GUIDE TO VIRTUE, THE MOST EFFECTIVE AUXILIARY OF RELIGION.'

Notes

1. # Professor Bell.
2. # Dr [Alexander] Crombie: Treatise on *The Etymology and Syntax of the English Language*; Concluding Remarks [1802].
3. George Campbell, *The Philosophy of Rhetoric* (1776).
4. # 'Multa renascentur, quae jam cecidere.' Horace, *Ars Poetica*, 70. [Many words which have now died out may again revive.]
5. # [Thomas] Astle, *The Origin and Progress of Writing* [1784].
6. Purple patches.

CHAPTER SIX

F.D. Maurice

F.D. Maurice (1805–1872) is best remembered today as a nine-teenth-century Liberal Anglican, or Broad Church, theologian, and as a leader of the Christian Socialist movement. However, his *curriculum vitae* also contained a period as a professor of English literature and history, and he had wide interests in education.

Born the son of a Unitarian minister, Maurice remained a member of that denomination at the age when he was ready to commence his university studies. He was able to enter Trinity College, Cambridge in 1823, since no religious tests were imposed at Cambridge at time of entry. He later transferred to Trinity Hall, where he took a first in the Civil Law classes, but he took no degree, as he was unwilling to subscribe to the Thirty-Nine Articles of the Church of England, which was a precondition of graduation. While at Cambridge, Maurice co-edited the *Metropolitan Quarterly Magazine*, for which he wrote articles attacking Utilitarianism and praising Romantic writers, especially Coleridge. Also while at Cambridge, he became a founder member of the Apostles' Club.

In 1831, Maurice entered the Church of England, and was ordained in 1834, becoming Chaplain to Guy's Hospital in 1836. In 1840, he became Professor of English Literature and History at King's College, London, adding the Chair of Theology to his duties in 1846. In 1848, he and other professors from King's College founded Queen's College in London for the education of governesses, Maurice being its first principal.

Maurice's liberal theological views made him deeply unpopular with some sections of the Church of England, with the result that his position at the Anglican and far from free-thinking King's College became increasingly difficult, and he was forced out in 1853 as a result of his disbelief in eternal punishment. His social commitment and his concern to extend education among sections of the population hitherto little touched by it led him to think in terms of a Working Men's College, and the first of these opened at Queen Square in 1854, with Maurice as principal. In 1866, he returned to Cambridge as Knightsbridge Professor of Casuistry,

Moral Theology and Moral Philosophy, but he still retained his position as Principal of the Working Men's College.

The first item included here is from *Has the Church, or the State, the Power to Educate the Nation?*, published in 1839, the year before Maurice began his work at King's College. In this extract, Maurice considers the education of 'the middle class,' a class which he believes to have a vital role to play in the great task of uniting the nation and preventing class conflict. The middle class has a particularly national, English character, making it quite different from the more internationally orientated aristocracy. Therefore, just as the aristocracy is educated in the international languages and literatures, Greek and Latin, the middle class should be educated in English.

The second item is Maurice's inaugural lecture as Professor of English Literature and History at King's College. Maurice sets out how he intends to connect the historical and literary studies with which he has been entrusted. He means to devote time to a detailed study of individual texts, in order to examine the language, but also to enable the students to become closely acquainted with each work, its author, and the age in which each work was written. Maurice thereby establishes the set text as a great institution in English studies. He also picks up and develops his ideas concerning the place of English in middle-class education, as he starts work in a college catering primarily for the middle classes in the capital: English literature, from Chaucer's *Canterbury Tales* onwards, is basically a middle-class literature. One of the most striking features of the lecture, however, is Maurice's religious conception of English history and literature, a conception which typified Broad Church beliefs and which helped to advance English studies in this mid-century period: God is at work in history, and therefore, by studying English history and its closely-related literature, English people will receive the education which God intended for them.

The final brief extract is from Maurice's later work, *Learning and Working* (1855), where, addressing himself to his former students at King's College, Maurice urges them, now that they have received their education, to go out and educate the working class. English literature can be for them, too. This is a significant moment, when the epitome of a middle-class subject is conceived as being appropriate for the working-class, too.

'Education of the Middle Class'

*
* *

This view of what the middle class is, and of the improvements which have taken place in it, may seem dismal. I could easily have made it less so, by alluding to the noble specimens we meet with of virtue and wisdom both among tradesmen and yeomen; but I have purposely set before you the gloomy side of the picture, that we may understand exactly what the difficulties are which we have to combat, and how they are to be met. By looking at the uneasy, turbulent members of a class, you may often ascertain what the whole class is in need of, whereas the satisfaction of the calmer members might mislead us. I think it evident then that there is a craving in them, first after a political position, secondly after a teaching as true and substantial as that which the professional class possess. They expect, in some way, that Education is to confer upon them both these benefits – that it is both to make them wise, and to give them an influence in the nation which they had not before. You must see that an Education, which strives to communicate information to them upon the same subjects which more leisurely people understand, only of an inferior kind, excites these cravings, but does not satisfy them. And in connection with the wishes of this class, we are able to discover a few of their wants. We see that they want to be set above the influence of mere talking men, to be gifted with the power of understanding hollow phrases and empty generalities – to have the faculty of trying words as the palate trieth meats. We see, that they have corrupted the language of their simpler forefathers, and that they want, in some way, to be taught to use their native tongue, so that it shall really be a vehicle for thoughts, and not merely a collection of sounds. The evidence of these necessities lies upon the surface; but if you think more you will perhaps perceive, that another deeper want is implied in these – the want of something which shall not only give this class a position of its own – not only make its members feel that their knowledge is sound, but which shall actually unite them to the other classes, causing them to understand, that they form one body with those whom they have been tempted to look down upon, as well as with those whose level they have been striving to attain. An Education not fulfilling these conditions cannot meet the wants and the wishes of the middle class, or be a substitute for the miserable Education which they have hitherto received.

Now what you would think it is most out of the province of Education to supply is, perhaps, that political position of which we see that the member of the middle class is so covetous. This (you may be inclined to say) can only be given him by a change in the order of society.

If he is able to unsettle the commonwealth he may get it, but this is not an object in which we desire to assist him; if he resort to any other means, he will of course be disappointed. I believe you are mistaken, and I should be very glad to convince you that you are mistaken; for it is a point concerning you as much as any tradesman or yeoman. It is not the sense of being superior to other men, I am sure, which makes the most high-minded members of the aristocracy value their position. I am not speaking now of that which is the highest of all reasons for gratitude, the power which their station confers upon them of being useful to their fellow creatures; this may belong to them in common with many others; but I mean that that which is properly the aristocratical feeling as it exists in the mind of the best man, (in whom of course it ought to be tested, because in worse men it is compounded with worse feelings) is not the sense of superiority, but the sense of connection with a family which has preserved its honour through many generations. This feeling which seems to me so precious, that I know not how to call that a nation which is not leavened with it, is then something distinct from any particular personal privileges; they belong to it, not it to them. How then is it communicated? It is communicated through Education. It comes to you through family records, through family pictures, through ancient halls and chapels, through venerable trees, through names traditionally hallowed. By these means men become endowed with that feeling which is the part that in their best moments they really prize of their civil position, which redeems the accidents of it from the dominion of vulgar pride, which gives even them a sanctity. But if this be so, the sense of a position may possibly be communicated to another class also through Education. It may be the want of that Education, and not the want of some external change, which has prevented them from realizing it. I know it is fancied that the only recollections of any deep interest are those which have a feudal and chivalrous character. The romance writer, who has had most effect upon the mind of this generation,[1] has done much to impress this opinion upon us. But it must be remembered that he belonged to a country which was differently circumstanced from our own, and indeed from most countries in Europe – a country never subjected to those impulses from the rise of towns and the formation of a second class, which, for good or for evil, so powerfully affected us and Germany, and, though in a different way, Italy and France. A Scotchman can know nothing, experimentally, of any feelings but those which belong to feudalism or to the religious movement after the reformation. But there is, I conceive, a very solemn interest (whether it may properly be called a romantic interest I know not) in the history of these movements in England, seeing that with them is connected the formation of our language, the establishment of our literature, the very awakening of the sense of a distinct national life. There is surely a dignity and a sublimity of its own, connected with the sight of an old town with some commercial hall recording its early franchises and the deeds of its municipal government, which, if it is very different from the sublimity of a baronial castle, may yet claim a place in our minds beside it. One cannot help feeling that precisely the difference, be it what it may, between a mere family and a nation has been produced by the addition of one of these elements to the other. Take away the family life, and I cheerfully allow that you reduce the nation into a set of restless warring atoms; but take away the other element, and you lose all personal distinctness; you have a continuous race, but you have not a set of distinct human beings. Doubtless, if you are determined to look at the town spirit as merely that which is setting itself in opposition to the other, it will present itself to you as a very mean, beggarly thing, living only in the moment, unconnected with the past and the future. But the moment you bring it in contact with historical recollections, the moment you bring the townsman of one age to feel himself connected with the townsman of another, by different links indeed from those which bind you to the former members of your own family, but still by most real links which the heart and the imagination are able to recognize, that moment this meanness and narrowness disappear. The busy member of the particular corporation, the fidgetty partizan in the particular borough controversy, belongs to burghers of another day, his corporation takes its place in the history of corporations, and bears upon the life of the nation. And when he himself feels this, without losing his activity he obtains quietness; he has a more solemn impression of the duty which he has to perform, but his mere self-importance is quelled; he rises from the state of a laborious pettifogger to the dignity of an English citizen.

I have spoken first of the tradesman, because I do not anticipate any difficulty in persuading you that the other member of the middle class, the yeoman, may be acted upon by very stirring historical associations. The connections of his fathers with the soil, with the old military achievements of England, with some of the most loyal and conspicuous deeds of the aristocracy has given him a kind of hereditary position which even the romancers have been willing to recognize. It is surely well, in the same class, among men whose relative position to the rest of the community marks them out as intended to mix in a school, to find the two habits of mind which, being fused together give permanency to a nation, so well embodied. The tradesman may be considered as emphatically the representative of the middle order, the yeoman as infusing into that character something of the spirit which belongs to the higher class. It will be the effect of our Education, if rightly conducted, to make these two elements really combine, and so to prevent either from being lost to the country.

But what must the nature of this Education be? We have seen that the middle class has or ought to have a peculiarly national character. Without it, as I said just now, we should not have become definitely English. Our knights connected us with the whole of Christendom: as warriors of the Cross, as bound by freemasonry to all the knights of every country, they had a Catholic, much more than a specifically national character. That character, for the sake of the nation, we would wish to see them retain; and for this end, we would give them a large Catholic cultivation, training them along with professional men in the two most Catholic languages. But the member of the middle class gave us the feeling of our distinct English position, that we were to be something within ourselves, not using a common Christendom language, but speaking a homely native tongue, – Saxons not Latins, islanders not Europeans. It seems to me, then, that the first object we should aim at is to give the middle class of this day a thorough, hearty understanding of that language which their fathers did so much to secure for us. The central point in their intellectual cultivation should be the study of their own tongue in its vigour and purity. Herein I distinguish the education of tradesmen from the education of professional men. The end is to call forth the humanity in each; but the humanity of those who have the one vocation, is best appealed to by languages which connect them with other nations as well as with their own – the humanity of the other, by a language which they can feel to be truly and actually their own. There have been great misunderstandings on this point, I think, from want of attention to the different position of the classes, and from transferring the experience of the one to the other. Scholars have said we cannot understand the English language, unless we understand the principles of language itself, through more comprehensive and fundamental languages. What, I think, they should have said, was, We cannot understand how the principles of language govern the usage of the English language, unless we have this previous culture. This assertion would have been most true. The relation between their own and other languages, was made comprehensible to them by the study of Latin and Greek; and without the feeling of that relation, it seemed to them as if they were only using the words of their own language at hazard. This is the experience of men who are marked out by Providence for the business of keeping up an intercourse with men of all countries, those who are to be strictly men of letters. But there were some who have been able to answer them. 'We can speak English and write English, and even be sure that we write and speak correctly, without this scholarship of yours; nay, we think that we speak more freely and simply for the want of it. It seems to us that we love it more than we should, if our minds were imbued with another language first, and if we looked upon this as only growing out of it.' This is the experience of men, whose business it is especially to work on their own soil, with the men of their own soil; to uphold the national exclusive spirit, which is in its own way as needful as the Catholic spirit. And I think the assertions in each case have been justified, only not as universal propositions. The scholars have showed a mastery over English, which has not been damaged, but actually conferred on them, by their classical knowledge. The other men have showed, that they could talk English clearly and beautifully, without any Latin or Greek. I do not believe the life of the English language would be preserved without either; by scholars only, or by mere Englishmen, and English women (to whom it is far more indebted for its preservation than to the men) only. They must act and react upon each other. I conceive then, that there would be no difficulty in giving a sound instruction in English, without communicating any other scholarship, provided only the person who gave it had himself been bred a scholar. I do not know whether there is such a thing as a tolerable English grammar, but I suppose it is not impossible that one may be written by a person who knows what grammar is, and what English is, who will profit by his experience of the classical languages, and will take care to assist himself with Cobbett and other men of native sense. But even if this is a dream, I believe that oral instructions in grammar, by a sound-headed man, who had himself studied diligently, would very much supply the want. In studying a foreign language, it may be impossible to dispense with formal rules involving a multitude of exceptions. But these are at best only temporary standing-places, by help of which, one is to rise gradually into the perception of grammatical laws and principles, which admit of no exceptions, or at least which explain to us any exceptions which caprice, a desire of euphony, or the circumstances of a particular age may have occasioned. In teaching our own language, it would seem that a judicious master might be able, by a series of well-chosen and orderly experiments, to lead his pupils into the perception of these principles without needing so much assistance from definitions and rules. Some valuable hints, respecting a method of this kind, may be seen in the Chapter on Language, in Biber's *Life of Pestalozzi*.[2] I am not sure that we ought to follow strictly this very able author's recommendations, or that there may not be a merit in the old rule system which he does not acknowledge. I am inclined to believe, that on many accounts, a set of authoritative announcements of even imperfect truths, or mere generalizations from experience, may be necessary as a preparation for our own discoveries, and that the obedient reception of them may be a good discipline for the mind. But the use of the one plan does not involve the rejection of the other. Exceedingly irksome as the mere learning of rules about a language, which we are actually speaking is, that very irksomeness may be useful if it is made a step to the very delightful exercise (I should think there were very few more delightful) of ascertaining what the laws are which we do actually follow, and must follow when we speak so as to make ourselves intelligible to others. This is one part of the study of language, but the mind of the pupil will become very cold and formal, though possibly very acute and ingenious, if it is made the only one. The consideration of words, of their connections with each other, of their origin and history, and of the new meanings they contracted as they came in contact with new subjects, is the other and vital part of it. How deep an interest boys at a very early age may take in this pursuit; what clearness, liveliness, honesty it gives to their minds; at the same time what a sense of awfulness and mystery in themselves, and in that language which they are every day using; consequently what a serious meditative habit it cultivates in them, without in the least destroying the gaiety of their spirits, I think we may all have observed. I can conceive scarcely any pursuit a teacher can engage in, which would bring him in so many rewards of increased acquaintance with his pupil's mind, and with his own, or one therefore for which it would be more his duty to train himself diligently and systematically. Of course he will perceive at once that the study of English words is connected with the study of English books, and can only proceed successfully when those books are of the best kind, and of a kind most especially to interest the pupil. He will therefore be able to save the funds of the school from the expense of nearly all the books which have been written to assist Education during the last half century. For he can by no means sanction the principle of using volumes composed by worthy men with good intentions, merely for the purpose of illustrating all possible abuses of language and confusions of thought. As a reward for this economy, he will request to be supplied with our old English chronicles, our principal poets, especially the earlier ones, because these tend so much to illustrate the growth of our language – in short, whatever of our native writings answer most nearly in spirit and clearness to those which the master of a Latin and Greek school would put into the hands of his scholars. These the teacher will read with his pupils formally and directly, with a view to give them a knowledge of the language. But as the history of the language and the history of the nation are inseparable, he will so arrange these studies as to communicate a living interest respecting them both together. And as it will be the English language in which he mainly instructs them, so it will be English history with which, by all possible contrivances, he seeks to impregnate their minds

– speaking of the history of other nations only as it bears upon this, giving no sort of course of history, but bringing before them particular transactions or series of transactions, illustrating them by the poetry of the period in which they occurred, and attaching them so far as he can to localities with which they are themselves familiar. The hint of this last method is given and followed out with admirable skill in the history of the Anglo-Saxons, published in Murray's *Family Library*,[3] a book, which, I conceive, should be introduced into every middle school, and might serve as a model for any writer attempting to provide a literature expressly for them. I do not imagine, however, that much new literature will be wanted for them. The best that any one could do would be to provide cheap school editions of our old authors, especially the chroniclers and the poets.

If you suppose that I am recommending this study because it is more entertaining than any other that could be chosen, you greatly mistake my intention. I think this might be made a very severe course of study; very much more severe than that which is pursued in our ordinary English commercial schools, or even in the Prussian schools, where so much seems to be taught. As I remarked, when speaking of the English grammar schools, many of the studies which enter into their apparently comprehensive course are really pursued among us; only they came in accidentally, as it were, to illustrate the books which the pupil is reading for another purpose, not as separate subjects which, without any feeling of their relation to each other or to him, he is at a certain hour to take up. The boy who is reading English history will, as a matter of course be exercised in English geography, and will be obliged to notice the geography of any other country with which England is brought into connection. This, I should suppose, would prepare him to think about the relations of places to each other much better than if you gave him lectures upon that distinct topic: and if there be in him a faculty for studying geography scientifically, it will in this way be awakened. You might give him many discourses upon natural philosophy, but I should fancy that the questions which he would ask, when he read in his history of the compass being discovered, or of a great change in men's opinions about the relation of the sun to the earth, might give rise to answers which would lead him just as far as he was able at that time to go, and open his way to further knowledge if he had the capacity for it. Another branch of the Prussian course involves a more difficult inquiry: I allude to composition. This, as you know, is no peculiarity of theirs; it forms a regular part of our grammar-school exercises, and rises naturally out of the study of language. It is, I conceive, nearly the hardest problem in practical Education to know how far this practice ought to be enforced or encouraged; and, if to any extent, by what means.

On the one hand it seems almost impossible to enter into the spirit of a language unless you write in it; on the other there is immense peril of introducing dishonesty into a pupil's mind, of teaching him to utter phrases, which answer to nothing that is actually within him, and do not describe any thing that he has actually seen or imagined. I do not in the least know how the good is to be compassed or the evil avoided, but I wish that persons who have thoughts and experience on the subject would produce them, and would steadily apply their minds to the consideration of all the puzzling questions which it involves. It seems as if it were almost a necessary part of a man's freedom that he should be able to express himself. It seems also as if it were necessary with our English habit of reserve, that we, above all others, should be taught and encouraged to express ourselves. And if the habit could be acquired without our looking upon it as a knack to *compose* or put certain words together, it would certainly be most desirable. At all events, the kind of Education I have described, an Education in the good English authors, seems to be that which would best cultivate the faculty of expression, and be most likely to preserve it from degenerating into what is artificial and insincere.

This is the course that I would propose as the general one for all boys in a middle school, supposing them not to stay longer than their fourteenth year... .

When the pupil has passed through his English course he will have perceived how much a knowledge of other languages would assist him in thoroughly mastering his own. Now then, I think, he should have the means (if his parents will allow him the time) of studying Latin. He will enter upon it in quite a different spirit from that in which he would have undertaken it at the beginning of his school career; he would then have had a notion that Latin was a fine accomplishment, to be desired because the squire's sons possessed it; he would have gone into it with no heart, it would not have had anything to do with what he was thinking or feeling; by this time he has discovered that it is worth something. He will set about the study with real earnestness; and though he may not become a scholar, the knowledge he acquires of it will be sound and sincere: otherwise all that he learns will be shop-Latin, worth very little while he has it, and soon to be forgotten, leaving behind it only a hollow sense of his consequence because he had once made such an acquisition. But to prove that no jealousy lest the trading class should rise to the same level with the professional class actuates us in giving this different direction to their pursuits, we might, I think, very well introduce here another study which forms no part of our grammar-school course. For the same reason that we give the pupil of the middle school, who can afford to stay longer than the ordinary period, the advantage of learning Latin, we might also, perhaps, contrive that he should have the means of learning Anglo-Saxon. It would be a good to all classes that this study should be more cultivated than it is; it would be a pleasant thing to think that the members of the middle class had some study which they could call their own, and it seems peculiarly consistent with the character I have given them, as expressly the English class, that this should be their accomplishment. Their previous practice in the English language would have led them to feel the use of this as well as of Latin, and hence they will pursue both with relish and enthusiasm.

It is not the actual amount of knowledge communicated in this Education to which I look as satisfying the wants, and in some degree fulfilling the wishes of our yeomen and farmers. It is in the reality and the security of the knowledge, in its penetrating and leavening quality, in its tendency to excite a thirst for fresh knowledge, and yet to prevent that thirst from being feverish, that its virtue will consist. Our student will have learned nothing to make him proud of himself, but he will have learned to understand himself; nothing to make him despise the place in society which he is appointed to fill, but much to make him know that he has a dignity which the highest place in society could not give him. That sense of having a country, which is wrought into him thus early, by the study of his country's language and his country's history, will not forsake him through life. Political agitators may tell him that it is a dream; they may ask him what this fine phrase, 'having a country,' is? when his neighbour rides in a carriage, and he walks on foot – when his neighbour makes laws, and he sells yarn; – he knows it is a reality for all that they say; he feels it to be so in his inmost being; and he knows, moreover, that what they call realities are dreams; that they want him to forfeit his position as a member of a nation, in order to assert his position as the member of a class. Moreover, he knows what words signify; large sounding phrases do not terrify him, or cause him to admire; he has a calm, solemn, patient, earnest spirit, the spirit of a man who is not living in the present moment, but feels himself bound up with the past and with the future; who has learned that every man is sent into the world to do something; and that it is not well for a man to wish he had something else to do than what is given him, but to do that and be still.

What, you will say, is all this to be the effect of a boy's learning English grammar and history? Not precisely. But I am obliged to tell you what part of his Education bears upon each portion of his life, although it is not one part, but the whole of it which really makes even that portion of his life consistent and true. It is the study of his own language and his own history, which directly connects itself with his *political* feelings, and delivers them from their bondage to what is material and worldly. But this instruction would be a monstrous inconsistency, it would be utterly ineffective and unmeaning if it stood alone. If we looked at history or language as secular studies, if we did not consider them as instruments given to us for the very purpose of destroying secularity, it would be extravagant to speak of them as producing any sobering, deepening effect upon the character. We regard them as such instruments, whenever we connect them with a higher discipline; whenever we ground our teaching upon the truth, that our pupils are spiritual beings, and make the first step of it an announcement of this truth to them... .

* * *

Notes

1. Sir Walter Scott.
2. George Edward Biber, *Henry Pestalozzi, and his Plan of Education* (1831).
3. Sir Francis Palgrave, *History of the Anglo-Saxons* (1831).

'Introductory Lecture' at King's College, London

Gentlemen, I avail myself of the privilege, ordinarily granted to a new Professor, of stating in an Introductory Lecture what I conceive to be the nature of my office, and the right method of fulfilling it. The practice is, I think, a reasonable one in all cases; and is, on some accounts, particularly expedient in mine. A person who is merely about to deliver a course of lectures upon a given subject may choose his own plan, may, in a great measure, determine his own object, and may hope that they will, by degrees, explain and justify themselves as he proceeds. But he who is admitted to be one of the lecturers in a school or a college has not the same freedom. He is bound to consider with himself, first, what place his particular department of instruction holds in the general plan of the institution to which he belongs; secondly, how he may conduct it in such a manner as to promote and not to thwart the plans of the teachers with whom he is associated. And it must, I think, be desirable that he should, at the very outset of his course, impart his views on both these points to his pupils.

This duty is enforced by some special considerations upon a Professor of English Literature and Modern History. These subjects appear, at first sight, to be somewhat disconnected with those to which your attention is called in the rest of your college course. You are probably aware that they have been often put forward as having a more direct claim upon the regard of young men in this day, than those which we here account the fundamental parts of education. You may have been told, that it would be far better if we made English our primary object, and treated Latin and Greek as accessory and ornamental studies. Now, as this opinion seems to be flattering to that branch of instruction which is committed to me, and as the flattery is of a kind which I believe to be dangerous, both to it and to you, I ought, I conceive, to tell you why I look upon my task as altogether a subordinate one, and what relation it seems to me to bear to those which, in importance and dignity, take precedence of it.

And it is more necessary for me to do this than it could be for my respected predecessor.[1] He had given proofs, at the time he came among you, of the influence which a classical education may exercise in forming an English scholar and poet. He might be excused from labouring to prove a connexion by argument, which he was able to illustrate by so satisfactory an instance, just as he might be also excused from showing, by any other evidence than that of his life, how well intellectual accomplishments may be combined with practical devotion to the wants of the humblest classes.

Gentlemen, there is an education which men acquire by moving about in the bustle and tumult of the world. It is an education not to be despised or undervalued. By means of it men acquire great readiness in speech and in action. It cures or diminishes some awkward unsocial peculiarities. Above all, it teaches a man practically that he cannot have his own way; for that there are thousands of others each of whom wishes to have his way. These are the lessons which are, without any study or meditation, brought home to a person who takes part in the business of such a city as this. Now the pursuits and the discipline of a college cannot impart this kind of knowledge, or can impart it but in a small degree; and, therefore, if they are to be of any avail, they must communicate some other kind of knowledge. They must aim at giving you some instruction which the world cannot give you, but at the same time which is necessary to make what it does give profitable and not mischievous. If you think a moment, you will discover what sort of instruction this must be. People who are moving about in society see all things in rapid change and succession. The one truth which they are sure not to discover by the light which their circumstances supply is that there is anything fixed and permanent. They see men's notions, opinions, modes of action, altering with every new age, with every different climate. There is nothing (nothing, I mean, of which they will take heed) to remind them that there is a standard by which all these opinions, notions, modes of action, must be measured. They see a multitude of natural agents, an endless variety of machines at work, to assist those natural agents in procuring for them the means of subsistence and comfort. There is nothing to tell them that these agents are subject to certain laws; that there are laws which regulate the forces and the actions of these machines. They hear and utter a multitude of words, it may be in different languages, which are necessary to the purposes of traffic or government, or persuasion. There is nothing to bring the thought clearly and definitely before them: these words which you speak are not mere counters; they, too, have laws and principles which govern them, and which prevent discourse from being a mere hubbub of voices. These discoveries (I repeat it) form no part of that teaching which is obtained by walking and acting in the world. And yet without these discoveries – without a conviction derived from some other source and impressed upon active and bustling men in spite of themselves, that there is a standard of what is right and true; that there are some principles which govern physical instruments, and whatever is invented by man to make them more effectual; and that words are not spoken at hazard, but follow a certain order, and are bound by certain links and affinities to those which were spoken ages ago, in circumstances the most different from our own, there would have been no system or security in the proceedings of men, no machinery to assist them, no commerce to connect them with each other. All these have been owing to the recognition of those fixed principles and laws of which, in the world itself, we are taught nothing. All these will perish when that recognition is lost. What the world, then, cannot dispense with and cannot bestow, you have a right to ask of these Schools and Colleges. You have a right to ask, Is there any law to which the life and actions of men may be referred, which may govern them and yet not rob them of their freedom? We answer this question by teaching you Theology, which one of the two greatest philosophers of the old world affirmed to be necessarily and essentially the highest science, because, in a higher sense than all others, it deals with that which is, and which is unchangeable;[2] which *the* greatest of all the old philosophers believed to lie at the foundation of all practical morality, and even of all political fellowship.[3] You have a right to ask us whether there are any laws which determine the movements of those bodies which compose this outward world, which assign their relations to each other, and according to which human art may regulate its own operations? We answer this question by teaching you Mathematics, to which both the philosophers of whom I just spoke assign the second place among sciences, as teaching us to see the constant and invariable laws of that which is in itself fluctuating. Finally, you have a right to ask that we should show you how it is that, amidst the varieties of human thought and speech, there yet seem to be some principles which are common to all, which explain the nature and determine the limits of language itself. We answer this question by leading you to study two Languages, in which you may see these principles most livingly at work; not subject to the caprices of circumstance or fashion, but in a great degree helping you to understand how those caprices may have conspired with other deeper and more important causes to give a shape and character to the dialects of Modern Europe. These three subjects form, then, as we believe, the ground-work of a College education. And the more I in my particular vocation, and each of the other Professors in his separate department, do homage to these, acknowledging that our own teaching is in the general scheme secondary to them, the more shall we maintain for it a high and honourable character; the more successful shall we be in preventing it from being useless to you.

It would be very unbecoming in me to illustrate this position in reference to those physical studies, of which there are so many able teachers among us. You will often, I am sure, be warned by them of the danger to which these studies are exposed, by the very circumstances which seem to be signs of their prosperity; how likely it is they will become superficial when they become popular; what fear there is that they will be confounded with those mechanical pursuits which derive from them all their virtue; how needful it is that they should be associated with what is purely and strictly scientific. But you may be less able to see why similar admonition should be necessary for those who are entering upon the study of English literature. It may seem to you that this is a property which, by the clearest right of inheritance, belongs to you, and that it is most unreasonable to require that you should seek your title to it in Theology, Mathematics, or the Languages of the old world. Unquestionably, it is your property, and it is our desire that you should, as soon as possible, enter into the possession of it. But I know that many who have fancied it was theirs have been cheated of all the fruits of it. A man takes up a volume of Shakspeare or of Milton – of Taylor or of Burke. He finds in it the same words which he has been used to hear in ordinary conversation or to read in the newspapers. Unawares, he brings the standard of thinking and judging which he has acquired from the writers and speakers of his own time, to bear upon these authors. He sets himself above them; he judges them. If he takes a fancy to them, he adopts them as favourites; if he dislikes them, he throws them aside. He pronounces this book agreeable and that disagreeable. What seems to him agreeable, he calls good; that which is disagreeable, he soon believes to be bad. And thus, he never really studies these writers at all. They do not improve him or educate him. He tries their practice by his rules, when it would have been far better for him to have learnt his rules by their practice. This comes to pass because he has not learnt

61

that neither literature nor anything else is valuable, except as it serves to emancipate us from that which is capricious and changeable, from the notions and habits which are peculiar to our own age; except as it connects us with what is fixed and enduring.

But if you do learn this lesson from your other studies – and I have shown you that they are particularly fitted to teach it to you – then see with what profit you may approach this particular one. You will not have to forget that it is your own language you are occupied with; that these words are the words you speak; that the authors you are reading were your own countrymen and ancestors. All these thoughts will be more than ever cherished by you, for there will be another to strengthen them. These words which I hear used – which I am using myself so constantly on low and trivial occasions, are yet not in themselves low or trivial. They are living words. They have their roots deep in our soil; they have been growing for generations. These English words are not mere words to buy and sell with any more than those Greek or Latin words which have passed out of the common uses of the world, and are become sacred. These, too, have been dedicated to the highest purposes – these, too, have expressed the calm and sedate thoughts of men who lived, not for their own time only, but for all times. These are not meant, any more than the others, to be mere utterances of momentary necessities or party spleen. They are prostituted in all lips – they will be prostituted in mine if they are not redeemed to true and worthy ends, if they are not uttered with a sense of responsibility for enjoying them. I think you must feel how much more really we shall enter into the possession of our own English stores if we begin with such thoughts of them as these. But these are the thoughts that unite this subject to the rest of your education, and when we lose sight of the purposes of that education we shall cease to entertain them.

I hope, then, I have convinced you that I am not degrading my office, but asserting its dignity, when I say that I do not wish it to stand alone, or to exalt itself above those other studies which have hitherto been thought more necessary. I hope I have shown you, that though it cannot supersede those studies, it carries out the intention of them, and may assist you more than they could do without it in rising above what is apparent and transitory to what is real and permanent. There are other points of connexion with two out of these three subjects, which I may be permitted to notice very briefly, as they will help you to understand the course which I have marked out for myself. It might occur very naturally to any one that the study of the classics, however favourable to the general cultivation of our faculties or even of our characters, would rather tend to check than to promote the development of proper English feeling. To be carried so far away from our own land, to be taught so much sympathy with men who lived in circumstances altogether different, might seem an unsuitable preparation for the growth of native affections and habits. A suspicion of a similar kind might attach itself to the study of theology. Though a sense of reverence would hinder you from saying that the knowledge of that which is essentially good, could ever hinder men from exhibiting one particular form of goodness, yet you might be inclined to fancy that theology had some high aims which would make it careless of this subordinate one; or you might even persuade yourselves that it discouraged national feelings, as exclusive and bad.

But a little consideration shows that both these impressions are unfounded. You cannot advance one step in the study of Roman or Greek literature, of Roman or Greek history, without perceiving that these people owed whatever was most remarkable in either of them to their nationality. They were, I need not tell you, entirely different from each other in their character and their cultivation. But they had this in common – this which distinguished them from all the countries over which they exercised sway: each man in them felt that he belonged to a nation; all the better and wiser men in them were better and wiser, because they identified themselves with their nation. This feeling expressed itself in all their acts and words. When it departed, they ceased to do anything that it is worth while to hear. This is the lesson above all others which our profane studies impress upon us. How is it with our sacred studies? Our theology is not delivered to us in maxims and propositions; it is unfolded to us in a history. This we assert to be the great indication of its reality – the great proof that it was meant for man. But that history is the history of a particular nation. It tells how one nation was selected and separated from the rest of the world that it might exhibit the relations of God to His creatures, His government, and His character. It teaches us that to live as a faithful citizen of that nation was one and the same thing with entering into the intentions and fulfilling the will of God – with being a sincere, brave, devout man. On the other hand, that indifference to national privileges was one and the same thing with being a hard-hearted, selfish, irreligious man. Thus, then, you see that these studies, though so different, harmonise wonderfully on this point. The contemplation of men feeling their own necessities, exercising their own powers, searching after a truth which was not made known to them, shows us that these wants can only be understood, these powers realized, this search carried on by men who have national union and national sympathies. The contemplation of men who were the subjects of a revelation – who were taught that they were under a Divine superintendence – who had learnt what they were to avoid and whom they were to trust – shows us that these blessings are received by men as members of a nation. How, then, gentlemen, must one feel who has been really trained in these pursuits? Must he not feel as the painter did when he had been musing upon the work of an elder artist? Must he not exclaim, 'I, too, am a citizen; I am the member of a nation?' Will he not be led to inquire, 'What is this nation to which I belong? Has it a history? Has it possessed men who were able to utter its deepest thoughts and exhibit its highest character as the poets and statesmen of Greece and Rome exhibited the feelings and character of their land, as the divinely-appointed and inspired prophets of the Hebrews showed forth the amazing purpose for which their nation existed?' This inquiry is suggested most naturally by those other studies in which you are engaged; and, therefore, on this ground also I must contend that those studies are a fitting preparation for mine, which ought to meet this inquiry and answer it.

Once more, you cannot fail to perceive that neither the history of the Jewish nation, nor the history of the great heathen nations is complete. Both alike are looking forward to something beyond the period which they embrace. Both alike want something to make their meaning thoroughly intelligible. When you read with what terrible judgments Jerusalem ceased to be – how the national life of Greece expired – how the republic of Rome vanished into a monstrous military despotism, you must needs ask – And what has come of all this? Have all the elements which composed these bodies dispersed and ceased to be? You have learnt already that you, as Englishmen, have a national position, as the Greeks, or Romans, or Hebrews had. But this information cannot satisfy you. The Greek had dreams of a universal government which his art and knowledge were to exercise over the world; the Roman empire actually embraced nearly all that was known of the earth; the Hebrew seer foretold that the destruction of his own particular commonwealth would be the beginning of a commonwealth for the universe. To what have their anticipations pointed? Has any general European or human society emerged out of the wreck of the old world, as well as that particular national society to which we individually belong? You will easily see that the reply to these questions should be contained in that part of my lectures which treats of Modern History. You ought to learn from them what that is which we call Christendom; how it is related to the rest of the world; how it is related to the different particular nations which compose it; how it is related to us the individuals of those nations. You can only have satisfaction on these points while you trace its history gradually from the point where it is connected with the histories of which I have just been speaking; and therefore here again we have an evidence how close the relation is between my province and that of your other lecturers.

In making these remarks I have partly anticipated an objection which might occur to some members of my class; and which would be still more likely to occur to those who only hear by chance of our institution and its arrangements. It might seem that far too weighty a task was assigned to one professor, when he was called upon to superintend two such spheres as those of English Literature and of Modern History. Undoubtedly, gentlemen, it is true that not merely one of these subjects, but some little corner or section of one of them, might very easily occupy and has actually occupied the exclusive labours of a life. And were it our main object to improve the knowledge which men generally possess of English Literature or of Modern History, nothing would be more desirable, if it were possible, than that men should be found who would devote themselves with conscientious zeal and diligence, to even minute portions of these studies. But I must remind you again that our object is *Education*; that we look upon all these subjects as instruments and not as ends; and that we are to use each instrument in that way in which it will most conduce to our end. Now, I conceive that the College in committing to me this double task, does not really give me a license to wander over a vast and unlimited field, but rather wishes to mark out certain boundaries which I must not transgress.

If I had been merely entrusted with the subject of English Literature, I might have puzzled myself to know to what point I should direct your principal attention, what centre I could find from which my different discussions upon it should radiate. I should have doubted whether I ought to speak to you chiefly of our Poets, or our Historians, or our Moralists, or our writers on Manners. I should have been at some loss to know whether I was to look at these works mainly in respect to their subject or their composition, or as connected with questions about the arts generally, and their influence upon civilization. On the other hand, if I had been merely required to treat upon history, whether it were the History of England or of Europe, I should not have well known whether to make my lectures very general or to aim as far as possible at minuteness – whether I were intended to give histories of facts or to indulge in disquisitions.

But now it seems to me that my course is tolerably clear. By connecting History with Literature the College admonishes me, that for the purposes of its education these subjects should be viewed in their relations to each other; that I am to look upon the literature of our country as it bears upon our history, and again that I am to look at modern history generally, as it bears upon our own particular nation. These hints I have found very valuable. They have removed much vagueness from my mind respecting the method which I ought to pursue. Chiefly by their help and by considering how best I might conform myself to the practice of the other professors, and so make my course a proper accompaniment to theirs, I have been led to adopt the plan which is explained in my syllabus, and on which I will here make some remarks:–

I. When I said that I wished to connect all our literary inquiries with the study of history, you will have seen that I was acting according to the method which you follow in your Greek or Latin course. There, the writings of the great men are inseparable from the history of the times in which they wrote; either would be unintelligible without the other. But it may strike you that in one respect I am departing from that precedent. With your classical professor you may read indeed the most remarkable books of poetry or of history, but you read them in a great measure for the sake of the language in which they are written. To become thoroughly acquainted with that language is not merely a means to the attainment of a knowledge of those books; it is a valuable end in itself; one to which the study of them may in one sense be considered subordinate. Perhaps you will fancy that in this point, at least, I must necessarily follow a different rule, because my language is one with which you have been familiar from your childhood. But I have told you already that that circumstance is not altogether in our favour; that our familiarity with certain words and phrases, and the habitual employment of them on vulgar occasions, may be rather hinderances than helps, to our really entering into the meaning of these words and phrases. An intelligent foreigner, though he may violate our idiom very often, has sometimes a much truer and deeper insight into our language than we have ourselves; because he really bestows study upon it, because he has become acquainted with our words in good books, and not merely in the drawing-room or the market place. It is not then on this account that I should wish to adopt a different principle from that which is recognised by your other teachers. Still less should I do so from any notion that by giving prominence to the study of words I should be leading you away from the study of history. On the contrary I believe that the history of our words is a part of the history of our nation; that the knowledge of the changes which a word has undergone in different periods, may often (as has been remarked by a great man) throw more light upon those periods than the history of a campaign. I am rather inclined to think that we shall find the study of words and constructions, the very link between literature and history, between the particular book we are reading and the age in which that book was written. I shall therefore adhere strictly to the practice with which you have been familiarised in your other pursuits, and make it my first object to lead you into the experimental study of your own language. I use this expression *experimental*, to distinguish the kind of study which I should wish to promote among you, and in which I think I can be useful to you, from one to which I should feel myself incompetent and which if I did not, would scarcely fall within my notion of the objects of this professorship. In general discussions about the formation of our language, I shall indulge very sparingly – for I do not see my way in them. When the occasion demands it, I will tell you as far as I know what theories other persons have had upon the subject, and whether it strikes me that there is any method of reconciling them. But quite independently of any such theories there is a way of observing the facts of our language, as they present themselves in the books of great authors, which seems to me both more interesting and more sure. We meet with a word in Shakspeare or in Bacon, the sound of which is familiar to us but which is evidently not used as we are wont to use it. What is the connexion? Is this word used in the same sense elsewhere by this author or his contemporaries? What other meanings has it in him or in them? What binds these different meanings together? Whence came the word originally? What changes has it passed through in earlier times? Does the particular force of it which we are considering indicate some perversity or affectation in an author? or does it indicate that he had a deeper understanding of the word than we have? Has it become stronger or weaker since? Has it become capable of expressing new forms of thought, or has it lost its capacity of expressing the old forms? What circumstances or changes of feeling may have affected it? Such are some of the questions which will arise, and which, however trivial the occasion that suggests them may seem, may if they are rightly followed out, lead us into very interesting and important discoveries respecting the state and progress of our nation, and of our own minds. One great value which they have in my eyes, is that they connect the Professor with his class; that they enable him to work out his problems, not apart from them but in conjunction with them; that they make him the guide to his pupils' thoughts, rather than the dogmatical utterer of his own.

It is obvious that the kind of inquiry I have described can only be pursued effectually by reading some book. You would soon be weary if I proposed to you some particular *word* for investigation in each lecture; but if the words occur in some great English classic you will feel that they deserve to be examined and that you are repaid for the trouble by the new pleasure with which you read him. Indeed every day will convince you more, that the study of an author's words and constructions has very much to do with the study of his character and genius. You will pass from the one very naturally into the other; nay, at times you will find them positively identified. And there will be a great advantage in beginning what is called Literary Criticism in this method. I have told you already what danger there is in one kind of criticism which is very common in this day. If you come to an author as masters and not as pupils, the punishment is that you never know anything of him. A young man must make his choice between his desire to judge for himself and his desire to be educated. If he will judge for himself in the sense in which those words are constantly used – that is to say, if he will make himself the judge and standard of all that he reads and hears, he cannot be instructed. Instruction means nothing to him, he has already assumed the position to which instruction is meant to bring him. I speak wrongly; instruction never would bring him to the point he has chosen for himself. It might confer on him a quick apprehension of what is right, a quick discernment in rejecting what is wrong; but it would never give him that sense of his own importance, that power of looking down upon other men which he has usurped without it. The more instructed he is the lower he will become in his own estimation; the less he will have of the appetite for censure, the more he will find to cherish and admire. In wise and thoughtful old men, the habit of admiration becomes sometimes even excessive; they are inclined to admire everything. Writings, which in their youth, they on the best grounds and without any arrogance undervalued, they can now see a merit in. Their grey locks which give them a right in our opinion to pronounce sentences of condemnation, seem in their minds reasons for withholding them.

I do not wish you to affect this maturity, nor would I affect it myself, but I do wish you to feel that as persons acquire deeper perceptions of things, they become more humble; and I do wish you to put yourselves in training to acquire more perception of what is good, and less of that morbid self-conceited desire to find fault, which is in a most fearful degree the disease of our times. Now nothing I believe is more likely to correct this tendency and to substitute true wholesome criticism for that which consists in pert sneers and the condemnation of what we have not taken pains to understand, than the real and earnest study of some good author. Every step that we advance will show us how much more there was in him than we suspected; how much he had really entered into things which we have only loose and vague notions of. The choice of his words, the structure of his sentences, will be indications to us as we examine them, that we are in the company of a man who has really thought and meditated, and who can perhaps put us in the way of thinking and meditating too.

And this course of proceeding will teach us far better than any other can, our author's weakness as well as his strength, what he cannot do as well as what he can. Those who have habituated themselves to condemn the great multitude of all the books they read and persons they see, are often righteously punished for this offence, by becoming utterly enslaved to some one writer or speaker. They feel they must have something to cling to, that they cannot wholly be satisfied with their own wisdom; and therefore they make to themselves some idol whom they look up to with cowardly deference and awe, and in whom they persuade themselves that all the wisdom of past and present time has centred itself. Now if you read books with the intention of learning from them, you will acquire a power of knowing when it is that they have taught you what they can teach, and what there is beyond which does not lie within their sphere, and which you must look for else-where. In like manner, when there is anything positively false or evil in the book, your dislike to it will not be the less but the greater, for the love that you feel to it and to its author. The more you care for a friend the more his faults grieve you; and I believe also the more acute you are in perceiving his faults. So that it is not necessary to stint our affection and admiration in order to secure ouselves from the dangerous conse-quences of their being foolish or blind.

I have spoken of the book and the author as if they were one; and, indeed, I think it is very hard to separate them. It is common, I know, to say – 'Such a book is very clever and interesting, but the person who wrote it was utterly worthless.' It may be true in certain cases, of books written to support some side in a political controversy, of diplomatic productions, of works describing mere manners, possibly (though I should hesitate long before I said so) of scientific treatises; but I do not think it can be true of books which compose the literature of a country. For the purpose of education at least, I am sure that if the man be worth-less the book is worthless; that no mere skill or knack he may have shown in the composition of sentences will repay us for the trouble or cost of studying him. A book must be the utterance of that which is in a man, or its words will not enter into us to do us any good. If then, I ask you to read an author with any attention, for any purpose but just that of supplying certain points of evidence, you may be sure that I believe there is worth in him; that there is that in him which deserves to be loved. We shall feel no temptation to gloss over any bad acts that may be distinctly proved against him. We shall not talk any nonsense about these acts being justified or hallowed by his genius. we shall not try to make out that bad means good, or good bad. All such courses, I be-lieve, besides being very immoral in themselves, tend to hinder instead of promote the free and genial study of literature. If you feel that you are not honest and simple with yourselves, or that your lecturer is not honest and simple with you; if you find he is trying to make out a case for a favourite hero, and is insulting your sense of right and wrong, the only effect will be a strong reaction against that which you were admir-ing, or he was encouraging you to admire. Neither if we are wise shall we conceal from ourselves the truth, the very painful and awful truth which every day brings home to our own experience and consciences – that speech and action are utterly different things, and that a man may have spoken words of deepest truth – true, not merely to themselves, but true to him – to which his conduct exhibited only a very faint correspondence. Certainly it is not meant to be so; but it is so, and a man knows little of himself who does not know that the faculty of speaking good words is apt to serve him with a miserable excuse for not doing good deeds. It would be cowardly to suppress these facts, or not earnestly to ponder them. But they do not interfere with the principle I have laid down – that we are to love an author who has spoken that which is true, and who, so far as we can make out, has spoken it because he felt it. I have said already that he may not have spoken the highest truth, and that we are not to delude ourselves with thinking he has given us all we want because he has given us something that we want. But still if he has given us anything – if he has enabled us to know ourselves better than we did before, we are to be thankful, and we are not to express our thanks by bestowing on him the shabby, heartless, newspaper praise, that he is a man of power, or talent, or genius; we must feel to him as a benefactor and a friend.

One course of my lectures, then, I should wish might always be devoted to the minute and critical study of some English author, primarily for the purpose of getting acquainted with his language; but secondarily, and by means of this, with the spirit of the book, with the character of the author, and with the age in which he wrote. For the purpose of studying the force and meaning of words, I believe a poet will be always most useful to us. For the purpose of studying the structure of sentences we must resort to our prose classics; the first being in my judgment the more important object, I have determined to begin with one of our poets. At first I had thought of introducing you to an historical play of Shakspeare, both because we have the fulness and perfection of the language in him, and because I should thereby compass my object of connecting your literary and historical studies together. But upon reflection, I have, for the present, abandoned this intention, and selected a short poem of another writer. The prologue to Chaucer's *Canterbury Tales* contains a most lively picture of the different classes and characters of his age; and I thought there was some advantage in making our first experiment upon a writer whose language would cause you a little trouble. You will have to construe him. You must seek for the meaning of his words, if you would understand him at all. We shall thus be forced into the track in which I hope we shall afterwards walk with great willingness and pleasure, and we shall have the advantage of commencing our inquiries respecting the

English language with a period when it was beginning to exhibit a distinct formation, and when it was still struggling with many foreign influences and admixtures.

II. There is one characteristic in this poem of Chaucer, which will strike you as soon as you have read it. You will observe how plain, homely, and practical it is; how much keen interest it exhibits in all forms of human life; how little it has of anything grand or heroic. If you continue your reading to the tales which this prologue introduces, you will find that these conclusions respecting his character were not formed from a hasty observation; that they are abundantly confirmed by an increased acquaintance with him. You will find that, though he might make use of Italian or classical fables, the personages in them become in his hands strictly human persons, not removed by any vast interval from ourselves or from the humble men and women who relate them. You will feel also, I think, very strongly, these are not poems for knights, but for citizens; if they are to be regarded as in any sense the commencement of our English literature, that literature had a much less grand and stately origin than we should perhaps wish to discover for it. I call your attention to the facts which will force themselves upon us in this course of lectures, because they will help you to see how that course is related to another which I intend should run parallel with it. These peculiarities of Chaucer are, I believe, in a remarkable degree, the peculiarities of English literature in all its stages; they mark the difference between it and other literatures; they show why it has a more strictly historical character than all others; why it is a better index of national feeling and a more instructive commentary upon national events than any other could be.

I have said that in your classical studies, history and literature are inseparable. To understand the age of Pericles you must read Sophocles as well as Thucydides; to understand the age of Augustus you must attend more to the odes and epistles of Horace than to Suetonius or even Plutarch. But though this is true, you will not fail to observe that the great tragedies of Greece do not really present any image of the world around them. They carry you back to traditions of a former period; they place you among a race of heroes; they tell you what Greeks at that time could conceive, and therefore, in one sense, what they were; but the violent contrast between them and the contemporary comedies proves that their worth consisted chiefly in this, that they created an ideal world into which men might escape from the corruptions and abominations of their common life. The same cannot be said of the Roman writers; but this must be said of them, that they were Court writers and not popular writers; that they exhibited the character of the period in which they lived only as that character was imaged in a few

71

refined and cultivated minds. Accordingly, if you want to understand the Roman people of that time, you may get more real information by reading Shakspeare's *Julius Caesar* than the compositions of all the able men who lived among them. Now, one or other of these qualities has passed into most of the literatures of modern Europe. All the nations which possessed any cultivation before the coming of Christ, felt that our nature must have some connexion with the Divine, and fixed upon certain beings – either actual persons or creatures of the imagination – as those in whom this connexion was realized. All the nations which believed that the union between our nature and the Divine had been once and for ever established in one person, inevitably looked upon it as endowed with a new character as well as a new glory. The reverence for strength was changed into the reverence for meekness, or, at all events, for strength doing homage to meekness. Still, in the Southern countries of Europe the new feeling was the almost exact counterpart of the old one. The Saints of the Church succeeded to the place of the Heroes; on them a reverence has been bestowed which has been always tending to idolatry, though certainly having no inevitable connexion with it. I am quite satisfied that some countries are intended to feel this reverence with a strength which is indeed dangerous, because human corruption is ready to avail itself of any strong feeling and to degrade it, but which may be the preservation of health as well as the occasion of sickness. To the existence of this reverence we owe, I believe, all great works of art; and where it does not exist in a very high degree, I do not suppose they will ever be produced. They never have been produced in our land; I do not say they never will, because I do not say that the great peculiar gift which has been vouchsafed to our land may not coexist with that which has been vouchsafed to other lands. But I do mean that what has been bestowed upon us has been an ample compensation for what has been denied us, and that to acknowledge this gift, and to preserve it is one of our first duties. We too have been taught that our humanity has been glorified by being taken into connexion with the Divinity, and have believed and confessed this great truth: but we have been led to build another conclusion upon it; we have learnt that not a few persons of really or reputedly transcendent virtue have had a grandeur conferred upon them by the mighty fact on which our faith rests; but that in virtue of it the life and acts of every human creature, down to the meanest beggar, have acquired a grandeur which make them worthy of the solemnest contemplation and study. This I believe to be the animating, life-giving principle of our great English books. They will be found less grand and chivalric than any; they will descend at times to lower descriptions than most; they will almost seem now and then as if they had no right to the factitious

dignity and conventional importance which belong to books and compositions – they deal so directly with realities. But hereby it comes to
pass that they are part and parcel of our national history – of our national life; that each reflects the image of the other; that we may judge
what one is by seeing what the other is; that we may interpret the purposes of God to our land by seeing how the events which have befallen
us bear upon the thoughts of the men who have appeared among us. A
few words will make my meaning more clear.

It might naturally have been expected that the Norman race as the
dominant party in our country, as that which connected us with foreign nations, and contained the chivalry of our land, would have been
the authors, or at least the inspirers of our literature. The reverse is
actually the case. It was not till this influence had become weakened,
till the old Saxon element in our nation had recovered its strength, that
we learnt to speak at all. We may, by a reasonable latitude of language,
reckon as part of our literature those books which were written by Englishmen to illustrate our annals, though they used the ordinary language of the Church; but these had not a Norman origin if they had not
an English one. Their authors and the class with which they were connected were much oppressed by the Norman princes, and had often a
real attachment to the soil. And no possible ambition to enlarge the
circle of our national compositions can tempt us to reckon among them
those French poems which were written by minstrels or gentlemen in
the courts of our princes, who despised England, and refused to speak
its tongue. It is, therefore, to that age of England in which the middle
class began to appear, that we owe the recovery of our language, and
with it the commencement of our literature. So soon as it did appear, it
took, as you will find when we come to speak of Robert of Gloucester's
Chronicles, an historical form. The class which was rising up in England, was never content to look upon itself as a new class. It asserted its
connexion with the oldest form of English life. But other influences were
wanting to give this literature the clear and marked form which it assumed in Chaucer. At the time when trade was commencing, when
towns were in the process of being established, when those powers were
gathering themselves together which were to counteract the power of
the baronial Castle, there began also a strong and decided religious
movement. A number of facts which I may produce hereafter will show
you what a close relation there was between all these circumstances
and the doctrine of Wycliffe, and how both acted together upon the
mind of Chaucer. And these observations will serve to account to you
for much that might seem strange to you in him. A tendency to coarseness accompanying very great delicacy of perception and feeling. A
propensity to dwell on some of the lowest and vulgarest exhibitions of

human life united to a lively sympathy with manly virtue and feminine grace. This is precisely what you would expect from a poet who had lost some of his reverence for that which time and authority had canonized; who had acquired a new and deep reverence for the worth and dignity of men as men; who shared in the earth-born feelings which belonged to those who were beginning to find out that they had a position in society, but who had these quickened and glorified by their connexion with certain moral truths which gave to each man and citizen the sense of his having a distinct and personal connexion with a divine and mysterious economy.

Now, if we pass on from the age of Chaucer to the age of Shakspeare, we shall see how all the feelings and influences which were then beginning to act upon our country had obtained a recognition for themselves, and yet had not superseded, but become mingled with, feelings and influences of an opposite kind. If we look at the writers who lived at the period of the Elizabethan reformation, we see in them the same qualities that we observed in Chaucer – only accompanied with a much wider range of observation, and with a clearer sense of the system and harmony that are in the world. You see the same love for what is real and actual, the same absence of anything grand or heroical; the same union of coarseness and delicacy; the same sense of the interest and importance of every form of human life; the same feeling that the deepest and saddest events and the most ludicrous are not to be presented in violent contrast with each other, nor yet to exclude one another, but enter successively and often together into the scenes of the world's drama.

In Shakspeare we find all these qualities in their perfection. You see in him, if possible, less delight in mere heroical qualities than in Chaucer, or in his own contemporaries. Every hero he speaks of is obliged to become a man, to take his station with the rest of his race. But one does not feel that he loses anything by this change – rather that he gains much. We become acquainted with the innermost hearts of men whom before we knew only by their fine holiday dresses; and we begin to feel that the most wretched heart is worthier of contemplation than the most magnificent costume. And the morality of his plays does not suffer because no strange and superior models are exhibited to us in them, nor even because so much is exhibited to us that is indifferent or evil, because there was given to him a wonderful apprehension of a scheme and order in the world, against which all the evil workings of man's will are striving in vain, and to which his greatest and loftiest imaginations cannot reach. This apprehension does not appear except occasionally in formal sentences; still less does it express itself in what is called by playwrights poetical justice, that is in the making the man who has had a righteous cause comfortable and the evil man uncomfortable, at the end of the fifth act; but it comes out in the whole scheme and construction of his drama, and makes us feel what a drama is. In that play, for instance, which is perhaps the most familiar to you of any, you have the clearest picture of Italian factions – of the servants carrying out the feuds of their masters – of selfish nobles – of lively, high-spirited, passionate young men. Within this, there is an inner circle of ardent and pure human love, not raised to any ideal excellence, but exhibited in its deepest and most fervent workings. Something still was wanting to bring all these into their relation with one another, to give us the sense of what is deeper and more perfect than even this love – to give us a sense of harmony and peace in the centre of this tumult and confusion. The Friar comes in with his basket of flowers and his graceful comparisons and emblems. There was no need to say more – no need to bring out into stiff and formal language what is meant; this little delicate indication serves more than much talking would do – it imparts to you a sense of order and harmony, and shows you that the world of strife is God's world still; that there is a life in it which can transfuse elements of confusion into quietness and peace. Thus these dramas, even when they turn upon fables, have always, if I may so say, an historical character; they show us not an ideal world, but the actual world, only with the idea of a divine regulation and government lying beneath it, and adjusting it. And, therefore, one is not surprised to find how many of these plays are actually historical; and we rejoice to find among them the dramas of our own national life, exhibiting the meaning and sense of those events which the ordinary historian gives us merely in detail. But even in the most purely imaginative creations of Shakspeare, even in that which is perhaps the most wonderful work of imagination in the world, and which the most enables us to understand what the faculty of imagination means – even in the *Tempest* you see how much Shakspeare is conversing with the objects of actual life and experience. Who can help connecting Caliban – his half dawnings of affection – his brutal instincts – his sense of his own dignity – his idolatry of Stephano and his bottle, with those pictures of savage life which were pouring in, in Shakspeare's time, upon the ears of Europeans, or with all the melancholy records of the way in which European civilization and Christianity have made themselves known to savages that have accumulated since?

Thus then in the second great age of English poetry, we find the same characteristics as in the first – the same practical and historical tendencies – the same illustrations of the state of belief and society. But what shall we say of Milton? How can a poem, so entirely removed from the sphere of ordinary life as his, have any connexion with the books we have spoken of hitherto? How can it have anything to do with the world by which he was surrounded? At first sight he seems to stand quite aloof, to be a poet of another country and another order. But if we study the facts more attentively, we shall come to a very different conclusion. We shall recognise in him the principle which we have seen pervading English literature; and the modification which it assumes will show us more clearly than anything else could, the character of the age in which he lived. In the Paradise of Milton we do not find high heroical human personages; we find a simple man and woman representing to us humanity itself in its relation to God and to the spirit of evil. He makes us feel that the attempt to be heroes – to be as Gods, is that attempt through which angels became devils – through which man became fallen; as in his other admirable poem he shows us that the refusal of the heroical character, the choice of humiliation, poverty, humanity, was the characteristic of him through whom Paradise is recovered. Here then we are arrived, if I may speak so, at the very essence of our English poetry. It is altogether different from that poetry in its plainer, more natural forms; but it contains the spirit which was hidden in their forms. In that period there was a mighty struggle going forward to separate what is spiritual and essential from the forms in which it is clothed. With what wisdom or success this struggle was conducted we may inquire hereafter. All that is necessary to my present purpose, is to remark that poetry of Milton's latter days, as it contains whatever is pure and holy in the political conceptions of his earlier life, throws back the most brilliant light upon these conceptions and upon the events that attested their strength or their feebleness.

The next age supplies us with another kind of evidence. Our dramatic literature during the latter part of the seventeenth and early part of the eighteenth centuries, was as little heroic as it had been during any future period. The idea of a great man never dawned upon the minds of those who constructed it. But, alas! the compensation for this want was gone. The feeling that humanity has something besides its own natural debasement, that it has been redeemed and glorified, was lost; therefore this debasement became that in which most of our writers delighted and revelled. They saw and knew nothing of men but this. But there must be something else; otherwise society could not exist. Another set of writers perceived this truth and set themselves to describe society as it does exist; to give a picture of it in all its outward appearances and semblances, to show us *manners* not *men*. These writers cannot tell us much of what is below the surface; they cannot materially contribute to the increase of our self-knowledge, that they like all we have spoken of hitherto, remarkably exemplify and expound the age which gave them birth.

A period of strong excitement followed, and poetry very different from this was demanded to satisfy its wants. Now, first, there was an attempt to introduce an heroic literature among us. The experiment was conducted by men of the greatest talent and influence, and for a time seemed most successful. But it was found that the heroes which were brought among us, had no variety of character, scarcely of costume; that they were chiefly remarkable for gigantic passions and crimes; that the interest in them was strongest when our minds were most irregular, tumultuous, and feeble. Therefore the admiration which they excited has, to a great degree, died away, and has been gradually more and more directed towards a poetry which was for a long while scorned, because it rested on the principle that the most deep and awful things are not those which are most strange and peculiar; that there are a wonder and mystery in common and daily occurrences; that poetry should dwell more in cottages than in palaces; that the hearts of men are more worthy of note than the deeds of heroes. I believe that both these kinds of poetry, like all that we have spoken of, illustrate remarkably the character of the times which have produced it, and show us what we must aim at if we would be that which Providence has intended us to be.

For, gentlemen, it is surely impossible to attribute the preservation of this character through so many ages, to chance. It is equally impossible to attribute it to human calculation and foresight, to suppose that Chaucer and Shakspeare laid a deep scheme of composing books which should exhibit certain peculiar qualities, and give a tone to the mind of their country. You cannot adopt either of these conclusions, and what then remains but that we should believe that a higher power has been at work, directing the destinies of our nation, educating it and forming it to fulfil a definite purpose? To bring out this truth; to show that our nation has had a regular growth and progress; that all outward events have been contrived to build it up; that each great man in the country in proportion as he has been really great, has been an instrument in its edification; to show what perversities of men have thwarted this intention, and how we may thwart it or promote it ourselves; this will be the design of my lectures on the Growth of our nation and its literature. I hope that I may be able to continue them as far as the reign of Henry VIII during the present term; the Elizabethan period, the period of the civil wars, and the eighteenth century, ought to furnish subjects for four other courses.

III. If I am able to interest you in this view of the progress of our own nation, I have no fear that you will enter with pleasure and profit upon the history of modern Europe. It is not my intention to give any lectures upon this subject during the present term, but I hope that the lectures which I shall deliver may furnish some hints respecting it, which we may be able hereafter to bring out and elucidate. Much as I am anxious to cultivate in you a national spirit, it would be the farthest thing from my intention to cultivate in you one national prejudice. In fact, if the national spirit be truly awakened, it will be found the best destroyer of national prejudice. When we feel that we have a great work to do, we shall be far more ready to acknowledge that all the other nations have their own work to do, and to wish them God speed in the doing it. And besides this, it will be quite impossible for us to advance one step in our inquiry into our own national position, without discovering that there is a higher position than this; that there are bonds which connect us – first with Christendom, then with the world. To ascertain what these bonds are – to know how we may realize them, will be one of our greatest objects in turning over the records of the past. For we shall find these records full of warning as to the causes which have separated the nations from one another, full of encouragements, I do also believe and hope, as to the possibility of their being some day united. And if it be true, as I have said, that our national literature throws the greatest light upon these records, we may derive from that also instructions which may assist us in accomplishing this great end. That great principle which I have shown you has animated the whole of it, that man, as man, is glorious – glorious only because there is a bond which connects him with the Divine nature, will carry us far in the belief that all the barriers which separate men, united in that acknowledgment, will be ultimately removed, and that then they will go forth to make all mankind partakers of the same fellowship. And I am well convinced, gentlemen, that just in so far forth as literary men do endeavour to stretch their thoughts abroad, and to interest themselves for their fellow-men, as made in the image of God, literature will flourish and win new triumphs; and that just so far as they shut themselves up in narrow circles, glorify themselves, flatter one another, and despise their brethren, literature will become a useless and a cursed thing, hateful to men and to God, which another Vandal irruption may take from us altogether. We are brought here to labour, each in his own vocation, that this evil may not overtake us. We shall labour most effectually when we are determining that we will use all the wisdom of every kind that is entrusted to us for other ends than the promotion of our own selfish vanity and consequence. The older colleges of our country bear witness, that these are not the purposes for which men are to learn and improve themselves. We must resolve, in the infancy of ours, that we will not build upon a feebler or narrower foundation. And it cannot do harm to remind you – it must be a consolation to me to remember, that these have been the views and feelings of those who have lived and laboured among you. They were the feelings of one who was taken from you in early life,[4] but who, before he came here, had consecrated to the highest and noblest purposes those powers of which we saw only the first blossom, but which were to expand themselves in a freer and purer air; of one[5] whom you lost when his faculties were ripened and matured, whose life was a struggle with acute and continual suffering, and who was permitted to show how little such suffering could diminish his kindness to individuals, or his zeal for his country and the Church; of one who has given proof that the highest and noblest exercises of a life may be reserved for the period of a serene old age.[6] I am sure that if these men were now among you, their deepest desire would be to impress upon you a truth which was uttered more than two centuries ago, not by a divine, but by a prince of natural philosophers – the wisest of political writers. Remember that those three studies, which I said lay at the foundation of all your knowledge (and what is true of them must be true of them, must be true of English Literature – of Modern History – of every other pursuit in which you are engaged):

> are to them that are depraved no better than the Giants' Hills.
>
> Ter sunt conati imponere Pelio Ossam,
> Scilicet atque Ossae frondosum involvere Olympum.
>
> But to those who refer all things to the glory of God, they are as the three acclamations, Sancte, Sancte, Sancte, – holy in the description or dilation of his works; holy in the connexion and concatenation of them, and holy in the union of them all in a perpetual and uniform love.[7]

Notes

1. Thomas Dale.
2. Aristotle.
3. Plato.
4. # Joseph Anstice, Esq., First Classical Tutor at King's College.
5. # Rev. Hugh James Rose, Second Principal of King's College.
6. # Rev. W. Otter, D.D., late Lord Bishop of Chichester, First Principal of King's College.
7. # [Francis Bacon], *The Advancement of Learning* [(1605), II.vii.6. The quotation contains a quotation from Virgil: 'Thrice they attempted to heap Ossa on Pelion, and then to pile leafy Olympus upon Ossa (Virgil, *Georgics* i.281–2).]

Preface to *Learning and Working*

*   *
*

…I am also bound to say something to those whom I have myself had a share in educating, and to whose kindness I owe more than I can express. I have broken a promise in the letter which some of them were so good as to draw from me, that I would reproduce some fragments of Lectures

I once gave them on English Literature; I believed I should keep the spirit of it better, if I could show them how they might carry out in practice the principles which I endeavoured to set forth in those Lectures. They had, in my opinion, one merit, and only one. They were formed upon the belief that all history and all literature exhibit God's education of mankind; that the history and literature of England exhibit the education of our people and of ourselves. I enforced this principle till I have no doubt my hearers were tired of what seemed to them an endless repetition. If, on looking back to the time we spent together, they have forgiven that fault, and the want of information and liveliness which they must have detected since they became acquainted with other teachers, it must be because they have felt that truth to be one, which however it was uttered and expounded, is needful for our time, and becomes alive when it is acted out. This I am sure is a right judgment; therefore, if I can help them to act, if I can point out to them a course of action, I am giving them the old Lectures revised and corrected, with the very commentary which they missed when they were first delivered. Let them understand that God has been educating them to educate their brethren of the working-class, and all that they learnt, all that they are still learning, all the work of their professions or trades, will acquire a new character, will be valued as it has never been valued before, will be changed from a weight into a power – from the routine of a machine, into the onward movement of a spirit.

*
* *

CHAPTER SEVEN

Charles Kingsley

Charles Kingsley (1819–1875) had a many-sided career, including work as a clergyman, writer, teacher and Christian Socialist leader. One of his jobs, though held for only one year, was as Professor of English Literature at Queen's College, London, a college started by some of the professors at King's College in 1848 with the aim of providing education for girls who were to become governesses. Kingsley was a friend of F.D. Maurice, who was himself Professor of English Literature and History at King's College, but who also became the first Principal of Queen's College.

Kingsley was a student at King's College, London, then entered Magdalene College, Cambridge in 1838, where he studied in both the Mathematical and Classical Triposes. He gained First Class Honours in the Classical Tripos in 1842, and was ordained in the Church of England the same year. He met Maurice in 1844 and became Maurice's disciple theologically. It was also in 1844 that Kingsley became Rector of Eversley in Hampshire, retaining the living until his death. After 1848, he became involved, together with Maurice, in Christian Socialism. This involvement brought him some enemies in the Church, and he was at one time forbidden by Bishop Blomfield to preach in the Diocese of London. In 1860, he became Professor of Modern History at Cambridge, but from 1863 went to Cambridge only twice a year to deliver lectures, and he resigned in 1869. He died in 1875.

Kingsley was a prolific writer, his work including poetry, a number of novels, the famous story *The Water Babies (1863)*, a study of the sea-shore, historical lectures and sermons. Apart from *The Water Babies*, he is probably best remembered for the novels *Alton Locke* (1849), *Yeast* (1849), *Westward Ho!* (1855) and *Hereward the Wake* (1866).

The two lectures here were inaugural lectures which Kingsley delivered at Queen's College in 1848, one being the prelude to his course on English Composition, and the other to his course on English Literature. In his lecture on composition, he sets out his intention to examine good authors, in order to study their use of language and provide the basis for helping his students to learn to write. He will adopt a 'historical' method in studying these writers, on the basis of the Broad Church idea that the history of a nation parallels the history of an individual. Therefore, an individual should learn to write different genres in the same order as these genres appeared in the national literature; poetry should be first, and prose, the highest form, should be last. Kingsley plainly sees himself as reacting against earlier writers on rhetoric and composition, with their preconceived ideas and abstract rules. Hugh Blair and Lord Kames are mentioned, as is 'the Pope and Johnson school of critics.' Kingsley stresses the need to approach the texts with reverence and humility, in order to learn the true principles of composition, principles which derive from God rather than from Hugh Blair.

The second lecture here, 'On English Literature', picks up the idea set out by Maurice in his inaugural at King's College, that literature gives the truest picture of a nation's history, because it is a history from the inside; it will also lead the student to God. Kingsley believes that it is necessary to look at the whole period of English literature, particularly including the contemporary, since students will read this anyway, and they should therefore be guided. Like Maurice, and later Henry Morley, he is resolutely against the use of 'Extracts' and 'Select Beauties'; students must study whole works, because a work of literature is an organic whole. Kingsley meets head on the question of nationalism in relation to the teaching of English literature, rejecting the need for any 'John-Bullism', but enthusiastically and unashamedly espousing the idea that English literature will give a more national tone to these girls' education. Turning one's back on 'dreary cosmopolitanism' is very much to be welcomed; it does not mean that foreign writers are not read, but well-educated English girls should have a strong English standard whereby to judge foreign thought.

'On English Composition'

An Introductory Lecture on English Composition is, I think, as much needed as one on any other subject taught in this College. For in the first place, I am not sure whether we all mean the same thing when we speak of English Composition; and in the next place, I believe that pupils themselves are very often best able to tell their teachers what sort of instruction they require. I purpose, therefore, to-day, not only to explain freely my intentions with regard to this course of Lectures, but to ask you to explain freely your own wants.

I must suppose, however, that the ladies who attend here wish to be taught how to write English better. Now the art of writing English is, I should say, the art of speaking English, and speech may be used for any one of three purposes: to conceal thought, as the French diplomatist defined its use: to conceal the want of thought, as the majority of popular writers and orators seem now-a-days to employ it: or again, to express thought, which would seem to have been the original destination of the gift of language. I am therefore, I suppose, in duty bound to take for granted that you come here to be taught to express your thoughts better.

The whole matter then will very much depend on what thoughts you have to express. For the form of the symbol must depend on the form of the thing symbolized, as the medal does upon its die; and thus style and language are the sacraments of thoughts, the outward and visible signs of the inward and spiritual grace, or want of grace, in the writer. And even where language is employed to conceal either thought, or want thereof, it generally tells a truer tale than it was meant to do. Out of the abundance of the heart the mouth must speak, and the hollowness or foolishness of the spirit will shew itself, in spite of all cunning sleights, in unconscious peculiarities or defects of style.

Hence I say style, as the expression of thought, will depend entirely on what there is within to be expressed, on the character of the writer's mind and heart. We all allow this implicitly in the epithets which we apply to different styles. We talk of a vigorous, a soft, a weak, a frigid, an obscure style, not meaning that the words and sentences in themselves are vigorous, soft, weak, or even obscure (for the words and their arrangement may be simple enough all the while). No, you speak of the quality of the thoughts conveyed in the words; that a style is powerful, because the writer is feeling and thinking strongly and clearly; weak or frigid, because his feelings on the subject have been weak or cold; obscure to you, because his thoughts have been obscure to himself – because, in short, he has not clearly imagined to himself the notion which he wishes to embody. The meaning of the very words, expression and composition, prove the truth of my assertion. Expression is literally the pressing out into palpable form that which is already within us, and composition, in the same way, is the composing or putting together of materials already existing; – the form and method of the composition depend mainly on the form and quality of the materials. You cannot compose a rope of sand, or a round globe of square stones – and my excellent friend Mr. Strettell will tell you, in his lectures on Grammar, that words are just as stubborn and intractable materials as sand or stone, that we cannot alter their meaning or value a single shade, for they derive that meaning from a higher fountain than the soul of man, from the Word of God, the fount of utterance, who inspires all true and noble thought and speech – who vindicated language as His own gift, and man's invention, in that miracle of the day of Pentecost. And I am bound to follow up Mr. Strettell's teaching, by telling you that what holds true of words, and of their grammatic and logical composition, holds true also of their esthetic and artistic composition, of style, of rhythm, of poetry and oratory. Every principle of these which is true and good, that is, which produces beauty, is to be taken as an inspiration from above, as depending not on the will of man but of God; not on any abstract rules, of pedant's invention, but on the eternal necessities and harmony, on the being of God Himself.

These may seem lofty words, but I do not think they are likely to make us lofty-minded. I think that the belief of them will tend to make us all more reverent and earnest in examining the utterances of others, more simple and truthful in giving vent to our own, fearing equally all prejudiced and hasty criticism, all self-willed mannerism, all display of fine words, as sins against the divine dignity of language. From these assertions I think we may conclude what is the true method of studying style. The critical examination of good authors, looking at language as an inspiration, and its laws as things independent of us, eternal and divine, we must search into them as we would into any other set of facts, into nature, or the Bible, by patient induction. We must not be content with any traditional maxims, or abstract rules, such as have been put forth in Blair and Lord Kames,[1] for these are merely worked out by the head, and can give us no insight into the magic which touches the heart. All abstract rules of criticism, indeed, are very barren. One may read whole folios of them without getting one step further than we were at first, viz. that what is beautiful is beautiful. Though, indeed, these abstract rules generally tend to narrow our notions of what is beautiful, in their attempt to explain spiritual things by the carnal understanding. All they do is to explain them away, and thus those who depend on them are tempted to deny the beauty of every thing which cannot be thus analyzed and explained away, according to the established rule and method. I shall have to point out this again to you, when we come to speak of the Pope and Johnson school of critics, and the way in which they wrote whole folios on Shakespeare, without ever penetrating a single step deeper towards the secret of his sublimity. It was just this idolatry of abstract rules which made Johnson call Bishop Percy's invaluable collection of ancient ballads 'stuff and nonsense.' It was this which made Voltaire talk of Hamlet, as the ravings of a drunken savage, because forsooth it could not be crammed into the artificial rules of French tragedy. It is this which, even at this day, makes some men of highly cultivated taste declare that they can see no poetry in the writings of Mr. Tennyson, the cause, little as they are aware of it, simply being that neither his excellencies nor his faults are after the model of the Etonian classical school which reigned in England fifty years ago. When these critics speak of that with which they sympathize they are admirable. They become childish only when they resolve to bind all by maxims which may suit themselves.

We must then, I think, absolutely eschew any abstract rules as starting points. What rules we may require, we must neither borrow nor invent, but discover, during the course of our reading. We must take passages whose power and beauty is univerally acknowledged, and try by reverently and patiently dissecting them to see into the secret of their charm, to see why and how they are the best possible expressions of the author's mind. Then for the wider laws of art, we may proceed to examine whole works, single elegies, essays, and dramas.

In carrying out all this, it will be safest, as always, to follow the course of nature, and begin where God begins with us. For as every one of us is truly a microcosm, a whole miniature world within ourselves, so is the history of each individual more or less the history of the whole human race, and there are few of us but pass through the same course of intellectual growth, through which the whole English nation has passed with an exactness and perfection proportionate of course to the richness and vigour of each person's character. Now as in the nation, so in the individual, poetry springs up before prose. Look at the history of English literature, how completely it is the history of our own childhood and adolescence, in its successive fashions. First, fairy tales – then ballads of adventure, love, and war – then a new tinge of foreign thought and feeling, generally French, as it was with the English nation in the twelfth and thirteenth century – then elegiac and reflective poetry – then classic art begins to influence our ripening youth, as it did the youth of our nation in the sixteenth century, and delight in dramatic poetry follows as a natural consequence, – and last, but not least, as the fruit of all these changes, a vigorous and matured prose. For indeed, as elocution is the highest melody, so is true prose the highest poetry. Consider how in an air, the melody is limited to a few arbitrary notes, and recurs at arbitrary periods, while the more scientific the melody becomes, the more numerous and nearly allied are the notes employed, and the more complex and uncertain is their recurrence, in short, the nearer does the melody of the air approach to the melody of elocution, in which the notes of the voice ought continually to be passing into each other, by imperceptible gradations, and their recurrence to depend entirely on the emotions conveyed in the subject words. Just so, poetry employs a confined and arbitrary metre, and a periodic recurrence of sounds which disappear gradually in its higher forms of the ode and the drama, till the poetry at last passes into prose, a free and ever shifting flow of every imaginable rhythm and metre, determined by no arbitrary rules, but only by the spiritual intent of the subject. The same will hold good of whole prose compositions, when compared with whole poems.

Prose then is highest. To write a perfect prose must be your ultimate object in attending these Lectures; but we must walk before we can run, and walk with leading-strings before we can walk alone, and such leading-strings are verse and rhyme. Some tradition of this is still kept up in the practice of making boys write Latin and Greek verses at school, which is of real service to the intellect, even when most carelessly employed, and which, when earnestly carried out, is one great cause of the public school and college man's superiority in style, to most self-educated authors. And why should women's writings be in any respect inferior to that of men, if they are only willing to follow out the same method of self-education?

Do not fancy, when I say that we must learn poetry before we learn prose, that I am only advancing a paradox; mere talking is no more prose than mere rhyme is poetry. Monsieur Jourdain in Molière's Comedy,[2] makes, I suspect, a very great mistake, when he tells his master, 'If that means prose, I've been talking prose all my life.' I fancy the good man had been no more talking prose, than an awkward country boy has been really walking all his life, because he has been contriving some how to put one leg before the other. To see what walking is, we must look at the perfectly drilled soldier, or at the perfectly accomplished lady, who has been taught to dance in order that she may know how to walk. Dancing has been well called the poetry of motion: but the tender grace, the easy dignity in every gesture of daily life which the perfect dancer exhibits answers exactly to that highly organized prose which ought to be the offspring of a critical acquaintance with poetry. Milton's matchless prose style, for instance, grows naturally from his matchless power over rhyme and metre. Practice in versification might be unnecessary if we were all born world-geniuses; so would practice in dancing, if every lady had the figure of a Venus and the garden of Eden for a play-ground. But even the ancient Greeks amid every advantage of climate, dress, and physical beauty, considered a thorough instruction in all athletic and graceful exercises as indispensably necessary, not only to a boy's but also to a girl's education, and in like manner, I think the exquisite models of prose with which English literature abounds will not supersede the necessity of a careful training in versification, nay, will rather make such a training all the more requisite for those who wish to imitate such excellence. Pray understand me, by using the word imitate, I do not mean that I wish you to ape the style of any favourite author. Your aim will not be to write like this man or that woman, but to write like yourselves, being of course responsible for what yourselves are like. Do not be afraid to let the peculiarities of your different characters show yourselves in your styles. Your prose may be the rougher for it, but it will be at least honest; and all mannerism is dishonesty, an attempt to gain beauty at the expense of truthful expression which invariably defeats its own ends, and produces an unpleasant effect, so necessarily one are truth and beauty. So far then from wishing to foster in you any artificial mannerism, mannerism is that foul enchanter from whom, above all others, I am sworn 'en preux Chevalier'[3] to deliver you. As Professor Maurice warned me when I undertook this lectureship, my object in teaching you about 'styles' should be that you may have no style at all. But mannerism can be only avoided by the most thorough practice and knowledge. Half-educated writers are always mannerists; while as the ancient canon says, 'the perfection of art is to conceal art'[4] – to depart from uncultivated and therefore defective nature, to rise again through art to a more organized and therefore more simple naturalness. Just as, to carry on the analogy which I employed just now, it is only the perfect dancer who arrives at that height of art at which her movements seem dictated not by conscious science, but unconscious nature.

I do hope then that the study, and still more the practice of versification, may produce in you the same good effects which they do in young men; that they may give you a habit of portioning out your thoughts distinctly and authentically in a more simple, condensed, and expressive style: that they may teach you what elevation of language, what class of sounds, what flow of words may best suit your tone of thought and feeling, that they may prevent in you that tendency to monotonous repetition, and vain wordiness, which is the bosom sin of most uneducated prose writers, not only of the ladies of the 19th century, but of the middle-age monks, who, having in general no poetry, on which to form their taste, except the effeminate and bombastic productions of the dying Roman empire, fell into a certain washy prolixity, which has made monk Latin a bye-word, and puts one sadly in mind of what is too truly called young ladies' English.

I should like then to begin with two or three of the early ballads, and carefully analyse them with you. I am convinced that in them we may discover many of the great primary laws of composition, as well as the secrets of sublimity and pathos in their simplest manifestations. It may be that there are some here, to whom the study of old ballads may be a little distasteful, who are in an age when the only poetry which has charms is the subjective and self-conscious 'poetry of the heart' – to whom a stanza of *Childe Harolde* may seem worth all the ballads that ever were written; but let me remind them that woman is by her sex an educator, that every one here must expect, aye hope, to be employed at some time or other in training the minds of children: then let me ask them to recall the years in which objective poems, those which dealt with events, ballads, fairy tales, down to nursery rhymes, were their favourite intellectual food, and let me ask them whether it will not be worth while for the sake of the children whom they may hereafter influence, to bestow a little thought on this earlier form of verse.

I must add too, that without some understanding of these same ballads, we shall never arrive at a critical appreciation of Shakespeare. For the English drama springs from an inter-marriage between this same ballad poetry, the poetry of incidents, and that subjective elegiac poetry which deals with the feelings and consciousnesses of man. They are the two poles, by whose union our drama is formed, and some critical knowledge of both of them will be, as I said, necessary before they can study it.

After the ballads, we ought, I think, to know a little about the early Norman poetry, whose fusion with the pure North Saxon ballad school produced Chaucer and the poets previous to the Reformation. We shall proceed to Chaucer himself; then to the rise of the Drama; then to the poets of the Elizabethan age. I shall analyze a few of Shakespeare's master pieces; then speak of Milton and Spenser; thence pass to the prose of Sidney, Hooker, Bacon, Taylor, and our later great authors. Thus our Composition Lectures will follow an historical method, parallel with, and I hope illustrative of, the Lectures on English History.

But it will not be enough, I am afraid, to study the style of others without attempting something yourselves. No criticism teaches so much as the criticism of our own works. And I hope therefore that you will not think that I ask too much of you when I propose that weekly prose and verse compositions, on set subjects, be sent in by the class. To the examination of these the latter half of each lecture may be devoted, and the first half hour to the study of various authors: and in order that I may be able to speak my mind freely on them I should propose that they be anonymous. I hope that you will all trust me when I tell you that those who have themselves experienced what labour attends the task of composition, are generally most tender and charitable in judging of the work of others, and that whatever remarks I may make will be such only as a man has a right to make on a woman's composition.

And if I may seem to be asking any thing new or troublesome, I beg you to remember, that it is the primary idea of this College to vindicate women's right to an education in all points equal to that of men; the difference between them being determined not by any fancied inferiority of mind, but simply by the distinct offices and character of the sexes.

And surely when you recollect the long drudgery at Greek and Latin verses which is required of every highly educated man, and the high importance which has attached to them for centuries in the opinion of Englishmen, you cannot think that I am too exigent in asking you for a few sets of English verses. Believe me, that you ought to find their beneficial effect in producing, as I said before, a measured deliberate style of expression, a habit of calling up clear and distinct images on all subjects, a power of condensing and arranging your thoughts, such as no practice in prose themes can ever give. If you are disappointed of these results it will not be the fault of this long proved method of teaching, but of my own inability to carry it out. Indeed I cannot too strongly confess my own ignorance or fear my own imbecility. I stand aghast when I compare my means and my idea, but I believe that 'by teaching thou shalt learn,' is a rule of which I too shall take the benefit, and having begun these Lectures in the name of Him who is The Word, and with the firm intention of asserting throughout His claims as the Inspirer of all Language and of all Art, I may perhaps hope for the fulfilment of His own promise, 'Be not anxious what you shall speak, for it shall be given you in that day and in that hour what you shall speak.'[5]

Notes

1. Hugh Blair, *Lectures on Rhetoric and Belles Lettres* (1783); Henry Home, Lord Kames, *Elements of Criticism* (1762). Both Blair's and Kames's work went through many editions.
2. *Le Bourgeois Gentilhomme* (1670).
3. Like a valiant knight.
4. 'Prima est, ne ars esse videatur.' (Quintilian, *Institutionis Oratoriae* I.xi.3.)
5. Mark xiii.11.

'On English Literature'

An introductory Lecture must, I suppose, be considered as a sort of art-exhibition, or advertisement of the wares hereafter to be furnished by the Lecturer. If these, on actual use, should prove to fall far short of the promise conveyed in the programme, hearers must remember, that the Lecturer is bound even to his own shame, to set forth in all commencements the most perfect method of teaching which he can devise, in order that human frailty may have something at which to aim; at the same time begging all to consider that in this piecemeal world, it is sufficient not so much to have realized one's ideal, as earnestly to have tried to realize it, according to the measure of each man's gifts. Besides, what may not be fulfilled in a first course, or in a first generation of teachers, may still be effected by those who follow them. It is but fair to expect that if this Institution shall prove, as I pray God it may, a centre of female education worthy of the wants of the coming age, the method and the practice of the College will be developing, as years bring experience and wider eye-range, till we become truly able to teach the English woman of the 19th century, to bear her part in an era, which as I believe more and more, bids fair to eclipse in faith and in art, in science and in polity, any and every period of glory which Christendom has yet beheld.

The first requisite, I think, for a modern course of English Literature is, that it be a whole course or none. The literary education of woman has too often fallen into the fault of our Elegant Extracts, and Beauties of British poetry. It has neither begun at the beginning, nor ended at the end. The young have been taught to admire the laurels of Parnassus,[1] but only after they have been clipt and pollarded like a Dutch shrubbery. The roots which connect them with mythic antiquity, and the fresh leaves and flowers of the growing present, have been generally cut off with care, and the middle part only has been allowed to be used – too often, of course, a sufficiently tough and dry stem. This method is no doubt easy, because it saves teachers the trouble of investigating antiquity, and saves them too the still more delicate task of judging contemporaneous authors – but like all half measures, it has bred less good than evil. If we could silence a free press, and the very free tongues of modern society; if we could clip the busy, imaginative craving mind of youth on the Procrustean bed of use and want, the method might succeed; but we can do neither – the young *will* read, and *will* hear; and the consequence is, a general complaint, that the minds of young women are out-growing their mother's guidance, that they are reading books which their mothers never dreamt of reading, of many of which they never heard, many at least whose good and evil they have had no means of investigating; that the authors which really interest and influence the minds of the young are just the ones which have formed no part of their education, and therefore those for judging of which they have received no adequate rules; that, in short, in literature as in many things, education in England is far behind the wants of the age.

Now this is all wrong and ruinous. The mother's mind should be the lode-star of the daughter's. Any thing which loosens the bond of filial reverence, of filial resignation, is even more destructive, if possible, to womanhood than to manhood – the certain bane of both. And the evil fruits are evident enough – self-will and self-conceit in the less gentle, restlessness and dissatisfaction in many of the meekest and gentlest; talents seem with most a curse instead of a blessing; clever and earnest young women, like young men, are beginning to wander up and down in all sorts of eclecticisms and dilettantisms – one year they find out that the dark ages were not altogether barbarous, and by a revulsion of feeling natural to youth, they begin to adore them as a very galaxy of light, beauty, and holiness. Then they begin to crave naturally enough for some real understanding of this strange ever-developing 19th century, some real sympathy with its new wonders, some real sphere of labour in it; and this drives them to devour the very newest authors – any book whatever which seems to open for them the riddle of the mighty and mysterious present, which is forcing itself on their attention through every sense. And so up and down, amid confusions and oscillations from pole to pole, and equally eclectic at either pole, from St Augustin and Mr Pugin, to Goethe and George Sand, and all intensified and coloured by that tender enthusiasm, that craving for something to worship, which is a woman's highest grace, or her bitterest curse – wander these poor Noah's doves, without either ark of shelter or rest for the sole of their foot, sometimes, alas! over strange ocean-wastes, into gulfs of error – too sad to speak of here – and *will* wander more and more till teachers begin boldly to face reality, and interpret to them both the old and the new, lest they mis-interpret them for themselves. The educators of the present generation must meet the cravings of the young spirit with the bread of life, or they will gorge themselves with poison. Telling them that they ought not to be hungry, will not stop their hunger; shutting our eyes to facts, will only make us stumble over them the sooner; hiding our eyes in the sand, like the hunted ostrich, will not hide us from the iron necessity of circumstances, or from the Almighty will of Him, who is saying in these days to society, in language unmistakeable, 'Educate, or fall to pieces! Speak the *whole* truth to the young, or take the consequences of your cowardice!'

On these grounds I should wish to see established in this College, a really entire course of English Literature, such as shall give correct, reverent, and loving views of every period from the earliest legends and poetry of the middle age, up to the latest of our modern authors, and in the case of the higher classes, if it should hereafter be found practicable, Lectures devoted to the criticism of such authors as may be exercising any real influence upon the minds of English women. This, I think, should be our ideal. It must be attempted cautiously and step by step. It will not be attained at the first trial, certainly not by the first Lecturer. Sufficient, if each succeeding teacher shall leave something more taught, some fresh extension of the range of knowledge which is thought fit for his scholars.

I said that the ages of history were analogous to the ages of man, and that each age of Literature was the truest picture of the history of its day; and for this very reason English Literature is the best, perhaps the only teacher of English History, to women especially. For it seems to me that it is principally by the help of such an extended literary course, that we can cultivate a just and enlarged taste, which will connect education with the deepest feelings of the heart. It seems hardly fair, or reasonable either, to confine the reading of the young to any certain fancied Augustan age of authors, I mean those of the 17th and 18th century; especially when that age requires, in order to appreciate it, a far more developed mind, a far greater experience of mankind and of the world, than falls to the lot of one young woman out of a thousand. Strong meat for men, and milk for babes. But why are we to force on any age spiritual food unfitted for it? If we do we shall be likely only to engender a lasting disgust for that by which our pupils might have fully profited, had they only been introduced to it when they were ready for it. And this actually happens with English literature: by having the so-called standard works thrust upon them too early, and then only in a fragmentary form, not fresh and whole, but cut up into the very driest hay, the young too often neglect in after life the very books which then might become the guides of their taste. Hence proceed in the minds of the young sudden and irregular revulsions of affection for different schools of writing: and all revolutions in the individual as well as in the nation are sure to be accompanied by some dead loss of what has been already gained, some disruption of feelings, some renunciation of principles, which ought to have been preserved; something which might have borne fruit is sure to be crushed in the earthquake. Many before me must surely have felt this. Do none here remember how, when they first escaped from the dry class-drudgery of Pope and Johnson, they snatched greedily at the forbidden fruit of Byron, perhaps of Shelley, and sentimental novel-writers innumerable? How when the luscious melancholy of their morbid self-consciousness began to pall on the appetite, they fled for refuge as suddenly to mere poetry of description and action, to Southey, Scott, the ballad-literature of all ages? How when the craving returned (perhaps unconsciously to themselves) to understand the wondrous heart of man, they tried to satisfy it with deep draughts of Wordsworth's celestial and pure simplicity? How again, they tired of that too gentle and unworldly strain, and sought in Shakespeare something more exciting, more genial, more rich in the facts and passions of daily life? How even his all-embracing genius failed to satisfy them, because he did not palpably connect for them their fancy and their passions with their religious faith – and so they wandered out again over the sea of literature, Heaven only knows whither, in search of a school of authors yet alas! unborn. For the true literature of the 19th century, the literature which shall set forth in worthy strains the relation of the two greatest facts, namely of the universe and of Christ, which shall transfigure all our enlarged knowledge of science and of society, of nature, of art, and man with the eternal truths of the gospel, that poetry of the future is not yet here: but it is coming, aye even at the doors; when this great era shall become conscious of its high vocation, and the author too shall claim his priestly calling, and the poets of the world, like the kingdoms of the world, shall become the poets of God and of His Christ.

But to return. Should we not rather in education follow that method which Providence has already mapped out for us? If we are bound, as of course we are, to teach our pupils to breathe freely on the highest mountain peaks of Shakespeare's art, how can we more certainly train them to do so, than by leading them along the same upward path by which Shakespeare himself rose – through the various changes of taste, the gradual developments of literature, through which the English mind had been passing before Shakespeare's time? For there was a literature before Shakespeare. Had there not been, neither would there have been a Shakespeare. Critics are now beginning to see that the old fancy which made Shakespeare spring up at once, a self-perfected poet, like Minerva full-armed from the head of Jove, was a superstition of pedants, who neither knew the ages before the great poet, nor the man himself, except that little of him which seemed to square with their shallow mechanical taste. The old fairy superstition, the old legends, and ballads, the old chronicles of feudal war and chivalry, the earlier moralities and mysteries, and tragi-comic attempts – these were the roots of his poetic tree; – they must be the roots of any literary education which can teach us to appreciate him. These fed Shakespeare's youth; why should they not feed our children's? Why indeed? That inborn delight of the young in all that is marvellous and fantastic – has that a merely evil root? No, surely! it is a most pure part of their spiritual nature; a part of 'the heaven which lies about us in our infancy'; angel-wings with which the free child leaps the prison-walls of sense and custom, and the drudgery of earthly life – like the wild dreams of childhood, it is a God-appointed means for keeping alive what noble Wordsworth calls:

> those obstinate questionings
> Of sense and outward things,
> Fallings from us, vanishings;
> Blank misgivings of a creature
> Moving about in worlds not realized;

by which:

Though inland far we be,
Our souls have sight of that immortal sea
Which brought us hither:
Can in a moment travel thither,
And see the children sporting on the shore,
And hear the mighty waters rolling evermore.[2]

And those old dreams of our ancestors in the childhood of England, they are fantastic enough, no doubt, and unreal, but yet they are most true and most practical, if we but use them as parables and symbols of human feeling and everlasting truth. What, after all, is any event of earth, palpable as it may seem, but, like them, a shadow and a ghostly dream, till it has touched our *hearts*, till we have found out and obeyed its spiritual lesson? Be sure that one really pure legend or ballad may bring God's truth and heaven's beauty more directly home to the young spirit than whole volumes of dry abstract didactic morality. Outward things, beauty, action, nature, are the great problems for the young. God has put them in a visible world, that by what they *see* they may learn to know the *unseen*: and we must begin to feed their minds with that literature which deals most with visible things, with passion manifested in action, which we shall find in the early writing of our middle ages: for then the collective mind of our nation was passing through its natural stages of childhood and budding youth, as every nation and every single individual must at some time or other do; a true 'young England,'[3] always significant and precious to the young. I said there was a literary art before Shakespeare – an art more simple, more childlike, more girlish as it were, and therefore all the more adapted for young minds. But also an art most vigorous and pure in point of style: thoroughly fitted to give its readers the first elements of taste, which must lie at the root of even the most complex aesthetics. I know no higher specimens of poetic style, considering the subject, and the belief of the time about them, than may be found in many of our old ballads. How many poets are there in England now, who could have written 'The Twa Bairns,' or 'Sir Patrick Spense'?[4] How many such histories as old William of Malmesbury, in spite of all his foolish monk miracles? As few now as there were then: and as for lying legends, they had their superstitions, and we have ours: and the next generation will stare at our strange doings as much as we stare at our forefathers. For our forefathers they were; we owe them filial reverence, thoughtful attention, and more – we must know them, ere we can know ourselves. The only key to the present is the *past*.

But I must go further still, and after premising that the English classics, so called, of the 16th and 18th centuries, will of course form the bulk of the Lectures, I must plead for some instruction in the works of recent and living authors. I cannot see why we are to teach the young about the past and not about the present. After all, they have to live now, and at no other time: in this same 19th century lies their work; it may be unfortunate, but we cannot help it. I do not see why we should wish to help it. I know no century which the world has yet seen, so well worth living in. Let us thank God that we are here now, and joyfully try to understand *where* we are, and what our work is *here*. As for all super-stitions about 'the good old times,' and fancies that *they* belonged to God, while this age belongs only to man, blind chance, and the evil one, let us cast them from us as the suggestions of an evil lying spirit, as the natural parents of laziness, pedantry, popery and unbelief. And therefore let us not fear to tell our children the meaning of this present day, and of all its different voices. Let us not be content to say to them, as we have been doing, 'We will see you well instructed in the past, but you must make out the present for yourselves.' Why, if the past is worth explaining, far more is the present, – the pressing, noisy, complex, present, where our workfield lies, the most intricate of all states of soci-ety, and of all schools of literature yet known, and therefore the very one requiring most explanation.

How rich in strange and touching utterances have been the last fifty years of English literature. Do you think that God has been teaching us nothing in them? Will He not *make* our children listen to that teaching, whether we like or not? And suppose our most modern writers *had* added nothing to the stock of national knowledge, which I most fer-vently deny, yet are they not actually influencing the minds of the young? and can we prevent their doing so either directly or indirectly? If we do not find them right teaching about their own day, will they not be sure to find self-chosen teachers about it themselves, who will be almost certainly the first who may come to hand, and therefore as likely as not to be *bad* teachers? …

* *
* *

The best method, I think, of working out these principles would be to devote a few lectures in the last term of every complete course, to the examination of some select works of recent writers, chosen under the sanction of the Educational Committee. But I must plead for *whole* works. 'Extracts' and 'Select Beauties' are about as practical as the worthy in the old story, who, wishing to sell his house, brought one of the bricks to market as a specimen. It is equally unfair on the author and on the pupil; for it is impossible to shew the merits or demerits of a work of art, even to explain the truth or falsehood of any particular passage, except by viewing the book as an organic whole. And as for the fear of raising a desire to read more of an author than may be proper – when a work has once been pointed out as really hurtful, the rest must be left to the best safe-guard which I have yet discovered, in man or woman – the pupil's own honour.

Such a knowledge of English literature would tend no less, I think, to the spread of healthy historic views among us. The literature of every nation is its auto-biography. Even in its most complex and artistic forms, it is still a wonderfully artless and unconscious record of its doubts and its faith, its sorrows and its triumphs, at each era of its existence. Wonderfully artless and correct – because all utterances which were not faithful to their time, which did not touch some sympathetic chord in their heart's souls, are pretty sure to have been swept out into wholesome oblivion, and only the most genuine and earnest left behind for posterity. The History of England indeed is the literature of England – but one very different from any school history, or other now in vogue; you will find it neither a mere list of acts of parliament, and record-office like some; nor yet an antiquarian gallery of costumes and armour, like others; nor a mere war-gazette and report of killed and wounded from time to time; least of all not a *Debrett's Peerage*, and catalogue of kings and queens, (whose names are given, while their souls are ignored) but a true spiritual History of England – a picture of the spirits of our old forefathers, who worked, and fought, and sorrowed and died for us; on whose accumulated labours we now here stand. *That* I call a history – not of one class of offices or events, but of the living human souls of English men and English women. And therefore one most adapted to the mind of woman; one which will call into fullest exercise her blessed faculty of sympathy, that pure and tender heart of flesh, which teaches her always to find her highest interest in mankind, simply as mankind; to see the Divine most completely in the human; to prefer the incarnate to the disembodied, the personal to the abstract, the pathetic to the intellectual; to see, and truly, in the most common tale of village love or sorrow, a mystery deeper and more divine than lies in all the theories of politicians or the fixed ideas of the sage.

Such a course of history would quicken women's inborn *personal interest* in the actors of this life-drama, and be quickened by it in return, as indeed it ought: for it is thus that God intended woman to look instinctively at the world. Would to God that she would teach us men to look at it thus likewise! Would to God that she would in these days claim and fulfil to the uttermost her vocation as the priestess of charity! that woman's heart would help to deliver man from bondage to his own tyrannous and all-too-exclusive brain! from our idolatry of mere dead laws and printed books – from our daily sin of looking at men, not as our struggling and suffering brothers, but as mere symbols of certain formulae, incarnations of sets of opinions, wheels in some iron liberty-grinding or Christianity-spinning machine, which we miscall society, or civilization, or worst misnomer of all, the Church!

This I take to be one of the highest aims of woman – to preach charity, love, and brotherhood: but in this 19th century, hunting every where for law and organization, refusing loyalty to any thing which cannot range itself under its theories, she will never get a hearing, till her knowledge of the past becomes more organized and methodic. As it is now, for want of large many-sided views of the past, her admiration is too apt to attach itself to some two or three characters only in the hero-list of all the ages. Then comes the temptation to thrust aside all which interferes with her favourite idols, and so the very heart given her for universal sympathy becomes the organ of an exclusive bigotry, and she who should have taught man to love, too often only embitters his hate.

I claim, therefore, as necessary for the education of the future, that woman should be initiated into the thoughts and feelings of her countrymen in every age, from the wildest legends of the past to the most palpable naturalism of the present; and that not merely in a chronological order, sometimes not in chronological order at all; but in a true spiritual sequence; that knowing the hearts of many, she may in after life be able to comfort the hearts of all.

But there is yet another advantage in an extended study of English literature – I mean the more national tone which it ought to give the thoughts of the rising generation. Of course to repress the reading of foreign books, to strive after any national exclusiveness, or mere John-Bullism of mind, in an age of railroads and free press, would be simply absurd – and more, it would be fighting against the will of God revealed in events. He has put the literary treasures of the continent into our hands; we must joyfully accept them, and earnestly exhaust them. This age is craving for what it calls catholicity; for more complete interchange and brotherhood of thought between all the nations of the earth. This spirit is stirring in the young especially, and I believe that God Himself has inspired it, because I see that He has first revealed the means of gratifying the desire, at that very time in which it has arisen.

But every observant person must be aware that this tendency has produced its evils as well as its good. There is a general complaint that the minds of young women are becoming un-English; that their foreign reading does not merely supply the deficiencies of their English studies, but too often completely supersedes them; that the whole tone of their thoughts is too often taken from French or German writings; that by some means or other, the standard works of English literature are becoming very much undervalued and neglected by the young people of this day; and that selfwill and irregular eclecticism are the natural results.

I must say that I consider the greater part of these evils, as the natural consequence of past miseducation; as the just punishment of the old system, which attached the most disproportionate importance to mere acquirements, and those mostly of foreign languages, foreign music, and so forth, while the 'well of English undefiled,'[5] and not only that – but English literature, history, patriotism, too often English religion, have been made quite minor considerations. Therefore so few of the young have any healthy and firm English standard whereby to try and judge foreign thought. Therefore they fancy when they meet with any thing deep and attractive in foreign works, that because they have no such thoughts put before them in English authors, no such thoughts exist in them.

But happily we may do much towards mending this state of things, by making our pupils thoroughly conversant with the aesthetic treasures of English literature. From them I firmly believe they may derive sufficient rules, whereby to separate in foreign books the true from the false, the necessary from the accidental, the eternal truth from its peculiar national vesture. Above all we shall give them a better chance of seeing things from that side from which God intended English women to see them: for as surely as there is an English view of every thing, so surely God intends us to take that view; and He who gave us our English character intends us to develop its peculiarities, as He intends the French woman to develop hers, that so each nation by learning to understand itself, may learn to understand, and therefore to profit, by its neighbour. He who has not cultivated his own plot of ground will hardly know much about the tillage of his neighbour's land. And she who does not appreciate the mind of her own countrymen, will never form any true judgment of the mind of foreigners. Let English women be sure that the best way to understand the heroines of the continent is not by mimicking them, however noble they may be; not by trying to become a sham Rahel, or a sham de Sevigné, but a real Elizabeth Fry, Felicia Hemans, or Hannah More. What indeed entitles either Madame de Sevigné, or Rahel, to fame, but their very *nationality*? that intensely *local* style of language and feeling which clothes their genius with a living body instead of leaving it in the abstractions of a dreary cosmopolitanism? The one I suppose would be called the very beau-ideal, not of woman, but of the French woman – the other the ideal, not even of the Jewess, but of the German Jewess. We may admire wherever we find worth; but if we try to imitate we only caricature. Excellence grows in all climes, transplants to none: the palm luxuriates only in the tropics, the Alp-rose only beside eternal snows. Only by standing on our own native earth can we enjoy or even see aright the distant stars: if we try to reach them, we shall at once lose sight of them, and drop helpless in a new element, unfitted for our limbs.

Teach, then, the young by an extended knowledge of English literature, thoroughly to comprehend the English spirit, thoroughly to see that the English mind has its peculiar calling on God's earth, which alone, and no other, it can fulfil. Teach them thoroughly to appreciate the artistic and intellectual excellencies of their own country; but by no means in a spirit of narrow bigotry: – tell them fairly our national faults – teach them to unravel those faults from our national virtues; and then there will be no danger of the prejudiced English woman becoming by a sudden revulsion an equally prejudiced cosmopolite and eclectic, as soon as she discovers that her own nation does not monopolize all human perfections; and so trying to become German, Italian, French woman, all at once – a heterogeneous chaos of imitations, very probably with the faults of all three characters, and the graces of none. God has given us our own prophets, our own heroines. To recognize those prophets, to imitate those heroines, is the duty which lies nearest to the English woman, and therefore the duty which God intends her to fulfil.

I should wish therefore in the first few Lectures on English Literature to glance at the character of our old Saxon ancestors, and the legends connected with their first invasion of the country; and above all at the magnificent fables of King Arthur and his times, which exercised so great an influence on the English mind, and were in fact, although originally Celtic, so thoroughly adopted and naturalized by the Saxon, as to re-appear under different forms in every age, and form the key-note of most of our fictions, from Geoffrey of Monmouth and the medieval ballads, up to Chaucer, Spenser, Shakespeare, and at last, Milton and Blackmore. This series of legends will, I think, as we trace its development, bring us in contact one by one with the corresponding developments of the English character; and unless I am much mistaken, enable us to explain many of its peculiarities.

Of course nothing more than sketches can be given; but I think nothing more is required for any one but the professed historian. For young people especially it is sufficient to understand the tone of human feeling, expressed by legends, rather than to enter into any critical dissertations on their historic truth. They need, after all, principles rather than facts. To educate them truly we must give them inductive habits of thought, and teach them to deduce from a few facts a law which makes plain all similar ones, and so acquire the habit of extracting from every story somewhat of its kernel of spiritual meaning. But again, to educate them truly we must ourselves have faith: we must believe that in every one there is a spiritual eye which can perceive those great principles when they are once fairly presented to it, that in all there are some noble instincts, some pure yearnings after wisdom, and taste, and usefulness, which, if we only appeal to them trustfully through the examples of the past, and the excitements of the present, will wake into conscious life. Above all, both pupils and teachers must never forget that all these things were written for their examples; that though circumstances and creeds, schools and tastes, may alter, yet the heart of man, and the duty of man, remain unchanged; and that while

> The old order changes, giving place to the new,
> And God fulfils himself in many ways,[6]

yet again 'Through the ages one unaltered purpose runs;'[7] and the principles of truth and beauty are the same as when the everlasting Spirit from whom they come 'brooded upon the face' of the primeval seas.

*
*   *

Notes

1. In the Classical world, the laurel symbolized the spirit of prophecy and poetry; one of the summits of Parnassus was consecrated to Apollo and the Muses, and came to be regarded as the seat of poetry and music.
2. Wordsworth, 'Ode: Intimations of Immortality from Recollections of Early Childhood.'
3. Young England was a group of young Tory politicians who, in the 1840s, tried to resurrect a rather romantic version of paternalistic feudalism.
4. 'The Twa Bairns' is usually known as 'The Twa Brothers.' Both 'The Twa Brothers' and 'Sir Patrick Spense' are medieval poems by unknown authors.
5. Spenser, *The Faerie Queene* IV.ii.32.
6. Tennyson, *Idylls of the King*, 'The Passing of Arthur,' l.408.
7. Tennyson, 'Locksley Hall.'

CHAPTER EIGHT

Appointment of a Professor of English Language and Literature at University College, London in 1865

During the period from the establishment of the Chair of English Language and Literature at University College in 1828 to the appointment of Henry Morley to this Chair in 1865, there was no settled view of what the subject was to be. Morley was the ninth incumbent, so the college had had a number of opportunities to ask itself what it wanted from this professorship and what the place of English was to be. The emphasis was variously on composition, rhetoric, philology and literature, while images of the subject included the patriotic, socially cohesive, morally and spiritually uplifting and the utilitarian. University College, with its traditional stress on useful knowledge, was particularly inclined to see the subject as being concerned with composition and the formation of style, but this was not the sole, exclusive model.

When Morley's predecessor, David Masson, moved on to Edinburgh in 1865 after thirteen years at University College, the Senate appointed a committee of eight professors to consider the applications for the vacant post. Their report is extremely thorough, analysing what they saw as the college's requirements as well as the qualifications of the various candidates to meet these requirements. The ability to teach composition was of paramount importance, but the successful candidate would also require a sound knowledge of the history and structure of the language, and would need to be able to provide students with the critical tools with which to judge literature for themselves.

There were fifteen candidates for the selection committee to consider. However, the main contenders, in the view of the committee, were J.W. Hales, who later became Professor of English Language and Literature at King's College, London, and Henry Morley. The extracts here focus particularly on these two candidates. Morley was the older man, and had more to show in terms of published scholarly work, as well as teaching at King's College, which was more directly relevant than Hales's experience to the teaching required at University College. In Morley's transfer from King's College to University College, different strands in the history of English studies were united.

Henry Morley stayed at University College from 1865 until 1889, a time of overall college expansion as well as growth in the numbers studying English. From 1878 he combined his University College duties with tenure of the Chair of English at Queen's College, London. Then, in 1879, he was also appointed one of the two examiners in English Language, Literature and History for the University of London, a position which gave him immense influence over the development of English studies, as the London examinations were sat in many of the new colleges which were springing up throughout Britain and the Empire.

Report of the Committee of the Senate

*
* *

...Your committee trust that they will not be thought to have slighted any of the other Candidates, because they arrived at the distinct opinion, that for our particular purpose Mr Hales[1] and Mr Henry Morley[2] were better qualified than the rest.

We think that the Professor of the English Language and Literature in our College, ought, if it were possible to unite all the qualifications which we think desirable, to be a thoroughly educated man, a man whose peculiar learning is based upon the sound scholarship which is the general training of English gentlemen. He ought to have made a systematic study of the English Language and English Literature: a systematic study of the Language, so as to be thoroughly conversant with its etymological structure, and the history of its formation through its successive stages; a systematic study of the Literature, so that his familiar knowledge of it may not be confined within the limits of one or two periods. He ought to have experience as a Lecturer, and to be able to lecture well: but he ought to be prepared not only to lecture, but to teach. We must bear in mind, and our Professor must bear in mind, that the practical end of our English Class is to teach our students to use their own language well both in speaking and writing.

The grammatical, etymological, and historical study of the language, no doubt brings with it other benefits. English Literature is rich in treasures; and the Professor may render good service to the student by directing him what to read, and how to estimate what he reads. Although we must express our conviction, that little good is done by lectures which give accounts of books and criticisms on books, unless the student goes on to read the books themselves. Without this further step, the information received from the lecturer is not knowledge, but a substitute for knowledge. But the practical object both of the study of the language and of the study of the literature is the attainment of correctness and facility in the use of our mother tongue; and for this object it is necessary that the students should have practice in composition, and should be trained to express their thoughts, and taught to correct whatever may be inexact or ungraceful in the expression of them. We should be very sorry to see any gentleman appointed to fill our English Chair, however elegant as a writer, or eloquent as a lecturer, who would not undertake the laborious duty of correcting the written exercises of his students, and gradually training them in the principles of rhetoric.

*
* *

Mr Henry Morley ... has achieved a reputation as a journalist. For fifteen years he has been associated with Mr Charles Dickens by writing for periodical publications edited by that gentleman; and for about the same time he has written regularly literary articles for the *Examiner*; and for the last four or five years he has been the sole editor of that paper. His lives of Bernard Palissy, of Jerome Cardan, and of Cornelius Agrippa, attest not only his researches into outlying regions of the domain of literature, but also a singular power of vivid and picturesque writing, and of delineating human feelings and characters. Mr Morley has made a most thorough and systematic study both of the English Language and English Literature. He has proposed to himself as the labour of his life a complete review of English Literature from the very origin of the nation and language to the present day.[3] His first volume, which is already published, contains first, in 116 pages, an Introductory Sketch of the Four Periods which he distinguishes in English Literature; and then a very full account of the origin and formation of the language, and of all its monuments, beginning with the Anglo-Saxon writers, and passing through the Early English Chroniclers and Poets to the end of his first period, that is, to the age of Chaucer. The second volume will be published in the spring; and Mr Morley has placed some sheets of it in our hands. This work appears to be of very great value. It is true that in his First Chapter, in which he discusses the affinities of languages, we miss the comprehensive grasp of the subject which thorough classical scholarship would have enabled him to take. It is likely that Mr Morley is not a classical scholar. It appears from his own very interesting statement, that his attention was accidentally turned to literature, when he had already entered upon life as a medical practitioner; and his abundant learning in English and in other modern literature must have been acquired since that time. When he has got

103

over this doubtful ground in his First Chapter, his chapters on the Celtic races in Britain, and the remains of Gaelic and Cymric poetry, are very instructive; and his account of Anglo-Saxon and Early English Literature is so full that it may be thought to be exhaustive. We cannot doubt that Mr Morley's knowledge of our later writers is equally full and exact. But besides the possession of this store of learning, Mr Morley has given proof of his practical ability as a Teacher. In 1857 he undertook the conduct of the Evening Class of English at King's College; and the class, which, when he began, consisted of twelve pupils had grown by the Session of 1860–61 to one hundred and fifteen. Mr Morley says that he lectured once a week in the Summer Session, and four times a week in the Winter Session, and five times when there were entries enough for an Anglo-Saxon Class. At the end of the Session in 1859 the authorities of King's College acknowledged his services by placing him on the permanent staff of the College as Lecturer on the English Language and Literature. For the first four years Mr Morley taught an Elementary Class as well as more advanced Classes; but for the last four years he has committed the care of the Grammar Class to a competent assistant, and lectured only to the Senior Classes. But it appears from the Prospectus that his lectures were not merely lectures on the literature, but included instruction in English Composition and the formation of style. Dr Hodgson, who is now conducting our English Class, has testified in favour of Mr Morley, and he writes thus: 'It seems to me that the grand aim of the Professor ought to be to make the students (many of whom are badly prepared) proficient in the use of their own language as the instrument for the expression of thought and feeling, whether by voice or by pen. To this great end everything else ought to be subordinated and made subsidiary.... . Now for this important and difficult task I believe that Mr Morley is better qualified and disposed than any other man known to me.' The whole of Dr Hodgson's letter is well worth reading: and it is to be observed that Mr Morley assents to Dr Hodgson's view of the duties of the Professor. In forwarding his letter he says, 'Whether right or wrong in its good opinion of me, it is written by one who knows how English ought to be taught.'

Mr Hales is a Fellow and Assistant Tutor of Christ's College, Cambridge. He took an honourable place (4th in the First Class) on the Classical Tripos in the year 1859. He was for three years and a half an Assistant Master at Marlborough, and then returned to Cambridge. His degree is evidence of his high Classical Scholarship: but his scholarship is of a character which makes it especially valuable for our purpose. His colleague Mr Peile says, 'I can myself speak from the fullest knowledge of the broad view he has always taken of the literature of Greece and Rome; not regarding them as something to be studied and explained solely in and for itself, but as phases of the human intellect, to be explained in their connexion with the history of the world. This view he has always most fully carried out. His classical knowledge is exempt from all suspicion of narrowness.' Mr Moule, Fellow and Classical Lecturer of Corpus Christi College, and a colleague of Mr Hales at Marlborough, says, 'Mr Hales's classical scholarship is at once so refined and so thorough, and so remarkable in the readiness and largeness of view, with which he brings his knowledge of the Greek and Roman Languages and Literature to bear on the study of the English, that I should regard these as among the most valuable of his qualifications for the vacant post.' Mr Sidgwick, Fellow and Assistant Tutor of Trinity College, after speaking of the good effects of his classical training, adds, 'He possesses moreover a breadth of view and capacity for generalisation, which Cambridge has no claim to impart.' But with this training in Classical scholarship Mr Hales states in his letter to the Council, 'that the English Language and Literature have been for several years my favourite studies.' And he has studied them in a regular and systematic way. Mr Peile says, 'Immediately after leaving Cambridge he turned his attention particularly to English Literature; and during more than a year's residence in London he applied himself to definite periods of that literature in the same spirit with which he had worked at Cambridge.' And then after speaking of his residence at Marlborough, and his study of German and French, and of his return to undertake College duties at Cambridge, he adds, 'In the middle of this various work he has still carried on that systematic study of our own literature, which entitles it to be called his peculiar line, the line which I am quite sure he prefers to any other.' Mr Skeat, a former Fellow of Christ's College, who has himself devoted several years of study to the English Language and Literature, says, 'I feel sure that his (Mr Hales's) attention to the structure of the English Language has kept pace with his knowledge of that of the older Classics. As to his acquaintance with English Literature this I know to be unusually extensive; and what is very striking in connexion with it, extremely accurate. I know his reading to have been not only general but particular; that he has not satisfied himself with a comprehensive view of both history and literature as a whole, but that he has also devoted himself to a minute, special, and detailed study of certain more important periods.' These testimonies to his thorough study of English are confirmed by other friends. And he has also experience of teaching the subject. Mr Bradley, the Head Master of Marlborough College, after speaking of Mr Hales' success during 3½ years in his work as an Assistant Master, goes on to say, 'But there was one line of work to which, during the whole of that time, his devotion was constant and uniform, and in which his success was eminent. From the time he first joined us, until the time when he returned to Cambridge to undertake

College work, Mr Hales took unceasing interest in promoting the study of English Literature in the School. With great skill and great success he aroused the interest of many boys in various parts of the school in the authors of their own language; and both by his direct teaching and indirect influence produced a marked and lasting effect. I feel quite sure, that, if appointed to the vacant Professorship he would show that he had a *rare gift* of stimulating and directing the minds of his pupils.' Mr Moule, who, it will be remembered, was one of his colleagues at Marlborough, speaks of his distinguished ability and success in teaching English in the highest class; and he goes on to say, 'Mr Hales's general power of teaching is singularly great; and his success in inspiring an audience with his own interest in a literary subject seems unfailing. His animation, clearness, and thoroughness of treatment, at once claim confidence and sympathy. It may be mentioned as a proof of his powers of dealing with various pupils, that he had been an eminently successful teacher in the London Working Men's College before he went to Marlborough, where he again achieved an equal success with two kinds of pupils so widely different as the highest classes of a Public School and the men and boys of a Wiltshire Night-school.' Other testimonials speak of his 'realising power,' – 'a power of throwing himself into a period,' and sympathising with its ways of thought and feeling, and a kindred power of winning the sympathy of his audience. Mr Gunson, the Tutor of Christ's College, says, 'Emphatically he possesses the gift of imparting to others the knowledge he himself possesses;' and he mentions his success in attracting a class of voluntary attendants in his College to a course of lectures on the ancient Greek Historians. Mr Brodribb of St John's College, a gentleman senior to Mr Hales, and formerly his private tutor, says, 'I have heard lectures which he has delivered on subjects connected with English History and Literature. In these lectures he showed a wide and varied knowledge, as well as a command of clear and appropriate language.' Mr Stephenson, a Fellow of Christ's College, and now Vice-Principal of the Liverpool College, says that Mr Hales 'has great power of clear and thorough explanation;' and that he knows by the direct testimony of some of Mr Hales' pupils at Marlborough, that he had 'the same power of making his teaching effective, and exciting the same interest in *them* which he felt himself;' and he adds, 'He has also, as I know from lectures which I have heard him deliver, great power of adapting himself to his audience, and being popular without being in the least superficial.' We have cited largely from Mr Hales' testimonials, because Mr Hales' merits can be known to us only through the testimony of his friends. Mr Henry Morley sent no testimonials, except the letter of Dr Hodgson; and our opinion of his claims rests upon his published works, and his own statements with respect to his success at King's College, which are sustained by the official documents of the College. Mr Hales' testimonials are well worth reading; for they differ from many testimonials, by not containing mere general praise, but speaking very definitely of definite points of excellence in Mr Hales.

Your Committee at their last meeting considered more fully the claims of Mr Hales and Mr Henry Morley, and were impressed still more deeply with a sense of their superiority to those of the other candidates: but in judging of the two, they arrived at the conviction that it was the safer and preferable course to recommend the appointment of Mr Henry Morley. There can be no doubt that at the present time Mr Morley possesses a wider and more thorough knowledge of English Literature and all that pertains to it than Mr Hales. Mr Hales is probably about fifteen years younger than Mr Morley; and with his devotion to the subject we might reasonably expect that some years hence his learning would be as great as Mr Morley's; but Mr Morley has his treasures ready for present use. It appears that Mr Hales has a singular power of teaching; but Mr Morley is also a successful teacher; and he has had experience in teaching in exactly the same way in which he would be required to teach among us, not only on the same subject, but with the same kind of pupils. Moreover, Mr Morley has established his reputation as an able and even a brilliant writer, and his reputation would redound to the advantage of the College. Mr Hales has written in literary journals; but his writings hitherto are known only to his friends. On the other hand Mr Hales possesses a great advantage in his early training and his classical scholarship. In these respects he is superior to Mr Morley, whose literary culture began at a later period of his life, and whose modern learning does not rest upon a thorough knowledge of the intellect of the ancient world. We think it likely also that Mr Hales would be able to give more of his time to the college, and to devote himself to us more than Mr Morley with his other engagements and duties can do; and we rate highly the benefit that might accrue to our students from familiar association with a young professor of the genial temper and character of Mr Hales. But notwithstanding these advantages, we were of opinion that the greater weight of qualifications lay in the scale of Mr Henry Morley; and we accordingly recommend him to the favourable consideration of the Senate.

Notes

1. J.W. Hales (1836–1914). See his essay, 'The Teaching of English.'
2. Henry Morley (1822–1894), the appointee.
3. *English Writers*, (11 volumes, 1864–1895).

CHAPTER NINE

The Schools Inquiry Commission

In the 1850s and 1860s, the country's educational provision was examined by three commissions, commonly known as the Newcastle Commission (1858–1861), the Clarendon Commission (1861–1864) and the Taunton Commission (1864–1868). English education had never been so carefully studied before. The three commissions looked at different sectors of education: Newcastle at so-called 'popular' education, Clarendon at what were termed the nine 'great' public schools, and lastly Taunton, the Schools Inquiry Commission, at what had not already been covered, the middle ground. The Taunton Commission report of 1868 refers again and again to 'middle-class education,' which it clearly saw as its own particular brief.

The Newcastle and Clarendon Commissions did not have a great deal to say about English, although it was not completely ignored by either. The Newcastle Commission was interested primarily in useful knowledge for elementary school children, and the Clarendon Commission was much more concerned with classics at the 'great' public schools than it was with English. The schools examined by the Taunton Commission were many and various, but with a preponderance of endowed grammar schools, whose central function was considered to be the teaching of classical subjects. The report, however, criticized these schools severely, pointing to their failure even to teach properly the classics, the very subjects to which they were supposed to devote their attention. It was out of this sense of failure of classics as the basis of education for the middle classes that a great deal of pressure was enabled to build up behind English studies.

Members of the Commission, and also many of those whom they interviewed, were very interested in English as an alternative to classics for the middle-class pupils in these schools, and a number of questions were asked about English. The evidence to the Commission included here is from Rev. G.G. Bradley and the Earl of Harrowby.

G.G. Bradley (1821–1903) was a pupil at Rugby under Dr Arnold, and then studied at University College, Oxford. He later returned to Rugby as a teacher, before becoming Headmaster at Marlborough in 1858. In 1870, he left Marlborough to become Master of University College, Oxford. In 1881, he succeeded his old friend, Arthur Penrhyn Stanley, Dr Arnold's biographer, as Dean of Westminster.

At the time of giving evidence to the Schools Inquiry Commission, Bradley was Headmaster of Marlborough. He was questioned closely about competitive examinations for the army, the Civil Service and the India Civil Service, and the effect which these examinations had on middle-class education. The question of 'cramming' seems inseparable from any consideration of these examinations, and it is easy to see how the early inclusion of English as a subject in these competitions served to identify English in many people's minds with cramming and crammers. This association was still present at the time of the Oxford debates in the mid-1880s, as is illustrated in Edward Freeman's article and in many of the letters to the *Pall Mall Gazette*.

Minutes of Evidence from G.G. Bradley

(Mr Acland)[1] What is your opinion of the effect of the several competitive systems now in operation, distinguishing the effect of the different competitions, and distinguishing also the different classes of society on which those competitions bear? – We manage to prepare very well for Woolwich[2] since the number of subjects has been reduced. Still the boy is overworked. You overwork a young soldier. He has to give up all games.

(Mr Baines)[3] Do you mean during the time of cramming? – I mean with ourselves, when preparing for Woolwich. We can prepare for Woolwich, and are generally successful with anyone we send up, but the boy has to work too hard, in mathematics for instance.

(Dr Temple)[4] For how long should you say? – For his last year quite. In one sense you cannot cram in mathematics; I speak with submission; but, on the other hand, you can push a boy on a great deal too far in mathematics; far beyond what he can digest, and much further than he should be pushed; but it is absolutely necessary to do so, if he is to compete with those who come from the private establishments of the crammers; and if questions are to be set in the higher mathematics; and you have to make him take up five subjects. You have to teach him French and German, and you will not teach him badly. A man who is a really good teacher will make him work his French and German very much as he would work his classics. But this thorough teaching is not tested enough at the examination; it hardly pays. Besides that, you have to cover a great extent of history, often in a way very detrimental to

education; to make him know all English history in addition to those other subjects, at an age when he is not ripe for the knowledge of all English history at all. In addition to that you have to teach him some other subject. With us, in one particular case, it was geology, where a boy had a great taste for geology, and he made himself a very good geologist. Oftener it is perhaps geography, or some subject which is not taught well. He has to know all geography, and you have to push him through a mass of knowledge which he probably soon forgets; but still as the number of subjects at Woolwich is limited to five, though a boy is overworked and over-pushed, yet we can teach him, and with success; but for the India Civil Service examination, as it stood thus far, we could not prepare if we would, and we would not if we could. I am in despair about it.

(Lord Taunton)[5] Why so? – Because the number of subjects is unlimited, and their scope is enormous, and you will not be elected unless you take up from four to eleven nominal subjects, really each of them *groups* of distinct and heavy subjects. For instance, the English 'subject' means a knowledge of the whole of the English literature; it means also the knowledge of all English history, including constitutional history; it means also the history of the English language. Those three form one 'subject.' The next subject is Latin. That includes not only the Latin language and composition, but the whole of Roman history, and the history of its literature. The next subject is Greek; that is the same. No one, or next to no one, has ever got through with these subjects alone, except perhaps in a year when there were 80 vacancies. Then a really able Oxford pupil of mine got in very low; he just got in with those subjects. Add to that French, including all French history, and the whole history of French literature, and the French language; and you cannot hope to get in with these; you must add to that some other subject; as many as 10 or 11 of these groups are sometimes taken up by young men, who may do none of them well yet take high places. Now, of course, it is impossible really to teach those subjects. The idea of teaching a boy the whole of English literature, as one of a large group of subjects, is ridiculous, and we cannot do it; nor can we teach a boy three physical sciences in six months; but it is done elsewhere, and with very great success.

(Mr Acland) What is the particular ground of your objection to the India Civil Service examinations? – In the first place it probably concerns us more than it does almost any other school, from the very large number of boys who come to us as the sons of clergy who have no definite openings in life. That is my excuse for taking up the question. We have, I should think, an unusually large portion of the upper boys who would be very glad to go to India. I think a third of my sixth form, a short time

ago, would gladly have gone to India if they could. On the other hand, I find it thus far impossible to prepare them with any effect on account of the large number of subjects which are absolutely necessary for success in the India Civil Service examinations. When it is said in defence of the present system that some get in with only four subjects, those who make the statement, perhaps, are scarcely aware that each of those subjects represents a large group of subjects, e.g., that the subject of English embraces the whole of English literature, the whole of English history, and the whole of the English language. No teacher who is worthy of his position at any school that professes to educate, could undertake to teach boys, by the time they left school, the whole of English literature, and the whole of English history, in addition to the number of other subjects that imperiously demand attention. Besides which the number of those who get in with four subjects is very small, and their place low; 35th was the highest place got by four subjects last year, and there were only 40 vacancies.

Do you think that any system which tends to encourage success by a low standard in a number of subjects [is] positively injurious to middle-class education? – I am absolutely sure of that; the attempting to make the young mind bestride too large a number of subjects I find every day enfeebles it, and deadens it, is fatal to all originality, and all real play of mind.

Do you consider that the position of the middle classes, who do not go to the universities, is one which requires a special protection in that matter, inasmuch as they are not supported by the university standard, which standard fixes the attention on a smaller number of subjects? – I should think there would be a very great danger of the education of those middle-class schools, which at all looked forward to the India Civil Service being deteriorated to the utmost possible extent by the attempt to prepare their pupils for that examination or any one conducted on similar principles.

Can you suggest any method by which such examination might concentrate the attention of the pupils on a number of subjects which would not be injurious to their education? – I think the simplest remedy, though perhaps a rough one, would be to limit the number of subjects that a candidate might take up. There are other remedies, one at present, I believe, under consideration, which might be equally effective.

(Lord Lyttelton)[6] Does what you have said about this system of cramming apply to the ordinary Civil Service examinations, and to the Army examinations? – No, I think not. The papers I have seen for direct commissions for the Army have struck me as extremely sensible; there is a great latitude of choice allowed, and there has been no encouragement, in the papers I have seen recently, to cram. They were very bad when

111

they began. As regards the ordinary Civil Service, I am afraid that there is a good deal of cram for them; but I cannot speak from my own knowledge; I can speak from my own knowledge as to the India Civil Service, from having thoroughly gone into the question, and the system of preparation which is most successful seems to me to be positively degrading.

(Dr Storrar)[7] Is it within your personal knowledge that the system which you have described as existing in the preparation for the India Civil Service is extensively pursued? – Yes.

(Sir S. Northcote)[8] Do you consider that either for good or for evil these systems of competitive examinations are a very powerful engine in working the education of the middle class? – They are becoming so.

And that, therefore, in any inquiry directed to the state of education, and the means to be taken for improving the education of the middle class, it would be important to pay attention to the mode and principles upon which those examinations are conducted? – I think most important, because otherwise these examinations may debauch your whole system of education.

Do you think it possible to conduct an examination of this kind, either limiting the number of subjects or not limiting them, in such a manner as to draw out the real knowledge of the boys, and their real powers, and to exclude the great advantages of cramming? Do you think that by a different system of setting purer and simpler questions, but observing the manner in which those questions are answered, better tests might be applied than are now applied? – Yes, I think a great deal might be done in that way. It would be beside the point, perhaps, if I were to talk too much of remedies that have occurred to me, but I think that a great deal might be done by a different system of examination. For instance, in English literature, in enabling a boy to get high marks for a real knowledge of a few great works, or of one kind of English literature, such as a good acquaintance with English poetry, or a real acquaintance with one period of English literature. At present the knowledge which pays is of the most superficial and useless nature.

* * *

(Mr Acland) In your opinion is the amount of marks for the different subjects entirely disproportionate to the amount of labour necessary to master them? – No; I do not so much quarrel with the distribution of marks. The English, which is an enormous subject, is marked very high, and if it were well examined for, and if it were not possible to get up English literature as it is got up, and to get high marks for it in three months, I should not object to it. Again, Mathematics are marked high, but the standard of the papers is so high that very few take up this subject, and fewer still are rewarded for it.

You mean that the fault is in the examination? – Yes, the examination is very much to blame. But the difficulty of examining fairly in so vast a subject as English is great.

I understood you to say that a person who had laboured very much, and become a good scholar, could not by any possibility get the amount of marks which he would get if he distributed the same amount of effort over several subjects? – Quite so. If many a young man who had got the Balliol scholarship were then with his present acquirements to stand for India, he would not have the remotest chance of success. Of course if he were to give the same labour to getting up all these different subjects, the same ability would make him succeed, but he would in my estimation be damaging his intellect and wasting his time. He would succeed if he diverted himself from the subjects he was following, and pored over manuals of English literature, and manuals of history, not reading a single great author or a single great historian, did some Sanscrit, some Arabic, or some moral philosophy, or some geology from a book, and a number of those subjects. In that case I have no doubt that the same ability would ensure him success.

(*Mr Baines*) As I understand, your objection is not so much to the existence of private tutors, whom you call 'crammers' as it is to the vast multiplicity of subjects in the examinations? – The examinations tend to cultivate one thing and one thing only – memory. The one thing rewarded in those examinations is memory. Of course a good private tutor would hate cramming, but unfortunately the 'crammer' succeeds.

We have had a witness of eminence who has expressed rather a strong opinion favourable to these private tutors, or 'crammers,' but the subjects with which he was connected were much more limited in their range. You perhaps would not express any opinion unfavourable to the private tutors, to that institution as it were, but simply to the degree of force which they are obliged to use to compress within a short time a vast number of subjects of instruction? – Quite so. There has become an organised system, so to speak, of cheating the examinations. And such a system is not likely to fall into the best hands.

* * *

Notes

1. Thomas Dyke Acland MP (1809–1898).
2. The Royal Military Academy.
3. Edward Baines MP (1800–1890).
4. Frederick Temple (1821–1902), later Archbishop of Canterbury.

5. Henry Labouchere, Baron Taunton (1798–1869), a prominent politician and Chairman of the Commission.
6. George William, Lord Lyttelton (1817–1876)
7. John Storrar MD of Hampstead.
8. Sir Stafford Northcote MP (1846–1911).

Dudley Ryder, Earl of Harrowby (1798–1882) was a Conservative politician, first as an M.P., then as a member of the House of Lords. He studied at Christ Church College, Oxford, where he gained a double First, and where he became a friend of Lord Taunton, later to be Chairman of the Schools Inquiry Commission. In 1819, he was elected as M.P. for Tiverton, a seat which he held until 1831. In the election of that year, he did not contest Tiverton again, but instead stood as a candidate for a Liverpool constituency. He was elected, and remained in the House of Commons as a Liverpool M.P. until 1847. In that year, he succeeded his father as second Earl of Harrowby. He later held the posts of Chancellor of the Duchy of Lancaster and Lord Privy Seal. As well as being a politician, he had intellectual interests, was a good linguist, an art expert, and a Fellow of the Royal Society.

The Earl of Harrowby appeared before the Commission primarily to make a plea for English. He was particularly concerned about boys who were going to be at school until the ages of only thirteen, fourteen or fifteen. They would never get far enough with classics to make it worthwhile, but they could read English literature, and this would greatly increase the moral and intellectual power of the nation. All the way through his evidence, the failure of Latin as an instrument of improvement is set against the potential of English.

Harrowby had the advantage of a close knowledge of the schools in Liverpool, and as a result of this, had ideas about how different schools might be set up for the different levels of the middle class, while allowing the possibility, for able students, of progression from one school to another. English would be most appropriate for the boys of the lower middle and middle middle class, for whom Latin was least appropriate, but even those of the upper middle class would benefit from English. One of the greatest obstacles to progress, Harrowby believed, was the attitude of the schoolmasters, or at least those who had studied at Oxford and Cambridge. It was they, rather than the parents, who wished to preserve Latin.

Minutes of Evidence from the Earl of Harrowby

(Lord Taunton) I believe your Lordship has given much attention to the subject of education in this country, and especially to that of the middle classes? – Yes. I ought perhaps to apologize for appearing before you, having very little practical experience on the subject, and having in vain endeavoured to gain lights on education in foreign countries of a similar kind, which I should have desired to do previously for the purpose of comparing what had been done elsewhere with what has been done, or with what might be done in England. My principal object in being not unwilling to appear before you is this, I wanted simply to enter a plea for English, that it shall have that place in the education of our people which Latin and Greek had in the education of the Romans and Greeks themselves; that we shall not consider a man well educated in this country who is not well acquainted with the classics of his own country, any more than a Greek would have been considered well educated who had never read Homer, or a Roman who had never read Cicero. I cannot but consider that our own language is placed in a degraded position under the present system of education. The English master is always considered a subordinate person, as a man who can teach reading and writing, and summing, or the lower parts of mathematics, and who is put into a corner and never treated as if he had to teach what I consider the noblest of languages, containing the noblest sentiments that any language can offer. It does seem to me, considering what our literature in the last 300 years has been, in poetry, in oratory, in divinity, in morals, and in fiction of every kind, that it is a scandal that our language in our education should be relegated to a corner as a thing that we ought almost to be ashamed of, and not made an essential part of the education of every liberally educated man. Further than that, not that I object to classics being a part of liberal education, I object that classics should be put as a necessary part of education for every person above all those who frequent the national schools, when I consider that what you have to deal with is a person who has to go into the ordinary concerns of life, and whose education you have to do with only perhaps till the age of 13 or 14, or 15. I am not for that purpose bound to consider what is the highest possible education, what is the highest abstract education, but what would most contribute to refine his taste and strengthen his reasoning powers, or in any way to raise him to the highest possible character of an Englishman, or even of an English gentleman, which the circumstances will permit. I take the problem as of an ordinary boy from ordinary classes going into an ordinary career in life, and over whom you have a control only till the age of 13, 14, or 15. Well then, I say, what is the best use to make

of those years during which you have control over him? You will not refine his taste, you will not make him read the *Aeneid* fluently, you will not make him read Cicero fluently, still less Greek. I put Greek out of the question, but you will not make him inclined to take up a Latin book again. What you will have done as far as I can see it is this; you will have made him toil not through, but among the difficulties of the accidence, and possibly through two or three preliminary books, such as Henry's books,[1] or books of that character. What will you have done by that? What advantage will he have gained? You will have occupied a certain portion of his time; you will have given him an indisposition to learn and a dislike for literature; possibly you may have enabled him to dissect some English words, and to know that this means one thing and this means another, but really that is all you have done for the education of his mind or his character. Now, I confess I look upon it not merely as an intellectual question, but as a moral question, and I do believe that it will be of the most infinite moral advantage to our nation if our youth of every class were accustomed to read our best books in literature from their earliest days, proportioned of course to their age and to their condition in various ways; but if they were accustomed to read the most interesting and profitable books in English literature, I believe the moral as well as the intellectual effect would be enormous. I believe it would increase the moral and intellectual power of the nation to an extent not to be conceived. I do believe that to put any lad into a position to have a taste for, and an acquaintance with the best works of our literature would be an advantage hardly to be calculated. Well, then, I conceive that the question is not whether classical learning is not a good thing in itself, but whether, in a given position, under given circumstances, you will force the accidence and the books of elementary instruction in a manner which appears to be rather an obstruction to the boy's learning anything else than a help to his acquiring that particular branch of knowledge, if you may so call it, to which he is professedly addressing himself. As to the idea that it is necessary to learn two languages for the purpose of learning one, I cannot conceive how that can be so, considering the number of men who have written well in our own language without knowing the classics; for instance, Hugh Miller,[2] and Shakspeare himself, as to whom there is a doubt about his being able to read Latin, and in a thousand other instances; or, looking only to the Romans and Greeks themselves, who certainly mastered their own languages without being acquainted with a foreign language, it does seem to me to be historically impossible to maintain that to acquire a good possession of one language you must also acquire a second. In the first place, as far as I see, with those lads who are only instructed for a short time, you do not give them the possession of any language; you give them a few of the difficulties of the language. You give them a certain exercise of memory, in its most distasteful form, where the boys are constantly asking themselves, 'What is all this about, and what does it lead to? What good is it?'

You do not attach much importance to the study of a grammar of a dead language such as Latin as an exercise of the mind, as a means of training the mind distinct from the use of the literature of that language, in case the study should not be pushed far enough to enable a boy to enjoy that literature? – In the first place, I do not believe that nine-tenths of those who are put to learn this, do really acquire any knowledge at all – that they really gain anything except a distaste for other things. I do not say that a person who has a literary taste, who has a logical faculty, who has a power for study, does not gain by it; but looking at the average advantage of the great number, I cannot but conceive that it is rather an obstacle than an advantage.

With reference to the practical objects of this Commission, what do you think we should recommend, which would tend more to encourage the study of English, and to discourage too much time being given to Latin, in the cases in which it was not likely to be found of much use to boys in their subsequent career? – My feeling would be to follow as far as the local circumstances would permit, the idea of the three collegiate schools at Liverpool.

I believe your Lordship has personally paid great attention to those schools? – Yes, I was interested in them some time ago, and I have had occasion to revive my interest in them lately. I was particularly struck with the organization adopted there. There are three schools under the same roof, but the boys do not of necessity pass by age or examination from one into another. They are differently graduated as to price, so that a father makes his choice and sends his son to the lower, middle, or upper school. In the lower school no Latin is taught, or if it is taught at all it is only for the purpose of explaining the prefixes and affixes, in the most rudimentary way. It is a good English education; then, as a means of enabling the boys who had distinguished themselves by a particular turn, what I may call a literary turn, to pass into a higher grade, there are periodical examinations, which give a title to a gratuitous passage into the next school, and so in the same way, for a gratuitous passage into the third school; the third school preparing for the Universities. In this way you have each of those schools well taught separately, without the functions of the one intruding on the other; but you still retain that which is of the highest importance to retain still in our country, that the poorest boys who have peculiar faculties for the purpose, shall be able by the cultivation of those faculties to rise to the highest position in church or state.

I presume you would not propose that the Legislature should interfere with the course of instruction in any school, except in the case of endowed schools? – No; as far as I can see I should act in this way – there is a vast number of grammar schools all over the country. I should like to club the grammar schools with some relation to locality, and I should like to say – '*You* shall be a good lower middle-class school; *you* shall be a middle middle-class school; and *you* shall be a higher middle-class school, that which is now called a grammar school.'

Do you mean by the expression 'clubbing' that you would bring them together in the locality or that you would leave them in the localities where they now are, only giving them a different direction for their studies? – Of course it is a very delicate matter to deal with endowments at all, at the same time I think the public mind is ripe for their being dealt with in some degree, and that with the help of the Charity Commissioners, and possibly of the Court of Chancery, and of Parliament in larger cases, indeed much as Parliament now deals with schemes sanctioned by the Charity Commissioners, that you might make a revision of the whole system. I think one great ground of apprehension in regard to dealing with grammar schools has been this: grammar schools having been no doubt originally founded mostly in connexion with the Church of England, there has always been an apprehension that if you dealt with endowments upon what may be called more modern notions, you would divert them from that purpose and alter their design. As far as I understand, there is now a course of action established in regard to grammar schools which will very much remove that difficulty. There is now a course of action pursued by the Court of Chancery by which the connexion of grammar schools with the Church is recognized, but the children of parents who are not connected with the Church or who object to instruction according to the Church of England, are admitted to receive the benefits of the instruction. If this is recognized as a basis of action I cannot but think that one great difficulty would be removed from the minds of those who object to interfering with the grammar schools. At present the difficulty is that the courts have recognized the grammar schools as of necessity, if I am rightly informed, implying instruction in Latin and Greek. There has been a modification of that from time to time in some of these schools under which modification English masters are appointed; but then how are they appointed? You get inferior persons. It is considered an inferior thing. All the force and honour of the school are involved in the higher classics, and English is not recognized as in itself an important study. There should be then some means by which a passage [can be made] from these lower grammar schools which should teach only English into the middle grammar schools and from the middle grammar schools into a higher class of schools, similar, as far as circumstances will permit, to that which I have described as existing at Liverpool. Schools should be secured. It is rather difficult to say how that should be effected. Of course that could only be done by endowments in some shape. Endowments might be founded, possibly by rating, possibly by private benevolence, possibly by appropriation of some of the funds of the grammar school, where they were enabled to bear the extra charge. I am very much inclined to think that there would be even in the existing grammar schools a very large provision towards that object. Of course it is not so easy in small towns as it is in a large town like Liverpool, where you can have the whole thing grouped together more simply, where it is a modern foundation and where the passage from one to the other is very much simplified, and where you have a liberal community to appeal to, to assist in providing any resources which were not already at hand. Still the principle might be kept in view, and I cannot but think to a very material extent. It seems to me to be one of the most important things in this middle-class Commission that it should try to vindicate for the English language its proper place, exclusively in the lower classes, but in the higher classes also never to be lost sight of. How many of our higher classes there are who pass away from Eton and Harrow without having read any one English classic and who know nothing of English but Dickens and Thackeray? It is a scandal. English reading of the highest order ought to enter into every part of every English education. Intellectually it has its value in every way, but morally, I consider the English language contains the highest morals of any language. It has the best literature as well as the most extensive. That the mass of our population, whether high or low, should be by our system of education excluded from the teaching of those subjects appears to me to be a remnant of the middle ages, a remnant of barbarism, and a mere antiquated adherence to tradition.

Do you think it would be impossible in cases where a boy could give ample time, from the circumstances of his parents, to pursue a really liberal education, to combine a good foundation in Greek and Latin with a thorough course of instruction in the English language? Would not they assist each other? – Yes; if we are speaking of the higher class. I believe they help each other. The real difficulty of learning is, that the boy does not want to learn. Give him the taste for learning, and he will learn fast enough. You begin with the broad end of the wedge, and say, 'First learn that which is of the least utility, and the least pleasant, and then you shall learn something which shall be agreeable.' I would sooner he began with learning *Robinson Crusoe* than the Latin accidence, anything to give a boy a taste for learning, a taste for knowledge of any kind, and the thing is done. There is no difficulty afterwards.

* *
*

(Lord Stanley) From your observation, which in these matters has been considerable, do you think that even among the higher classes more than one boy in, say, half-a-dozen, carries away from school any real knowledge of Latin, not to speak of Greek, such as would enable him to read a Latin work some years afterwards, with any pleasure to himself? – I believe not. I should say a much smaller proportion than that. I recollect old friends of mine who came to the private tutor with me, who had passed through all the classes of a public school, and could not read Latin at all. They were very sensible men in subsequent life, but when you gave them such a thing as the *Westminster Grammar*[3] to read, it is not surprising that they had not acquired a taste for Latin.

Your theory is, that in the time during which they have not been learning, but professing to learn classics, they might really, many of them, have acquired a taste for English literature, whereas at present, they had been sickened of reading altogether? – That is so.

According to your experience, are you not aware that in the middle classes generally, the wish of the parents is that the boy should learn English, but that the wish of the schoolmaster following the old tradition, is that the boy should be well-grounded, as it is called, in classics? That is so as far as I can see, and I think I saw a practical evidence of it in this, in a single fact – I was the other day at a school in Lambeth, a very extensive middle-class school. I asked what proportion of the boys' parents wished them to learn Latin, and the answer was – 2½ per cent.

(Mr Acland) What sort of school was that? That is a school at which the payments are very low, 7s. 6d. a quarter, is it not? – About 10s. a quarter, I think. We are speaking of the lower middle class. I am not now speaking of the highest. As to French, the proportion was about 25 per cent.

(Lord Stanley) Your theory is that this tradition of exclusive devotion to classical literature has been handed down among teachers from the time when there was no available literature except classical literature? – That is exactly my feeling. From generation to generation the teachers have gone upon this idea, and they cannot comprehend anything else. In regard to the lower school at Liverpool, I was asking – 'Who are your best teachers?' and the reply was – 'The best teachers are the men trained at Battersea and at St Mark's.[4] They have learned English thoroughly and systematically, and they are the best teachers we can get'; but the fact is that a gentleman educated at the Universities does not

know how to teach English. It has never been taught him. He has picked it up by conversation and his own reading, if he has at all.

A man in the higher grades of life, may now leave the university without having read a line of Shakspeare or Milton, and possibly with only the barest possible acquaintance with the outlines of English History? – Yes.

He may leave the University having taken a degree? – Yes. Some of the St Mark's and the Battersea trained men were excellent in the thorough knowledge of English. They took passages from Milton, read them backwards and forwards, and put them into other order, and they were obliged to parse them and explain them. The same faculties were exercised there in construing Milton as in construing Latin, only there was an interest in the one and there was no interest in the other. I believe in America, in the same way, in all their common schools they make English an essential element of their teaching. I believe it is a tradition, and nothing else, that keeps our population from the enjoyment of their own classical language.

*
* *

(*Dean of Chichester*)[5] Do you not think female authors write very good English? – Very good English.

Have they generally learned Latin? – They have generaly learned very little Latin. I believe that the learning of a good style does not proceed from the rules of grammar, but from familiarity with good conversation and good authors. It is notorious that all the best books in every language have been written before the grammar of the language was composed, or before the rules were understood.

*
* *

(*Mr Baines*) I quite understand your Lordship not to undervalue Latin in any of its uses, for instance, as a foundation for modern language? – Yes, French or Italian, or Spanish.

But simply to raise a superior and prior claim for English? – Yes, above all things, let us not neglect English.

You would admit the great utility of Latin for scientific men, for those who have to travel, for those engaged in business, and who must have a knowledge of the languages of foreign countries. In all those cases you do not in the least mean to undervalue Latin? – No; but then I do not expect when you deal with the education of the lower middle class, that a very large proportion of them would be deriving an advantage even from such openings as you were suggesting. At Lambeth, I said: 'Why is this boy going to learn Latin?' and the reply was, 'Because his father is a chemist, and he wants him to go into the chemical line.' Another was the son of a schoolmaster, and he looked to his son going to one of the Universities. Those are specific and exceptional cases. But if the whole system of education has been such that for the sake of those three or four all the rest were to be drudging through matter which was of no use to them, and which obstructed them in more important things, I should say you are sacrificing the major to the minor object.

* * *

(*Mr Acland*) If I understand you right, you would make the two necessary elements [in the education of the lower middle class] English and arithmetic? – English and arithmetic, good fluent reading, good exercises, dictation, writing from recollections of a good paper in the *Spectator*, which had been read over night, arithmetic carried as far as you possibly could, and of course good spelling and good handwriting.

Taking those as the formal or instrumental elements of education, what would be the subjects in the way of direct information and the communication of facts and of knowledge; which would you think most important? – English history, good biography, modern and ancient, Plutarch's *Lives*, for instance, in translation, that should be first of course. I am always presuming that there is a sound religious basis, and that I think would be very much increased by the knowledge of English, as almost all our best English books are strongly imbued with a religious character directly or indirectly.

* * *

Have you fully considered the practical difficulty of giving a boy a lesson in English when he knows no other language but his mother tongue, and telling him to get that up with an equal degree of accuracy to what would be required in the case of learning another language? – I do not think you practically get that accuracy from nine out of ten of the boys with whom you deal in that way now. I see boys going to the University every day who cannot put a Latin sentence into form, and what have they gained directly or indirectly?

Do you think those boys would have arrived at greater precision of mind and greater grasp of language if they had been taught English? – I think so; I think if they had read *Robinson Crusoe* and been examined in the fact of *Robinson Crusoe*, they would have learned much more than they have done. They would have learnt a vast deal from the book itself, and they would have acquired a taste for knowledge and for geography and an interest in foreign parts.

* * *

Notes

1. I have been unable to trace this author.
2. Hugh Miller (1802–1856). A popular writer on various subjects, particularly geology and its bearing on the evolution question.
3. William Camden, *Institutio Graecae Grammatices Compendiaria: in usum Regiae Scholae Westmonasteriensis* (1617). Editions of this work were still appearing in the nineteenth century.
4. Training colleges for teachers.
5. Rev. Walter F. Hook (1798–1875).

CHAPTER TEN

Museum and English Journal of Education

A sequence of four articles dealing with English studies was published in the *Museum and English Journal of Education* in March, April, May and June 1867. There is no indication of authorship. The journal survived with this title for only six years, from 1864 to 1869. It was, however, formed by the merger of three other journals, the *Museum* (1861–1864), the *English Journal of Education* (1843–1864) and the *Pupil Teacher* (1857–1863). It published a wide range of articles which would have been of interest to teachers, teacher trainers and all those involved with educational issues.

These four articles deal with the teaching of both language and literature. The first reviews three books: an edition of a Shakespeare text and two collections of literary material, all of which have been published for the student market. Each of these books is the first of a series, and this is seen as demonstrating that English has already arrived as an academic subject, although encouragement and assistance are required. The writer is careful to insist that he has no wish to see classics superseded, but English has many advantages, both in teaching grammar and in imparting the higher influences of literature. The second article, only a short section of which is included here, considers the place which would be appropriate for English in different sorts of schools. It should be admitted as a partner with classics even in the great public schools, but in middle-class education English should be recognized as being more important than Latin. The third article focuses on the content and method of teaching English at elementary level. The content includes composition, the history and development of the English language, etymology, a 'portion of some standard English author' and an introduction to some simpler modern poets. The use to be made of the literature is essentially mechanical, with many exercises recommended. The final article considers the teaching of English at a more advanced level. Again, the main stress is on language: the philosophy of language, division of languages into families, Anglo-Saxon and Middle English, etymology, and close examination of words and idioms. There is also literature, however, and here the subject matter must be attended to as well as the language.

'The Study of English Classics'

It is the design of the works noted below,[1] as explained in the preface to the first of them, 'to encourage and assist the study of English literature as an essential and systematic part of a liberal education.' The words are happily chosen; for fortunately, that study does not now require to be originated; it needs only encouragement and assistance. That study is now prosecuted, not only in our colleges, but also in our schools, in a way, and to an extent which were unknown not many years ago. We have passed from the stage in which 'elegant extracts' were used merely as a means of teaching to read or to declaim; and we now recognise the importance of our national literature as 'an effective instrument of mental training and refinement.' The improved methods of studying the language have conduced greatly to this result. The teacher of English does not now merely teach his pupils 'to read and write the English language with propriety,' – an end often professed but seldom accomplished, – but he uses the language and literature in combination as a valuable instrument of mental culture, and his professional status has risen proportionately with the elevation of his aims. The value and richness of our literature as such have always been admitted in theory; it has been reserved for the present generation to demonstrate the value of its study as a discipline. The real benefit of a classical education lies, for the great mass of men, not so much in the positive knowledge acquired, as in the method pursued in acquiring what may afterwards be forgotten. There are hundreds of men who, after spending years in the study of Latin and Greek, are unable to translate a line of Horace or of Homer. Were these years, then, so much time wasted? Has their labour been lost? Certainly not; many benefits of the training survive, just as strength of muscle and grace of motion survive the gymnastic or calisthenic exercises which have been long ago disused. The knowledge of words, and facts, and systems may have vanished; but the strength and acuteness of judgment, the accuracy of thought, the refinement of taste remain, and are being daily and hourly exercised upon objects as far as possible removed from the mental gymnasium in which they were first developed.

Now it is the aim of English scholars in the present day to apply the same processes which have been employed for centuries in the study of the ancient classics to the classics of our own language. That the English language is of the same value as Latin or Greek as an instrument of discipline, we by no means maintain. There are many things to prevent this. It is a living language, constantly changing with its growth; they are dead languages, fossilized and permanently fixed. It is an analytic language, meagre in inflections and abounding in circumlocutions; they are synthetic languages, comparatively perfect in organisation, rich in inflection, and pre-eminently nice in syntax. Above all, English is the mother tongue, and can be understood without any, or with but little, of that mental effort which a foreign language requires, and in requiring which its main value as a discipline consists. It is, moreover, in constant use, and therefore constantly liable to abuse; hence its employment in the elevating and refining processes of education is open to the objection that, like the beasts in Peter's vision, it is 'common and unclean.'[2]

With all this, however, the English language admits of precisely the same methods being applied to its study as are applied to the study of the classical tongues. There may be (there is, we admit), a difference in degree; in kind there is none. Questions of exactly the same nature come up for discussion in the one case as in the other. The development of analysis has shewn that the main relations of the parts of the sentence are the same in all languages. The exercise involved in breaking down a sentence, so as to get at its real meaning is an exercise in thought, even more than in words; and it can be performed as well in English as in Greek, in some respects better. Indeed, it is only because English is our mother tongue, and we therefore understand its utterances for the most part intuitively, and without the laborious process of formal analysis, that this fact has been so long overlooked. But our very familiarity with the language makes the process more intelligible, and the result more enjoyable when, under the direction of a skilful teacher, the analysis is performed. It is generally admitted that we do not read an ancient author with profit or enjoyment, until long study has enabled us to dispense, to a great extent, with grammatical technicalities; but in the case of a native author we reach this stage much sooner. We prosecute our scientific investigations, so to speak, in a country that is familiar to us, every feature of which we can understand, with every aspect of which we can sympathise.

Let it not be supposed that we wish the study of English to supersede the study of classics. Our argument simply claims for English a place amongst those languages which are recognised as useful as disciplinary studies. We have admitted throughout the superiority of the classical languages in this respect, and we have stated our reasons for making the admission. But there are hundreds who are shut out from the full benefits of a classical education; and we wish to shew, in the first place, that in their case the study of native classics may be made productive of benefits the same in kind, as the study of foreign or ancient classics in the case of those who are more highly favoured. This, it may be said, is very true as regards grammatical knowledge, and as regards the value of grammar as a mental discipline; but it takes no account of the higher influences of a classical education, – influences to be felt rather than described, – arising from contact with great minds, and acquaintance with perfect models of style. In reply we ask, in the case of how many are these influences appreciated? Is it not true that the proportion of men trained in our classical schools who ever reach the point at which contact with the great minds of antiquity becomes a reality, is pitiably small? And if we were to bestow half the time and attention upon the masterpieces of our own literature that we give to these, is it not reasonable to expect that we should find ten men who would be elevated and strengthened by this study for every one who really profits by the other? As regards style, the extent of the influence of classical studies must be similarly circumscribed. We do not question the effect of the study of the ancient models upon our great scholars and best writers; but the number of these in any generation is lamentably small. In the case of the great mass of those who receive a classical education, this influence upon style is inappreciable. We have, indeed, we again repeat, no desire to underrate the importance of the study of classics; but we have a strong conviction that in the case especially of those who do not, or cannot, make this study a life-labour, the study of the native classics would, as regards style, quite as much as regards thought, exercise an influence both wider in extent and greater in degree, than can be produced by the far-off glimpses of majesty to which nine-tenths of our classical students are accustomed. No one will deny that the current style of the present day, even from the pens of professed classics, is loose and inaccurate in the extreme. And it is so mainly, we suspect, because our attention is absorbed by an unmanageable mass of current literature, most of it indifferent in style, much of it positively bad, and we leave ourselves no time to examine the masterpieces of men who treated composition as a work of art. We can conceive of no better, or more rational, remedy for this decadence of style than the systematic study of our older authors.

But we are inclined to go a step farther than this, and to maintain that the scientific study of English grammar, or rather of grammar in English, is for Englishmen the best introduction to the study of the ancient tongues. Many men have declared that they never understood the grammar of their own language until they had learned that of Latin or of Greek, and have hence rather hastily concluded that English grammar cannot be understood until that of some more purely synthetic language has been mastered. There is here a grain of truth lying on the surface of a whole mass of error. That grammatical principles are not learned in English is not the fault of English grammar, but solely of the method of teaching it. At the very root of the assertion we have quoted lies the fact that the great principles of grammar are universal, else the study of Latin grammar could never have been made available in elucidating the principles of that of the mother tongue. It must be admitted, therefore, that these principles are applicable to English; and being so applicable, it seems a strange inversion of the order both of nature and of art, to delay their application to a living language until a dead language has been acquired. We reach the unknown through the known in everything else; we make a boast of reaching the known through the unknown in the study of our own language!

The anomaly admits of an easy explanation. The understanding of a Latin author compels attention to principles; the understanding of an English author does not. We do not require to take an English author to pieces, sentence by sentence, clause by clause, and word by word, in order to reach his meaning. We at once grasp the thought intuitively, and with so much ease that the principles of construction escape our notice. But in the case of a foreign author, a learner is compelled to go through the process of analysis, at first laboriously, and afterwards unconsciously, when his mastery over the principles involved has made them a part of his mental nature. Now it is in the process referred to that the principles are evolved, and that a minute and accurate knowledge of grammar is acquired. And our position is that, if, in spite of our familiarity with English, we were to insist upon subjecting it to the same process, we should arrive at these principles all the sooner, just because we are familiar with the ground on which we search for them. Further, and this is the main point in this part of our argument, if our pupils did so acquire them, they would not find Latin Grammar to be the bewildering *terra incognita* that it is to most of them. They would come to it furnished with a frame-work of principles into which they had only to fit a new series of facts. Granting that the classical languages afford wider scope than our own for grammatical exposition, such exposition will be all the more profitable that the general principles are already known. Granting that peculiarities have to be pointed out, and modifications to be explained, this can only be done by comparison, and comparison here implies a known standard which can be constantly and safely appealed to. Indeed, classical teachers set themselves a stupendous task when they attempt to teach unknown principles through an unknown language, double labour surely both to themselves and to their pupils. But in point of fact, in teaching classics, we do constantly draw our illustrations, either by analogy or by contrast, from our own language; yet we are told that we cannot understand English Grammar, except through Latin and Greek!

That the analytic process by which grammatical principles are evolved, can be applied to English, as well as to Latin and Greek, and with the same or similar results as regards both grammatical knowledge and mental training, needs no demonstration at our hands. It is the daily practice of every good teacher, and his own experience will best confirm the truth of our statement. It requires, moreover, but a moment's reflection to shew the utility of this kind of teaching to the classical student. We have already said, that if he has thoroughly mastered the more general relations of the parts of the sentence in his own language, he will have the less difficulty in understanding the structure of sentences in Latin and in Greek. But we go farther than this, and maintain that if he were accustomed to treat of such constructions in English sentences as the absolute phrase, the appositional relation, the relation of attribute and substantive, of dependent and principal clauses, of protasis and apodosis, of the double object to the verb, and many others that might be quoted, he would come to the study of classical syntax with a mind thoroughly prepared for grappling with its peculiarities and difficulties, and his progress would be all the more easy and all the more rapid. Yet so completely is all this ignored at present, that in many of our best Latin grammars, it is considered necessary to begin with definitions of the parts of speech, as if it were unsafe to presume that even the alphabet of grammar had been, or could be, learned in the mother tongue.

We have dealt with the question, hitherto, mainly on its scientific or technical side. We have said very little regarding the wealth of English literature, its richness in those higher qualities which are pre-eminent in their educative power. In this connection we do not presume to reopen the well-worn question of the comparative value of the ancient and the modern learning. All that we maintain is, that there is in our native literature a wealth of pure and noble thoughts, and of lofty imaginings, as well as a body of scientific truth and of practical knowledge, sufficient to inform and elevate the minds of Englishmen, and to fit them for the highest duties of life, though they should never read a line in any language but their own. If we are asked to point to examples of such results as these, we reply, that it will be time enough to ask for examples when the process has been thoroughly tried. As yet it has not been so, unless in exceptional cases. On the other hand, we might adduce instances not a few in which the minds that most powerfully influenced their age, and all succeeding ages, did not bear the impress of the classical stamp in any marked degree. To take the highest example first: all critics admit that we cannot ascribe much of Shakespeare's greatness to classical training, or indeed for that matter to instruction of any kind, though all his works testify to his devotedness to the native literature, such as it was in his day. We know that the genius of Scott, dormant during the period of his classical education, was enkindled by our native ballad literature, and the romances of chivalry. In Wordworth and Burns we have an intense love of nature and of human nature bursting forth in rapturous song. But we have no wish to cut off our students from wandering over foreign pastures. If they feed upon them, truly feed upon them, and do not merely hurry over them with an occasional nibble, their minds will be all the stronger therefor, their sympathies all the wider, their position as thinkers and as men all the higher. Yet we conceive that a mind formed on the study, the close and careful study, mark, of Shakespeare alone, might imbibe so much of his spirit, might gain such an insight into human character and the springs of human action, such strength of thought and refinement of taste, and at the same time such mastery of language, as to entitle it to compare with the results of any other process of training. Contact with such minds as those of Hooker, and Bacon, and Addison, or Milton, and Wordsworth, and Tennyson, if, we must again observe, it be real contact, and not merely a distant view, – cannot fail to arouse the intelligence where there is any germ of life, or to ennoble the willing spirit. Nor would style be anything but improved by the study; at all events, these models are within the comprehension, as they are certainly within the reach of all. For while it is admitted that devotion to the ancient learning enables the few to reach pre-eminence, it can hardly be doubted that the similarly systematic study of the native masterpieces would carry the many to a much higher altitude both of taste and of knowledge than they at present attain. But the two courses of study are by no means exclusive of one another; we have endeavoured to shew how, on the contrary, they may be made mutually helpful. And if it be true, as is often alleged, – as was alleged but a few weeks ago by Mr John Stuart Mill,[3] – that a large proportion of our youth spend years of classical study absolutely in the dark, we ought surely to welcome a proposal which promises to let in upon them a little of that light of heaven, which is as essential to life and growth in the realm of mind as in that of nature.

We have been led into these remarks by an examination of the works mentioned at the head of this article. They are one in their design, – that of encouraging the systematic study of English; and they are very similar in plan. The Messrs Nelson's *Literary Reader*, edited with great care and sound judgment by Canon Robinson, is the best introduction we have seen to the study of English prose. It differs from the ordinary historical compendiums, in that it confines the attention to the really great authors. It differs from the ordinary books of extracts, in that it is not a series of fragments, but affords a specimen of each author's writings sufficiently long and connected to enable us to study the peculiarities of his language and mode of thinking. We are thus brought face to face with the men themselves, and are enabled to read their lineaments, and to feel that we know something about them at first hand. Better have this knowledge of a few men, than a superficial and outside acquaintance with the mere names of the hundreds of authors that are passed in rapid review in the pages of our histories of literature. These compendiums are very useful in their own place, but they do not give us literature itself, but only the author's views 'about it and about it.' The book before us, however, while really a manual of literature, is well adapted for studying English prose historically, and to this end it contains an introductory essay, tracing briefly the development of this side of our literature. Prefixed to the extracts from each author, there is a biographical sketch and an account of his works. At the end of the volume there are philological and critical notes, which help materially to elucidate the text in the case of the older authors. In the same editor's edition of *King Richard II*, though there is not the same originality of plan as in the *Reader*, there is the same scholarly tone, the same just appreciation of educational requirements.

Mr Morris's *Specimens of Early English*, which brings down the survey of our literature from the middle of the thirteenth century, to the close of the fourteenth, has many features in common with Canon Robinson's *Reader*. Its main design is to present to the student literature itself, and not a mere description of it; and so, by bringing him into immediate contact with the authors, to emancipate him from the dubious guidance of literary histories. Mr Morris expresses, in his preface, the same view with regard to the early period that we have already stated with reference to the later, that the brief extracts usually presented to the students 'are quite inadequate to convey any clear notion of the dialect, grammar, and vocabulary of the writers.' His extracts, therefore, as in the former case, 'present continuous narratives of considerable length.' The study of these *Specimens* does not presuppose any systematic knowledge of Anglo-Saxon; but they form the connecting link between the oldest and the more recent forms of the language. An interesting and, educationally considered, a most profitable field of study is thus opened up, towards which the editor's labours in this volume contribute most valuable assistance. The Grammatical Introduction is an exceedingly able and concise survey of the peculiarities of the dialects in use in England in the thirteenth and fourteenth centuries; and this, together with the notes and the Glosssary, contain all that is necessary to enable the student to read even the most difficult extracts at once with profit and with pleasure.

We hail the publication of these volumes with unfeigned satisfaction, not merely because they are valuable in themselves, but still more because they are each 'the first of a series.' It is now some years since the Messrs Nelson projected a series of 'English Classics,' of which their *Literary Reader*, noticed above, is the first issue. We are glad to notice also, that the delegates of the Oxford Clarendon Press, under whose auspices Mr Morris's elegant volume is produced, announce a corresponding series, under the able superintendence of Professor Brewer.[4] We earnestly hope that these projects may meet with the encouragement they so well deserve, and that they may be the means of removing from our educational system the reproach under which it has too long lain, of neglecting the rich stores which our native literature unquestionably contains.

Notes

1. #Hugh G. Robinson, *The Literary Reader: Prose Authors; with Biographical Notices, Critical and Explanatory Notes, &c.* (London and Edinburgh: T. Nelson & Sons, 1867).
   Shakespeare, *King Richard II; with Historical and Critical Introductions, Grammatical, Philological, and Miscellaneous Notes, &c.*, adapted for the use of pupils in Training Colleges, &c. by Hugh G. Robinson (Edinburgh: Oliver and Boyd; London: Simpkin, Marshall, and Co., 1867).
   R. Morris ed. *Specimens of Early English, selected from the Chief English Authors, A.D. 1250 to A.D. 1400, with Grammatical Introduction, Notes, and Glossary* (Oxford: Clarendon Press, 1867).
2. Acts x.14.
3. Inaugural address delivered to the University of St. Andrews, 1 February 1867.
4. J. S. Brewer (1809–1879), Professor of English Language and Literature at King's College, London.

'On the Teaching of the "English Language and Literature"'

*   *
 *

... Our subject ... requires us to take into consideration, what the teaching of English literature involves; and this may very soon be defined. For it simply contemplates the turning to purposes of education our time-honoured and classical English writers. It is taken for granted, of course, that every educated and accomplished Englishman has read Shakspeare's plays, Milton's *Paradise Lost*, Bacon's *Essays*, Dryden's *Fables*, Addison's contributions to the *Spectator*, and others of the great works that are identified with our native tongue, and will live and die with it. These, we say, are supposed, with more or less truth, to be familiar to educated men, but how far in the majority of cases does that familiarity reach? How many are as conversant with the *Paradise Lost* as good classical scholars are with the *Iliad*? When we urge the more general and systematic employment of standard English authors as staples of education, we mean to insist on nothing less than a patient, thorough, exhaustive study of them in every respect. Such a study will leave nothing untouched. It will spread itself alike over the thoughts and the words. It will take cognizance of idioms; it will treasure up sentiments and maxims; it will explain allusions, and trace out parallelisms; in short, it will not rest till the very life and spirit of the author have in a measure been transfused into the student.

The practical details of this study – the methods of teaching which must be pursued to give reality to it – belong to another part of our general subject; it is enough now to indicate the *nature* of the study and the *direction* of the teaching.

It may here be observed, that what we are now insisting upon for English schools, is a recognised part of the French school system. Mr Arnold, in his interesting account of the French Lyceums,[1] tells us, that Fenelon, Voltaire, Boileau, Massillon, Bossuet, and Montesquieu, are established classbooks, and are read in all the forms in combination with the ordinary Greek and Latin authors. Mr Arnold says, indeed, that 'the French literature possesses prose works, and perhaps even poetical works, more fitted to be used as classics for schoolboys, than any which English literature possesses.' We cannot admit the truth of this statement, so far at least as poetry is concerned. Goldsmith's *Traveller*, Wordsworth's *Excursion*, Gray's 'Elegy' and Odes, some of Dryden's Fables, the *Paradise Lost* of Milton, such plays of Shakspeare as *Julius Caesar*, *Macbeth*, *King John*, *Richard II*, and *Henry VIII*, suggest a course of poetical literature, not only higher in tone, superior in genius, to anything that can be found among the literary treasures of France, but also far more valuable, in an educational point of view, supplying more materials for the exercise of the scholar's faculties, involving more difficulties, requiring more research. Then, again, as to prose, we scarcely need fear a comparison, when we call to mind the stores from which we are at liberty to draw. We ought not to be at a loss to find English prose classics for schoolboys, when we remember that we have the First Book of the *Ecclesiastical Polity*, the *Essays* and *Advancement of Learning* of Bacon, the *Areopagitica* of Milton, the Biographies of Walton, the *Sermons* of South, the Miscellaneous Prose Works of Dryden, the *Essays* of Addison, the Histories of Gibbon, Robertson, and Hume, and many other compositions equally admirable for style and matter.

No doubt many of these authors are not as a whole suitable for school purposes. They are not, for one thing, in a very accessible or manageable form. What then would be wanted, if they were made use of as we contend they should be, are portions or extracts printed separately, and edited with a direct view to make them serviceable as text books. But this is a want that would be readily met as soon as its existence was satisfactorily entertained. The demand, when it comes, will infallibly create the supply.

We must not overlook the History of English Literature. Some instruction on this subject should accompany the study of the standard authors. It is incumbent on every one who claims to be an educated man, to have a general acquaintance with the great literary epochs of his country, with the authors who shed the light of their genius on each epoch, and with the nature and merits of the works which they left behind them. But here neither teacher nor student will encounter any difficulty. There is more than one manual which deals with the subject in a clear, concise, and methodical way, and the study of any particular author will be properly accompanied and supplemented with the study of the literary history of the age to which he belongs.

* * *

Note

1. Matthew Arnold, *The Popular Education of France* (1861).

'On the Method of Teaching the "English Language and Literature" – II'

We have already remarked that the English Language and English Literature cannot take the place in education to which they are entitled, until more thorough and systematic methods of teaching them come to be generally understood and adopted. The study of the dead languages, however imperfectly they may be taught, involves of necessity some labour and mental effort. The study of a foreign language, however superficial, has yet in it some disciplinary virtue. On the other hand, to make one's native tongue even a moderately effective instrument of education, it must be taught with scientific accuracy and stimulating force. For the words are for the most part so familiar, and the idiom is so much a matter of course, that a general acquaintance with the subject-matter is soon obtained, and there seems little to exercise the powers of attention, understanding, and reasoning.

134

How then should English be taught? Some attempt to answer this question is the object of this paper, and we will endeavour to make our suggestions as practical as possible, and to illustrate them by exhibiting, as far as the conditions of an article in a public journal will allow, the actual processes and methods by which the work should be carried on.

We will begin, then, by dividing the teaching of our subject into the two heads of *elementary* and *advanced*.

The elementary teaching of English must at the outset be at once simple, colloquial, and practical. To very young children nothing scientific or abstract in connection with language can with any advantage be exhibited. But if due attention be paid to what young children are capable of understanding and turning to good account, a beginning may be made with them betimes, and the foundations of a complete and systematic course of English laid at a very early age.

The first attempt then must be associated with the reading lesson. And this lesson will give opportunity for two processes, obvious enough, no doubt, and not altogether overlooked by any teachers, but seldom carried out as systematically and efficiently as they should be. One of these is *the explanation of the meaning of words*. To this we must suppose that every teacher pays some attention, but the explanation is for the most part given in a dry, technical, dictionary-like style, that very often only substitutes one hard word for another, and at all events paints no picture before the mind's eye, and so leaves no vivid image for memory to treasure up. And yet the subject is one that gives scope for animated description and graphic illustration. The teacher must not indeed cumber his class, at this stage, with learned etymologies or with verbal analysis. He may, however, by calling in the aid of simple acts or objects, by the use of his black board, by some readiness of mental resource on his own part, make a word imprint itself on the minds of his scholars with something of the power of a living reality. Let us take a few words as they suggest themselves to us, and use them to illustrate our position.

There is, for instance, the word *impetuous*. The dictionary tells us that this word means *vehement* or *hasty*, and the teacher may content himself with telling his class the same thing. If he does, he will not leave any very lasting impression on their minds. On the other hand, if he starts with the image embodied in the word, and illustrates its meaning by the description of a man rushing headlong at an object, and then after having conveyed to his class the general notion of haste and violence contained in the word, applies it in several ways, as for instance, to the course of a river, the action of a spirited horse, the impatience of a hot-tempered person, he will fasten that word on the memory by associations which will probably be indelible.

Take again the word *disproportion*. The teacher may fall back on his dictionary and explain this word to be *want of proportion or symmetry*. If he does, he has, like many greater men, explained *obscurum per obscurius*.[1] A slight sketch on the black board will give a very different result. Let him illustrate *disproportion* by a figure exhibiting the characteristic, and a brief comment on such a figure will do everything that is necessary.

There are many words of frequent occurrence in elementary reading-books, the meaning of which may be thus conveyed by the method of *picturing out*, and in this way not only will the interest of the lesson be deepened, but the pupil will have his vocabulary enriched, and his appreciation of the force of words daily more and more developed.

The other process to which we referred as being fitted for very elementary teaching, is that of exercising a class in the use of language. We do not by this mean the practice of written composition, but something that may even precede that. It is of course customary with all teachers to examine their classes on the subject matter of the book they have just read. In doing this, some little training is necessarily given in the use of language. But what we recommend is, that there should be an examination on the language as well as the subject matter of the lesson. This may be carried out in several ways. The pupils may be required to repeat the substance of a paragraph in their own words, and their manner of doing so may be criticised and corrected by their teacher. Again, particular expressions may be pressed on their notice, and associated with certain ideas and thoughts. Phrases and idioms also may be picked out by the master and written down on the black board, and the pupils may be called upon to use these phrases and idioms, and to work them up into new combinations. The learners should be encouraged and aided in every way to acquire freedom and nicety of speech, and teachers should never accept disjointed, broken, incoherent, ungrammatical answers to questions put in the course of an oral lesson. Englishmen are as a rule somewhat slow of speech, clumsy in expression, painfully feeling after words, apt to clothe their thoughts in unfinished forms. Something would be done towards remedying this if children were carefully trained from the outset in readiness and fulness of expression.

To the exercises here proposed let there be added, as the class becomes fit for it, the practice of writing on the slate short abstracts of some simple narrative, fable, or description, and then all, we think, will be done for the teaching of English that can be attempted before the first course of lessons in grammar is entered upon.

To the consideration of how English grammar is to be taught we now pass.

In the earlier stages of this subject no text-book should be used. The practice of setting a portion of some popular manual to be learnt by heart day after day, as the readiest course to a knowledge of grammar, may at once and for ever be exploded. This time-honoured artifice for making a dead book do the work of a living teacher, so long prevalent in many schools, should at once be relegated to the limbo of all educational and other follies and blunders. The text-book, of course, has its use, and may at a somewhat more advanced point in the course, be introduced in subordination to the oral lesson, but even then it must derive a good deal of its efficacy from the comments and illustrations of the teacher.

The first step then in the teaching of grammar, is the classification of the parts of speech. The reading lesson will again furnish the point of departure. The teacher may begin by calling the attention of his class to the fact that, on the open page before them, there are several different sorts of words.

There is, of course, a difference of great and small, of hard and easy, at once perceptible to every one, but the difference to which he has to draw attention is difference of use and meaning, difference of *kind*. Thus some words stand for things that they can see, others for actions that they do; some words have a meaning when taken by themselves, others seem to have no significance unless when used in connection with other words of more dignity and weight. Hence the ground of classification. The teacher must accordingly at once introduce his class to this process. And the noun is the part of speech with which he must begin.

Let him call upon his class to give him the names of a variety of objects which are before their eyes, and let him write them down on the black board. When he thinks his list long enough, he may bid his scholars take notice that all these words are *names*, names of things that they can see. So there are other words which in the same way are *names* of things that can be heard, felt, thought about.

These *names*, then, form a class of words by themselves, and this class grammarians are accustomed to call *nouns*; which, we may add, are after all the same thing as *names*.

Having got so far, he will have no difficulty in drawing out from his pupils the ordinary definition of a noun.

He must then require them to pick out the nouns in some passage which they have read, and at [the] same time to *verify* the selection by stating of what sort of thing each word selected is the name.

The part of speech which should next be dealt with is the verb, and this will best be explained and defined by exhibiting it in connection with the noun. Let the teacher produce a list of nouns which are names of living agents, and let him attach to each agent its appropriate action, and he will thus be able to convey a clear and intelligible notion of the nature and properties of the verb.

At this point too he may venture to introduce his class to the simple sentence in its most elementary form, and to the terms *subject* and *predicate*. When he has made the notion of these things clear to them, he may proceed to the other parts of speech which can be best explained by reference to their position and functions in the sentence.

The personal pronouns, for instance, may be introduced as substitutes for a noun subject, and thus their character and the reason for the name given them may at the same time be elucidated. The adjective, again, may be exhibited as an enlargement of the noun, and by a succession of examples wherein the relation of the former to the latter is practically illustrated, the definition may at length be drawn from the class itself. In the same way the adverb should make its first appearance, in accordance with its name, in juxtaposition with the verb; its wider use as a modifying word for any attributive may afterwards be explained.

The remaining parts of speech, viz., the preposition and conjunction, will present no difficulty; care however must be taken, not only to explain their respective functions, but to shew the intrinsic difference between them.

Multiplied examples and illustrations, the constant use of the black board, testing questions, practical exercises, frequent repetition, must all combine to make the teaching thorough and effective.

Supposing now that in this way the class have got a clear notion of the different parts of speech, the functions they perform, and the grounds of their classification, the teacher may take up the subject of grammatical inflection. Beginning with the noun, he must explain its conditions of number, case, and gender. The changes which the verb undergoes in relation to mood, tense, and person, must next be pointed out. Then will most naturally and properly follow explanations and illustrations of what is commonly called the primary rule of syntax, – the agreement of the verb with its subject. In speaking of the conditions of singular and plural, it obviously suggests itself to the mind to call attention to the effect of a singular or a plural noun on the verb with which it is put into grammatical relation. So for a similar reason an account of the cases of nouns should be accompanied with an explanation of the rule, that a transitive verb governs the objective case. We may add, that the pronouns, retaining as they do more of the inflections once characteristic of our language, are best fitted for illustrating the nature of case, and the government of verbs and prepositions. The teacher, therefore, should have recourse to them for this purpose, and, after shewing, for example, how a verb causes *him* to be used after it instead of *he*, should substitute a noun for the pronoun, and then to make his class understand that, though the noun does not change its form as the pronoun does, yet it is the custom to speak of it when in that condition as being in the objective case. Thanks to the grammatical simplicity of our language, there is little more in the way of inflection to teach in our elementary course. The comparison of the adjective, the varieties of the adverb, and a few more simple points of etymology and syntax, will complete the primary or introductory course of lessons on English grammar.

A second and more comprehensive course must then be taken up. Of this the more extended analysis of sentences should form a prominent feature; and some such clear and simple manual as Mr Dalgleish's work on analysis[2] should be adopted as the text-book for the class. Frequent exercises in composition should also now begin to form part of the course, and the teacher should from time to time exhibit specimens of ungrammatical English, and leave his class to discover the mistakes and correct them. Some indeed have condemned this latter practice, as tending to produce a dangerous familiarity with bad grammar, but the objection seems futile. The error is never presented apart from its correction, and whatever association is established in the mind will be against and not for that particular combination. It may be observed in passing, that there are a great many trifling inaccuracies of grammar current in the every-day conversational idiom of educated people, and teachers would really do good service to the interests of language if they would take note of these, and specially call the attention of their pupils to the improprieties and their correction. How constantly, for example, are the words *lie* and *lay* confounded. How persistently is the wrong case used after the verb *to be*, or in such combinations as 'There is nothing left for you or I.' How often do we hear people say, 'moreover than that,' 'it is tiresome to a degree,' 'he was affected by it like I was myself,' &c. But indeed if a teacher will be at the pains of examining one of the popular novels of the day, he will be able to supply himself from its pages with an ample store of 'frightful examples' to set before his class.

With regard to exercises in composition, it must be observed that care should be taken to make them progressive and systematic. These should be, first, the *synthesis* of simple sentences; then the combination of a principal sentence with its subordinates, or of two or more principal sentences; lastly, the composition of paragraphs and themes. Beginners are apt to find a difficulty in connecting their clauses. They have not the art of neatly dovetailing one sentence into another, and of employing with harmony and precision a variety of conjunctional words. They generally string a succession of statements together by a monotonous and tedious repetition of the conjunction *and*. Now to make a lesson in composition really effective, it is not enough to require an exercise to be written, and then to correct it in a general and superficial way, by simply marking the grammatical or verbal errors. The teacher must do far more than this. He must dissect the composition step by step. He must minutely criticise whatever is feeble, clumsy, redundant, unidiomatic. He must by way of contrast exhibit the same thoughts in a comely and appropriate dress. Roger Ascham, in his *Schoolmaster*,[3] insists very emphatically on the advantage of translation and re-translation, as the readiest way to familiarity with the Latin tongue. An approximation to this has been attempted in the teaching of English by the introduction of *paraphrasing*. This exercise has long had a prominent place in the examinations for certificates, conducted under the auspices of the Committee of Council on Education.[4] It is very much to be doubted, however, whether it is one that can be strongly recommended. At all events it is not every kind of writing that can be advantageously paraphrased. To convert in this way a passage of Addison, or Hume, or Macaulay, is to pull down fine masonry, and build a rough wall with the materials. And, indeed, the paraphrases of a good many students are nothing better than awkward inversions of the original order, or bare substitutions of more or less synonymous words.

It is a useful exercise, however, to translate poetry into clear and simple prose, or to take a passage from some writer addicted to long intricate passages, and sesquipedalian words, and to reduce it to short periods, and easy Saxon English. Benjamin Franklin tells us that, when the sense of his deficiencies, and the ambition to be a correct writer, stimulated him to the work of self-education, he took especial pains to acquire a good style. His plan was to read over a paper in the *Spectator* some five or six times, till the thoughts and, to some extent, the language, became imprinted on his memory. He then laid aside the book, and sat down to reproduce the essay. When he had accomplished this to the best of his ability, he compared his composition with the original, and took note of his errors and shortcomings in language and sentiment. The value of such an exercise is unquestionable, and it may well be recommended to teachers, as deserving a place among their educational appliances and methods.

At the stage we are now considering, the lessons in English grammar should enter more fully into the points touched on in the earlier stage of the course.

Some knowledge of the history and progress of the English language should be imparted, and illustrations should be given of the more important changes which have from time to time taken place in the idiom, grammar, and vocabulary of our native tongue.

* *
*

We must add, that a text-book on English grammar should, at this second stage of the elementary course, be put into the hands of the class. It should be carefully got up, but should not be allowed entirely to supersede oral teaching, for which indeed it ought to serve as a basis. For this end the work of Morell is well adapted,[5] and it is accompanied by a good and ample series of exercises. A grammar has also been lately published by Mr Dalgleish,[6] which forms a companion text-book to his analysis, and which is fitted, both as to compass and arrangement, for the use of schoolboys. The master must consult deeper and more advanced works on his own account, for there is no subject with regard to which it is more important that the teacher, even of the elements, should have a full and mature acquaintance, than in the case of grammar. Finally, to make this elementary course complete, a portion of some standard English author should be selected, and used with the class as a model and a study.

The author chosen should be one of our later ones, simple, correct, and elegant in style; interesting and not abstruse, or too abstract in subject matter. Some of Addison's papers in the *Spectator*, portions of Goldsmith, or of Johnson's *Lives of the Poets*, Washington Irving's graceful and polished sketches, or Southey's *Life of Nelson*, may be referred to as samples of the sort of book that should be adopted. It must be very thoroughly studied, and may be made available for several purposes. It will serve as a reading book, and the parsing, analysis, and all other grammatical exercises, may be taken from it. It should, in fact, be gone through, paragraph by paragraph, with this view. The teacher may complete his elementary course by introducing his class to some of our simpler and more modern poets. A book of Cowper's *Task* or of Wordsworth's *Excursion*, Thomson's *Seasons* or Campbell's *Pleasures of Hope*, would be well adapted for this purpose. Large portions of the poem selected should be committed to memory, the language and imagery should be critically noted, all allusions, metaphorical expressions, and peculiar idioms, carefully explained, and the subject-matter, as it were, translated into simple grammatical prose.

Such then is the course which we venture to recommend as fitted to lay a solid foundation for the more advanced study of the English language and literature. It seems to us to take in all the more essential features and divisions of the subject, and, if properly taught, it ought not only to supply a store of knowledge, but to furnish also a considerable measure of discipline. Very much of course depends on the manner of teaching, on the energy, clearness, intelligence, and aptitude of the teacher. He must remember that it is an essential part of his business to enlist the co-operation, and thus to develop the reasoning powers of his scholars. The study of language is fitted to train the mind to the exercise of some of its most important processes. It involves the principles of generalisation and critical analysis; it calls forth the habit of drawing inferences; it quickens the insight into distinctions and differences of things; and, in accordance with the significant fact, that one Greek term stands both for *word* and *reason*, – in leading men to express themselves with accuracy and precision, it teaches them also to think coherently and cogently.

Notes

1. the obscure through the even more obscure.
2. Walter Scott Dalgleish, *Grammatical Analysis* (1865).
3. Roger Ascham, *The Schoolmaster* (1570).
4. The Committee of the Privy Council on Education was set up in 1839, with Dr James Kay-Shuttleworth as secretary, to supervise the use of parliamentary grants in National and British schools. This committee was merged with the Education Department in 1856.
5. John Morell, *A Grammar of the English Language* (1857).
6. Walter Scott Dalgleish, *Outlines of English Grammar and Analysis for Elementary Schools* (1867).

'On the Method of Teaching the "English Language and Literature" – III'

The elementary course of English teaching, laid down in the last number of this Journal, will, if thoroughly carried out, leave the pupil in a condition to enter upon a more profound and scientific study of the subject. It remains for us to examine how this study is to be prosecuted. And we will endeavour to make what we say available, as well for the teacher who has to instruct and guide others, as for the solitary learner who, without an instructor, sets himself manfully and energetically to the work of self-improvement.

At the stage to which we have now come, the scholar is supposed to have acquired a sound knowledge of the leading principles and chief facts of English grammar, to have a general acquaintance with the history and constitution of the language, to be able to write it correctly and idiomatically, and to have become partially familiar with a few at least of the standard works of the literature. What remains to be done is to build on this substantial foundation, to deepen and extend the knowledge already given, to trace out the causes of the effects exhibited, to make theory more exhaustive and scientific, and practice more masterly and refined.

I. In the first place, if he would leave nothing untouched that bears upon his subject, the teacher must go to the very beginning of things, and open to his class some views of the *origin of language*. It will be enough in ordinary cases to touch lightly on this theme. Suggestions for further research into it may be thrown out for the benefit of those who are disposed to carry on the inquiry. One or two points may be so dwelt upon as to interest and profit all. Such a point is what is called *onomatopoeia*. It has been made a question how far language is the result of imitation. It is certain at least that very many words in all languages are formed on this principle. It will be the business of the teacher to illustrate this by exhibiting to his class a collection of such words. The names of very many animal sounds are of this kind. When we speak of the *neigh* of the horse, the *purr* of the cat, the *yelp* of the dog, the *croak* of the raven, we at once perceive the imitative character of the term, and feel how the sound echoes to the sense. We may refer again to sounds like *slap, clip, rush, crash, wrench*, as at once by their very sound suggesting the acts of which they are the symbols. Other points that bear on the origin of language, and that seem fitted to supply interesting material for class-teaching, are *primary roots, the prevalence of metaphor in speech, the power of language as a distinguishing faculty of the human race*.

The student who wishes to obtain some general knowledge of this interesting subject, will find what he wants clearly set forth and discussed in the admirable little books lately published by the Rev. F.W. Farrar.[1] Those who are anxious to study it more deeply may be referred to the writings of Max Müller[2] and Donaldson,[3] and to Rénan's work, *De l'Origine du Langage*.[4]

II. Another topic which must be dealt with in our course, and dealt with fully and carefully, is the classification and affinities of languages. Without venturing to discuss very elaborately the question of one primitive language from which all existing forms of speech are derived, the teacher must shew that existing languages are divisible into *families*, and that of these the three chief are the *Indo-European*, the *Semitic*, and the *Mongolian*. He must go on to exhibit to his class the various languages which in each of these families stand to one another in a co-ordinate relation. Herein his attention will chiefly be confined to the *Indo-European family*. He must trace out its historical and geographical conditions; he must specify the different groups of which it consists, such namely as the *Hellenic*, the *Celtic*, the *Gothic*, the *Sclavonic*; he must enumerate the various languages which belong to each group. He will thus be led on to point out the true position of the English language among the languages of the world, to refer it to the particular *family* to which it belongs, and to exhibit its undoubted pedigree. Into the mysteries of comparative grammar it will not be his business to enter, but he ought to give his class some practical illustrations of that affinity of languages about which he has been talking to them. It will not be difficult to make such illustrations intelligible and interesting, even to the mere student of English. Such a one has been taught to regard his native language as consisting of two elements, the Saxon and the Latin. He is accustomed to refer one class of words to the former, another to the latter. It will be a new discovery for him when he is led to see that words which stand most widely apart from each other as belonging to those opposite elements, are nevertheless akin by virtue of a common descent from a remote ancestor. The numerals and the pronouns furnish the most obvious examples of this affinity. A selection of words, however, may easily be made which would make it plain to any intelligent learner. As instances, we may suggest a comparison between *know* and *noscere, stand* and *stare, write* and *scribere, ear* (to plough) and *arare, earth* and *terra, yoke* and *jugum*, &c.

We must repeat that we do not recommend – in connection with the study of English, or with the teaching of it as a branch of general education – any profound or elaborate research into the affinities of language or the principles of comparative grammar. We only suggest in this way what can be done in passing, the giving of just as much insight into the subject as a well-educated Englishman ought to have, as much as is necessary to a right appreciation of the conditions of the English language. When this has been accomplished, the student is ready to concentrate his attention on the language itself. He has learnt something about the innate faculty of language, about those elementary forms in which it originally manifested itself, about all those modifications and changes which have gradually called into existence distinct varieties of language, each with its proper name and local habitation. He now knows whence his mother tongue has sprung, and what are its alliances and connections. He will be all the better able to trace its progress, and to analyse its constitution.

III. Professing, then, to recommend a comprehensive and somewhat ambitious course of study, we would insist on the importance of taking up with English as near the well-head as possible. Start with the stream, high up among the heathy hills and wild pastures, and follow it down to where its broad bosom swells with the invading tide of ocean. In plain words, we would give the study of Anglo-Saxon an early and a prominent place in the programme we are laying down. The importance and advantage of this study appear to us very obvious. Unless some attention be paid to it, the learner will never arrive at a complete knowledge of his native tongue. It alone can introduce him to the 'inner life' and essential laws of English speech. It alone can shew him the consistency and harmony of what would otherwise appear to be arbitrary or anomalous in the language. To Anglo-Saxon belong very many of the prefixes and suffixes in present use, together with all that remains to us of grammatical inflexion. In Anglo-Saxon, we find the key to that complicated and seemingly inconsistent orthography which is the perplexity of foreigners striving to learn our language. To Anglo-Saxon we can trace many of those rough provincialisms that vex polite ears, and puzzle refined understandings. Moreover, in learning Anglo-Saxon, some good mental discipline will be found. Its inflexional character, its definite and concrete terminology, the fact that it is, if not a dead, yet at least an antiquated and obsolete form of speech, makes it a not altogether inadequate or contemptible substitute for Latin as an educational instrument. In every case, then, where the aim is to teach English thoroughly and radically, we advise the teaching of at least the outlines of Anglo-Saxon. There are now ample resources and appliances for accomplishing this. Those who only seek to make the institution elementary, will find all they need in a little work by the Rev. W. Barnes, entitled *Se Gefylsta, or the Helper*.[5]

This work supplies an outline of the declensions of nouns, adjectives, and pronouns, and of the conjugation of verbs, together with a delectus and vocabulary. For those who wish to carry the study further, there is Vernon's *Guide to Anglo-Saxon*,[6] based on Rask's *Anglo-Saxon Grammar*,[7] together with various extracts and editions of Anglo-Saxon writers.

It will, of course, be the aim of the teacher to make his lessons in Anglo-Saxon practically useful, that is, to make them especially illustrative of modern English. Thus, in exhibiting the declensions of nouns, he will have the opportunity of shewing the original character and position of such a plural form as *oxen*. There were in earlier English, as we know, many more such forms, as for example, *hosen, arwen, housen, eyen*. Now, these forms correspond with the nominative plural of Anglo-Saxon nouns of the first declension (according to Rask's classifiication), which ends in *an*, as *eagan, uxan, steorran*, &c.

* *
*

IV The next subject in the course will be the history of those modifications and changes by which the language of Alfred's time became the language of Elizabeth's... .

* *
*

V So far then the history of the language, its growth and development, have been provided for. There remain other points of view in which it has to be regarded, other facts and features of it in which instruction must be given. Next in order, therefore, we suggest the study of English Etymology. This will involve an examination of *general principles*, and of *particular instances*. It is with the general principles that the teacher should mainly concern himself. Thus, in the case of words derived from the Latin, he will have to shew the sort of change they undergo in order to become naturalised. He will direct the attention of his class to such obvious facts as that a great number of Latin words ending in *tio* become English by the simple addition of *n*; that a considerable number are enfranchised by the mere conversion of *tas* into *ty*; that in some cases a word is derived from the supine of a Latin verb, as for example *accept, reject, convict*; in other cases from the infinitive mood, as *discern, consent, impute*. He will distinguish between those words which have been imported direct from the old Latin tongue, and those which, though Latin by descent, have passed through an intermediate French state. It will be made to appear how in this way many words owe their particular form to the accident of entering the language mediately or immediately from their native stock. This alone accounts for the difference in structure between *receive* on the one hand and *accept* on the other, both being derived from compounds of *capio*, but the one coming direct from the Latin supine *acceptum*, the other from the present *recipio*, through the French *recevoir*.

Closely connected with the subject of etymology is that of the structure of words, or word-building, as it is sometimes called. The handling of this subject will give opportunity for shewing how the different classes of words have grown up from primitive roots; by what internal literal changes, and by what external accretions, they have come to symbolise modified or enlarged ideas. Under this head the teacher will deal with the whole matter of prefixes and suffixes and compound words.

In a course of lessons on structural and derivative etymology, care must be taken not to encumber or overload the pupil with materials. A discursive, unmethodical treatment of the subject must also be avoided. The point is to grasp and exhibit a few general principles and laws, and to bring forward a sufficient number of the most appropriate illustrations. It will be for the learner to apply the rules, and to carry out on his own account the etymological researches to which he has been introduced. It must be remembered again, that the practical value of etymology lies in the clearer insight which it gives into the true meaning of words.

VI. The examination, therefore, of the exact force and meaning of words, forms another branch of our subject, and the teacher and the student will find it not one of the least interesting. There are many words in our language which form excellent anatomical subjects, if we may so speak. The dissection of them, the investigation of the ideas and images they embody, of the changes of meaning they have undergone, will, in the hands of a skilful manipulator, very easily fix the attention, and very considerably enlarge the information of a class of learners. Take, for instance, a word of which we have ourselves just made use, the word *investigation*. It is one thing to know its general meaning, and another to get at its full significance by an examination of its origin. As soon as we connect it with the Latin *vestigium* and *vestigare*, we at once have the image before the mind's eye of the dog tracking his prey, the hunter pursuing his game. The word leaves a more vivid impression on the understanding, the symbol becomes more real. But we need not dwell on this topic. Archbishop Trench has awakened attention to the history that lies hid in words, to the pictures which, when their inner sense is penetrated, they suggest to the imagination. He has opened a mine which the educator will find his profit in working. A recommendation of his *Study of Words*, and *English, Past and Present*,[8] may very appropriately be introduced at this point, for these interesting and original works supply copious materials for the sort of teaching we are describing, and, by the method in which these materials are dealt with, make any very minute directions on our part superfluous. We may observe, however, that there is no element in the teaching of the English language that is more experimental and demonstrative than this. It can be exhibited as palpably and effectively as the experiments in chemical science. If the mind of the teacher himself is sufficiently well stored, if he is orderly and systematic, has the faculty of analysis and classification, he may deliver a course of lessons that will awaken the interest and secure the attention of even his less active and diligent pupils.

To this end the black board must be the great mechanical instrument with which he works, and, instead of taking his words at random, he must group them in accordance with some law of their constitution, or some principle which they represent and embody in common.

VII. Passing on to another division of our subject, we have to consider the study of *idioms* as an important part of the general study of the English language. There are certain combinations of words to which we give the name of idioms, because they are peculiar to the language, stand in a particular relation to it, and are in special harmony with its essential character. Idiom in language, therefore, may be compared to what in persons is sometimes called *idiosyncrasy*. Hence the study of idiom is necessary to attaining a thorough insight into the genius of a language. It will indeed be most successfully prosecuted in connection with the study of the national literature. The teacher must, however, in order to make his course of instruction complete and exhaustive, deal with it as a specific point. In this way he will enable his class to appreciate its nature, and to follow it up in connection with their own reading.

Let him then select a passage of English as thickly inlaid with distinctive idioms as may be, and after reading this aloud, let him call attention to the idiomatic phrases, and shew, as far as he can, wherein their peculiarity consists, and through what mental process they seem to have been evolved.

Among the modifications which the language has from time to time undergone, not the least striking and significant is change of idiom. This may be illustrated in many ways. For example, there is a difference in the use of some of the prepositions now and at an earlier period. An Elizabethan writer would probably say *accompanied with*, where we say *accompanied by*. *Of* formerly expressed relations now denoted by *on* or *by*. Sir P. Sidney has the expression *to feed of tougher knowledge*, to *depend of poetry*. In the Bible we constantly meet with such a use of *of* as the following, 'I am found *of* them that sought me not.' *For* was commonly introduced before the infinitive mood, as for instance, 'This is that Elias which was *for to come*.' The pronomial compounds *herein*, *whereby*, *thereof*, *wherefrom*, were once greatly in vogue; they are now nearly superseded by the relative pronoun and a preposition. Particular phrases again occur in our older writers, which no modern writer would venture upon. Thus Bacon speaks of *entertaining thoughts into the head*, of being *laboured* (i.e. urged), *to do a thing*; Chaucer has the phrase *to lie on one's might*, where we should say, *to lie in one's power*; Hooker talks of *these beaten paths wherewith men have been inured*. Clarendon has the expressions, *bestowed to such persons as he thought fit; he indulged to himself pleasures of all kinds.*

The examples have been selected at hazard; they will at all events serve to illustrate the point we are considering, and will suggest to the teacher or the student what he is to look for and to examine.

VIII. And now we seem to have touched on every leading division of the subject. We have, at least, proposed a course of instruction which introduces the learner to some of the primary facts concerning language, which leads him to become acquainted with the pure and primitive form of his mother-tongue, which enables him to trace its history and to mark the orthographical, verbal, and syntactical changes which century after century have taken place in it, which will give him the power and the habit of explaining the origin and the signification of words, and of analysing and comparing idioms. Prepared by such a course, he must enter upon a laborious critical study of classical English authors. In pursuing this study, he must exercise and apply all the philological knowledge which he has acquired, and must deepen and extend it. Guided by what he has been taught, he will know how most profitably to read his books. And it cannot be too strongly insisted upon that the study of English literature must not be a trifling, superficial dilettante business. It ought to be as severe and as thorough as 'the getting up' of Greek and Latin authors for an Oxford class.

The attention of the student must be directed equally to the subject matter and to the language. As to the former, he must labour to make the high and noble thoughts his own. He must follow and weigh the arguments, and treasure up the images and figures. He must read, not to cram himself or to quote, but to digest, to assimilate, to imbibe nourishment and intellectual life. He must not only *read*, therefore, but *meditate*. The subject-matter that he gleans from the pages of his author must filter through his brain, and, as it were, saturate his mind. Let him then often question himself or be questioned on what he has read, and let him from time to time reproduce the thoughts and arguments in his own words.

In dealing with the language of the work he is studying, he must follow the suggestions which this article has already thrown out. Let the words and phrases be carefully analysed, and any peculiarities of use and meaning diligently noted. A list of words employed in any exceptional way should be made, and a collection of phrases and idioms accumulated. Illustration by means of parallel passages from other writers must not be overlooked, and the ear must be trained, and the taste educated to appreciate elegancies and detect roughness or inequalities of style. No study of English is thorough that does not provide for the practice of composition, and it is possible, we believe, for the student to catch the tone and to imitate the style of the author on which he is engaged. But the style of one who has digested the best writings of our best writers can hardly be wanting in point, vigour, and grace. It is not, perhaps, out of place, in concluding this paper, to suggest a course of English literature, the mastery of which would make the student no mean master of the English tongue, and not inadequately versed in his country's noble literature.

Such a course would, in poetry, include Chaucer's 'Prologue' to *The Canterbury Tales*, Sackville's 'Induction,' the first book of Spenser's *Fairy Queen*, select plays of Shakespeare, Milton's *Paradise Lost* and *Comus*, Dryden's *Fables*, Pope's *Essay on Man* and some of his epistles and satires, Thomson's *Seasons*, Gray's poems, Cowper's *Task*, with selections from Wordsworth, Scott, Byron, and Tennyson.

For a course of prose authors, we recommend the following: Wycliffe's New Testament, St Luke's Gospel, Ascham's *Schoolmaster*, Part I, Hooker's *Ecclesiastical Polity*, Book I, Bacon's *Essays* and *Advancement of Learning*, Raleigh's *History of the World* (selections), Sir T. Browne's *Hydriotaphia*, Cowley's *Essays*, Milton's *Areopagitica*, Dryden's *Essay on Dramatic Poetry*, South's *Sermons* (select), Addison, select papers in

Spectator, Johnson's *Rasselas*, Hume's *History of the Reign of Elizabeth*, Burke's *Thoughts on the Present Discontents*, Macaulay's *Essay on Lord Clive*.

To some this may appear a very formidable catalogue, though in truth it leaves many of our standard writers altogether out of account. It exhibits, however, a chronological series of representative authors, and from it a selection can be made by those who have neither time nor inclination to grapple with the more extended course.

And now, we beg leave to commend the suggestions offered in this paper to the favourable consideration of all who are interested in the business of education. We might, undoubtedly, have handled our subject more effectually, but we do not hesitate to assert that, even as we have put it, there is a very strong case in favour of the English language and English literature as an essential part of an Englishman's education. If so much can be made of the subject, if it offers such scope for the teacher as it appears to us to do, is it really necessary to depend so exclusively as we are doing on the languages and literatures of Greece and Rome for mental culture and mental discipline? We are not the enemies of what is called classical education. We do not desire to supersede Greek and Latin. But while we recognise their merits, we denounce their monopoly. If the experiment can only be fairly tried, we shall look with confidence on the fruit that will be reaped from a generation imbued with the great results of modern science, and nurtured with the kindly milk of their native literature, and their noble mother-tongue.

Notes

1. F.W. Farrar, *Chapters on Language* (1865).
2. See also Friedrich Max Müller's letter to the *Pall Mall Gazette*, included in this volume, pp. 238–41.
3. John William Donaldson.
4. Ernest Rénan, *De l'Origine du Langage* (1848).
5. William Barnes, *Se Gefylsta – the Helper: an Anglo-Saxon Delectus* (1849).
6. Edward Vernon, *A Guide to the Anglo-Saxon Tongue* (1846).
7. Rasmus Rask, *A Grammar of the Anglo-Saxon Tongue*, translated from the Danish by Benjamin Thorpe (1830).
8. Richard Chenevix Trench, *On the Study of Words* (1851) and *English Past and Present* (1855).

CHAPTER ELEVEN

Henry Sidgwick

Henry Sidgwick (1838–1900) was a philosopher, who became Knightsbridge Professor of Moral Philosophy at Cambridge in 1883. However, he had started his academic career in the field of classics, only exchanging his lectureship in classics for one in moral philosophy in 1869. Yet, prior to this actual change of direction, he had long had philosophical interests, and had worked with others to broaden Cambridge undergraduate studies through the inclusion of philosophy. He was also a leading figure in moves to improve female education, and in 1869 devised a scheme which finally led to the opening of Newnham Hall in 1876.

In 1867, Sidgwick was a contributor to a collection of essays edited by F.W. Farrar, *Essays on a Liberal Education*. There was a heavy Cambridge bias among the contributors, only one of whom had no connection with Cambridge. Sidgwick's essay, 'The Theory of Classical Education,' was an attack on the pre-eminent place given to classics in the education of the middle and upper classes. In their place, Sidgwick pressed the claims of both English and natural science.

In some ways, Sidgwick's arguments in favour of English anticipate John Churton Collins's point that whatever classical teaching was retained would become more efficacious as a result of the introduction of a new element, English. In many ways, though, Sidgwick went further in wishing to replace classics in the education of many boys. A schoolmaster, he argued, should be a 'missionary of culture,' and the literature which he taught should explain, as far as possible, 'the intellectual life of our own age.' This meant largely English literature. If English literature were taught, it would make it possible to exercise some influence over what people actually read: they would read the authors whom they had studied at school. This was plainly not the case when they had studied classics at school.

Sidgwick's essay dealt with both English language and English literature, but the extract included here is concerned with literature.

'The Theory of Classical Education'

* * *

In the eyes of many persons … the most important of the direct utilities supposed to be conveyed by a classical education is still that for which a classical education was originally instituted, acquaintance with the Greek and Latin literatures. In the first place, just as the ancient languages were called a master-key to unlock all modern European tongues, so the ancient writings are said to be indispensable to the understanding of all the best modern books. 'If,' says Dr Donaldson, 'the old classical literature were swept away, the moderns would in many cases become unintelligible, and in all lose most of their characteristic charms.'[1] A moment's reflection will show this to be a most strange and palpable exaggeration. For instance, Milton is the most learned of our poets: nay, as a poet, he is generally said to be obtrusively learned, learned to a fault. Yet how grotesque an absurdity it seems to assert that *Paradise Lost* would 'lose most of its characteristic charm' to a reader who did not understand the classical allusions and similes. The real state of the case seems analogous to that which we have just discussed. A knowledge of classics is indispensable, not to the general reader, but to the historical student of modern authors: without it he can enter into their ideas and feelings, but not the antecedents which determined those ideas and feelings. He cannot reproduce the intellectual *milieu* in which they lived; he can understand what they said, but not how they came to say it. But for the general reader, who has no wish to go so deep, classical knowledge does not do much more than save some trouble of referring to dictionaries and histories, and some ignorance of quotations which is rather conventionally than really inconvenient. Many allusions to the classics explain themselves; many others are explained by the context; and the number of those that remain incomprehensible to a person who has read histories of Greece and Rome, and knows as much about the classics as he must inevitably pick up from a good course of English literature, is not very considerable. We may grant that 'literature can only be studied *thoroughly* by going to its source.'[2] But the conception conveyed in this word *thoroughly* assumes an exalted standard of reading, which, if carried out consistently, would involve an overwhelming encyclopedic study of literature. For the modern authors whom the stream of fame has floated down to us, and whom we do read, contain numerous allusions to preceding and contemporary authors whom we do not think of reading, and require, in order to be *thoroughly* understood, numerous illustrations from preceding and contemporary history which we have no leisure to procure. We content ourselves with the fragmentary lights of a casual commentator. I do not see that it would be so dreadful if classical allusions were apprehended by the general reader in the same twilight manner. It may be very desirable that we should read everything more accurately and thoroughly; but let us have one weight and one balance. The historical study of literature, for the completeness of which I allow classics to be indispensable, is a most interesting and improving pursuit, and one which I hope will gain votaries yearly. But, after all, the branch of this study which seems to have the greatest utility, if the space we can allot to it is limited, is surely that which explains to us (as far as is possible) the intellectual life of our own age; which teaches us the antecedents of the ideas and feelings among which, and in which, we shall live and move. Such a course, at this moment of history, would naturally contain a much larger modern than ancient element: it would be felt in framing it more imperatively necessary to represent French, German, and English thought of recent centuries, than to introduce us to any of the older influences that combined to determine our immediate intellectual antecedents.

*
* *

… 'It is admitted,' says a *Quarterly* reviewer (summing up very fairly the Report of the Public Schools Commission), 'that education must be literary, and that of literary education, classical learning must be the backbone.'[3] Whether I should agree with this or not, depends upon the sense in which 'backbone' is interpreted: at present classical learning forms, so to say, the whole skeleton; and the result is, that, to a very large number of boys, what is supposed to be a purely literary education, what is attacked as being exclusively a literary education, is, paradoxical as it may sound, hardly a training in literature at all. For surely it is essential to the idea of such training that it should have some stimulating power; that it should inspire a fondness for reading, educe the capacity for enjoying eloquence and poetry, communicate an interest in ideas; and not merely guide and chasten such taste and interest if they already exist. The instruments of literary training ought to be not only absolutely admirable, but relatively attractive. If we wish to educate persons to enjoy any kind of art, I do not say that we are not to put before them things hard to appreciate, but we must certainly put before them also things that they will find easy to appreciate. I feel sure that if the schoolmaster is ever to be, as I think he ought to be, a missionary of culture; if he is to develop, to any extent, the aesthetic faculties of other boys than those who have been brought up in literary homes, and have acquired, before they come into his hands, a taste for English classics, he must make the study of modern literature a substantive and important part of his training. It may be said that some part of

153

ancient literature, especially Greek, is ever young and fresh; and no doubt, in most good schools, some boys are made to feel this, and their path becomes flowery in consequence. But the majority want, to stimulate their literary interest, something that can be read with more ease, in larger portions: something, moreover, that has a visible connexion with the life of their age, which exercises so powerful a control over their imaginations. I do not know that, if difficulties of language were put aside, some ancient historians, such as Herodotus, might not be more attractive to boys from their freshness and *naïveté*, than any modern ones. But just when the difficulties of language are beginning to be got over, boys cease to relish this *naïveté*. They want something that speaks to their opening minds and hearts, and gives them ideas. And this they are seldom able to find to a great extent, in the ancient works they read. This is true, I know, of some at least among the minority who study classics at school and college with all the stimulus of uniform success; much more is it true of the majority who fail or are but indifferently successful. If such boys get imbued with literary culture at all, it is not owing to the classical system; it is due to home influence, to fortunate school friendships, to the extra-professional care of some zealous schoolmaster. In this way they are taught to enjoy reading that instructs and refines, and escape the fate of the mass, who temper small compulsory sips of Virgil, Sophocles, Tacitus, and Thucydides, with large voluntary draughts of James, Ainsworth, Lever, and the translated Dumas.[4]

I wish this occasional and irregular training to be made as general and systematic as possible; and I feel sure that whatever classical teaching was retained, would become more efficacious by the introduction of the new element; and this not merely because every new mental stimulus that can be applied to a boy is immediately felt over the whole range of his work, but because the boy would gain a special motive for learning Latin and Greek, which he had hitherto been without, and the want of which had made his studies (to use the words of a *Quarterly* reviewer) 'a prolonged nightmare.' He might not at once begin to enjoy the classics: his progress might be still so slow, and his attention so much concentrated on the form of his authors, as to allow him but a feeble interest in their substance. But he would be cheered by the hope of this interest becoming daily stronger: he might distinctly look forward to the time when Sophocles would be as dear to him as Shakespeare, when Cicero and Tacitus would stir him like Burke and Macaulay. Again, some modern literature has a direct power of revealing to us the charm of ancient literature, of enabling us to see and feel in the older masterpieces what the *élite* of each generation could see and feel for themselves when the language was once understood, but what for the mass requires an interpreter. Some, for instance, would perhaps be ashamed to confess how shallow an appreciation they had of Greek art till they read Goethe and Schiller, Lessing and Schlegel. No doubt there are boys who find out the beauties for themselves, just as there are some to whom it would be a feast to be turned into a room full of fragments of antique sculpture. But our system is framed for the mass, and I feel convinced that the mass require to appreciate both the one and the other a careful preparation, the most important part of which would be supplied by a proper introduction into education of the element I am advocating.[5]

Further, I am disposed to think that the literary education of even the best boys is liable to suffer from the narrowness of the existing system. In the first place, there is a great danger in the predominance that classics are made to gain over their minds, by the indiscriminate eulogy and unreserved exaltation of the ancient authors *en masse*,[6] which they frequently hear. They are told, dogmatically, that these authors 'are perfect standards of criticism in everything that belongs to mere perfect form,' that 'the laws that regulate external beauty can only be thoroughly known through them,' that 'they utterly condemn all false ornament, all tinsel, all ungraceful and unshapely work;' and the more docile of them are apt to believe these dogmas to a degree that warps and oppresses the natural development of their critical faculties. The truth is, that the best classical models only exemplify certain kinds of perfection of form, that several writers that boys read exemplify no particular perfection at all, and that some illustrate excellently well the precise imperfections that the enthusiast I have quoted enumerates.[7] How can it be said, for instance, that there is no 'false ornament' in Aeschylus, no 'tinsel' in Ovid, no 'ungracefulness' in Thucydides, no 'unshapely work' in Lucretius? In what sense can we speak of finding 'perfect form' and 'perfect standards of criticism' in such inartificial writers as Herodotus (charming as he is) or Xenophon! There is perhaps no modern thinker, with equal sensitiveness to beauty of expression, who (in those works of his which have been preserved to us) has so neglected and despised form as Aristotle. Any artist in words may learn much from Cicero, and much from Tacitus; but the profuse verbosity of the one, and the perpetual mannerism of the other, have left the marks of their misdirection on English literature. I am simply repeating what are now the commonplaces of cultivated criticism, which can no longer be charged, on the whole, with being servile towards antiquity; but education is less emancipated, and as long as these sweeping statements of the perfectness of ancient literature are reiterated, a demand for careful limitation seems necessary.

But secondly, it can hardly be said that the artistic training which might be given by means of ancient literature (which I should be sorry to seem to undervalue) is given under our present educational system. A few attain to it self-taught: and even these are liable to all the errors and extravagances of such self-education.But what effort is made to teach literary criticism to the great majority in our schools (or even in our universities)? Are they encouraged to judge as wholes the works that they so minutely analyse? to attain to any synthetical apprehension of their excellence? The point on which the wisest admirers of ancient art lay most stress is the completely organic structure of its products and the instinct for complex and finely articulated harmony that is felt to have guided the production. But in so far as schoolboys (with a few exceptions) are taught to feel the beauty of these products at all, it is the beauty of parts, and even of minute parts that they are taught to feel. And, from the mode in which these beauties are studied for purposes of composition it is not only a partial, but generally a perverted appreciation that is attained. In the effort to prepare his mind for composition, a boy is led to contemplate his authors under conditions as unfavourable to the development of pure taste and sound criticism as can possibly be conceived. He is led to break the diction of great masters into fragments for the purpose of mechanical ornamentation, generally clumsy and often grotesque. His memory (as an advocate exultingly phrases it) is 'stored with precious things:' that is, it is stored with long words, sounding epithets, imposing circumlocutions, salient extravagances and mannerisms: so that his admiration is directed to a great extent to what is *bizarre*, fantastic, involved, over-decorated in the admirable models he studies: and even of what is really good he is apt to spoil his delicacy of apprehension, by the habit of imitating and introducing it unseasonably. I am aware how much careful training may do to correct these vicious tendencies: but they are likely to exist in overwhelming force as long as the imitative instinct is so prematurely developed as it is now, and applied to a material over which so imperfect a command has been gained.

*
*   *

Notes

1. John Donaldson, *The New Cratylus* (1839), p.10.
2. # Dr Temple [Frederick Temple (1821–1902), later Archbishop of Canterbury, a leading member of the Schools Inquiry Commission, whose report was published in 1868].
3. [R. H. Cheney], 'Public Schools,' *Quarterly Review*, 116 (1864), 181.
4. # I must be pardoned for using the names familiar to my generation. I have

no doubt there are other favourites now. [Nineteenth-century popular writers: G.P.R. James (1801–1860) was a prolific writer, who wrote many historical novels inspired by Scott, including *Richelieu, Darnley, Mary of Burgundy* and *Henry Masterton*. Harrison Ainsworth (1805–1882) was another imitator of Scott, whose novels included *Sir John Chiverton, Jack Sheppard, Rookwood*, and *The Admirable Crichton*. Charles Lever (1806–1872) wrote novels set mainly in Ireland or on the Continent, including *Charles O'Malley, Roland Cashel* and *The Knight of Gwynne*. The Alexandre Dumas whom Sidgwick has in mind is probably Dumas the Elder (1802–1870), whose best-known works included *The Three Musketeers* and *The Count of Monte Cristo*.]

5. # The *Quarterly Review*, a journal that does not often clamour for rash and premature reforms, says ([Charles Badham, 'French Education'], 117 [1865], 418): 'Much more is it a thing to wonder at and be ashamed of, that, with such a literature as ours, the English lesson is still a desideratum in nearly all our great places of education, and that the future gentry of the country are left to pick up their mother tongue from the periodical works of fiction which are the bane of our youth, and the dread of every conscientious schoolmaster.'

We may add that the question, whether native literature is to be systematically taught, has long been decided in the affirmative both in France and in Germany.

6. # I allow that there are some exceptions to this statement; for instance, one of the most exquisite artists in language, Euripides, has been perhaps unduly depreciated. Still I think I have fairly described the general tendency.

7. #Mr Thring [Edward Thring. See his letter to the *Pall Mall Gazette*, included in this volume, pp. 254–5].

CHAPTER TWELVE

J.W. Hales

J.W. Hales (1836–1914) was, as we have seen, defeated by Henry Morley in the selection procedure for Professor of English Language and Literature at University College, London in 1865. Hales was a Fellow of Christ's College, Cambridge, who went on to spend most of his working life at King's College, London. He worked there first of all as a master in the school from 1867, and then the following year as a lecturer in the evening classes. In 1877, he became Professor of English Language and Literature, a post which he held until 1903. He also became a Professor of English at Bedford College, London (a women's college), was Examiner in English for the University of London, and from 1889 to 1893 was Clark Lecturer in English Literature at Trinity College, Cambridge.

Like Henry Sidgwick, Hales was a contributor to *Essays on a Liberal Education* (ed. F.W. Farrar) in 1867. Most of the essays in this work were concerned with aspects of classical education. Sidgwick, however, urged attention to English and to natural science, and there were separate essays on both these subjects. Hales's essay, 'The Teaching of English,' is concerned mainly with 'advocating the claims of the English language to a place among the subjects of English education.' By studying their own language, rather than two foreign, dead ones, boys would, amongst other benefits, arrive at a much better understanding of the workings of language, and learn to write their own language.

Towards the end of the essay, Hales moves on to literature, albeit briefly. For most boys, ordinary mortals rather than exceptional luminaries, Virgil would never be the object of voluntary study, whereas English literature might be. They should, therefore, be taught English literature, which would then provide them with material which they could return to throughout life. If a solid foundation of education based on English were laid at school, this might be later built upon, rather than being simply forgotten.

'The Teaching of English'

It may seem strange that there should exist any necessity for advocating the claims of the English language to a place among the subjects of English education. But this is not more strange than true. None of our better schools, with certain notable exceptions, dream of giving any attention to it. There is a gross want of adequate treatises dealing with it. No encouragement is given to the studying such treatises as these are: consequently, the Englishman grows up in mere ignorance of his native tongue. He can speak it, because he has heard it spoken around him from his earliest years. If he has been born and bred in what is called well-educated society, he speaks it 'with propriety.' He shudders duly when he hears it spoken with impropriety. But his accuracy is of a purely empirical kind. If society were suddenly to countenance and adopt some outrageous solecism, there would be nothing for him but to submit. The language might be changed just as manners are. Propriety in the one case is pretty much what it is in the other. In a word, the ordinary knowledge of English is altogether one of facts, not of principles; is thoroughly superficial, not fundamental. English is an unknown tongue in England. Something is known of French, of German, of Latin, of Greek – of most languages, with this remarkable exception.

But I propose now confining myself to a consideration of its absence, not from the country at large, but from our schools.

To begin with, how comes it to be conspicuous by its absence from our schools? While in French schools, French is taught; in German schools German; why is English excluded from English schools? The principal answers to such a question are: 1. That a deep-rooted prejudice in favour of Latin, as the basis of what linguistic education there is, has been handed down from generation to generation, ever since the Dark Ages. 2. That another triumphant judgment has pronounced that the English language is too irregular to be capable of being systematically taught. Such has been, and is, the power of these two prejudices, that the English language never has had, and has not that attention paid to it which, as the medium of communication between so many myriads of people, as the obvious and natural basis of their education, to say nothing of the great literature belonging to it, it might naturally expect and demand.

With regard to the predominant influence of Latin, I shall here say the less, because that subject is discussed at length in another essay contained in this volume.[1] But I must point out how detrimental to the study of our mother-tongue that monopoly has proved. It has thrown it completely into the shade, has dwarfed and stunted it. It has driven English away from the doors of our better schools, 'to seek a shelter in

159

some humbler shed.' The heir has met with no favour; a stranger has occupied his place. No doubt much of this fatal estrangement has been due to the narrow spirit in which the so-called classical studies have been pursued, which cannot live on in the light of a broader scholarship. In that linguistic dispensation which seems dawning, no language is called common or unclean. Latin can no longer stand aloof from the languages of modern literatures as if they were some inferior things, of suspicious contact. That old exclusive *régime* is gone by for ever; a truer, more catholic philology recognises the interest and importance of subjects that have for many centuries been regarded with the most languid indifference, or the supremest contempt. Thus, whatever conclusion may be arrived at respecting the time and attention that may be still given to the old monopolies, there can be no doubt that the manner of the study of these should be thoroughly revised; that that Pharisaic element which still lingers tenaciously, should be most carefully expelled from it; that modern languages, instead of being industriously ignored, should be perpetually recognised, both to illustrate, and to be illustrated. But till this current century, the influence of Latin has not only not been helpful; it has been deleterious. The classical languages have been the only wear; and so satisfied and delighted with them have men been, that not a native thread, not a home-dyed colour, not a domestic pattern could be tolerated. When in course of time the growth of a class that could never affect to be learned, but yet needed some instruction, made imperative the paying some slight attention to the language of the people, then most severely did the influence of Latin damage the rising study. The vulgar grammar-maker, dazzled by the glory of the ruling language, knew no better than to transfer to English the schemes which belonged to Latin. 'Jungebat mortua vivis.'[2] He never dreamt that the language, for which he was practising his rude grammatical midwifery, might have a character of its own, might require a scheme of its own. He knew, or thought he knew, what the grammar of any language ought to be, and he went about his work accordingly. What chance had our poor mother-tongue in the clutch of this Procrustes? The Theseus of linguistic science, the deliverer, was not born yet.[3] So the poor language got miserably tortured, and dislocated, and mangled. Who can wonder if it failed to thrive under such treatment? if it grew haggard and deformed? All the passers by were on the side of Procrustes; and, when the victim shrieked at some particularly cruel stretch of its limbs, they called it disorderly, reprobate, vicious. In these two ways then, the dominance of Latin proved baneful to the study of English; it for many a day made that study seem despicable and unworthy – in effect, suppressed it; and, when at last it could no longer be suppressed, then still it overshadowed and withered it.

Hence, then, arose that second prejudice mentioned above as obstructing the study. The language, coerced into subjection to laws foreign to its spirit and found rebellious, got a bad name, and the usual consequences followed. It became a proverb of refractoriness. It was anathematized as utterly lawless and hopeless. Its guardians did not understand its character; they judged it by their own narrow standard; they could not conceive that there were more things in heaven and earth than were dreamt of in their philosophy; they consigned this hapless nonconformist to profound neglect. It was mad, and there was no method in its madness, they said. They took no pains to investigate its hallucinations; these did not deserve so much consideration.

No wonder, then, the study of English did not prosper. Men were content with Latin; they were discontented with English. This discontent tended to perpetuate itself, as it restrained those investigations which, if pursued, would have put an end to it for ever. The language was in fact condemned without a hearing. And there was no appeal from the sentence of that ill–informed court which condemned it. The mere fact that the classics were in possession of the field, told with fearful power against the timid claimant for a place in it. Possession gives a vast advantage in all matters. In matters of education it gives an almost insuperable advantage. Parents are, for the most part, well content that their children should be educated much as they were. They are not likely to quarrel with the *propria quae maribus*[4] of their youth. Distance lends its enchantment to that and such like horrors. Moreover, as to what changes may be necessary, they put their trust in the schoolmaster to whom they confide their offspring. Schoolmasters as a race – whatever glorious exceptions there may be – cannot be expected to embrace readily alteration and change: they have learnt their part once and for all, and will not usually be anxious to unlearn or relearn it. They have mastered more or less adequately one particular system of training, and do not care to modify or abandon it. Then if we consider how extensive the machinery of any established system – how endless its handbooks, how enormous the literature belonging to it – we shall see yet more fully what a supreme advantage possession is, and what powerful incentives there always are to conservatism in educational subjects. The educational literature of English is yet in its very infancy.

These three considerations – the general unreadiness in schools to change their routine, the particular unreadiness to change it in the present case, the distinct reluctance to change it in favour of English, if any change at all were made – do, I think, sufficiently account for the forlorn condition in which the study of English now is, and distinctly show that no inference can fairly be drawn from that condition to the disparagement of its capabilities as an educational subject. They demonstrate emphatically that that condition is the misfortune of English, not its fault. The language has been weighed in the balances certainly, and found wanting; but this result has been due to the incompetence of the weighers. On this point I wish especially to insist, that English has never yet received a fair trial. Till very late years indeed it has been left in the hands of empirics and sciolists. Better men have occasionally wondered whether it was not worthy of more honourable treatment, whether it was in truth so bad as it was painted. 'Ex nostratibus aliqui,' writes Wallis in the seventeenth century, 'quod tamen mirandum est nescio quam perplexam somniant et intricationem linguae nostrae rationem, ut aegre possit grammaticae leges subire.'[5] But our countrymen went on dreaming so. In a word, our language has been, ever since the Norman Conquest, the victim of prejudices. For more than a century it was thrown altogether in the background; not till the close of the fourteenth century did boys in schools translate their Latin lessons into it; not till the latter half of the nineteenth have boys begun to study it.

* * *

But is English teachable? One might imagine the language showing the same indignation at such a question as the Jew showed when seemingly suspected of incapability of revenge. 'Hath not a Jew eyes? Hath not a Jew hands, organs, dimensions, senses, affections, passions, &c.?'[6] I have already explained how it comes to be possible that such a question can be asked. The inflectional virtues of Latin and Greek have blinded the world to all other virtues. English, mostly lacking them, has been stigmatised as wholly grammarless.[7] But inflections are not the soul of grammar. A language does not become ungrammatical when it passes out of that stage. The main function of grammar is concerned with more perpetual and imperishable matters. That function ceases only when a language loses its articulateness – ceases to serve for the expression of thought – ceases to be a language. However deficient the English language may be in case-endings and such grammatical landmarks, – in power of expression, in delicacy, in elasticity, in versatility, it is not deficient. So that it presents endless varieties of that grammatical culminating subject of inquiry and interest – the sentence. What an inestimable, inexhaustible mine of study is here! Then the very compositeness of the language adapts it singularly well for the teacher's use. It furnishes him at once with abundant material. He must be dull indeed who can be at a loss for subjects for lessons in English. No doubt, should English once take its place as a vulgar school-subject, innumerable text-books would quickly spring into existence. Consider of what a long growth our existing Latin and Greek school-book literature is; and consider how unsatisfactory it still is!

What I should wish to propose is, that the linguistic studies of all our schools should begin with English, should then proceed with the dead languages in the case of boys who are likely to have leisure to study them to any profit, and in other cases should proceed with English and living languages.

The study of language in English schools should begin with English – should begin at home. The way of learning is, and must be, rough and thorny; and I do not expect what I now propose will make it smooth and all roses. But if the road can be improved at all, if but a few flowers can be got to grow along it, and the torn feet can find a moment's respite, this is well worth the doing. Obviously, what is most earnestly to be wished for and aimed at in the formal commencement of a child's education, is to excite his interest in his studies – to give them some meaning to him, let him have some inkling of their use. Their full meaning will not be revealed to him for many a year; that will grow more and more clear to him all his life long, if he develops into a thoughtful man. But some meaning, some practical significance his studies must have for him from the beginning, if he is to pursue them with pleasure – that is, with the highest degree of profit. He cannot stretch a hand through time to catch the far off interest of years. If, then, he is to learn intelligibly, he must see that there is some sense in his studies, that these are not mere arbitrary burdens laid on his youthful shoulders. Otherwise, things will go but drearily with him. He will repeat with the mouth, not with the understanding. His memory will be well stocked; but what is vastly more important, his mind will remain listless. Now, if we introduce a boy to the study of language by putting into his hands a Latin grammar and bidding him master the declensions, how will the case stand with him? How does the case stand with him? What wretched drudgery those early schooldays are! Is it one of the 'penalties of Adam'[8] that they should be so? Is it altogether boys' fault that their elementary tutors find them so recalcitrant? Is it wholly through the dulness of their nature that they do not love the Conjugations at first sight, or conceive a passionate attachment for the Irregular Verbs? What a queer thing their nature would be if it did kindle in them either flame! At all events, it does not. And the ordinary boy's early life is spent in a war of independence against his Primer. What is the genitive case of the Third Declension to him, or he to it? Then, for the teacher, is the work more inspiriting for him? Can his enthusiasm relieve and dissipate the direful tedium? Can he brighten these lacklustre exercises?

> Pater ipse colendi
> Haud facilem esse viam voluit.[9]

'Through me you pass into the city of woe,' might well be inscribed over the doorway of the lower departments of our classical schools. 'All hope abandon, ye who enter here.'[10]

I venture to believe that if the commencement of the classics were postponed for a while, and the time so saved devoted to some attention to English, great advantage would accrue. Consider how expedient and profitable it is to turn to account the boy's powers of observation, to enlist them in the service of his education. Why not, then, if you wish to provoke him to the study of language, bring them to bear on the language he hears spoken around him? Here is a world full of interest all round him. Why not encourage him to gaze well at it and air his nascent faculties there, instead of rudely dragging him forth into a *terra incognita*, where to him prevails outer darkness? Can such a wild, precipitate relegation profit? You divorce peremptorily his studies and his daily life, so that he cannot discern any sign of any association between them. You dismiss him into a far country amongst voices that are strange and harsh to his young ears. Why not rather win him to listen to the voices that speak around him? Are the words they utter not profitable for doctrine? Do they contain no lessons that are worth the learning? Are they, too, not the constituents of a mighty language?

Let his study of language begin with his native language. Let his first lessons in that science be based on that language which is already to some extent familiar to him – illustrated, interpreted, made meaning by that. Surely, this is the rational course. Having gathered so from the specimen that lies ready to hand, some notion of what a language is, let him, if you please, proceed to another language, dead or living.... .

* * *

... The 'compound sentence' in Latin is studied at several of our higher schools with much success. Thorough able teaching of a high intelligent sort is brought to bear upon it, and the fruit is good. What was dark, is illumined. But in schools of a much lower social order, the 'analysis of sentences' has been proved to be a perfectly possible lesson-subject for pupils of no considerable age. Before the adoption of the Revised Code,[11] it was very commonly taught in National and British Schools,[12] and found to be within the reach of pupils who enjoyed so few out-of-school advantages as do the children who attend them.

I venture to believe then, that by beginning our study of language with English, and beginning it in the above-sketched way, great gain might be secured both in respect of the study of language, and also in respect of general intellectual awakening and activity. 'We free our language,' says Ben Jonson, advocating the claim of the national tongue to some formal attention and treatment, 'from the opinion of rudeness and barbarism, wherewith it is mistaken to be diseased; we show the copy of it and matchableness with other tongues; *we ripen the wits of our own children and youth the sooner by it, and advance their knowledge.*'[13] And yet Jonson knew no truer mode of dealing with English than binding it to the framework of the Latin grammars of his time, and constraining it into the same shape. He saw clearly enough what facilities of education were being wasted, what pearls were being trodden under foot. But he, and many another thinker[14] before and since, saw and deplored this wilful waste (what woeful want comes of it!) in vain.

In schools where, rightly or wrongly, Latin and Greek form the staple of the studies, I am convinced those languages would thrive the better, if the medium through which they are taught were better understood. At present we teach *ignotum per ignotius*.[15] Our grandfathers avowedly followed the same method with regard to Greek. The grammars of that tongue over which they groaned and detested life, were written in Latin. The old lexicons rendered in Latin the meanings of the words which that bewildered young ancestry 'looked out.' That remarkable arrangement has been repealed. But has the young student of to-day a much superior knowledge of the now current, the obvious, medium of instruction? May not his posterity wonder how he could make satisfactory progress, when he understood so meagrely the language in which his learning was tendered to him? We teach our children to walk, before we send them to the dancing-master. How obscure, how incomprehensible, must be, and is, a great part of the school-books in vogue, because the users of them have not been taught something of their mother-tongue! How can a boy be expected to know what a case is – what is meant by the subject, by the predicate of a sentence, by a dialect, by illative, causal, and other innumerable like terms which abound in his grammar, if he is not taught? An intelligent boy, we are told, will 'pick up' these important bits of knowledge.[16] But what of the boys that are not intelligent? And is their name unit or legion? And in the case of the intelligent boy, is this 'picking up' method quite safe and satisfactory? Will his ideas be sufficiently clear and lucid, or will they not rather be somewhat obscure and turbid? Yet in these matters definiteness and accuracy are essential. A confused notion is worse than none; and the clever boy, as will happen under some systems of education, is worse off than the dullard.

In schools whose pupils are not destined to proceed from them to a University, or to a life of studious leisure and opportunity, English should, I think, be made the prominent linguistic and literary study. Their time is too limited for any pretence at mastering Latin and Greek, and should not be squandered *operose nihil agendo*.[17] What hope could they have of ever enjoying Virgil in the original? That poet will but become to their imagination the sort of magician – the sayer of dark sentences – that he was to the Middle Ages. They will dig but little gold from that profound mine: they cannot give to this work the necessary *labor improbus*.[18]

> Διώκει παῖς ποτανὸν ὄρνιν,
> πόλει πρόστριμμ' ἄφερτον ἐνθείς,[19]

for is not the public detriment grievous, when the energies of young scholars are misdirected and wasted? But it may be said that though the youth cannot reach the goal, yet the running is good for him. This is quite true; but there are goals and goals, and each one with its own course, its own difficulties, its own advantages. Which one is the best for this youth? I may presume to suggest that that study has many recommendations, which seems most possible to pursue in what moments of leisure the student may have in after life. Would there be much hope of his returning to his Virgil, and pushing on his studies in that direction? (Of course I speak of the ordinary mortal, and not of any exceptional luminary.) I think not. His imperfect knowledge of the language, coupled with its excessive difficulty, his ignorance of the ideas which permeate and inspire it, his consequent incompetence to appreciate and sympathize with its sentiment and tone, seem to render any such hope preposterous. For him in all truth it is

> not better done, as others use,
> To sport with Amaryllis in the shade,
> Or with the tangles of Neaera's hair.[20]

He does not know how to conduct himself before such presences. He knows nothing of their classical ways and arts. To him they seem uninteresting and frigid. In fact, he is not at all at his ease in their society, he cannot converse naturally with them, justly estimate and admire their calm placid beauty, their noble, dignified grace. He must find society more accordant with his tastes and abilities. For such an one, surely his native language and literature should be made the foundations of his linguistic and literary education. On these he will be able to build subsequently, to continue the structure commenced at school:- and consider how broad these foundations are. It is not unfrequently said that these subjects do not present sufficient difficulties to the learner. This is an ancient traditional objection, which surely cannot survive much longer. It is the voice of times that knew nothing whatever about the English tongue, that did not perceive it had idioms and characteristics of its own; in whose mind familiarity had bred contempt. I suppose to a Greek, the use of those fine, subtle particles, whose precise influence is to us so difficult to determine, seemed perfectly obvious and natural.

Was Virgil conscious how well-nigh insuperable the language he wrote was, what a world of trouble his ablatives were creating for his future readers, what a forest of *cruces*? Should English ever become a dead language (a wholly improbable supposition) would it be thought devoid of difficulties? Would the scholiasts and commentators find no place for their acumen? Indeed, are they now without work, the editors of our English classics, the authors of treatises on our English language? Is Shakespeare's diction always so transparent? Can the reader never help understanding what Milton means? To go back to earlier English writings, any one who opens Mr Morris's *Specimens of Early English*,[21] for instance, may soon encounter difficulties in abundance, difficulties not only of a verbal kind. But I have already, above, glanced at this accusation that English is ill-adapted for the teacher's purposes. I do not think it has much weight.

Much more might be said on this subject. But I shall not now attempt to say it. I shall be now content if in any way I have excited or fostered a doubt in any reader's mind as to the wisdom of the educational course at present followed in this country, – as to whether we avail ourselves satisfactorily of the means at our service, or rather, strangely ignore and neglect them.

Notes

1. Henry Sidgwick, 'The Theory of Classical Education,' extracts from which are included in this volume, pp. 151–7.
2. 'He joined the dead to the living' (Virgil, *Aeneid*, viii.485).
3. In Greek legend, Procrustes was a robber who laid all who came into his hands in an iron bed. They were then either stretched or had limbs shortened until they fitted the bed. Procrustes was finally killed by Theseus, here seen as the deliverer of English.
4. A rule of grammar: 'Propria quae maribus tribuuntur' – You may call those things masculine which appertain to males. This became the title of a popular Latin grammar.
5. 'It is a wonder, which I however do not understand, that some of our countrymen foolishly dream that the nature of our language is so confused and complicated that it can hardly submit to grammatical rules' (John Wallis, *Grammatica Linguae Anglicanae*, 1653).
6. *The Merchant of Venice*, III.i.55–7.
7. # [George] Gascoyne in his 'Steele Glass' (1576) bids his readers pray –
   That Grammar grudge not at our English tong
   Because it stands by monosyllaba
   And cannot be declined as others are.
8. Adam was banished from Eden with the curse, 'In the sweat of they face shalt thou eat bread' (Genesis, iii.19).
9. For he, the sire, ordained it so to be,
   Nor willed earth's harvests to be garnered free. (Virgil, *Georgics*, i.121.)

10. Dante, *The Divine Comedy*, 'Inferno,' iii.8–9.
11. i.e. before 1862.
12. Schools run by the National Society for Promoting the Education of the Poor in the Principles of the Established Church, and its Non-Conformist rival, the British and Foreign School Society.
13. Ben Jonson, *The English Grammar*, Preface. The date of the first edition is not known, but it was included in Jonson's *Works* (1640).
14. # See quotations from [Richard] Mulcaster's *Elementarie* (1582), and [John] Brinsley's *Grammar School* (1612) in *Education in Early England*, by F.J. Furnivall (1867).
15. the unknown through the even more unknown.
16. # What tutor has not perpetually to notice and deplore his pupil's ignorance of English? I have again and again found errors in the compositions of pupils, at the University and elsewhere, that sprang solely from inability to understand the English original.
17. busily engaged in doing nothing (Seneca, *De Brevitate Vitae*, I.xiii).
18. sustained work.
19. Like a boy chasing a winged bird,
    He brings woe on all his people (Aeschylus, *Agamemnon*, 394–5).
20. Milton, 'Lycidas,' 67–9.
21. Richard Morris, *Specimens of Early English* (1866).

CHAPTER THIRTEEN

John Seeley

Sir John Seeley (1834–1895) was educated at the City of London School and Christ's College, Cambridge. He graduated in the Cambridge classical tripos in 1857, then worked there briefly as a classical lecturer. In 1861, he returned to the City of London School as composition master, but left there before his friend, E.A. Abbott was appointed headmaster, and moved on to become Professor of Latin at University College, London in 1863. In 1865, while at University College, Seeley was at the centre of a storm of controversy over *Ecce Homo*, a study which he wrote of the life and teaching of Jesus. In 1869, he followed Charles Kingsley as Professor of Modern History at Cambridge, specializing in modern political history. It is as a historian that Seeley is principally remembered.

Seeley allied himself with the Broad Church in matters of theology, enthusiastically espousing the idea of a National Church. Teaching English literature in schools was an effective way of providing the culture that such a National Church required.

This article was first published in *Macmillan's Magazine* 17 (1868), when Seeley was still Professor of Latin at University College. He is much more aware than most of the writers on English studies in the mid-nineteenth century of the need to educate 'the whole nation,' and sees that education will have to be radically different from what it has been hitherto. It is in this new educational landscape that English comes into its own.

'English in Schools'

* *
* *

… All that a gentleman asks of a schoolmaster for his son is booklearning; the higher moral education, almost all that is included under the word 'cultivation,' he furnishes himself, by his own example, by the society, by the books in the midst of which his children are reared. But the problem before us now is to educate the whole nation. We have to educate a class who have none of these domestic traditions, no inherited refinement, no common stock of literature forming an intellectual atmosphere around every child. If we teach this class what we have hitherto taught the other class, the result will not be the same. For them the schoolmaster must do much more, because the parents and the home have done much less. To them he must become a kind of priest or missionary of culture. He must no longer content himself with imparting naked facts, or rules, or book-learning, as though he taught those who are surrounded with other ennobling and refining influences. On the contrary, he must consider that just so much enlightenment, breadth of view, liberality, and magnanimity as he can contrive to impart to his pupils, just so much and no more will they carry with them into the world. If then the present classical system is inadequate already as the instrument of education to a class, much more will it be found inadequate to the civilizing of a nation.

*   *
  *

… I am pleading for a class which have no intellectual atmosphere around them; in the conversation to which they listen there is no light or air for the soul's growth; it is a uniform gloomy element of joyless labour, bewildering detail, broken with scarcely a gleam of purpose or principle. Such a boy goes to school, and at fourteen he is taken away, having read a book and a half of Caesar's *Commentaries*, two or three epistles of Ovid, and a book of Xenophon. In his mind, at the end of this time, what images have been deposited? There are some chaotic conceptions of Caesar exhorting his troops, and of Grecian soldiers marching indefinitely through Asia at the rate of so many parasangs a day. What happened when these soldiers reached their destination it is likely enough he has never found out, because that is recorded in another part of the book. Towards cultivating his imagination and taste, towards enlarging his contemplations, this is all that has been done, whatever may have been done for his reason and memory. This is all that has been done in the only years of his life that are redeemed from money-making, the only years in which the missionaries of civility and cultivation can reach him. He goes back to the mill with no conception gained of a larger life, of a freer and clearer atmosphere, sharpened, if you will, a little, but cultivated not at all.

Even this statement is hardly strong enough. It is bad that his education should not have put him in the way of becoming a thoughtful and cultivated man. But that it should leave him in total ignorance of the literature of his own country is more; and worse than this, it means that he is left not merely uncultivated, but absolutely uncivilized. He can have no link whatever with the past, he can have no citizenship, no country. Classical studies may make a man intellectual, but the study of the native literature has a moral effect as well. It is the true ground and foundation of patriotism. Now that the Americans, the Germans, the Italians, are almost drunk with the sense of their national greatness, it would surely be well if our own population could be brought to think of England otherwise than as a country where wages are low, manners very cold, the struggle for life intolerably severe. In the past we might find food for self-respect; surely we might find something interesting to tell our boys about their ancestors. We too are a great historic nation; we too have 'titles manifold.' This country is not some newly-discovered island in the Northern seas; even this London is no mere dreary collection of shops. It is literally true that in this city, in which I am now speaking to you, *Hamlet* was first brought out. The Long Parliament sat within two miles of you; Milton is buried in Cripplegate Church. These are simple facts, but it is the province of education to make them sink into the mind, and influence the character. The name of Milton sounds like any other name to those who have not pondered over his verses. I call that man uncivilized who is not connected with the past through the state in which he lives, and sympathy with the great men that have lived in it. And that the English people in general, and not merely a small class of them, should be civilized in this sense, does not seem to me a Utopian dream. Ordinary English boys seem to me quite capable of appreciating great thoughts. They seem to me quite capable of taking delight in the achievements and writings of their ancestors. No doubt they are liable to be led astray; they will not take most naturally to the best books; a little gentle constraint, as I have said, has to be used; their books must be prescribed for them at first, until the effort of coping with a great writer, the labour of following a high flight, has begun to be felt as invigorating and refreshing. But the chief thing they want is the opportunity and the guidance. The good books do not fall in their way, and they have no one to tell them what is good. What then might they not do, what growth in liberality and magnanimity might we not expect from them, if for four years of boyhood at least such books were forced into their hands, and such guidance were given to them?

Yet, certainly, if we only looked around us it might seem a most Utopian dream. If we judged of what can be done by what has hitherto been done, we should pronounce it impossible that the lower half of our population could ever receive either cultivation or civilization, we should conclude that things must remain always as they have so long continued, and that a small number of cultivated men will always live in England in the midst of a vast half-barbarous population. We should think ourselves happy that this half-barbarous multitude belongs to the better class of barbarians, that it is hard-working, tolerably honest and good-natured, and that its worst faults are narrowness and dulness. What higher hopes could we form if we looked at the lower section of the middle class, and marked the small traces left upon the ordinary Englishman by several years of education? He has all the good qualities that nature gave him; he is industrious, conscientious, benevolent, persevering. But what remains to him of his education? What marks him out as civilized? Has he any high or liberal pleasures? Has he any intellectual dignity, any breadth of view? Does he ever generalize, ever philosophize? Has he any worthy end in life, any ideal? Or does he creep and labour, and 'discuss the sewage question,' and provide for his family?

From the past of our country, from the masterpieces of our literature, would come most naturally the influence that might give back to the Englishman his self-respect. All the pride and strength of an aristocracy comes from the sense of ancestry, and every member of a historic nation, may have something of this sense and something of the pride that springs from it. He has but to make himself familiar with the past. There is something in what Mr Carlyle says, that the true Bible of every nation is its own history. And these same English people whose deficiencies we have been lamenting, are at the same time – the coincidence is worth noting[1] – singularly ignorant and incurious about English history... .

*
* *

Notes

1.   The word in the original text is 'nothing,' but the sense demands 'noting.'

CHAPTER FOURTEEN

E.A. Abbott

E.A. Abbott (1838–1926) had been briefly a Fellow of St John's College, Cambridge, but had resigned when he married. In 1865, at the early age of 26, he had become headmaster of the City of London School. There he introduced English literature throughout the school, though pupils also continued with classics. Each term the sixth form studied one Greek play and one Shakespeare play. He introduced some comparative philology, and even taught some of his senior pupils Sanskrit. Abbott was a Church of England clergyman, closely identified with the Broad Church, and was a friend of Sir John Seeley, a leading Broad Church figure. In addition to his work as a headmaster, he published a number of books, including studies of the gospels, sermons, an edition of Bacon's *Essays*, a study of John Henry Newman, text-books, and practical books on the teaching of Latin, as well as English language and composition.

This article appeared in 1868 in *Macmillan's Magazine*, which also published articles on English studies by Seeley and Huxley at about this time. Abbott approached the question of English very much from a schools' perspective, and he made it clear that he was thinking primarily of middle-class schools. English, as Campbell had written forty years earlier, was a particularly appropriate subject for boys who would leave school at fifteen or sixteen, 'intended for commercial pursuits.' It would help to devulgarize them. At the same time, like Maurice in his inaugural address at King's College, he made it clear that he was not trying to oust Latin and Greek completely.

Abbott was concerned to counter charges that English was all about cramming, and he clearly saw Civil Service examinations as one of the main reasons why the subject had come to be regarded in this way. He had little interest in teaching the history of English literature – a fruitful field for the crammers. Instead, in the tradition of Coleridge, Maurice and Kingsley, he argued for the teaching of whole texts.

'The Teaching of English'

The following remarks, concerning the teaching of English, can lay no claim whatever to attention except so far as they are the results of experience. It will, therefore, be best to entrust the care of theories to the more able hands of Professor Seeley, whose suggestions originated the practice described below; and, plunging at once into work, to imagine our class before us, the books open (say a play of Shakespeare, *Richard II*, for example), the boys expectant, and the master ready. It is quite certain, however, that the latter fiction – I mean the readiness of the master – will depend to some extent upon the distinctness of his conception of his object. Let us, therefore, apologize for keeping the class and our visitors a few moments waiting while, without theorizing whether the study of English be desirable, or necessary, or worthless, we ask ourselves what object we wish to attain by this study.

I answer, not the knowledge of *words*, or of the laws of *words* (except in a secondary degree), but, in the first place, the knowledge of *thoughts* and the power of *thinking*, and, in the second place, the attainment of the idea of 'a book,' as a work of art.

If English is to be regarded merely as an instrument for training boys as the classical languages train them, from that point of view English does very imperfectly what Latin and Greek do far more perfectly; and, should I ever be converted to that belief, I would at once give up English studies altogether.

There has been a great deal of exaggeration on this subject. The merit of the classical languages, as a method of training, when tolerably well taught, is precisely that which Mr Lowe, in his remarkable speech at Liverpool, refused to recognise in them.[1] They force boys to 'weigh probabilities.' Out of the ten or twenty meanings of the Latin word 'ago' found in a dictionary, a boy must select the right meaning by 'weighing probabilities' and pondering the context. Inflections give additional scope for the hunting and digging faculties. A boy has to disentomb nominatives, hunt after accusatives, eliminate all manner of other possible constructions of a dative until he is forced to the 'dativus commodi,' and the like. Surely no one will maintain that in these respects the training afforded to English boys by their own uninflected language is equal to the training afforded by Latin or Greek.

Hence the study of English as a study of *words* will be, comparatively speaking at all events, a failure, and likely also to superinduce a petty word-criticizing spirit of reading which is to be avoided. For these reasons, both etymology and grammar ought, in the study of English, to be kept in strict subordination to the study of thought. The great question ought always to be, 'What does the author mean?' and the continual requirement from the pupils ought to be, 'Put the meaning exactly into your own words.' Of course, directly the question is asked, 'What does the author mean?' grammar and etymology will at once step in under their proper ancillary character, doubly valuable because used as servants. They will not merely afford their usual mental training, they will also disabuse boys of the notion that grammar and etymology are infernal machines destined for their torture.

Wherever grammar and etymology illustrate the laws of thought, there they have their place in English studies; but where they do not illustrate, or cannot be made to appear to boys to illustrate thought (as for instance where etymology simply illustrates the laws of euphony), they ought to be carefully kept out of sight. Thus, if we take *Richard II* (I.ii), 'Thou art a traitor and a miscreant,' I should think the derivation of 'miscreant' far more important than that of 'traitor,' and the process of thought traceable in the former or even in the latter) word far more important than the law which drops the *d* in both words. In the same passage, a few lines above, 'Each day still better other's happiness,' if you were to ask young boys what is the meaning of the verse, and then, when some careless boys would show (as I think some would show, and know that some have shown) that they had misunderstood it, were to ask them to parse 'better,' I think even the average boy, instead of feeling aggrieved by the question, would have a new light shed upon parsing and grammar, on finding their aid useful for the understanding even of his native language.

But now I come to the great objection, which is, as I think, felt by many old experienced schoolmasters. 'There is no work,' they say, 'no digging, in all this; the boys cannot get it up; there's nothing to get up – no lexicon to be turned over, no grammar to be thumbed; the masters must lecture the boys; the boys are merely the recipients, and, at best, repeaters of what they have received.'

I don't think this is so. It is true there will be comparatively little turning over dictionaries and very little use of grammars in preparing an English lesson. But is it not a most valuable result that boys should be taught that the mere looking-out of words does not constitute mental work? Is it not work for boys that they should be forced to *think*, that they should be obliged to turn over, not lexicons, but *thoughts*, and perpetually be compelled to ask themselves, 'Do I understand this?'

But it may be said, 'You cannot get boys to do this.' On the contrary, – and this is almost the only point on which I speak with perfect confidence, – I am sure you can. Boys may not do it at first; but as soon as they perceive the kind of questions which they must be prepared to answer, they will work most thoroughly and satisfactorily in preparation. The great business of the master will be to prevent them from working too hard, and from accumulating a number of pieces of philological and grammatical information which, as not tending to illustrate the meaning of the author, must be stigmatized as *cram*. The derivations alone of the words in a single play of Shakespeare would take several hours of a boy's time. Therefore the master will not merely, with great self-denial, suppress his rising inclination to pour out his own superfluous knowledge, and to convert words into pegs whereon to hang his dissertations, he will also encourage his pupils to keep to the point, and nothing but the point, directing their labours (and this will be absolutely indispensable at first) by giving them at the conclusion of every lesson some indications of the difficulties which they must be prepared to solve in the next lesson. In a word, there must be this understanding between master and pupils: that the former, though he may ask more, is to be contented if the latter shows that he understands exactly what his author means, and has formed an opinion about the truth or falsehood of it. Other questions may be asked, but warning should be given of them beforehand.

And now let us return to our pupils whom we left patiently perusing their *Richard II*. Last week they received notice of the questions that would be asked, with the exception of those that arise natuarally from the passage, most of which they are expected to anticipate without warning. I turn to the bottom boy. '"The which he hath detain'd for lewd employments." – What was the original meaning of the word "lewd"?' He answers, or ought to answer (for notice has been given of this question), as his dictionary tells him, 'connected with the laity.' 'What process of thought is traceable in the change of meaning which the word has undergone?' He cannot answer: the question passes to the top, and you are told that 'it was thought that the laity were not so good as the clergy, and so the name came to be considered a reproach.' Perhaps you extract from another boy that 'by degrees the word came to express that particular kind of badness which seemed most unclerical.'

That is of the nature of a luxury. We pass to a more solid question:

> 'We thank you both: yet one but flatters us
> As well appeareth by the cause you come.

Explain the construction in the second line. Put the argument into the form of a syllogism, showing the suppressed major. Is it correct or incorrect?' This question brings a clear-headed boy to the top, or near it, and we pass on:

'That he did plot the Duke of Gloster's death
Suggest his soon-believing adversaries,
And consequently like a traitor coward
Sluic'd out his innocent blood.

Illustrate, by the derivations of the words, the Shakespearian use of "suggest" and "consequently."

That which in mean men we entitle patience
Is pale cold cowardice in noble breasts.

Give reasons for justifying or condemning this maxim. What are the two faulty extremes between which lies the virtue patience? What is the mean between cowardice and the other faulty extreme? "Yet can I not of such tame patience boast." – 'What is the difference between "patience" and "tameness", "tameness" and "cowardice"?'

Then come two questions of which notice has been given. 'What marked difference is there between Richard's language before and after his return from Ireland? Explain it. What is there in common between Hamlet and Richard?' After obtaining satisfactory answers evincing thought and study, and coming not far short of the mark, you can, if the class seems worthy of the information, guide them, by a series of searching questions carefully arranged, to a more complete answer than they have been able, unassisted, to give.

Then, passing to the subject of rhythm – '"As near as I could sift him in that argument." – is there any rule with reference to the number of syllables in a Shakespearian line? How would you scan this verse?

Setting aside his blood's high royalty,
And let him be no kinsman to my liege,
I do defy him, and I spit at him.
Call him a slanderous villain and a coward,
Which to maintain I would allow him odds
And meet him, were I tied to run afoot.

Analyse this sentence, pointing out the main proposition or propositions, parsing "setting" and "let," and expressing the whole sentence in a number of affirmative and conditional sentences.

Ere my tongue
Shall wound mine honour with such feeble wrong
Or sound so base a parle, my teeth shall tear
The slavish motive of recanting fear.

Expand the metaphor contained in the two first lines into its simile. Is it in good taste? Give reasons for your answer. Explain the meaning of "feeble wrong." Give the derivations and meaning of "parle." What is

177

the metaphor in "sound so base a parle?" What is the derivation of "motive," and how does the derivation explain the Shakespearian and the present use of the word?'

I have foreborne, for space's sake, to show how the answers to such questions, even when not entirely satisfactory, would give evidence of preparation, above all of mental not merely manual book-thumbing preparation, and would afford to the teacher a test of the diligence of his pupils as well as a means of developing their intelligence. Many may think these questions absurdly easy. I should be glad if they were found so; but my experience indicates that boys ranging in age from thirteen to sixteen will not find such questions too easy, and that for younger boys much easier questions would be necessary.

* *
*

I cannot quit this part of my subject without expressing my very strong belief that a knowledge of the processes of induction and deduction, and of the relation between a metaphor and simile, and the manner in which the latter is expanded into the former, ought to be communicated to boys earlier than is now customary. We want to teach boys to think. Now thought has metaphors for its materials, logic for its tools. And therefore to set boys on the study of thought without a knowledge of logic or of metaphor is to set them building a castle of shifting sand, – soon built, soon unbuilt. It is possible to teach 1. the processes by which we arrive at the knowledge, or what we call the knowledge, of general and particular propositions; 2. the stages of such processes in which we are most liable to be deceived; 3. a few of the commonest fallacies corresponding to those different stages, without making boys 'smatterers;' and if a teacher knows what he wants to teach, and confines himself to it, it may be taught in an hour and a half, and tested every day throughout the term. As regards metaphors, boys should be made not merely to get up the definition of 'metaphor' and 'simile,' which is of little or no use by itself, but, as soon as they have attained the idea of proportion, to expand each metaphor into its simile by supplying the one or two missing terms of the proportion. Thus, 'the ship ploughs the sea.' 'How many terms are here given?' 'Three.' 'How many do you want for the simile?' 'Four.' 'Supply the missing term, and give the whole proportion.' 'As the plough is to the land, so is the ship to the sea.' And in 'the mountain frowns,' the two missing terms could of course be supplied in the same way. This might be taught thoroughly to upwards of sixty boys, between the ages of eleven and fourteen, in less than half an hour; and it would be difficult to overvalue such a stimulant and test of intelligence.

After receiving this preliminary information, a boy would need nothing more in order to prepare for his English lesson but a dictionary and a handbook. I daresay it is possible to find many faults in all existing dictionaries and handbooks, particularly in dictionaries; but still, with such treatises as Dr Angus's *Handbook*[2] and Chambers's *Etymological Dictionary*,[3] a teacher can work away pretty well. And when I hear the cry for English teaching met with the cry for English text-books, I am tempted to think of the old proverb about the workman who found fault with his tools.

This brings us to the question of text-books, by which I mean authors edited with notes. I frankly avow that, unless they give very little and very carefully-selected information, they seem to me worse than useless. Of course I admit that for Early English or even for Elizabethan writers text-books are desirable. But it is evident to me that, if an English book is edited with answers to all questions that can fairly be asked, all obscurities explained, all necessity for thought removed, then, though such books may exactly suit crammers for Civil Service examinations, they are useless for us; there is an end of the training which we desire. The notes ought only to illustrate historical questions, explain archaic words or idioms, give parallel passages, and now and then hints to direct the reader to the meaning of a very difficult passage. They ought not to explain fully any obscurities, nor paraphrase any sentences, nor completely elucidate any thoughts.

I do not believe in 'extracts' or 'specimens,' except where Early English is being studied more for the words than the thoughts. In different schools the matter may present itself under different aspects; but at many middle-class schools there must always be a great number of boys who may get no idea of literature or of the meaning of 'a book' at home, and it therefore seems necessary that they should have the opportunity of acquiring that idea at school. Even in the lowest classes I should prefer to use a book that should contain tales or poems complete in themselves, however short.

For the same reason, I should not trouble myself much about the 'History of English Literature,' at all events till the pupils had reached the highest classes in the school, when such a study would imply something more than mere cram. I cannot help thinking that, in the middle and at the bottom of most schools, the study of a 'history of literature' would be little more than ornamental cram. Besides, there is the question of time. If it could be combined with the study of authors, well; but where could you find the time?

I would have each of the lower classes working at two subjects, one a longer book for home reading, the other a short poem, for school-work. The home book should be studied for the book as a whole; boys should not be troubled with detail, but merely be examined occasionally in the plot, characters, &c. in such a way as to bring out for them the drift of the book and purpose of the author. The shorter poem should be thoroughly studied with all minutest details. The home-work should teach boys what is literature, the school-work what is thought. A beginning might be made with *Robinson Crusoe* and Byron's 'Sennacherib.' or some other short, intelligible, and powerful poem; then *Ivanhoe* and 'The Armada'; then Plutarch's 'Coriolanus' and the *Horatius Cocles*, Plutarch's 'Julius Caesar and Gray's 'Ruin seize thee'; Plutarch's 'Agis and Cleomenes' and 'The Battle of Ivry'; then *Marmion*; then the 'Allegro' and 'Penseroso,' or *Comus* then (in the class in which those boys leave who are intended for commercial pursuits) Pope's *Iliad*; then part of the *Paradise Lost*; then part of the *Fairy Queen*; then Chaucer's 'Knight's Tale' or Dante's 'Inferno' (in English) or the *In Memoriam*, or some of the poems of Dryden, Pope, or Johnson. It would be well, if time could be found for it, to include in the subjects of the highest class some specimens of Early English. For though the study of Early English approximates to the classical studies, yet it cannot be denied that the philological knowledge obtained from the study of Early English pronouns, and of the employment of the subjunctive, and an acquaintance with the obstacles, impediments, and barrenness which made Early English what it was, contribute in no slight degree to the exact understanding of the expressions of Elizabethan and of Modern English.

A play of Shakespeare might be read during another term throughout almost every class in the school. Shakespeare and Plutarch's *Lives* are very devulgarizing books, and I should like every boy who leaves a middle-class school for business at the age of fifteen, suppose, or sixteen, to have read three or four plays of Shakespeare, three or four noble poems, and three or four nobly-written lives of noble Greeks and Romans. I should therefore like to see Plutarch's *Lives* in the hands of every English schoolboy; or, if it were necessary to make a selection, those biographies which best illustrate one's 'duty toward one's country.'

Now let me answer one objection. It may be said, 'The object you have described is desirable, but can be attained by the study of Latin and Greek, and does not necessitate the study of English. There are metaphors and syllogisms, thoughts as well as words, in the classical languages, and not in English merely. Why cannot all this be done in Latin and Greek?'

I answer, 'Is it done?' Can any classical master deny that often, when he has wished to elucidate the thought of his author, some enveloping difficulty of οὐ or μή has extinguished the thought in a mist of words? Of course you meant to point out to your pupils that, from one point of view, the Ilissus is as important as, or more important than, the Mississippi; that whether it be Brasidas with five hundred men, or Napoleon with five hundred thousand, it matters nothing as regards the principles on which cities and battles are won or lost: you intended, no doubt, to make your pupils feel the exquisite Sophoclean irony which sets poor strutting Oedipus spinning like a cockchafer for the amusement of gods and men; but did you? I am afraid that you have almost persuaded yourself that you did; but a regard for truth must induce you to confess, on second thoughts, that Brasidas was smothered in his case, and the Sophoclean irony extinguished by a tribrach in the fifth foot. Or, if you thought of it, you found it was getting late, and you could not do your forty lines, or your page and a half, unless you 'kept to the point.'

Classical scholars are like Alpine travellers, who ascend a mountain on the pretext of a glorious prospect, or scientific observations; but ninety-nine out of a hundred climbers find that when they have reached the top they are too tired to see anything, and that it is so late that there is nothing to see; and then, coming down again by the most difficult way they can select, they secretly confide to their most intimate friends their private conviction that the exercise is the great thing after all.

No doubt Latin and Greek might be taught much better than they often are. I do not envy the teacher who can teach them, without obliging his pupils to 'weigh probabilities;' but, for the study of thought, English is evidently more ready to our hand, because in other languages that study cannot commence till they have been translated into English.

I do not think that English can ever supersede or do the work of Latin and Greek, even for boys who leave school at the early age of fifteen. But, on the other hand, I venture to suggest that Latin and Greek may be unable to do the work of English. I am convinced that the study of English may be undertaken so as to interest, stimulate, and develop the student; that it is perfectly compatible with the discipline and competition of very large classes; that its success, as also the success of other studies, depends, to some extent, upon the way in which it is taught, but that, even when taught tentatively by those who will be very glad to receive hints how to teach it better, it may produce results not altogether unsatisfactory.

Notes

1. Robert Lowe, MP, former Vice-President of the Committee of Council on Education, who was closely identified with the 'payment by results' system. The speech referred to was made to the Philomathic Society in Liverpool on 22 January 1868.
2. Joseph Angus, *A Handbook of the English Tongue* (1862).
3. *Chambers's Etymological Dictionary*, ed. James Donald, (1867).

CHAPTER FIFTEEN

Matthew Arnold

Matthew Arnold (1822–1888), the son of Dr Arnold of Rugby, was well known as a poet, critic and analyst of the cultural state of the nation, as well as being an HMI (Her Majesty's Inspector of Schools). He was educated at Winchester, Rugby and Balliol College, Oxford. He graduated with second-class honours in 1844, but made up for what was regarded as a comparative failure by gaining a fellowship at Oriel College, Oxford in 1845. After a period as private secretary to Lord Lansdowne, 1847–1851, he became an HMI in 1851, and continued in this post until 1886, just two years before his death.

Arnold's career as a poet lay in the early part of his life, and was completely over by the time he was 45. He was elected Professor of Poetry at Oxford in 1857, and was re-elected for a further five years in 1862, but the appointment reflected his growing reputation as a critic rather than as a poet. He was the first layman to be elected to the Chair, and also the first to lecture in English instead of the traditional Latin. This professorship did not necessitate giving up his position as an HMI, or indeed enable him to give it up, since only occasional public lectures are required of an Oxford Professor of Poetry, and the remuneration is paltry.

Arnold's Oxford lectures formed the basis, together with contributions to periodicals, of the volumes of essays which he published, *On Translating Homer* (1861), *Essays in Criticism* (1865), *Culture and Anarchy* (1869) and *Literature and Dogma* (1873). It is these essays which established his reputation as a Victorian sage. Towards the end of his life, he made lecture tours of the United States in 1883 and 1886.

The extracts printed here are not from Arnold's essays, but from his general reports as a schools' inspector, written between 1852 and 1880. They deal with elementary schools, and are therefore focused almost exclusively on working-class education. For both elementary-school pupils and the young pupil teachers, Arnold believed that more study of English literature would be beneficial. For most of this period, elementary schools laboured under the Revised Code (1862), chiefly remembered for the system of payment by results. This code controlled very rigidly what was taught in schools by laying down in detail the skills which would be tested and paid for. School managers had no choice but to see that pupils were well drilled to pass tests in subjects which would bring government grants to the school. The only provision for English literature under the Revised Code was for recitation of poetry, yet even in this poor form it seemed to Arnold 'the special subject which … produces most good.' There was, therefore, huge potential to do still more.

General Report for the Year 1852

* * *

On one other topic, in connection with the subject of pupil-teachers, I am anxious to touch in conclusion. In the general opinion of the advantages which have resulted from the employment of them, I most fully concur; and of the acquirements and general behaviour of the greater number of those of them whom I have examined I wish to speak favourably. But I have been much struck in examining them towards the close of their apprenticeship, when they are generally at least eighteen years old, with the utter disproportion between the great amount of positive information and the low degree of mental culture and intelligence which they exhibit. Young men, whose knowledge of grammar, of the minutest details of geographical and historical facts, and above all of mathematics, is surprising, often cannot paraphrase a plain passage of prose or poetry without totally misapprehending it, or write half a page of composition on any subject without falling into gross blunders of taste and expression. I cannot but think that, with a body of young men so highly instructed, too little attention has hitherto been paid to this side of education; the side through which it chiefly forms the character; the side which has perhaps been too exclusively attended to in schools for the higher classes, and to the development of which it is the boast of what is called classical education to be mainly directed. I attach little importance to the study of languages, ancient or modern, by pupil-teachers, for they can seldom have the time to study them to much purpose without neglecting other branches of instruction which it is necessary that they should follow; but I am sure that the study of portions of the best English authors, and composition, might with advantage be made a part of their regular course of instruction to a much greater degree than it is at present. Such a training would tend to elevate and humanize a number of young men, who at present, notwithstanding the vast amount of raw information which they have amassed, are wholly uncultivated; and it would have the great social advantage of tending to bring them into intellectual sympathy with the educated of the upper classes.

General Report for the Year 1860

*   *
*   *

The candour with which school inspectors in France avowed to me their dissatisfaction with the school-books in use there, led me to reflect on the great imperfection exhibited by our school-books also. I found in the French schools good manuals for teaching special subjects – a good manual for teaching arithmetic, a good manual for teaching grammar, a good manual for teaching geography; what was wanting there, as it is wanting with us, was a good *reading-book*, or course of reading-books. It is not enough remembered in how many cases his reading-book forms the whole literature, except his Bible, of the child attending a primary school. If then, instead of literature, his reading-book, as is too often the case, presents him with a jejune encyclopaedia of positive information, the result is that he has, except his Bible, no literature, no *humanizing* instruction at all. If, again, his reading-book, as is also too often the case, presents him with bad literature instead of good – with the writing of second or third-rate authors, feeble, incorrect, and colourless – he has not, as the rich have, the corrective of an abundance of good literature to counteract the bad effect of trivial and ill-written school-books; the second or third-rate literature of his school-book remains for him his sole, or, at least, his principal literary standard. Dry scientific disquisitions, and literary compositions of an inferior order, are indeed the worst possible instruments for teaching children to read well. But besides the fault of not fulfilling this, their essential function, the ill–compiled reading-books I speak of have, I say, for the poor scholar, the graver fault of actually doing what they can to spoil his taste, when they are nearly his only means for forming it. I have seen school-books belonging to the cheapest, and therefore most popular series in use in our primary schools, in which far more than half of the poetical extracts were the composition either of the anonymous compilers themselves, or of American writers of the second and third order; and these books were to be some poor child's Anthology of a literature so varied and so powerful as the English! To this defectiveness of our reading-books I attribute much of that grave and discouraging deficiency in anything like literary taste and feeling, which even well-instructed pupil-teachers of four or five years' training, which even the ablest students in our training schools, still continue almost invariably to exhibit; a deficiency, to remedy which, the progressive development of our school system, and the very considerable increase of information among the people, appear to avail little or nothing. I believe that nothing would so much contribute to remedy it as the diffusion in our elementary schools of reading-books of which the contents were really well selected and interesting. Such lessons would be far better adapted than a treatise on the atmosphere, the steam-engine, or the pump, to attain the proper end of a reading-book, that of teaching scholars to read well; they would also afford the best chance of inspiring quick scholars with a real love for reading and literature in the only way in which such a love is ever really inspired, by animating and moving them; and if they succeeded in doing this, they would have this further advantage, that the literature for which they inspired a taste would be a good, a sound, and a truly refining literature; not a literature such as that of most of the few attractive pieces in our current reading-books, a literature over which no cultivated person would dream of wasting his time.

General Report for the Year 1871

*
*   *

In the extra subjects fixed by the fourth schedule of the New Code,[1] all the examinees, except those presented in recitation, were examined on paper. The rate of failure in the paper-work was nearly 40 per cent; 902 papers were examined, and 358 of them were marked *failure*.

This schedule of extra subjects is very valuable; by it, and by it alone, does the Department extend its care beyond the providing the mere instruments of knowledge to the providing knowledge itself. The order and plan by which this is provided is of the very highest importance. The schedule cannot at present be regarded as furnishing more than an inchoate plan; it will require to have all its parts developed and co-ordered, and better text-books than those now in use will have to be created. I showed to a distinguished physiologist the papers in physiology which had been worked under the present schedule; he told me that every one was quite worthless, and that apparently the method and text-books by which the subject had been taught were quite worthless too.

If this is the case with branches of knowledge so distinctly marked off and so clearly conceived as the natural sciences, how much more is it the case with that immense indeterminate field called literature. Here, above all, neither plan nor order of study exists, nor any well conceived choice of books; yet here, above all, these are necessary. What is comprised under the word literature is in itself the greatest power available

185

in education; of this power it is not too much to say that in our elementary schools at present no use is made at all. The reading books and the absence of plan being what they are, the whole use that the Government, now that its connection with religious instruction is abandoned, makes of the mighty engine of literature in the education of the working classes, amounts to little more, even when most successful, than the giving them the power to read the newspapers.

General Report for the Year 1872

*
* *

'Recitation' is the special subject which produces at present, so far as I can observe, most good. The great fault of the instruction in our elementary schools (of the secular part of it, at any rate) is, that it at most gives to a child the mechanical possession of the instruments of knowledge, but does nothing to *form* him, to put him in a way of making the best possible use of them. As things now are, the time is not ripe for laying down a theory of how this is to be thoroughly done and following it; all that can be said is, that what practically will be found to contribute most towards *forming* a pupil is familiarity with masterpieces; familiarity with them, for the less advanced pupil, in a very limited number and with each object of his study standing singly; for the more advanced pupil, in a series arranged according to some well-planned order. If the 'recitation' is carefully watched, as to the authors and pieces selected, it does give us something, though only a commencement, of that which for the less advanced pupil is needed. I can already see the good effects of it, and they may be extended much further. Music, now that instruction in it is made universal, ought to lay the foundation in the children of our elementary schools of a cultivated power of perception; 'recitation', in the present absence of any attempt even to raise their reading into something of a literary study, must be relied upon for carrying the power of perception onward.

*
* *

General Report for the Year 1876

*
* *

A stir of life is certainly more and more visible again in our schools. Scholars and teachers alike show it, and I have good hopes for the future. In what is properly to be called culture, in feeling, taste, and perception,

186

the advance is least; and this is, perhaps, inevitable. Even second year students still show, in this respect, an astonishing crudeness. 'Doctor, can you fulfil the duties of your profession in curing a woman who is distracted?' or again, 'Can you not wait upon the lunatic?' – these are paraphrases of Shakespeare's *Canst thou not minister to a mind diseased*, from which I am even now fresh. 'The witches who are under the control of Hecate, and who love the darkness because their designs are best accomplished then, have assembled at their meeting place with no other protection than a wolf for their sentinel, and by whose roar they know when their enemy Tarquin is coming near them.' It seems almost incredible that a youth who has been two years in a training college, and for the last of the two years has studied *Macbeth*, should, at his examination, produce such a travesty of the well-known passage in that play beginning, *Now witchcraft celebrates*. Yet such travesties are far too common, and all signs of positive feeling and taste for what is poetically true and beautiful are far too rare. At last year's meeting of the British Association the President of the Section for Mechanical Science told his hearers that, 'in such communities as ours, the spread of natural science is of far more immediate urgency than any other secondary study. Whatever else he may know, viewed in the light of modern necessities, a man who is not fairly versed in exact science is only a half-educated man, and if he has substituted literature and history for natural science, he has chosen the less useful alternative.' And more and more pressure there will be, especially in the instruction of the children of the working classes, whose time for schooling is short, to substitute natural science for literature and history as the more useful alternative. And what a curious state of things it would be if every scholar who had passed through the course of our primary schools knew that, when a taper burns, the wax is converted into carbonic acid and water, and thought, at the same time, that a good paraphrase for *Canst thou not minister to a mind diseased*, was *Can you not wait upon the lunatic*! The problem to be solved is a great deal more complicated than many of the friends of natural science suppose. They see clearly enough, for instance, how the working classes are, in their ignorance, constantly violating the laws of health, and suffering accordingly; and they look to a spread of sound natural science as the remedy. What they do not see is that to know the laws of health ever so exactly, as a mere piece of positive knowledge, will carry a man in general no great way. To have the power of using, which is the thing wished, these data of natural science, a man must, in general, have first been in some measure *moralised*; and for moralising him it will be found not easy, I think, to dispense with those old agents, letters, poetry, religion. So let not our teachers be led to imagine, whatever they may hear and see of the call for natural science, that their literary cultivation is unimportant. The fruitful use of natural science itself depends, in a very great degree, on having effected in the whole man, by means of letters, a rise in what the political economists call *the standard of life*.

General Report for the Year 1880

I find that of the specific subjects English literature, as it is too ambitiously called – in plain truth the learning by heart and reciting of a hundred lines or two of standard English poetry – continues to be by far the most popular. I rejoice to find it so; there is no fact coming under my observation in the working of our elementary schools which gives me so much satisfaction. The acquisition of good poetry is a discipline which works deeper than any other discipline in the range of work of our schools; more than any other, too, it works of itself, is independent of the school teacher, and cannot be spoiled by pedantry and injudiciousness on his part. Some people regard this my high estimate of the value of poetry in education with suspicion and displeasure. Perhaps they may accept the testimony of Wordsworth with less suspicion than mine. Wordsworth says, 'To be incapable of a feeling of poetry, in my sense of the word, is to be without love of human nature and reverence for God.'[2] And it is only through acquaintance with poetry, and with good poetry, that this 'feeling of poetry' can be given.

Good poetry does undoubtedly tend to form the soul and character; it tends to beget a love of beauty and of truth in alliance together, it suggests, however indirectly, high and noble principles of action, and it inspires the emotion so helpful in making principles operative. Hence its extreme importance to all of us; but in our elementary schools its importance seems to me to be at present quite extraordinary. I hope that, instead of its being confined to children in the Fifth and Sixth Standards, this excellent discipline of poetry will be retained for the children of the Fourth Standard, and brought into use universally for at least these three standards.

Happily, the poetry exercise has, as I have said already, become popular in schools, and it will, I am confident, become more and more so. Sir John Lubbock[3] says that in some board schools in Lambeth he asked the children which they preferred of four of their subjects of instruction – grammar, history, geography, and elementary science – and that a very large majority were in favour of elementary science. I do not quite understand how he took his comparison; he does not mention whether the children whose votes he took were all of them learning all these four subjects or not. But, at any rate, if he will come into Westminster and will ask the children in the schools there who are taking two class subjects and two specific subjects, poetry being one of these latter, which of the four they prefer, I think I can assure him that he will find a most decisive majority for poetry.

The choice of passages to be learnt is of the utmost importance, and requires close and intelligent observing of the children. Some years ago it was the fashion to make them learn Goldsmith's *Deserted Village*, at the recommendation, I believe, of the late Lord Lyndhurst;[4] or rather he had given high praise to this poem, and recommended it as a poem to be got by heart, and so it was supposed that the children in our elementary schools might with advantage learn it. Nothing could be more completely unsuitable for them, and this being soon proved by the event, the use of the poem for the purpose in question has happily almost ceased. That the poetry chosen should have real beauties of expression and feeling, that these beauties should be such as the children's hearts and minds can lay hold of, and that a distinct point or centre of beauty and interest should occur within the limits of the passage learnt, all these are conditions to be insisted upon. Some of the short pieces by Mrs Hemans, such as 'The Graves of a Household,' 'The Homes of England,' 'The Better Land' are to be recommended, because they fulfil all three conditions; they have real merits of expression and sentiment, the merits are such as the children can feel, and the centre of interest, these pieces being so short, necessarily occurs within the limits of what is learnt. On the other hand, in extracts taken from Scott and Shakespeare, the point of interest is often not reached within the hundred lines which is all that children in the Fourth Standard learn. The judgment scene in *The Merchant of Venice* affords me a good example of what I mean. Taken as a whole, this famous scene has, I need not say, great power; it is dramatic poetry of the first order, it is also well within our school children's comprehension, and very interesting to them. Teachers are fond of selecting it to be learnt by heart, and they are quite right. But what happens is this. The children in the Fourth Standard begin at the beginning, and stop at the end of a hundred lines; now, the children in the Fourth Standard are often a majority of the children learning poetry, and this is all their poetry for the year. But within these hundred lines the real interest of the situation is not reached, neither do they contain any poetry of signal beauty and effectiveness. How little, therefore, has the poetry exercise been made to do for these children, many of whom will leave school at once, and learn no more poetry! The conclusion I wish to draw is, that the teacher should always take care that the year's poetry of a class shall contain the best poetry in the piece chosen for them, and the central point of interest in it; not be mere prelude and introduction to this centre of interest. To secure this, the teacher may without scruple plunge into the middle of a scene or a passage, and make his children take their hundred lines there explaining to them, of course, the situation at the point where they begin. If they remain another year, they can take a new passage or scene under the same conditions. This is a far better course than to throw a year away, as is frequently done now, upon comparatively ineffective poetry, with the intention that the child, if he remains at school, may next year continue the same passage and reach the point of interest.

I insist at such length upon this poetry exercise, because of the increasing use of it, and because of its extreme importance. Stress is laid upon the necessity of the children knowing thoroughly the meaning of what they recite, and it is assumed that to secure their knowing this is the simplest matter in the world, and that not to secure it proves inexcusable negligence in the teacher. I am more and more refusing to pass children who do not know the meaning of words which occur in what they recite, but I proceed gradually and with caution. If I had begun by rigidly rejecting every child ignorant of the meaning of every word in what he recited, I should never have got the poetry exercise established in my schools at all. The scanty vocabulary of our school children, and their correspondent narrow range of ideas, must be known and allowed for if one is to guide their instruction usefully. I have found in London schools children of twelve years old, able to pass well in reading, writing, and arithmetic, who yet did not know what 'a steed' was. I found in a good school the other day a head class of some thirty, only one of whom knew what 'a ford' was. 'Steed' is a literary word, 'ford' is a word of country life, not of town life; still they are words, one is apt to think, universally understood by every one above five years old. But even common words of this kind are not universally understood by the children with whom we deal. Very many words are in their reading lessons passed over as certainly known to them, to which they attach no meaning at all, or a wrong one. The poetry exercise is invaluable by causing words to be dwelt upon and canvassed, by leading the children to grasp the meaning of new words, and by thus extending the range of their ideas. But the slowness and difficulty of the process, which are as incontestable as its high value, must be borne in mind, and we must have patience with that slowness and difficulty.

I should like, above all, to see this poetry exercise made no longer an extra subject, but a part of the regular work of the school, which would then consist of the three elementary matters, of the class subjects, and of this.... .

*
* *

Notes

1. The Revised Code of 1862 instituted the system commonly known as 'payment by results,' and defined very rigidly the subjects for which payments would be made. From 1870 there was some relaxation of this very rigid code, introducing what Arnold refers to here as the New Code.
2. Letter to Lady Beaumont, 21 May 1807.
3. Sir John Lubbock (1834–1913), banker, scientist and MP.
4. Lord Lyndhurst (1772–1863), three times Lord Chancellor.

CHAPTER SIXTEEN

John Churton Collins

John Churton Collins (1848–1908) was educated at King Edward's School, Birmingham and Balliol College, Oxford. His academic record at Oxford was undistinguished, with a Third in Classical Moderations in 1870 and a Second in the School of Law and History in 1872. However, Collins read widely in English literature while at Balliol, and when he left Oxford he earned his living mainly through his knowledge of English literature. He wrote literary articles and reviews, edited literary texts, and coached candidates for Civil Service examinations in English literature. In 1880 he began a career in University Extension teaching, which was for many years his professional mainstay. University Extension, which was the precursor of modern university extra-mural departments, began in Cambridge, but was rapidly taken up by Oxford and London. Collins worked for both London and Oxford, remaining in the employ of London for a continuous period of twenty-seven years.

Nevertheless, Extension work neither provided the status which Collins desired, nor did it pay well, nor leave him as much time as he wished for pursuing scholarship. He therefore applied for university chairs of English as they became vacant, most famously for the Merton Chair of English Language and Literature at Oxford in 1885. However, it was not until 1904, just four years before his death, that he became Professor of English at Birmingham.

The first item included here is an extract from a review in the *Quarterly Review* of *From Shakespeare to Pope* by Edmund Gosse. Gosse had recently delivered the Clark Lectures on English literature at Cambridge, and these had now been published by the university press. The book had been eulogized in many reviews, but was in fact full of errors. Collins's review was unsparingly vicious, but he used it as a springboard for his campaign on behalf of English studies. In the event, Collins's attack on Gosse somewhat backfired, since it was so savage that Gosse's plight aroused a good deal of public sympathy, and Collins was regarded by many as having behaved in an ungentlemanly manner. There was also a suggestion that Collins was taking out on Gosse his own disappointment at not having won the Merton Chair, especially since he referred to this chair in the review as an example of how the cause of literature was cheated.

Collins argued that the amateurishness of which Gosse's work was an example needed to be rooted out from English studies, and the teaching of English needed to be established on a proper basis. For Collins this meant literature, not philology. It also meant linking the study of English literature with the study of classics, for without classics, English literature could not be properly understood. Furthermore, its worth could not be effectively judged unless studied alongside Greek and Roman literature, because the classics were, using Matthew Arnold's word, 'touchstones' against which modern literature should be measured.

The second extract, also from the *Quarterly Review*, is from an article set out in the form of a review of the *Petition addressed to the Hebdomadal Council for the Foundation of a School of Modern Literature*. Collins makes the contemporary battle between the defenders of classics, on the one hand, and the Modern party in education, on the other, the main peg on which to hang his polemic. He is seeking to ally English with classics as a literary study, and thereby to gain the support of the classicists for English. Once again, philology is the identified enemy, a study which has but a lowly place 'as an instrument of culture.'

Review of *From Shakespeare to Pope,* by Edmund Gosse

That such a book as this[1] should have been permitted to go forth to the world with the *imprimatur* of the University of Cambridge, affords matter for very grave reflection. But it is a confirmation of what we have long suspected. It is one more proof that those rapid and reckless innovations, which have during the last few years completely changed the faces of our Universities, have not been made with impunity. We are no sticklers for the old regime, no advocates of a policy of ultra-Conservatism. We think that the Universities have done wisely in extending the ancient boundaries of education, and that those boundaries might with advantage be extended still further. We should, for example, be heartily glad to hear that Oxford and Cambridge had provided as amply for the interpretation of Modern Literature as they have for the interpretation of Ancient: that the *Laocoon* was being studied side by side with the *Poetics*, and *Macbeth* side by side with the *Agamemnon*. But there are certain points on which the Universities cannot be too Conservative. There are certain points on which any departure from prescription and tradition is not merely to be regretted, but to be deprecated. Whatever concessions Oxford and Cambridge may find it desirable to make in consulting the interests of modern life, it should be their first care to guard jealously their own prerogatives. Of all revolutions, that would be the most disastrous to learning and culture which should subject University legislation to popular control. Six centuries have not altered the relative position in which Oxford and Cambridge stand to the outside world. In the infancy of civilization they preserved learning from extinction. As civilization advances, they have the more difficult task of preserving it from corruption. They have no longer to combat barbarism and dulness, sloth and ignorance, but to counteract the mischievous activity of agencies scarcely less antagonistic to all that it is their glory to uphold.

It may sound paradoxical to say that the more widely education spreads, the more generally intelligent a nation becomes, the greater is the danger to which Art and Letters are exposed. And yet how obviously is this the case, and how easily is this explained. The quality of skilled work depends mainly on the standard required of the workman. If his judges and patrons belong to the discerning few who, knowing what is excellent, are intolerant of everything which falls short of excellence, the standard required will necessarily be a high one, and the standard required will be the standard attained. In past times, for example, the only men of letters who were respected formed a portion of that highly cultivated class who will always be in the minority; and to that class, and to that class only, they appealed. A community within a community, they regarded the general public with as much indifference as the general public regarded them, and wrote only for themselves, and for those who stood on the same intellectual level as themselves. It was so in the Athens of Pericles; it was so in the Rome of Augustus; it was so in the Florence of the Medici; and a striking example of the same thing is to be found in our own Elizabethan Dramatists. Though their bread depended on the brutal and illiterate savages for whose amusement they catered, they still talked the language of scholars and poets, and forced their rude hearers to sit out works which could have been intelligible only to scholars and poets. Each felt with pride that he belonged to a great guild, which neither had nor affected to have anything in common with the multitude. Each strove only for the applause of those whose praise is not lightly given. Each spurred the other on. When Marlowe worked, he worked with the fear of Greene before his eyes, as Shakspeare was put on his mettle by Jonson, and Jonson by Shakspeare. We owe *Much Ado About Nothing* and *The Alchemist* not to men who bid only for the suffrage of the mob, but to men who stood in awe of the verdict which would be passed on them by the company assembled at the Mermaid and the Devil.

As long as men of letters continue to form an intellectual aristocracy, and, stimulated by mutual rivalry, strain every nerve to excel, and as long also – and this is a condition equally important – as they have no temptation to pander to the crowd, so long will Literature maintain its dignity, and so long will the standard attained in Literature be a high one. In the days of Dryden and Pope, in the days even of Johnson and Gibbon, the greater part of the general public either read nothing, or read nothing but politics and sermons. The few who were interested in Poetry, in Criticism, in History, were, as a rule, those who had received a learned education, men of highly cultivated tastes and of considerable attainments. A writer, therefore, who aspired to contribute to polite literature, had to choose between finding no readers at all, and finding such readers as he was bound to respect – between instant oblivion, and satisfying a class which, composed of scholars, would have turned with contempt from writings unworthy of scholars. A classical style, a refined tone, and an adequate acquaintance with the chief authors of Ancient Rome and of Modern France, were requisites, without which even a periodical essayist would have had small hope of obtaining a hearing. Whoever will turn, we do not say to the papers of Addison and his circle in the early part of the last century, or to those of Chesterfield and his circle later on, but to the average critical work of Cave's and Dodsley's hack writers,[2] cannot fail to be struck with its remarkable merit in point of literary execution.

But as education spreads, a very different class of readers call into being a very different class of writers. Men and women begin to seek in books the amusement or excitement which they sought formerly in social dissipation. To the old public of scholars succeeds a public, in which every section of society has its representatives, and to provide this vast body with the sort of reading which is acceptable to it, becomes a thriving and lucrative calling. An immense literature springs up, which has no other object than to catch the popular ear, and no higher aim than to please for the moment. That perpetual craving for novelty, which has in all ages been characteristic of the multitude, necessitates in authors of this class a corresponding rapidity of production. The writer of a single good book is soon forgotten by his contemporaries; but the writer of a series of bad books is sure of reputation and emolument. Indeed, a good book and a bad book stand, so far as the general public are concerned, on precisely the same level, as they meet with precisely the same fate. Each presents the attraction of a new title-page. Each is glanced through, and tossed aside. Each is estimated not by its intrinsic worth, but according to the skill with which it has been puffed. Till within comparatively recent times this literature was for the most part represented by novels and poems, and by those light and desultory essays, sketches and *ana*,[3] which are the staple commodity of our magazines. And so long as it confined itself wihin these bounds it did no mischief, and even some good. Flimsy and superficial though it was, it had at least the merit of interesting thousands in Art and Letters, who would otherwise have been indifferent to them. It afforded nutriment to minds which would have rejected more solid fare. To men of business and pleasure who, though no longer students, still retained the tincture of early culture, it offered the most agreeable of all methods of killing time, while scholars found in it welcome relaxation from severer studies. It thus supplied a want. Presenting attractions not to one class only, but to all classes, it grew on the world. Its patrons, who half a century ago numbered thousands, now number millions. And as it has grown in favour, it has grown in ambition. It is no longer satisfied with the humble province which it once held, but is extending its dominion in all directions. It has its representatives in every department of Art and Letters. It has its poets, its critics, its philosophers, its historians. It crowds not our club tables and news-stalls only, but our libraries. And so what was originally a mere excrescence on literature in the proper sense of the term, has now assumed proportions so gigantic, that it has not merely overshadowed that literature, but threatens to supersede it.

No thoughtful man can contemplate the present condition of current literature without disgust and alarm. We have still, indeed, lingering among us a few masters whose works would have been an honour to any age; and here and there among writers may be discerned men who are honourably distinguished by a conscientious desire to excel, men who respect themselves, and respect their calling. But to say that these are in the minority, would be to give a very imperfect idea of the proportion which their numbers bear to those who figure most prominently before the public. They are, in truth, as tens are to myriads. Their comparative insignificance is such, that they are powerless even to leaven the mass. The position which they would have occupied half a century ago, and which they may possibly occupy half a century hence, is now usurped by a herd of scribblers who have succeeded, partly by sheer force of numbers, and partly by judicious co-operation, in all but dominating literature. Scarcely a day passes in which some book is not hurried into the world, which owes its existence not to any desire on the part of its author to add to the stores of useful literature, or even to a hope of obtaining money, but simply to that paltry vanity which thrives on the sort of homage of which society of a certain kind is not grudging, and which knows no distinction between notoriety and fame. A few years ago a man who contributed articles to a current periodical, or who delivered a course of lectures, had, as a rule, the good sense to know that when they had fulfilled the purpose for which they were originally intended, the world had no more concern with them, and he would as soon have thought of inflicting them in the shape of a volume, on the public, as he would have thought of issuing an edition of his private letters to his friends. Now all is changed. The first article in the creed of a person, who has figured in either of these capacities, appears to be that he is bound to force himself into notice in the character of an author. And this, happily for himself, but unhappily for the interests of literature, he is able to do with perfect facility and with perfect impunity. Books are speedily manufactured, and as speedily reduced to pulp. It is as easy to invest a worthless book with those superficial attractions which catch the eye of the crowd, as it is a meritorious one. As the general public are the willing dupes of puffers, it is no more difficult to palm off on them the spurious wares of literary charlatans, than it is to beguile them into purchasing the wares of any other sort of charlatan. No one is interested in telling them the truth. Many, on the contrary, are interested in deceiving them. As a rule, the men who write bad books are the men who criticize bad books; and as they know that what they mete out in their capacity of judges to-day is what will in turn be meted out to them in their capacity of authors to-morrow, it is not surprising that their relations should be similar to those which Tacitus tells us existed between Vinius and Tigellinus – 'nulla innocentiae cura, sed vices impunitatis.'[4] The *Edinburgh* and *Quarterly Reviews* appear unfortunately to have abandoned, for the most part, to Reviews of a very different character the censorship of current publications.

Meanwhile all those vile arts which were formerly confined to the circulators of bad novels and bad poems are practised without shame. It is shocking, it is disgusting to contemplate the devices to which many men of letters will stoop for the sake of exalting themselves into a factitious reputation. And the evil is fast spreading. Indeed, things have come to such a pass, that persons of real merit, if they have the misfortune to depend on their pens for a livelihood, must either submit to be elbowed and jostled out of the field, or take part in the same ignoble scramble for notoriety, and the same detestable system of mutual puffery. Thus everything which formerly tended to raise the standard of literary ambition and literary attainment has given place to everything which tends to degrade it. The multitude now stand where the scholar once stood. From the multitude emanate, to the multitude are dedicated, two-thirds of the publications which pour forth each year in myriads from our presses –

        viviamo scorti
Da mediocrità: sceso il sapiente
E salita è la turba a un sol confine
Che il mondo agguaglia.[5]

All this is no doubt inevitable, but what we sincerely trust is not inevitable is the corruption of that small minority, whose standards are not the standards of the crowd. The nurseries and strongholds of that minority are the Universities. At the Universities are still studied in a spirit too narrow indeed, but reverently and conscientiously, those masterpieces which, so long as they shall continue to be studied, will be of power to purify and exalt. There, amid the din of voices blatant without – the puffing and the cant, the gushing and the cackle – the still small voice of sincerity is clear. No shallow dilettantism has as yet found footing there. No sciolist, no pretender, no dishonest worker, has ever escaped detection and condemnation there. Nothing which falls short of a standard, as high perhaps as it could possibly be, is tolerated either in those who teach, or in those who seek honours in the schools. What work is done, is done as legislators, whose moral and intellectual ideals have been derived from Thucydides and Aristotle, from Plato and Sophocles, would necessarily insist upon its being done. And may this continue. For as long as this continues, as long as the Universities remain true to tradition and true to themselves, so long amid the general corruption will Art and Learning be sound at the core.

But we have lately observed symptoms which are, we fear, no uncertain indications that even the Universities have not escaped contagion. It is not our intention here to offer any remarks on the extraordinary innovations which have recently been made in the old system, both at Oxford and Cambridge.[6] That the majority of them are mere reckless experiments, that some of them are positively pernicious, and that almost all of them are fraught with peril, is, we think, unquestionable. If any proof of what these innovations are likely to lead to were needed, it would be afforded by the volume which stands at the head of this article. We have already pointed out the enormous responsibility which rests with the Universities at the present time. We have shown what was indeed self-evident, that unless they continue to oppose the true faith to the false faith, the high standard to the low standard, the excellent to the mediocre, the sound to the unsound, the prospects of literature are mournful indeed. It is therefore with the greatest regret that we have had placed in our hands, dated from Trinity College, Cambridge, and published by the University Press, a work which we do not scruple to describe as most derogatory to all concerned in its production. Whether this volume is an indication of the manner in which the important subject with which it deals is studied at Cambridge, we do not know. We sincerely trust that it is not. But of two things we are very sure; first, that a book so unworthy, in everything but externals, of a great University has never before been given to the world; and secondly, that it is the bounden duty of all friends of learning to join in discountenancing so evil a precedent.

Not the least mischievous characteristic of the work is the skill with which its worthlessness is disguised. From title to colophon there is, so far as externals are concerned, everything to disarm suspicion, everything to inspire trust. An excellent index; unexceptionable type; unexceptionable paper;

> Chartae regiae, novi libri,
> Novi umbilici, lora rubra, membrana
> Directa plumbo, et pumice omnia aequata.[7]

On opening the volume our confidence redoubles. We turn to the Preface. We there learn that the substance of the work was delivered in the form of lectures to members of the University of Cambridge in the Hall of Trinity College:

> It has been no small advantage to me that among the distinguished listeners to whom I have had the honour of reading these pages, there have been more than a few whose special studies have rendered them particularly acute in criticising. In consequence of such criticism I have been able profitably to revise the work, to add evidence where it seemed wanting, to remove rash statements, and to remould ambiguous sentences.

In the course of the work we learn that many 'eminent friends' have been anxiously consulted; for 'in an enquiry of this nature,' observes the author, 'exact evidence, even of a minute kind, outweighs in importance any expression of mere critical opinion.' As we are not concerned with Mr Gosse's eminent friends, but only with Mr Gosse himself, we shall merely remark that we quite absolve Professor Gardiner and Mr Austin Dobson from all complicity in Mr Gosse's delinquencies.

Of all offences of which a writer can be guilty, the most detestable is that of simulating familiarity with works which he knows only at second hand, or of which he knows nothing more than the title. That a Lecturer on English Literature should not know whether the *Arcadia* of Sidney, and the *Oceana* of Harrington, are in prose or verse, or, not knowing, should not have taken the trouble to ascertain, is discreditable enough; but that he should, under the impression that they are poems, have had the effontery to sit in judgment on them, might well, in Macaulay's favourite phrase, make us ashamed of our species. And yet this is what Mr Gosse has done. In one place (p. 26), he classes and compares the *Arcadia* with *The Faery Queen*. In another place (p. 75), he classes and compares it with Giles Fletcher's *Christ's Victory and Triumph*; while on p. 26 the *Oceana*, coupled with the *Arcadia*, is compared, on the one hand with Spenser's poem, and on the other hand with Phineas Fletcher's *Purple Island*.[8] Of the gross chronological blunder of which he is guilty, in placing the *Oceana* with the *Arcadia*, and *The Faery Queen* in the 'great generation,' when the *Oceana* was published in 1656, a period long subsequent to the time of which he is speaking, we say nothing. It is easy to see what has misled him with regard to the *Oceana*, and his error certainly furnishes a very amusing illustration of his method of investigation, He has confounded James Harrington, the prose writer, who was born in 1611, with Sir John Harrington, the poet, who was born in 1561; and the title *Oceana* having a very poetical sound, he has jumped to the conclusion that it is a poem.

On p. 108, he informs us that Garth's 'Claremont'[9] is 'a direct imitation of Denham's 'Cooper's Hill'.[10] If he had taken the trouble to read Garth's poem, he would have seen that, beyond the fact that it derives its title from the name of a place, and that it is written in heroics, it has simply nothing in common with 'Cooper's Hill.' Denham's poem is, as we need scarcely say, a poem describing the prospect from Cooper's Hill – St Paul's, Windsor, the Thames, the valley of the Thames – and with that description are interwoven such reflections as these objects severally call up; it then goes on to describe with singular animation, a stag-hunt; and it concludes with some remarks bearing immediately on contemporary politics, suggested by the view of Runnymede. Garth's poem, on the other hand, is simply a *jeu d'esprit* written on the occasion of the name of Claremont being given to the villa founded at Esher by the Earl of Clare. As a stream took its rise in the hill on which the mansion stood, welling up in a grotto where there was an echo, it struck Garth that he might make out of this a pretty story in the manner of Ovid. And so, with a few general remarks on the venality of poets who are ready to flatter without distinction any one who will pay them, and with the assurance that his own desire to please his noble patron springs from the most disinterested motives, he goes on to say that he has no intention of describing Claremont and its beauties. That theme he leaves to a nobler muse; his task is merely to tell:

how ancient fame
Records from whence the villa took its name

and the legend of Montano and Echo, modelled on the legend of Narcissus and Echo, in the third book of the *Metamorphoses* begins. With that legend we do not propose to trouble our readers. It is as easy to see what has misled Mr Gosse in this case as in the other case. Indeed, Garth himself has set the trap, and a reader who went no further than the title and the first words of the preface, would be certain to be caught... .

* * *

If we turn from the matter of Mr Gosse's volume to the style and the diction, it is equally surprising that any University could have sanctioned its publication. How even the reader for the press could have allowed such words as 'preciosity,' 'recrudescence,' 'solidarity,' 'rejuvenescence,' 'alembicated,' or such phrases as 'the lively actuality of a newsletter,' 'a personal sympathy with vegetation,' 'the excitement of resuscitation,' and the like, to pass unchallenged, is to us inexplicable. Was there no one who could save Mr Gosse from making himself ridiculous by such eloquence as this: 'We who can see this Orpheus-like Charles torn to pieces by the outraged liberties of England, and that comely head floating down the Hebrus of the Revolution'? (p. 81). Could the Delegates of the Cambridge Press have been blind to the ludicrous impropriety of permitting what was intended to be a serious treatise on English Literature to be prefaced by a copy of silly verses? – in which the author, an official of the University, assures his readers that he is:

Less than bird or shell,
More volatile, more fragile far than these.

Nor does the bad taste – to call it by no harsher name – which is conspicuous throughout the book, less jar on us. Speaking, for example, of Waller's 'Battle of the Summer Islands,'[11] Mr Gosse observes, 'My own belief is that the astute Waller, having property on the Islands, wrote his heroic poem and circulated it among wealthy and noble friends as an advertisement.' Can Mr Gosse possibly be ignorant that Waller was a gentleman? So again, when he talks of the 'tattling monkey-tongue' of Pope, we have an example of one of the most detestable fashions of modern times – we mean the pert irreverence with which very little men are in the habit of speaking of great men.

And now we bring to a conclusion one of the most disagreeable tasks which it has ever been our lot to undertake. Our motives for undertaking it have already been explained. Had Mr Gosse's volume been published in the ordinary way, we need scarcely say that we would not have noticed it. Had its errors and deficiencies been pointed out in the literary journals, we should probably have comforted ourselves with the thought, that what had been done once need not be done again. But when we saw that it came forth, carrying all the authority of a work published by a great University, and under the auspices of the most distinguished community in that University, and that so far from the literary journals estimating it at its true value, and placing students on their guard against its errors, Review vied with Review in fulsome and indiscriminating eulogy,[12] we felt we had no choice. It was simply our duty, our imperative duty, in the interests of literature and in the interests of education, to speak out. That duty we have endeavoured to perform temperately and candidly. We have perverted nothing. Had it been our object to make game of the book, it would not, we can assure Mr Gosse, have been very difficult. Though we have, we own, been strongly tempted to comment as severely on his delinquencies as they certainly deserve, we have deliberately forborne. We have even refrained from discussing matters of opinion. We have confined ourselves entirely to matters of fact – to gross and palpable blunders, to unfounded and reckless assertions, to such absurdities in criticism and such vices of style as will in the eyes of discerning readers carry with them their own condemnation. When we consider the circulation secured to this volume from the mere fact of its having issued from so famous a press, and under such distinguished patronage, it is melancholy to think of the errors to which it will give currency. We only hope that our exposure of them will have the effect of serving in some degree to counteract the mischief.

Now the Universities must know, or ought to know, that this kind of thing will not do. If they are resolved to encourage the study of English Literature, it is their duty to see that it is studied properly. If it is not studied properly, the sooner they cease to profess to study it the better. No good can possibly come from Dilettantism. No good can possibly come from unskilled teaching. To tolerate either is to defeat the purposes for which the Universities are designed, is to initiate corruption which will inevitably spread, is to establish precedents which time will confirm. We have already pointed out the responsibility which rests with the centres of education in days like these, and it is, therefore, with just alarm, that we find them countenancing, in any subject represented by them, such work as the work on which we have been animadverting.

But whatever be the faults of Mr Gosse's book, it will not, we hope, be without its use. If it illustrates comprehensively the manner in which English literature should not be taught, it may, on the 'lucus a non lucendo'[13] principle, direct attention to the manner in which it should be taught, and on that subject we propose to make a few remarks. The first fact which the Universities ought to recognize is, that a literature, which is represented by such poets as Shakespeare and Milton, as Pope and Wordsworth, and by such prose writers as Bacon and Hooker, as Gibbon and Burke, is a very serious thing, much too serious a thing to be abandoned either to unskilled teachers or to philologists; that it is a literature not inferior in intrinsic merit to the literatures of the Ancient World, that it is, therefore, from an historical point of view, worthy of minute, of patient, of systematic study; and that, regarded as an instrument of culture, it is – if studied in a liberal and enlightened spirit – of the utmost value and importance. But of this, to judge from such books as Mr Gosse's on the one hand, and by such editions of the English classics as the Clarendon Press provides on the other hand, the Universities appear at present to have no conception. We are very far from wishing to speak disrespectfully of the Clarendon Press publications, for they are, so far as they go, sound and thorough – the work, as a rule, of accurate and painstaking scholars. But their radical defect lies in the fact, that they do not sufficiently distinguish between philology and literature. Instead of regarding a great poem or a great drama as the expression of genius and art, they appear to regard it merely as a monument of language. They dwell with tedious and unnecesary minuteness on points which can interest none but grammarians and philologists, and out of this narrow sphere they seldom or never travel, unless perhaps to explain some historical allusion, to discuss some problem in antiquities, or to accumulate wholly superfluous parallel passages. In the Clarendon Press edition of Milton, for example, nothing is so common as to find a quarter of a page of notes... .

No one could say of the author of notes like these that he displays either want of industry or want of learning, but such notes are, from an educational point of view, all but useless; they are even worse; they render what should be an agreeable and profitable study, simply repulsive. They serve no end; they satisfy no need. It is on this ground, therefore, that we think the Clarendon Press series unsatisfactory. They err not on the side of superficiality or on the side of crude and imperfect learning, but on the side of too narrow a conception of the scope and method of interpreting literature; they err, in short, as Pope taunted Kuster and Burmann[14] with erring:

> The critic eye, that microscope of wit,
> Sees hairs and pores, examines bit by bit,

but fails to see:

> How parts relate to parts, or they to whole,
> The body's harmony, the beaming soul.

That pedantry is, when allied with learning, a far less evil than dilettantism, no one would dispute. Such a study of the English Classics as the Clarendon Press editors prescribe, is not, indeed, calculated either to enlarge a youth's mind or to refine his taste; it is still less calculated to awaken rational curiosity, or to inspire a love of literature for its own sake; but, regarded as a mode of discipline, it may possibly, in some cases, be of service in forming and confirming habits of accuracy, and, within certain limits, habits of thoroughness, and in training and strengthening the memory. But this cannot be pleaded in favour of dilettantism. Of all the pests that beset and impede culture, dilettantism is by far the most mischievous. It is to real learning precisely what the phantom sent by Juno to deceive Turnus was to the real Aeneas. It assumes its form; it brandishes what seem to be its weapons; it mimics its gait; it simulates its speech. But it is a mockery and a fraud. It serves only to delude and mislead. Nor is this all. It is not simply an intellectual, but a moral evil. It encourages those lazy and desultory habits into which young students are especially prone to fall. It tends to render them indifferent to the distinction between accuracy and inaccuracy, between truth and falsehood. It emasculates, it corrupts, it strikes at the very root of that conscientiousness and honesty, that absolute sincerity, which is, or ought to be, the first article in the creed of every scholar and of every teacher.

But the time will, we trust, come when Oxford and Cambridge will see the necessity of raising the study of our national literature to its proper level in education, and when neither dilettantism nor pedantry will be permitted to stand in the way of that study. But before that can be done, they must recognize the distinction between philology and literature, between the significance of the 'Literae Humaniores' as interpreted by verbal critics, and their significance as interpreted by such critics as Lessing and Coleridge. They must think less of the letter and more of the spirit. They must cease to dwell solely on what is accidental, and see the necessity for penetrating to the essence which is the life. Philological criticism is to criticism, in the proper sense of the term, what anatomy is to psychology. Each has its importance, each is in a manner related, and each should be studied, but who would dream of confounding them? The scalpel, which lays bare every nerve and every artery in the mechanism of the body, reveals nothing further. The *Agamemnon* and *Macbeth* are as little likely to yield up the secret of their life to the verbal scholar.

Much has recently been talked about the continuity of history, and the erroneous views which must necessarily result from studying it piecemeal. The continuity of literature is a fact of even more importance, and the persistency with which that fact has been ignored has not only led to errors infinitely more serious than any which can be imputed to historical teachers, but has rendered our whole system of dealing with literature, whether historically, in tracing its development, or critically, in analysing its phenomena, as inadequate as it is unsound. One of the most remarkable illustrations of this is the fact, that the study of our own literature is, in all our schools and colleges, separated on

principle from the study of the literatures of Greece and Rome. Its teachers are, as a rule, men who make no pretension to classical learning, or,
if they possess it, never dream of applying it to the interpretation of
English. Not long ago an eminent London publisher announced a series of annotated English Classics, one of the chief attractions of which
was that it was to be edited by 'none but men who had made a special
study of their mother tongue,' as 'the belief that a knowledge of Greek
and Latin was a qualification for editing English authors was,' so ran
the prospectus – 'a belief which the projectors of the series did not share.'
Now the literatures of Greece, Rome, and England, are radically and
essentially connected. What the literature of Greece is to that of Rome,
the literatures of Greece and Rome are to that of England. A scholar
would at once see the absurdity of separating the study of Roman literature from the study of Greek literature, for the simple reason, that
without a knowledge of the latter the former is unintelligible. We wonder what would be thought of a man who should profess to interpret
the *Aeneid* without possessing an adequate acquaintance with the Homeric Poems, with the Attic Drama, with the poetry of Alexandria; or
of a man who set up to expound the *Odes* of Horace, or to comment on
the style of Sallust and Tacitus, who was ignorant of Greek lyric poetry
and of Thucydides. We wonder what would be the fate of an editor of
the *Georgics* who knew nothing of the *Works and Days*; of an editor of
the *Bucolics*, who knew nothing of the Sicilian Idylls; or of an editor of
Terence, who knew nothing of the New Comedy.

The absurdity of separating the study of our own classics from the
study of the classics of Greece and Rome is equally great. Not only
have most of our poets and all our best prose writers, as well in the
present age as in former ages, been nourished on the literature of Greece
and Rome; not only have the forms of at least two-thirds of our best
poetry and of our best prose derived their distinctive features from those
literatures; not only has the influence of those literatures, alternately
modifying and moulding our own, determined its course and its characteristics; but a large portion of what is most valuable in our poetry is
as historically unintelligible, apart from the Greek and Roman Classics, as the Epic and Lyric Poetry of Rome would be apart from the Epic
and Lyric Poetry of Greece. Take, for example, the poetry of Milton. It
would not be too much to say, that the literature of antiquity was to
Milton's genius what soil and light are to a plant. It nourished, it coloured, it developed it. It determined not merely his character as an
artist, but it exercised an influence on his intellect and temper scarcely
less powerful than hereditary instincts and contemporary history. It at
once animated and chastened his imagination; it modified his fancy; it
furnished him with his models. On it his taste was formed; on it his

style was moulded. From it his diction and his method derived their peculiarities. It transformed what would in all probability have been the mere counterpart of Caedmon's *Paraphrase* or Langland's *Vision* into *Paradise Lost*; and what would have been the mere counterpart of Corydon's Doleful Knell, and the satire of the Three Estates, into 'Lycidas' and *Comus*. The poetry of Gray, again, can only be fully appreciated, can only, in the proper sense of the term, be understood by those who are familiar with the literatures from which its characteristics and its inspiration are derived. And what is true of the poetry of Milton and Gray is true of the poetry of innumerable others. There is much in the very essence of Spenser's poetry, there is much in the very essence of Wordsworth's poetry, which must be absolutely without meaning to readers ignorant of the Platonic philosophy, to readers ignorant of the *Phaedrus* and the *Phaedo*. Indeed the whole history of our early literature is little less than the history of the modification of Teutonic and Celtic elements by classical influences, as the history of the later development of that literature is the history of the alternate predominance of Classicism and Romanticism. It was the Roman drama, slightly modified by the Italian playwrights of the Renaissance, which determined the form of our Romantic drama. On the epics of Greece and Rome are modelled our own epics. Almost all our didactic poetry is professedly modelled on the didactic poetry of Rome. One important branch of our lyric poetry springs directly from Pindar; another important branch directly from Horace; another again directly from the Choral Odes of the Attic dramatists and Seneca. Our heroic satire, from Hall to Byron, is simply the counterpart, often indeed a mere imitation, of Roman satire. The Epistles which fill so large a space in the poetical literature of the seventeenth and eighteenth centuries derived their origin from those of Horace. To the *Heroides* of Ovid we owe a whole series of important poems. From them Chaucer borrowed the material for the most delightful of his minor works; on them Drayton modelled his *Heroical Epistles*, and Pope his 'Eloisa to Abelard.' The tone, the style, the method, of such narratives as Beaumont's *Bosworth Field* and Addison's *Campaign*, themselves the subject of numberless imitations, are borrowed unmistakably from Lucan. Martial and the *Anthology* have furnished the archetypes of our epigrams and our epitaphs, and Theocritus and Virgil the archetypes of our Pastorals. Of our Elegiac poetry, to employ the term in its conventional sense, one portion is largely indebted to Theocritus, Moschus, and Virgil, and another portion still more largely indebted to Catullus and Ovid, to Tibullus and Propertius. Indeed it would be no exaggeration to say, that if the influence individually exercised by each of the Greek and Latin poets, we do not say of the first but of the second order, on our own poets were fully traced, each would afford ample matter for a bulky treatise.

But if this is the case with our poetry, how much more strikingly is it the case with our prose! No one can appreciate more than we do the sweetness, the simplicity, the grace of such prose as Maundeville's, as Malory's, as Bunyan's; and that our language would, had it pursued its course unmodified by classical influences, have been fully equal to the production of such prose, is all but certain. But Maundeville, Malory, and Bunyan, are not the names which rise to our lips when we speak of the masters of prose expression. The history of English eloquence commences from the moment when the Roman Classics moulded and coloured our style – when periodic prose modelled itself on Cicero and Livy, when analytic prose modelled itself on Sallust and Tacitus. From Hooker to Milton, from Milton to Bolingbroke, and from Bolingbroke to Burke, this has been the case. The structure of their periods – allowing, of course, for differences of idiom – the evolution of their periods, their rhythm, their colouring, their tone are, when they rise to eloquence, precisely those of rhetorical Roman prose. It is commonly supposed that when, during the latter half of the seventeenth century, the long sentence began to be broken up, and the style which Addison and his school subsequently perfected became fashionable, the change is to be attributed to the influence of French writers. Nothing could be more erroneous. The style of Hobbes, Sprat, and Cowley, the style subsequently of Dryden and Temple, is as Latin as that of Hooker and Milton; but with a difference. Instead of going to the diction of Livy and to the rhetorical works of Cicero for their models, they went to Quintilian, to the Younger Pliny, and to Cicero's colloquial and epistolary writings. And what is true of them is true of Addison. The serious style of Addison is modelled, as closely as any style could be, on that of the *De Senectute* and the *De Amicitiâ*.[15]

It was the influence partly perhaps of Machiavelli and Guicciardini, but it was the influence mainly of Thucydides and Sallust, of Livy and Tacitus, which revolutionized our historical composition, which gave us Bacon for Capgrave, and Knolles and Herbert for Fabyan, and which was to determine the form, tone, and style of the great works which are the glory of our historic literature – of the great work of Clarendon in the seventeenth century; of the great works of Robertson, Hume, and Gibbon in the eighteenth century; of the great work of Macaulay in the nineteenth century. It was on the Orations of Cicero that Wyatt modelled the speech which is the earliest example in our language of oratorical eloquence; and, from that day to this, the speeches to which, if we wished to vindicate our fame in oratory, we should point, are the speeches which have followed most closely the same noble models. No names stand so high on the roll of our Parliamentary orators as the names of Bolingbroke, Pulteney, Chesterfield, the two Pitts, Burke and Fox; and no names stand higher on the roll of forensic orators than those of Somers, Mansfield, and Erskine. It is notorious that they all gloried in their familiarity with the ancient masterpieces – the masterpieces of Demosthenes and Cicero – and have all left testimonies of their obligations to them. And what has moulded our secular oratory has moulded our sacred oratory. On no part of our prose literature can we look with greater pride than on the sermons of our Classical Divines; and assuredly no part of our literature owes more to the influence of Greece and Rome. The dawn of the Renaissance found our pulpit oratory represented by a few rude and jejune homilies, scarcely rising above the level of the *Sawles Warde*[16] or the *Ayenbite of Inwyt;*[17] its close left us enriched with the Sermons of Hall and Donne, of Taylor and South, of Barrow and Tillotson. If this marvellous transformation is to be explained partly by the progress which secular literature had made, and partly by the influence of the writings of the Fathers, it is to be explained mainly by the influence – the direct influence – of those writers, to which the Fathers themselves were so greatly indebted. Hall and Donne, for example, are in style and diction close imitators of Seneca; and to Seneca, as the author of the *Consolatio ad Marciam* and the *Consolatio ad Helviam*, belongs, it may be added, the honour of having furnished models for the *Oraisons Funèbres* of the French, and for what corresponds to the *Oraisons Funèbres* in our own language. From Plato, Taylor learned the secret of his involved harmonies, and on Plato and Chrysostom he fashioned his diffuse and splendid eloquence. What South would have been apart from the influence of the ancient masters may be easily seen by comparing the passages in which he gives the rein to the coarse vigour of his native genius, and the passages on which his fame rests. The inexhaustible fertility of Barrow's intellect is to be attributed as unmistakably to the assimilative thoroughness with which he had studied the Greek and Roman Classics, as the pregnant energy of his expression bears the impress of Thucydides and Aristotle. What style is more purely Ciceronian than the style of Tillotson, than the style of Sherlock, than the style of Atterbury?

But no portion of our literature is rooted more deeply in the literature of antiquity than our criticism. Dryden has somewhere remarked that:

> One poet is another's plagiary,
> And he a third's till they all end in Homer.[18]

Till the end of the last century, it may be said with literal truth that from the publication of Wilson's *Art of Rhetoric,*[19] in 1553, it would be difficult to mention a single theory on the principles of composition, a single important critical canon, with the exception of the doctrine of the unities of time and place, which are not to be traced originally to the ancient critics. It is a great mistake to suppose, as it almost always is supposed, that we derived our principles of criticism from France. Our own criticism and French criticism sprang from a common source. It was derived directly from Aristotle and Longinus, from Cicero, from Horace, from Quintilian, and from the author of the *Dialogus de Oratoribus*, all of whom had been studied in England long before they had been translated into French.... .

We contend, therefore, that the history of English Literature can never be studied properly unless it be studied in connection with the literatures of Greece and Rome, and that to study it without reference to those literatures is as absurd as it would be to study the history of ethics and metaphysics, or the history of sculpture and architecture, without reference to the ancient schools. It may perhaps be urged that, as Celtic and Teutonic elements enter so largely into the composition of the English temper and the English genius, and that as the literatures of modern Italy, of France, and of Germany have successively affected our own, it is, from an historical point of view, as necessary to take them into consideration as it is the older literatures. This is partly true, but this is not practical. In no school of literature could a student be expected to read, in addition to Greek and Latin, half-a-dozen other languages, and among those languages Celtic, Anglo-Saxon, and German. And even if this were practicable, comparatively little would be gained. Neither Caedmon's *Paraphrase* nor the *Tain Bô*[20] would throw much light on the genesis of *Paradise Lost*, nor would the *Ayenbite of Inwyt* throw much light on the genesis of the Sermons of Taylor and Barrow. The only modern literature which has materially affected us is the Italian. But it is useless to discuss impossibilities. The question simply resolves itself into this, whether, if English Literature is to be seriously studied, it should be studied in connection with the literatures of the modern world, as is, we believe, now being proposed at Oxford; or whether, on the other hand, it should be connected with the study of the Classics. In what way that question should be answered we have endeavoured to point out.

But if in tracing the development of our literature it is necessary at every step to refer to the ancients in studying the literature itself, in regarding it, that is to say, in its spiritual, its ethical, its aesthetic aspects, in considering its structure and its style, how greatly do we gain by comparing its masterpieces with the masterpieces of Greece and Rome. To go no further than the tragedies of Shakspeare: what could be more interesting, what more profitable, than to compare them with the tragedies of the Attic stage, to compare them, for example, with the tragedies of Sophocles; to note how the same truths, the same passions, the same sentiments, find utterance in both; to observe how similarly each deals with the great problem of destiny and free-will, with the doctrine of the mean, with the doctrine of retribution, with the relations of the State to the individual and of the individual to the State; to mark how subtly in each the real and the ideal are blended; to compare their use of irony, to watch the same art working in obedience to the same eternal and unchanging laws directing them in the mechanism of their expression, and the same inspired wisdom guiding them in their interpretation of life. How much, for instance, would a comparative study of *Macbeth* and the *Agamemnon*, of *Henry V* and the *Persae* reveal. What better commentary is to be found on those marvellous fictions which, in the phrase of their creator, hold the mirror up to human nature, than the writings of the subtlest analyst of human nature who has ever lived, the author of the *Ethics* and of the third book of the *Rhetoric*? Indeed, if some scholar would illustrate the dramas of Shakspeare by pertinent references to Aristotle's treatises, he would add greatly to the interest of both, for it would be seen with what exactness each of these students of human nature, though separated by nearly two thousand years, has arrived independently at the same truths, and corroborate each other. We contend then that Aristotle contributes to the elucidation of Shakspeare, as Shakspeare contributes to the elucidation of Aristotle.[21] That such poems as 'Lycidas' and the 'The Progress of Poesy' have been the delight of thousands, who have never opened a Greek or Roman classic, is no doubt true, but it would be absurd to pretend that their pleasure would not have been increased tenfold had they been scholars; it would be absurd to pretend that the full significance, the race, so to speak, and flavour of either the one poem or the other could have been appreciated by them. A reader who knows nothing of Sophocles and Virgil may feel the charm of such a diction as the Laureate's,[22] of such a diction as the diction of *In Memoriam*, or the diction of *The Princess*; but how much will he miss, how many of the ὠκέα βέλη φωνᾶντα συνετοῖσιν[23] must fall flat on him.

But apart from particular reasons for associating the study of English Literature with that of the Literature of Antiquity, – apart from considerations of historical development and the interpretation of this author or that author, there remains the great fact, that by the universal consent of civilized mankind the ancients have in almost every department of the Literae Humaniores approached most nearly to perfection. Out of their very names have been coined synonyms for the excellencies which severally distinguish them. What they have wrought has become archetypal. They stand, indeed, in the same relation to polite letters as the Old Masters stand to painting. It is possible, no doubt, for a painter, whose eyes have never rested on a Dutch or an Italian masterpiece, to produce work of a very high order, and it is certainly possible for a poet who has never read Homer or Horace, to write poetry which Homer and Horace would not have been ashamed to own. But what applies to an artist will not apply to a critic. A man, who set up as a judge of pictures without being familiar with the chief works of the Great Age, or if he knew them, knew them only by copies, might pass for a connoisseur with the crowd, but would find his opinions little appreciated by experts. It is the same, or should be the same with the critic, with the student of Literature. The Homeric Poems, the *Aeneid* and *Georgics*, the Attic Tragedies, the Lyrics of Pindar and Horace, the best of the Platonic Dialogues, the best Orations of Demosthenes and Cicero – these are his Michael Angelos, his Da Vincis, his Raphaels. These are his standards, these are his touchstones. We are no bigoted admirers of the ancients. We believe that the great tragedies of Shakspeare are, considered merely as works of art, at least equal to the *Oedipus Rex*, and that if they be estimated by the powers of mind displayed in them they would, in sheer weight of intellectual bullion, make the dramas of Aeschylus, Sophocles, Euripides, and Aristophanes, massed together, kick the beam. No discerning judge would hesitate to say that the comedies of Molière are incomparably superior to the comedies of Terence. We should be quite prepared to prove categorically that Burke's speech on the Nabob of Arcot's debts and on conciliation with America are greater oratorical feats than the *Verrines* or the *Antonian Philippics*. We rank Burns with Catullus, we rank Dryden above Juvenal. We think Walpole and Gray wrote better letters than the younger Pliny, and we should pronounce the *History of the Decline and Fall* to be a more impressive monument of human genius and of human skill than the *History of the Peloponnesian War*. But this does not prove, as is often absurdly asserted, that familiarity with the works of modern writers would, in the education of a student of literature, be an equivalent for familiarity with the works of the ancients. By none indeed has this been more emphatically pointed out than by those who have themselves been the most distinguished ornaments of our vernacular literature. 'Let persons of limited conception,' says Burke, in a passage which educational legislators would do well to remember, 'think what they will of classical learning, it has ever been and ever must be the first principle of a taste, not only in the Arts, but in life and morals. If we have any priority over our neighbours, it is in no small measure owing to the early care we take with respect to a classical education which cannot be supplied by the cultivation of any other branch of learning.'[24] But it is useless to discuss a question about which, among competent judges, there never have been and there never can be two opinions.

On all grounds, then, on historical, on critical, on general, the necessity of associating the study of classical literature with that of our own, if our own is to be studied properly, is obvious, and it is equally obvious that if this is to be done, it can be done only with the aid of the Universities. Why Oxford and Cambridge should not deem the interpretation of our national literature as worthy of their serious attention as the study of our national history – how it has come to pass that, while the most liberal and enlightened views prevail with regard to the teaching of history, the teaching of literature is either neglected altogether, or abandoned contemptuously to dilettants and philologists – is a problem which we at least are quite unable to solve. But it points, we think, to the great defect, to the only serious defect in our University system. From the days of Pope, Oxford and Cambridge have been commonly taunted, and we fear justly, with attaching too much importance to philology, with regarding the works of great poets and of great orators, not as the expression of genius and art, but as mere material for verbal criticism, as mere monuments of language. Until lately, the literary and aesthetic value of the Greek and Roman classics has undoubtedly been too little considered, the method of interpreting them being almost exclusively the method of the technical scholar, a method which cannot be too highly appreciated when regarded as a means to an end, or too strongly condemned when regarded as an end in itself. We have, however, recently observed with pleasure that, on the subject of classical exegesis, more liberal views are beginning to prevail. We wish we could discern the same promising symptoms in the case of our own Literature, but here unhappily the dominion of philology is absolute. How obstinately indeed University legislators, or at all events an important section of them, appear to be bent on discountenancing any other than a philological interpretation of that Literature has recently received a memorable illustration. About three years ago, a party at Oxford, who were strongly in favour of an intelligent study of our national classics being encouraged in the University, and who were anxious to raise English Literature to its proper level in education, so far prevailed as to obtain the consent of Convocation to the foundation of an English Chair. A Chair of English Literature was accordingly founded and liberally endowed. A Board of Electors was appointed. As there was already a Chair of Celtic, a Chair of Anglo-Saxon, a Chair of Comparative Philology, and as therefore the philological study of English had been amply provided for, it was confidently expected that the choice of the electors would fall on the sort of teacher contemplated by the originators of the movement. But Philology triumphed. The Board discovering, that though the language of Caedmon and the language of Oisin had received the attention they deserved, the dialect of Robert of Gloucester and William of Shoreham had not, determined to seize this opportunity to remedy the defect. Availing themselves of a quibble on the word 'language' – for the Statute authorizing the foundation of the Chair happened, by a mere accident, to couple the word 'language' with 'literature' – they succeeded in ignoring the object for which the Chair was founded, and proceeded to elect, at a permanent salary of about £900, a Professor for the interpretation of Middle English. Such was the fate of a movement which might, and probably would, have formed an era of incalculable importance in education. It is indeed half-painful, half-ludicrous, to reflect that at the present moment, in Oxford alone, upwards of £3000 a year are expended on the interpretation of writings which are confessedly of no literary value, and of interest only as monuments of language, while not one farthing a year is spent on the interpretation of works which are the glory of our country.

We have, however, little doubt that an anomaly so extraordinary and so disgraceful will not be tolerated much longer. We feel confident that English Literature, in the proper sense of the term, will sooner or later receive the recognition to which at the centres of culture it is assuredly entitled. Our only fear is either that it may be considered too exclusively with reference to itself, or that it may be assigned a place in some other part of the curriculum than that part to which, as we have endeavoured to show, it properly belongs. It would, we submit, be a great mistake to make it form a portion, as some propose to do, of the curriculum of a School of Modern Literature and to treat it only in connection with Modern Literature. It would be a still greater mistake to attach it collaterally, as others propose, to the curriculum of the Modern History School, and to consider it mainly in its relations to Modern History. To prescribe, on the other hand, an independent and uncomparative study of it, to deal with it, that is to say, as a subject bounded by and complete in itself, would be equally objectionable because equally insufficient. Its proper place is the place which we have indicated – with the literatures which are at the head of all literatures, with the literatures which nourished it, moulded it, which best illustrate it.

What is needed, and we venture to add imperatively needed, is the institution of a school which shall stand in the same relation to pure literature, to poetry, oratory, and criticism, as the present school of history stands to history, and as the present school of Literae Humaniores stands to philosophy. In both these schools, in the former as it is about to be constituted, in the latter as it always has been constituted, the historical and philosophical classics of the old world are most properly associated with those of the new. No hard-and-fast line is drawn between philosophers and historians who write in Greek or Latin, and philosophers and historians who write in English. Both are studied not for the light which they may happen to throw collaterally on the structure and history of language, but for the light which they throw on the subjects which are severally treated by them. Herodotus and Thucydides are accordingly included in the same curriculum as Clarendon and Gibbon. The *Republic* and the *Ethics* are read side by side with the *Essay on the Human Understanding* and the *Enquiry concerning the Principles of Morals*. Thus not only are the masterpieces of ancient and modern philosophy brought home to the student, but their relations to each other are rendered intelligible. 'The work,' says the Regius Professor of Modern History at Oxford,[25] 'which I have come to do is to point out that the work of Kleisthenes, of Licinius, of Simon of Montfort, are parts of one living whole, a whole of which every stage needs to be grasped by the same faculties, to be studied by the same methods.' Why, we would ask, should not the same view be taken of the work of Sophocles and Shakspeare, of Cicero and Burke? Are they not also 'parts of one living whole'? Is not poetry, poetry; oratory, oratory; criticism, criticism in whatever language they may be expressed? And is not the study of literature the study of its development generally, and of its masterpieces particularly? Why the works of a philosopher or a historian who writes in a classical language should be studied as illustrating philosophy and history, while the works of a poet or of an orator who writes in a classical language should be regarded as mere material for construing, – why University men should be expected to know in what way modern metaphysics have been affected by Plato and modern ethics by Aristotle, and should not be expected to know in what way modern poetry has been affected by Homer and Horace, and modern oratory by Demosthenes and Cicero – we cannot understand. But of one thing we are quite sure, that it is high time, both in the interests of classical literature and of our own literature, to take this question into serious consideration, and to see whether the institution of such a school, or of some school similar to such a school as we have suggested, be indeed practicable. What the nation has a right to expect from the Universities is, that they should provide as adequately for the dissemination of literary culture as they have provided for other branches of education. And this we contend they can never do if, on the one hand, for the study of the two leading and master literatures of the world, the literatures which are and must always be the basis of the education of which we are speaking, they substitute the study of what certain educational theorists are pleased to call modern equivalents; and if, on the other hand, they continue to exclude our own literature from their curriculum.

Of the necessity of the Universities directing their attention to this

important subject, no further proof is required than the contrast between the high standard of classical, historical, and scientific teaching
throughout the kingdom and the deplorably low standard, all but universal, in the teaching of English literature. In many places it is degraded into mere cram-work, into prescribing so many pages of a primer
or manual to be got by heart. In other places it goes no further than the
purely philological study of single works. If a more enlightened exegesis is anywhere employed, it is the result of simple accident. And
what is true of the standard of teaching is true of the standard of production. A work analogous to the work which stands at the head of this
article would, we believe, in any other department of learning and culture, be impossible. One tithe of its blunders and absurdities would
have ruined instantly a book treating of Greek or Roman poetry, or
discussing some point in modern history. No one indeed can compare
an average review or magazine article on a classical, a historical, or a
scientific subject, with an average article dealing with a purely literary
subject, without being struck with the immense superiority of the former
to the latter. The first we feel to be the work of a man who has had an
efficient training, who is master of his subject, who is possessed with
his subject, and who is conscious that he is addressing readers who
will meet him halfway. In the second, we are fortunate if we do not find
all the indications of half-knowledge and of gross ignorance, and of
half-knowledge and gross ignorance conscious of being able to assume
without detection the garb and semblance of intelligence and learning.
An editor of a scientific or historical Review has not the least difficulty
in finding contributors who are able to write up to the high level required in such subjects. It is notorious that editors of literary Reviews
are constantly under the necessity of accepting articles, the inferiority
of which they are themselves the first to admit. For the existence of this
extraordinary anomaly, the Universities, and the Universities only, are
responsible. We owe it to them – and it is to their honour – that the
standard is so high, and those who maintain it so numerous in the one
case. We owe it to them – and it is not to their credit, that the standard
is so low, and those anxious to raise it so few, in the other case. And till
they are prepared to take active measures, and to extend to the study of
literature, and especially to the study of our vernacular literature, the
protection they have extended to other branches of education – so long
will this state of things continue; so long will mediocrity, sciolism, and
ignorance prevail; so long will our presses continue to pour forth such
books as the book on which we have been animadverting, and so long
will our leading literary journals continue to pronounce them 'volumes
not to be glanced over and thrown aside, but to be read twice and consulted often.'

Notes

1. Edmund Gosse, *From Shakespeare to Pope* (1885).
2. *The Gentleman's Magazine* was edited by E. Cave from 1731 to 1754, then by Richard Cave from 1766 to 1778. *The Annual Register* was commenced and published for many years by R. Dodsley.
3. literary gossip, as in 'Virgiliana' or 'Shakespeariana.'
4. 'They take no care to be free of guilt, but only to secure one another's impunity' (Tacitus, *Histories*, I.lxxii).
5. 'We live, led by mediocrity: the wise have sunk, the vulgar mounted, to one plane, thus levelling all' (Giacomo Leopardi, Canto 'Ad Angelo Mai').
6. A commission was set up under the Oxford and Cambridge Act of 1877, resulting in a number of statutes in the years that followed. These brought about great changes in the life and organization of the university.
7. 'royal paper, new volumes, new decorated ends for the cylinder, red straps, cover with lines ruled with lead, and all polished with pumice-stone' (Catullus, *Carmina*, xxii.6–8. This is a description of papyri.).
8. # As this may seem incredible to those of our readers who do not know what modern bookmakers are capable of, we will give the passages with their contexts in full... .
9. Samuel Garth, 'Claremont' (1715).
10. John Denham, 'Cooper's Hill' (1642).
11. Edmund Waller, 'Battle of the Summer Islands' (1645).
12. # One of our leading literary journals terminated a review which, though extending to six columns, did not point out a single error, with these words: 'It is a volume not to be glanced over and thrown aside, and we recommend the student of English Poetry to read it twice and consult it often' [*Athenaeum*, No. 3030 (21 November 1885), p.662]. Such is sometimes the value of 'review' advertisements.
13. 'A grove, so called because you cannot see into it' – a ridiculous derivation by which a thing is supposed to obtain its name from a quality which it does not possess. Quintilian wrote, 'Lucus, quia, umbra opacus, parum luceat.' – Lucus, a grove, is so called because, from the dense shade, there is very little light there (*De Institutione Oratoria*, I.vi.34).
14. *Dunciad*, iv.233–236. Ludolph Kuster and Peter Burmann were, respectively, German and Dutch classical scholars.
15. # This is an interesting question, and as our opinion may appear paradoxical, we will place side by side what will be allowed to be a typical sample of Cicero's literary style, and what will be allowed to be a typical sample of Addison's style. And the truth of what we have asserted will, we think, be at once apparent... .
16. An early Middle English homily.
17. A work in Kentish dialect Middle English by Dan Michel, being a translation of *Le Somme des Vices et Vertues* by Frère Laurent. Editions had been published by the Roxburghe Club in 1855 and the Early English Text Society in 1866.
18. This quotation does not seem to be from Dryden. However, Robert Burton wrote something similar in 1621: 'we can say nothing but what hath been said... . Our poets steal from Homer' (*The Anatomy of Melancholy*, 'Democritus to the Reader').
19. Thomas Wilson, *The Arte of Rhetorique* (1553).

20. An Old Irish prose epic, not translated into English until 1904.
21. # There is not, of course, the smallest reason for supposing that Shakspeare ever read a line of Aristotle, either in the original or in a translation.
22. i.e. Tennyson.
23. swift arrows, striking to the wise.
24. #Letter to Parr, *The Works of Samuel Parr*, J. Johnstone, ed. (1828) I, 200. 'It is with the deepest regret,' writes Scott, referring to his neglect of classical studies, 'that I recollect in my manhood the opportunities of learning which I neglected in my youth, and through every part of my literary career I have been pinched and hampered by my ignorance; it is a loss never to be repaired'[John Gibson Lockhart, *Memoirs of the Life of Sir Walter Scott* (1837), I, 13].
25. Edward Freeman, one of the most vociferous opponents of proposals to introduce English studies at Oxford. See his article included in this volume, pp. 277–93.

Review of the Petition Addressed to Oxford's Hebdomadal Council

It is with no small satisfaction that we are able to announce, that our recent article on English Literature at the Universities has not been without effect. The serious deficiency, which it pointed out in an important department of education, is now generally acknowledged. The necessity of endeavouring to supply that deficiency is admitted on all sides, and the opinions, which three months ago we appeared to be alone in maintaining, have been corroborated by such a consensus of authoritative opinion, that it would be impossible for any Council of educational legislators to disregard them. It will be remembered that what we advocated was this: the recognition on the part of the Universities of the claims of the Literae Humaniores, in the proper sense of the term, to a place in the curriculum of Academic study. We pointed out, that the time had come when it was necessary to distinguish between a literary and philological study of the Greek and Roman Classics, between their interest as monuments of language and their value as the expression of genius and art. We urged the claims of our own literature to a place in the curriculum of the same school, not simply on account of its growing importance as a subject of study throughout the kingdom and in the colonies, and the consequent necessity of the Universities providing adequately for its interpretation, but because of its intimate, its essential historical connection with ancient Classical literature, and because of its efficacy as an instrument of culture, if studied side by side with and in the light of the literatures which nourished, moulded, and coloured it. We showed how by thus associating the three leading and master literatures of the world, and by thus encouraging a liberal and enlightened treatment of them, each would gain in interest and value, as each would gain in efficacy and vitality: the study of the Greek and Roman Classics would at once, we contended, be placed on the only footing on which in modern times it is possible to justify it; and the study of our own literature, rescued from the degradation into which pedantry, dilettantism, and sciolism have sunk it, would be raised to its proper level in education.

We were of opinion, therefore, and are still of opinion, that if, under these conditions, English literature were admitted to a place in our Universities, a great deficiency in the economy of Modern education would be supplied, and the classical side of education would immensely gain. But nothing, we are convinced, could be more disastrous – disastrous alike to culture, to learning, to letters – than to attempt to substitute our own literature and the literatures of the modern world for those of Greece and Rome, or even to admit those literatures to a place in the curriculum – we are speaking of the Honour curriculum – unless in close association with the ancient Classics. Culture would suffer: for what competent judge, from Jonson to Arnold, has ever had two opinions about the relative educational value of the archetypal masterpieces of antiquity and the noblest monuments of Teutonic and Romantic Art? Learning and Taste would suffer: for what exegesis could be historically and critically sound, which did not trace formal characteristics to their origin, did not apply the standards and touchstones common to those who have been truly initiated and rightly taught? Letters would suffer necessarily and inevitably, necessarily and inevitably as effects follow causes. We entirely agree with Dr. Craik[1] that, if the study of English Literature be not inseparably connected with the classical curriculum, the Universities will do wisely, both for their own sake and for the sake of education generally, to continue to exclude it from their Schools.

It is therefore with just alarm that we hear, that the Hebdomadal Council at Oxford are, in obedience to a petition recently presented, considering the desirableness of founding a School of Modern Literature, a school in which English Literature is to hold a prominent place, and in which Classical Literature is, if retained at all, to be retained as a subordinate or optional subject. Now, if any confidence could be placed in the firmness and wisdom of University legislators, they might be safely left to decide this question for themselves. But, unhappily, no such confidence can be placed in them. During the last ten years, their Councils have been torn by two factions – the one representing the spirit of progress and experiment, and labouring to adapt University education to the practical requirements of modern life by developing it on the positive and scientific side, the other clinging with uncompromising tenacity to the old methods and to the old traditions. So far the two parties, though constantly opposed to one another, have not come into any violent collision. The modern party have refrained from meddling with the questions in which their opponents are most interested, the constitution and economy of the Classical Schools, and have contented themselves with providing for the subjects which more immediately concern them – for the study of natural science in all its branches, for the study of modern history, of political economy – for the study, in short, of all those subjects which belong to what is called the Modern as distinguished from the Classical side of education. This party, which is increasing yearly in numbers and influence, has the immense advantage of being in union with popular opinion, and of having as its allies all who believe that the object of education is not to cultivate, but to plant; not to elevate and refine, but to provide on the one hand what will be practically useful in practical life, and to provide on the other hand what will further the interests of scientific as distinguished from literary culture. The fact, that the Greek and Latin languages are no longer spoken, is with them a sufficient reason that they should be no longer read. Not very long ago one of their leaders publicly observed that, as an acquaintance with English History was more desirable than an acquaintance with Greek History, he saw no reason why Gregory of Tours should not be preferred to Thucydides. Indeed the sentiments of these revolutionists with respect to Classical Literature cannot be better expressed than in the words of a letter, recently written by Mr John Bright[2] to a correspondent, who had asked him whether in his opinion the classics of modern Europe were, from an educational point of view, an equivalent for the classics of Greece and Rome... .

The opinions of these revolutionists are every term gaining ground, and their policy is now aggressive. Indeed nothing is more certain than that, if a stand is not made against them, they will soon get the management of the Universities into their power, and the strongholds of Classical culture, assailed from within and assailed from without, will be in the hands of its professed opponents. Such a revolution would, in truth, be nothing less than a national calamity.

The crisis has now come; the test question is defined and under discussion; and the test question is this: Whether the study of our national literature – for its admission to a place in the curriculum of the University is now, we believe, virtually settled – is to be associated with the study of the Greek and Roman Literatures, or whether it is to be disassociated from those Literatures and to form the nucleus of a curriculum of Modern Literature? On the decision of that question depends – depends, we believe, permanently – the future of the higher education of this country, and of all that is involved in the maintenance of the standard of that education. If a school, an Honour School of Literature be founded at Oxford, as it has already been founded at Cambridge – with what success we have recently seen – in which the Classics do not form an essential part of the course, the immediate result will be the depression and subordination of the Classical element in University culture; the ultimate result will be the elimination of the classics from the curriculum of liberal education, and their retention merely as material for philological study.

That there are ample reasons for fearing that the important movement, which is now on foot, is in danger of being misdirected, and of involving in its misdirection incalculable mischief to education, is unhappily only too apparent. In our former article we protested against the transformation of a Chair, originally founded in the interests of literary culture, into a Chair designed merely to further the interests of philological learning. We have now to protest against something much more serious. The perversion of the Merton Chair was, it seems, merely a preliminary step. A Professor, elected on such a theory of the scope and functions of a Chair of Literature, is to be succeeded by a School, framed in accordance with the same theory of the scope and functions of a School of Literature. What the constitution of that school is to be, Professor Max Müller has recently explained. It is:

> to consist of three branches – Teutonic, Romanic, and Celtic. The Teutonic is to be subdivided into an English, German and Scandinavian section; the Romanic into a Southern (Provençal and Italian), a Northern (French), and possibly a third section comprising Spanish and Portuguese. These are as yet *pia vota* only; but I have that faith in young Oxford that, with certain modifications, and possibly after some hesitation, some such scheme will be carried.[3]

And 'some such scheme' is now embodied in the 'Petition' which stands at the head of this article. When we observe that in this 'scheme,' drawn up by Professor Max Müller and his disciples, the Greek and Roman classics have no place at all, and that the whole is evidently designed purely in the interests of philology; and when in addition we remember the great influence which Professor Max Müller exercises in Oxford, all who have the cause of literary culture at heart may well tremble for its prospects at the present crisis. We trust, however, that the Hebdomadal council will not permit themselves to be either deluded or misled. They have far more important interests to consult than the interests of a sect of technical scholars. What is expected from them has, during the last three months, been proclaimed definitely and imperiously by the voice of the whole nation. They are asked to make adequate provision for the cultivation of the Literae Humaniores, not in the philological, but in the proper sense of the term; and especially for the cultivation of our vernacular literature. They are asked to provide for the efficient education, not only of those students who will, on quitting the Universities, follow pure literature as a profession, or at all events become contributors of more or less importance to it, but of those who will become its apostles and exponents in other capacities – who will fill the Chairs of Literature which the modern side of education is every year multiplying – multiplying in the provinces, multiplying in the Colonies; who will be enlisted in the same service, as teachers in our Public Schools, as University Extension Lecturers, as Lecturers at Girton, Newnham and similar seminaries, as Lecturers in the innumerable Institutes scattered up and down the country. They are asked to send forth teachers conversant, not with the origins and antiquities of Literature, not with its barbarous and semi-barbarous experiments, its *Bersah Sagas*, *Tain Bôs*, *Beowulfs* and *Chansons de Roland*, but with its masterpieces and mature expression. They are asked for critics, they are asked for initiators; they are not asked for philologists. They are asked – for they are the legislators of the centres of culture – to provide, as efficiently as they can, for the training of those who will emerge from their schools to create the literature and especially the popular literature of the future, and whose aims and tone as writers will be in a large measure determined by early impressions. They are asked to educate those who are to educate the world. Up to the present time these men have been obliged to take their training into their own hands, and to pursue it collaterally with the sort of training which the Universities are competent to give. But, in pursuing this independent path, they have had too often to pursue it at the heavy price of receiving no share in the prizes which are the rewards of Academic distinction. Not that Oxford and Cambridge are indifferent to literary eminence, or have no pride in such of their sons as do them honour. If philologists and technical scholars enjoy the substantial rewards of learning – the mere loaves and fishes – it would be ungenerous to forget the many instances of men who, having succeeded after a life of poverty and depression in achieving literary fame, have lived to see that fame gracefully recognized in an Honorary Fellowship or an Honorary Degree.

The Hebdomadal Council will, we think, do wisely, if, at this momentous crisis, they pay serious attention to the opinions which our recent article has elicited. These opinions are now lying before us. Some of them are in the shape of private letters, which we now publish for the first time with the consent of the writers; others have appeared during the last six weeks in the columns of the *Pall Mall Gazette*,[4] a journal which has honourably distinguished itself by the ability and consistency with which it has supported us in pleading the cause of Literature and Education.

The first point, to which we would draw attention, is the authoritative and comprehensively representative character of these opinions – is the fact that they have emanated, not from men who are of probationary or secondary repute, or who belong to a particular calling, but from men pre-eminently distinguished in all walks of life; from the Archbishop of Canterbury, from the Cardinal Archbishop of Westminster, from the Lord Chief Justice, from the late Lord Chancellor, from men who fill or have filled the first places among English School Masters or University teachers, from the Bishop of London, from Archdeacon Farrar, from the Dean of Winchester, from the present Head Masters of Rugby, of the City of London School, of Wellington, of Clifton; from the most cultivated of contemporary statesmen, Mr Gladstone, the Earl of Lytton, the Earl of Carnarvon, Mr John Morley; from the most distinguished man of science now living, Professor Huxley; from men of letters like Mr Froude, Mr Matthew Arnold, Sir Theodore Martin, Mr Addington Symonds, Mr Courthope, Mr Walter Pater, Mr Frederic Myers; from men not less distinguished in other spheres of intellectual activity, from Professor Bonamy Price, Professor Max Müller, Professor Alfred Goodwin, Professor John Hales; from Heads of Houses in the University itself, from the Master of Balliol, the Master of University, the Rector of Lincoln, the President of Trinity, the Provost of Oriel, the President of Magdalen, the Warden of All Souls, from the Principal of the Nonconformist College. The second point, to which we would direct attention, is the remarkable uniformity with which these opinions, thus various in their sources, corroborate the views expressed by us in our recent article. On the necessity of our Universities providing adequately for the study of Literature, and particularly English Literature, as distinguished from Philology, there is not, if we except Professor Max Müller, an obstinate philologist, a dissentient voice.

* *
*

Not less definite and emphatic are the opinions which have been expressed as to the necessity of associating, in any School or Course of Literature, which may be provided or prescribed, the study of our own Literature with the study of ancient Classical Literature… . Nothing that we could say could add weight to these thoughtful and impressive remarks.

The necessity then of the University making adequate provision for the systematic study of literature, and especially for the systematic study of our own literature, is so generally acknowledged, that the advocates of the movement are no longer required to prove it desirable, but to show how, without injury to the curriculum of University studies as at present constituted, it can be rendered practical. This is the problem before the Council, and it is obviously a very difficult and a very complicated one. Indeed it may be admitted at once that, whatever scheme may finally be adopted, the choice will have to lie, not with the scheme which is open to no objections, but with the scheme which is open to fewest objections. And that which will be open to fewest objections will be that which is least calculated to disturb existing arrangements, and which, with the minimum of innovations, will yet attain the ends at which a School of Literature should aim. The scheme which most readily suggests itself, and which Mr Matthew Arnold, Canon Percival, and Mr Courthope appear to propose, is the modification of the present classical curriculum by the introduction of English Literature as a special subject, either in Moderations, or in the Final Schools, or in both. But there seem to us serious objections to this. If introduced into Moderations, it would, unless it were reduced to proportions wholly incommensurate with its importance and wholly incompatible with an adequate study of it, seriously interfere with the prosecution of the studies peculiar to that examination. Nothing is more important than the preservation of a high standard of exact scholarship, and the aim of Moderations is, and should continue to be, the preservation of that standard. If, again, it were introduced into the Final Literae Humaniores School, it would, as that School is now constituted, stand as a subject isolated not only from what is cognate to it in classical literature, but what is cognate to it in education; it would stand with Greek and Roman History, with Logic, with Comparative Philology, with Moral and Political Philosophy. Had the old School of Literae Humaniores, which included, with History and Philosophy, Poetry, Oratory, and Criticism, been left standing, the curriculum might no doubt have been modified without difficulty in the way which Mr Arnold suggests. But that basis no longer exists. The old school has gone, gone, it may be added, to the regret of all who do not share the modern rage for experimentalizing, and who are inclined to suspect that our fathers were at least as wise as ourselves.

We do not believe, therefore, in the modification of the curriculum of any existing school. Such a course would, we are convinced, lead to nothing but confusion and perplexity. As things now are, each school has a distinctive character and a definite aim. The aim of Moderations is, on the one hand, to secure and guarantee exact classical scholarship, and on the other hand to teach students to apply that scholarship to its proper use – the elucidation of the poetry, criticism, and oratory of Greece and Rome. The aim of the Final School of Literae Humaniores is to supplement the literary course thus admirably initiated in Moderations with the austerer discipline of Philosophy and Science. Now the introduction of English Literature into the curriculum of either of these schools would obviously be most injudicious. It would seriously interfere with the classical element in Moderations. It would be entirely out of harmony with the subjects studied in the Final School.

We are satisfied that the true solution of the problem would be the foundation of a new Final School, of a school which should not supersede, which should in no way interfere with the present Final School of Literae Humaniores, but which should correspond to it, and which should stand in the same relation to it as the old Law and History School used to stand to the old Literae Humaniores School. In the former times a student would take his honours in Literae Humaniores, and would then proceed to prepare himself for his second school, the School of Law and History, and it was within the reach of any man of intelligence and energy to take a first class in both courses. If he had not the energy or inclination to aspire to honours in both schools, it was open to him to take his choice between them, and to graduate in honours in 'Law and Modern History,' instead of in honours in 'Literae Humaniores.' This second school was abolished on the ground, no doubt, that as the subjects represented in it had no direct connection with the subjects prescribed in the curriculum of the preceding school, it was impossible for students to attain with a year's reading, even though that reading had been aided by reading pursued collaterally with their Literae Humaniores studies, a sufficiently high standard. But these objections would not apply to a School of Literature, for a portion of the work required for it would already have been accomplished in Moderations, and another portion of that work, the perusal namely of the lighter part of our own literature, would, so far from interfering with the preparation for Literae Humaniores, form, as indeed it now does, a pleasant relaxation for leisure hours.[5] Thus the student could take his honours in Literae Humaniores, and would still have a year before him for the severe and systematic study, which the school we are advocating would necessarily exact. On the other hand, men who were less energetic, or whose tastes and aims were purely literary, would be enabled to graduate in honours in Belles Lettres instead of graduating in honours in Philosophy, Philology, and Ancient History, just as in former times it was open to men to graduate in Law and History, instead of graduating in Literae Humaniores. We think, however, that the University would do well to require of every candidate for the Honour School of Literature that he should have obtained at least a third class in the School of Literae Humaniores. For a purely literary curriculum would undoubtedly be too thin. Poetry, Rhetoric, and Criticism can never, from an educational point of view, be equivalents for Logic, and Moral and Political

Philosophy, and the elimination of those solid elements from the curriculum of culture would constitute a serious deficiency even in the education of a literary critic. In our opinion no student should be entitled to a degree in Arts, who had not an adequate acquaintance with the *Ethics* and the *Republic*.

If, again, we regard the constitution of the proposed school in its relation to the constitution of existing schools, we shall see how little it would disturb existing arrangements, and how easily and naturally it would supply an obvious defect in the classical course. The aim of Moderations is, as we have seen, to enable students to read the chief Greek and Roman Classics with facility and accuracy, to give them a minute acquaintance with particular works, or with portions of particular works, and to initiate them in the rudiments of literary criticism and of literary history, so far at least as they relate to the Greek and Roman Classics. But all this is supposed to be accomplished in about two years, for Moderations is merely an intermediate school, and with Moderations the course of pure literature, thus admirably inaugurated, abruptly terminates. The classical student is then hurried on without option to the final School of Literae Humaniores, a school in the preparation for which he passes at once from Poetry to History, from Oratory to Ethics, and from Literary Criticism to Logic. If he chooses to abandon Classics, it is of course open to him to select any final school he pleases. He can, if he is so minded, betake himself to Mathematics, or to Natural Science, or to Jurisprudence, or to Modern History, or to Theology. But what he cannot do is to complete his literary education, is to consolidate and extend those studies of which he had in Moderations been able to do little more than lay the foundations. We shall not be suspected of undervaluing the educational value either of Natural Science or of Modern History, and still less of Mathematics and Theology. Nor are we disposed on the whole to find fault with a curriculum, which is obviously designed to blend a certain amount of literary culture with the severe discipline of philosophy and science. But no students are, we repeat, entitled to greater consideration on the part of the Universities, than those whose future calling will be to disseminate literary culture, to deal directly with literary criticism and with literary history. Now it is surely most unreasonable that a class of students, who are to occupy so important a place in letters and culture, should have no opportunity of completing their education, should have no option but to break off the studies peculiarly suited to them just when those studies are beginning to be of real service, and might and ought to be extended. A Final School of Literature on the lines we propose is therefore as desirable in the interests of classical culture, as it is in the interests of the study of English. Its formal constitution might, we think, be modelled on the constitution of the present Literae Humaniores School. In the curriculum of that school are included, as we have seen, Greek and Roman History, Logic, Moral and Political Philosophy, the History of Philosophy and a Special Subject. Now if for Greek and Roman History were substituted the General History of the Greek and Roman Literatures; for Moral and Political Philosophy, the General History of English Literature; for Logic and the History of Philosophy, Historical and Aesthetic Criticism; and for the Special Subject, which ranges from Textual Criticism to Comparative Philology, a critical examination of prescribed works, we should have a framework corresponding, or nearly corresponding, in its proportions to what is now partly a School of History, partly of Philology, and partly of Philosophy.

Thus the school we contemplate would group the subjects included in its curriculum thus. First would come Poetry; then would come Rhetoric, and Rhetoric would naturally subdivide itself into Oratory proper and into History, or rather into historical composition regarded as Rhetoric. Lastly would come Criticism, which might in its turn be appropriately subdivided into Historical Criticism, in other words, the History of Literature, and into Aesthetic and Philosophical Criticism. In the department of Poetry the classical portion should consist of passages for translation, selected from the leading poets of each era of Greek and Latin Literature, from Homer to Theocritus, from Lucretius to Prudentius, with elucidatory comments. The English portion should consist of questions framed with the object of ascertaining that the chief poems of each era had been thoughtfully perused, and that prescribed masterpieces, – the 'Prologue' and the 'Knight's Tale,' for example, the first and second books of *The Faery Queen*, half-a-dozen of Shakspeare's best dramas, the *Paradise Regained*, six books of the *Paradise Lost*, the *Absalom and Achitophel*, *The Rape of the Lock*, and the like – had been critically studied. In the department of Rhetoric the works offered for examination should, like the works offered for examination in Philosophy in the sister school, be specified by the Board of Studies, and what those works should be might be safely left to the discretion of the Board. In the Historical portion of the Department of Criticism papers should be set on the general history of the three Literatures, with a view to testing knowledge of their evolution and idiosyncrasies. And in addition to these papers a special paper on the direct and indirect influence of the Greek and Roman Literatures in moulding and modifying our own, and in particularly influencing the work of particular writers, ought undoubtedly to form a feature of the examination. Aesthetic, philosophic, and technical criticism should be represented by the *Poetics*, the third book of the *Rhetoric*, the *De Antiquis Rhetoribus*, the *De Structurâ Orationis*, and the *De Sublimitate*, in Greek; in Latin, by the *Brutus*, the *De Oratore* or a portion of the *De Oratore*, by the *Dialogus de*

Oratoribus and the tenth book of Quintilian. And to these should be added that immortal treatise which stands with the *De Sublimitate* at the head of the higher criticism – the *Laocoon*.[6]

If this scheme could be carried out, it would, it seems to us, not only serve to maintain that high standard of scholarship on which our Universities justly pride themselves, and without which the study of languages which are no longer spoken would be worse than useless, but it would, by extending the period of preparation from the period of school-life to the age of about three-and-twenty, enable students to peruse at least a third of what is most excellent in the pure literature of Greece, Rome, and England. It would enable them to make themselves masters of the great critical treatises – or of portions of those treatises – of which we have spoken, and of such works in English as represent what is best in the criticism of three centuries, from Sidney's *Apology* to Arnold's Homeric Lectures. It would enable them to encroach so far on Philosophy as to make the *Phaedrus* and the *Phaedo* their own – golden discourses, as precious, as indispensable, to the student of poetry as to the student of metaphysics. It would enable them to study analytically the *De Coronâ*, the *Philippics*, and *Olynthiacs*, the great Oration of Aeschines, the great Oration of Isocrates, an oration or two of Lysias, half-a-dozen of the best orations of Cicero, two or more of best orations of Burke. It would afford them ample leisure for such an acquaintance with the histories of Herodotus and Thucydides, of Sallust, Livy, and Tacitus, of Clarendon, Hume, and Gibbon, as would be sufficient for the purposes of rhetorical culture. It would enable them to peruse and compare the masterpieces of the Attic and Roman Drama with the masterpieces of our own Drama; the two noblest Epics of the Old World and the yet nobler Epic of the New; the *Odyssey* and *The Canterbury Tales*; the *Metamorphoses*[7] and *The Faery Queen*; the lyrics of Pindar and Horace, and the lyrics of those among our own poets, who acknowledged Pindar and Horace as their masters, or who have, in finding other sources of inspiration, rivalled, and more than rivalled, ancient artists. It would enable them to make themselves as familiar with the *Essay on Criticism* as with the *Ars Poetica*; with the Satires of Dryden, Pope, and Johnson, as with the Satires of Horace, Persius, and Juvenal; with such poems as *Alastor* and the 'Atys,' on the one hand, and the *Rape of the Lock* and the 'Coma Berenices' on the other,[8] with the gems of the *Anthology* and the gems of Martial, as with the gems of our own not less brilliant Florilegia. It would enable them to pursue consecutively the course of Philosophic and Didactic poetry, from the *Works and Days* to the *De Rerum Naturâ*, from the *De Rerum Naturâ* to the *Georgics*, from the *Georgics* to the *Essay on Man*, and from the *Essay on Man* to the *Excursion*; of Pastoral and Idyllic poetry, from the Sicilian Idylls to the *Bucolics* of Virgil, from the

Bucolics to the 'Mosella,' and from the 'Mosella' to such pieces as have in successive epochs of our own literature, from the appearance of the *Shepherd's Calendar* to the appearance of the English Idylls, been typical of the same class. It would enable them to understand the relations and to estimate the debt of our Narrative poetry to the *Argonautica* of Apollonius, to the *Peleus and Thetis*, to the *Heroical Epistles*, to the *Pharsalia*, to the *Thebaid*, to that brilliant Idyllic Epic, and that not less brilliant Allegoric Epic which, with other poems, once too much over-rated, now too generally neglected, constitute Claudian and Prudentius the link between ancient and modern poetry.

But it is easy to legislate on paper, and we are of course well aware, that such a scheme as we have suggested is open to many reasonable objections. It may be urged that the curriculum, which we have sketched, is on the one hand much too wide, and on the other hand much too narrow. How, it may be asked, are Thucydides, Tacitus, and Gibbon to be approached only on the rhetorical side;[9] or how is a line to be drawn between Plato as he illustrates poetry, and Plato regarded generally in his relation to Metaphysics? Many will contend, that an acquaintance with the chief monuments of Anglo-Saxon literature is to a student of English Literature at least as indispensable as a knowledge of the Greek and Roman Classics. Others will no doubt ask, why the chief master-pieces in the principal literatures of modern Europe should not be sub-stituted for works of less intrinsic value in ancient tongues; why, for example, in a curriculum which finds room for the Sicilian Idylls and the *Metamorphoses*, room should not be found rather for the 'Inferno' or the 'Purgatorio,' for *Faust* or for Molière's comedies? The Master of Balliol[10] and Mr Matthew Arnold, both agreeing in the necessity for connecting the study of the Classics with the study of English, would confine the curriculum of instruction to 'standard authors.' Others will protest against separating the study of literature from the study of history, pleading, and pleading with reason, the intimate connection between them. Others again will contend for the retention of philology, not on the ground of its identification with literature, but on the ground of its being one of those tangible subjects which are at once better adapted for purposes of teaching and purposes of examination than such volatile essences as the Excellent and the Beautiful. They will complain, with Mr Pater, 'that the fine flower of English poetry or Latin oratory or Greek art will fade in the long, pedantic, mechanical discipline; perhaps the "cram" which is the necessary accompaniment of a system of examination.'[11]

No one can appreciate more than we do the force of these objections. But in a problem so complicated as the determination of the best, and at the same time the most practical, method of legislating for a School of Literature, it is not, as we have already remarked, with the scheme which is open to no objections, but with the scheme which is open to fewest objections, that the choice must lie. It would, no doubt, be very desirable that, in addition to acquiring an adequate acquaintance with what is best in the works of the Greek, Roman, and English Classics, the student should acquire an adequate acquaintance with what is best in the writings of the Classics of Italy, France, and Germany, that he should be able to discuss the relative merits of the *Beowulf* and of Caedmon's *Paraphrase* in the original, and that he should possess a competent knowledge of philology and a competent knowledge of history. But to expect all this to be accomplished in the time now allotted to education is obviously absurd. Either Greek and Latin must be sacrificed for Anglo-Saxon and modern languages, or Anglo-Saxon and modern languages must be sacrificed for Greek and Latin. Philology must be cultivated at the expense of literary history and criticism, or literary history and criticism must be cultivated at the expense of philology. It would be an insult to Oxford to suppose, that she would sanction the institution of a School of Literature in which the *Beowulf* superseded the *Iliad*, the *Chanson de Roland* the *Aeneid*. Nay, it would be scarcely less derogatory to her, if she conferred this precedency on the maturest manifestations of Modern Art. It would defeat all the ends at which a School of Literature should aim, if Philology were forced into prominence, or even placed on an equal footing with those methods of exposition, by which alone the study of ancient and modern poetry, oratory, and criticism, can be rendered effective and fruitful. We are very far from under-rating the importance of Philology. In its highest departments it is a branch of learning of immense interest and value, and it is justly entitled to a place in the front rank of sciences. In its humbler departments it is an instrument without which the literary student would be helpless. But it must not be confounded with what in its higher departments it has little or no concern, and with what in its lower departments it serves only to assist. It must not be confounded with Literature. Up to the present time it has, in consequence of that confusion, been allowed to fill a place in education altogether disproportionate to its insignificance as an instrument of culture. As an instrument of culture it ranks, in our opinion, very low indeed. It certainly contributes nothing to the cultivation of the taste. It as certainly contributes nothing to the education of the emotions. The mind it neither enlarges nor refines. On the contrary, it too often induces or confirms that peculiar woodenness and opacity, that singular coarseness of feeling and purblindness of moral and intellectual vision, which has in all ages been characteristic of mere philologists, and of which we have appalling illustrations in such a work as Bentley's *Milton*. Nor is this all. Instead of encouraging communion with the nobler manifestations of human energy, with the great deeds of history, or with the master-pieces of Art and Letters, it tends to create habits of unintelligent curiosity about trifles. It too often resembles that rustic who, after listening for several hours to Cicero's most brilliant conversation, noticed nothing and remembered nothing but the wart on the great orator's nose. It is the privilege of Art and Letters to bring us into contact with the aristocrats of our race. It is the misfortune of Philology that, in its lower walks at least, it necessitates familiarity with a class of writers who probably rank lowest in the scale of human intelligence. The proper place of Philology in its higher phases, and of Philology in its higher phases we have not been speaking, is with the sciences. So far as it is related to Literature, it is related as the drudge is related to his master, as the key of the jewel-casket is related to the treasures it unlocks. Nor will the absurdity of forcing Philology into undue prominence in popular education be less apparent, if we regard it from another point of view. Those who can appreciate it as a science, and who are likely to be interested in what it teaches, are and always will be in a very small minority. And to how few even of this small minority, unless indeed they become teachers or specialists, will it ever be of much practical use, either directly in informing, or indirectly in educating. Those on the contrary, who appreciate Literature as distinguished from Philology, will in point of numbers quadruple, and more than quadruple, the former class. And two things are certain. Whatever may be the future calling of these students, the positive knowledge they will have attained will, unlike a knowledge of Philology, be of immense and immediate service to them; the liberal training to which, in the course of acquiring that knowledge, they have been submitted, will, unlike the narrow and narrowing discipline of mere philological culture, send them forth with enlarged minds and with cultivated tastes. Can there be any question then about the relative claims of Literature and Philology to precedence in the economy of education?

The truth is, that these two classes of students, separated by differences of temper, by differences of genius, by differences of taste, should be separately provided for. The inevitable result of forcing Philology into prominence in a School of Literature will be to defeat the purposes of the School. It will be to sacrifice the education of that large majority, who are capable of benefiting from literary studies, and are not capable of benefiting from scientific studies, to the education of a small minority. It will be an attempt to amalgamate elements which always have met and always will meet in oppugnancy. The instincts and faculties, which separate the temperament of the mathematician from the temperament of the poet, are not more radical and essential, than the instincts and faculties, which separate the sympathetic student of

Philology from the sympathetic student of polite Literature. And of all the sciences Philology is the most repugnant to men of artistic and literary tastes. It was the subject of the sarcasms of Milton and Dryden in the seventeenth century. It was an inexhaustible topic for the scorn and ridicule of the wits of the eighteenth century; and it has assuredly not met with much sympathy from the most distinguished men of letters in the present century. No one can doubt, that it has been the predominance of the philological element in the classical curriculum which has had the effect of inducing generation after generation of men, on whose writings the impress of Classicism is most unmistakably stamped, to turn with contempt from the schools, and to take their education into their own hands. No one can doubt, that it has been the predominance of that element, which has created so wide a gulf between the life that is stirring in our Universities and the dominant system. We well remember how, when it was once humorously suggested to the late Rector of Lincoln,[12] that the following lines from the *Dunciad* should be inscribed in letters of gold over the doors of the Classical Schools, he replied with a smile, 'Substitute letters of lead, and you have my entire approval':

> Since man from beasts by *Words* is known,
> *Words* are man's province: Words we teach alone
> When Reason doubtful, like the Samian letter,
> Points us two ways, the narrower is the better.
> Plac'd at the door of Learning youth to guide,
> We never suffer it to stand too wide;
> To ask, to guess, to know, as they commence,
> As Fancy opens the quick springs of sense.
> We ply the memory, we load the brain,
> Bind rebel wit, and double chain on chain;
> Confine the thought, to exercise the breath,
> And keep them in the pale of Words till death.
> Whate'er the talents, or howe'er design'd,
> We hang one jingling padlock on the mind.

But the recent Regulations have, we are glad to see, entirely removed this stigma from University teaching; and in the Classical School Poetry, Oratory, and History, are no longer under the old degrading yoke. It now remains to see, whether the new School of Literature is to return to the ancient bondage and mark a retrograde movement, or whether, on the contrary, it is to strengthen, to consolidate, to complete what the Classical Schools have during the last few months happily initiated. No sensible man would grudge Philology the recognition which is its due in every University. There is not the smallest reason why it too should not have its school and its curriculum, but we protest against that school being the School of Literature, and that curriculum being the curriculum of Arts.

We have adverted to the objections which may, with more or less plausibility, be urged against a School of Literature constituted as we would propose to constitute it, But we have not yet touched on the objection which will probably carry most weight with the multitude. The School, which we propose, not only requires as an indispensable qualification, both in those who teach and those who learn, the possession of classical scholarship, but its curriculum is based on, and indissolubly bound up, with the Classics. Its effect therefore – and let the blunt truth be admitted – will be to exclude from its course all but classical scholars. Now this, we shall be told, is monstrous. Is it not, it will be asked, a School of English Literature that is needed, and ought a School of English Literature to be other than what its name implies? Are our youth, it will be angrily urged, to be excluded from the study of Modern Literature, because they are not acquainted with the literatures of antiquity? Are they to know nothing of Shakspeare, of Burke, of Molière, because they know nothing of Sophocles, of Cicero, of Terence? Is the student to receive no instruction about the virtues and niceties of his own tongue, because he is ignorant of the Greek and Roman tongues?

Our answer to this is simple. The School which we are advocating, and the School for which any University when providing for the introduction of a new branch of study into its curriculum ought first to legislate, is an Honour School. And the function of an Honour School is to establish and maintain the highest possible standard of instruction and attainment in the particular subject represented in it, to base discipline, not on what is secondary and derived, but on what is original and typical. It is to teach those who are in their turn to become teachers, to educate those who are to educate others. We contend then, that no man should be entitled to the diploma of an Honour School of Literature whose education has not fulfilled these conditions – who has not traced what is best in Modern Literature upward to its source, who is not intelligently familiar with the literary masterpieces of the ancients, who has not received the impress of classical culture.

Whether in addition to an Honour School it would be desirable to establish a Pass School of Literature may be a matter for future consideration. For our own part we have little doubt that, whether desirable or not, it will sooner or later become necessary. In that case there is of course no reason at all why the great writers of one or more of the chief European Literatures should not be substituted, optionally, or absolutely, for the Greek and Roman Classics, and studied in conjunction with our own Classics. In that case there is no reason why such a school, as would meet the approval of Mr Bright and the most advanced of the modern party, should not be founded. For the functions of a Pass School are not the functions of an Honour School. We are, however, of opinion that it would be desirable even in a Pass School to require a certain amount of classical knowledge from the students. It should not in any case be an alternative school for the present pass Literae Humaniores; for a smattering of Aristotle and Tacitus is certainly preferable to a smattering of Shakspeare and Goethe.

To conclude. Whatever may be the decision of the Council at Oxford, whatever may be the fate of this movement, we shall at least have the satisfaction of feeling, that we have done all in our power to admonish, all in our power to prevent misdirection. In the interests of Literature and in the interests of culture we have pleaded for an institution, which will be beneficial or mischievous, a blessing or an evil, according to its constitution. The effect of that plea has been to mature a crisis, the full significance of which is not discernible to the common eye, but which is in truth one of the most momentous that has ever occurred in the history of education. Let us not deceive ourselves. What is now at stake is nothing less than the future of the higher culture of our country, whether expressing itself practically in teaching or reflectively in Art and Letters.

Classical Literature can never, it is true, become extinct, but it can lose its vogue, it can become, what Mr Bright calls it, a luxury, become the almost exclusive possession of mere scholars, become in short influentially disassociated from the world of Letters and the world of Art and culture. Every step in the progress of this alienation is a step in the progress of its decline. Philology cannot save it. Technical scholarship cannot save it. It must be linked with life to live, with the incarnation of what it too is the incarnation to prevail. Associate it as Poetry with Poetry, as Philosophy with Philosophy, as Oratory with Oratory, as Criticism with Criticism, and it will be vital and mighty. The University of Oxford has now to decide, whether this is to be done or not, or whether so far from this being done the Classics are to be ostracized from those dominions, over which for so many centuries they have reigned supreme, and the Dii Minores[13] of later and lesser dynasties set up in their place; whether in a School of Literature, in a School in which Poetry is represented, we are to look in vain for the names of Homer and Sophocles, of Virgil and Horace; whether the study of Criticism is to be divorced from the study of Aristotle and Quinctilian, and the study of Oratory from the study of Demosthenes and Cicero. This is the question – this and nothing less than this – now awaiting decision at the chief seat of English national culture.

Notes

1. See Craik's letter to the *Pall Mall Gazette*, included in this volume, pp. 264–5.
2. See Bright's letter to the *Pall Mall Gazette*, included in this volume, pp. 259–61.
3. See Max Müller's letter to the *Pall Mall Gazette*, included in this volume, pp. 238–41.
4. Many of the letters which Collins refers to are collected in this volume, pp. 236–76.
5. # In addition to this, a youth would bring up from school a certain amount of literary knowledge. Indeed we see no reason why he should not when he matriculates have made considerable progress in his English studies. The Universities, through their Scholarships, are virtually the dictators of the Public Schools, and we have little doubt that, if a paper on English Literature formed a recognized portion of the examination for Classical Scholarships, progress would be secured. The character of the questions set would determine the character of the instruction given, and would thus go far to remedy the defective teaching of which the Head Master of Clifton College complains. In speaking of the relation of the Universities to the Public Schools, we cannot forbear expressing a hope, that they will not countenance the recent extraordinary innovation of the Head Master of Winchester School. We are surprised that the Governors of that ancient institution should not have thought it their duty to intervene. If discountenanced by the Universities, it will seriously affect the interests of the School; if countenanced by the Universities, it will seriously affect the interests of culture. [Rev. William Andrewes Fearon had cut the teaching of Latin verse for some boys, replacing it with Shakespeare, history and geography.]
6. # Which could of course be studied perfectly well in one of the many excellent English translations.It is a proof of the indifference of the Universities to critical literature, that neither Lessing's masterpiece nor the *De Sublimitate* has a place in the curriculum of any school. The neglect into which the *Treatise* of Longinus has fallen is inexplicable. No nobler, no more suggestive, no more stimulating work has come down to us from antiquity. Yet there is not even a good modern edition of it. If some competent scholar would prepare a careful recension of the text, with notes and a translation, he would supply a real want. Will not Mr Jebb [Sir Richard Jebb, editor and translator] help us?
7. # No classical work has exercised more influence on modern poetry, especially in England and Italy, than the *Metamorphoses*.
8. # A comparative study of Shelley's *Alastor* and the 'Atys' would do more to make a student realize the fundamental and essential differences between Ancient and Modern Poetry than volumes of commentary; just as a comparative study of the 'Coma Berenices' and Pope's Mock Heroic, would show him how much they have sometimes, and in particular branches, in common.
9. #And yet classical historical composition, now almost extinct, is as purely a work of art, and as worthy of being studied as a work of art, as a great poem or a great oration. If the matter concerns the student of history and the political philosopher, the expression and the style concern the literary critic. The study of their great Histories from this point of view was held

by the Ancients to be one of the most important departments of rhetoric. To take an example: it is one thing to master the matter of Ségur's narrative of the great catastrophe of 1812 [Philippe Paul de Ségur, *Histoire de Napoléon et de la Grande Armée pendant l'Année 1812* (1825)], and of Thucydides' narrative of the great catastrophe of 413 B.C. [*History of the Pelopponesian War*]; it is quite another thing to understand, in what consists the immeasurable superiority of Thucydides to Ségur as a dramatic artist.

10. Benjamin Jowett (1817–1893).
11. See Pater's letter to the *Pall Mall Gazette*, included in this volume, pp. 241–2.
12. Mark Pattinson (1813–1884).
13. Lesser gods.

CHAPTER SEVENTEEN

Letters to the *Pall Mall Gazette*, 1886–1887

A central feature of Collins's campaign on behalf of English studies was a canvass of the views of eminent people, conducted under the auspices of the *Pall Mall Gazette*. In a later book, Collins set out as follows the questions which he had asked:

> 1. Was it desirable that the Universities should provide systematic instruction in English Literature?
> 2. Was it desirable that a distinction should be made between Philology and Literature, and that the instruction provided should be instruction in Literature as distinguished from instruction in Philology?
> 3. Was it desirable that the study of English Literature should be indissolubly associated with the study of ancient Classical Literature?[1]

Those canvassed, virtually all of them men, may be roughly divided into the following categories: university dons, headmasters of public schools, prominent clerics, politicians and men of letters.

Some of the suggestions deal with how English literature might be slotted into the existing provision at Oxford, and the labels 'Literae Humaniores,' 'Moderations,' and 'Final Schools' are used freely. Collins describes briefly the School of Literae Humaniores in his review of *From Shakespeare to Pope*; the arrangements concerning Moderations and Finals may be gleaned from the letters written by John Percival and W.J. Courthope and from Collins's review of the *Petition Addressed to the Hebdomadal Council*.

The letters collected here were all published in the *Pall Mall Gazette* and subsequently in *English Literature and How to Study It* (*Pall Mall Gazette* Extra, No. 32, 1887).

W.W. Merry (1835–1918) was at this time Rector of Lincoln College, Oxford. He was a classical scholar who had been a student at Balliol from 1852 to 1856. He became a Fellow of Lincoln College in 1859 and then Rector in 1884. He was primarily a Greek scholar, and was an editor of Homer and Aristophanes. He was also a popular preacher in Oxford.

In his letter, Merry focuses on the need to link any English studies at Oxford firmly to classics, and sees some benefit to classics deriving from this link.

Letter to PMG

Should a School in English Literature be established in the University of Oxford I should take it for granted that the subject would be taught in connection with the Greek and Latin classics. It seems to me the only scholarly method of such a study. A knowledge of the classics may not indeed be necessary to the ordinary reader for the appreciation and enjoyment of English literature; but it is quite indispensable to the student of English literary history. Without such a knowledge much of the matter and form of our literature can have no intelligible meaning. Its development must seem to be merely accidental without constant reference to the models on which it has been shaped. And the study of English Literature in this place in connection with that of the classics should have the further effect of giving more life and reality to the method of studying Greek and Latin authors.

T.H. Warren (1853–1930) was the President of Magdalen College, Oxford. He had been a student at Balliol, and had obtained Firsts in Classical Moderations in 1873 and in Literae Humaniores in 1876. He had been elected to a fellowship at Magdalen in 1877, becoming a classical tutor there in 1878 and President in 1885, an office which he held until 1928. Warren was very prominent in Oxford University affairs, and was for many years a member of the Hebdomadal Council. As well as being a Greek scholar, he wrote poetry in English and was Oxford Professor of Poetry from 1911 to 1916.

As someone heavily involved with policy-making at Oxford, in his response Warren gives no hostages to fortune, but he does go so far as to say that he believes the study of modern European literature, including English, would be both 'admirable' and 'delightful.' It would, however, need to be intimately connected with classical studies. Warren uses the word 'philology' to indicate what this 'modern school' might be like, but he means philology as a broad, literary and historical, as well as linguistic, study.

Letter to PMG

With regard to the introduction of modern languages and studies into the Oxford curriculum, there are two points on which I feel strongly. The first is that if we are to have a modern school, be it of English, French, German, Italian – any or all of these – such a school should be a School of Philology in the old, wide and true, and not in the new, narrow and false sense of that term – a school, that is to say, mainly of literature, and not of grammar and etymology. The second is that such a School of Modern Literature should make its studies intimately connect with and follow and depend upon the study of the Greek and Latin classics. I regard the literature of civilized Europe as one continuous whole, of which the later monuments cannot be properly understood without an understanding of the earlier upon which they are based. I say 'if' because I am not prepared at present to state how such a scheme could be fitted into the existing classical schools at Oxford; but that a wider study of the Greek and Latin classics as literature, followed by a study of the literature of modern Europe, would in itself be an admirable and delightful discipline, I have no doubt.

Friedrich Max Müller (1823–1900) was a Fellow of All Souls and Professor of Comparative Philology at Oxford, and was well known as an orientalist and philologist. He was born in the small duchy of Anhalt-Dessau, and studied first at the University of Leipzig. He covered many subjects there, but his main area of interest was Sanskrit. He then moved on to the University of Berlin, where he studied comparative philology under Franz Bopp, as well as philosophy. In 1848, Max Müller came to Oxford, first becoming Taylorian Professor of Modern European Languages in 1854, then Professor of Comparative Philology in 1868, a title which he held till his death, although he retired from active duties in 1875. He was appointed to a life fellowship at All Souls in 1858. Max Müller's interests were very wide-ranging, but centred particularly upon comparative philology, comparative mythology and comparative religion. He was well known for his Broad Church views.

In this very carefully argued letter, Max Müller rakes over the history of the establishment of the Merton chair and the appointment to it of Napier, an appointment in which Max Müller was himself involved. He defends the decision made by the electors to the Chair, and defends Napier against charges of being merely a philologist with no interest in literature. Max Müller hopes to see a School of Modern Literature at Oxford, in which English literature will have a place.

Letter to PMG

I have no hesitation in saying that I think the University of Oxford ought to do a great deal more for encouraging a scholar-like study of English literature than it has done hitherto. Foreigners have often asked me how it is that Oxford men ride so well and write so well, although there is at Oxford neither a riding-school nor a school of English literature. My answer has always been that no amount of teaching would ever produce a Ruskin or an Archer,[2], but at the same time I have had to confess, particularly in conversation with Americans, who often come to Oxford for the sole purpose of studying English literature, that our not having a professor of that subject seemed to me a serious blemish. However, I knew my old university long enough to feel convinced that at the first opportunity that blemish would be removed. Public opinion at Oxford is very sensitive, and we have now a body of young masters resident in the university who, if they once know what Oxford is in duty bound to do, will never rest till it is done. We have succeeded in passing statutes for endowing Chairs of Chinese, Celtic, Archaeology, Anthropology, Rabbinical Literature, all subjects which do not appeal to popular fancy, but which nevertheless, when once recognized as desirable, were most heartily welcomed at Oxford. Other professorships, some of extreme importance, such as Egyptology, Assyriology, are sure to follow as soon as funds become available for endowing them, but precedence over all was readily granted to the long-desired Chair of English Literature which last year (1885) was most liberally endowed by Merton College.

Those who really cared for the success of an English school at Oxford felt, and felt rightly, that everything would depend on the choice of the first occupant of the Chair of English. Although the framers of the statute have been blamed for calling it a Chair of English Language and Literature, I do not see how they could well have called it otherwise. We have not one Professor of the Greek Language and another of Greek Literature. We expect our Professors of Greek, Latin, Hebrew, Celtic, Chinese, &c., to be first of all sound scholars, and afterwards well read in some branches of their respective literatures. It will happen, no doubt, that one professor is more given to scholarship, while another is more widely read in literature; but that is the same in all universities. Every subject has now become so specialized and subdivided that ten Professors of Greek would have ample work to do in a university. But as that professorial Elysium is still far distant, all we can do at present is to see that no one should be allowed to lecture on literature who does not possess a sound and scholar-like knowledge of the language.

It is well known that we had excellent candidates for the Merton Chair. There were some with the highest testimonials as students of English literature, and others equally distinguished as students of English philology. The difficulty was to find a man who had given proof of real qualification to lecture both on language and on literature. In spite of the eloquent remonstrances of many most eligible yet not elected candidates, I still believe that the electors – the Warden of Merton, the Librarians of the British Museum and the Bodleian, Professor Freeman, and myself – have hit on the right man. Mr Arthur Napier is young and full of enthusiasm: that is worth something. He has been tried, and has not been found wanting, in two such universities as Berlin and Göttingen; he is known as a first-rate philologist, and came before us at the same time with the best credentials as to his knowledge of English literature. Those who in their ignorance can persuade themselves that the electors to the Merton Chair of English were capable of 'practising a fraud on letters'[3] would do well to consult the printed testimonials of Professor Napier before using such unwarranted language.

But you will be glad to hear that Professor Napier, undeterred by all bow-wows and pooh-poohs of disappointed candidates, has not been idle in the cause of English Philology and Literature at Oxford, and I believe I am divulging no secrets in alluding to his constant efforts to see a School of Modern Literature established among us. Until young men are allowed to take their degrees in Modern Literature, it is hopeless to expect that they will attend professors' lectures. We have had such men as Taine lecturing at Oxford on Modern Literature, and they have had audiences such as the Bishop of Chester had when he gave his public lectures on English History.[4] That School of Modern Literature is meant to consist of three branches, Teutonic, Romanic, and Celtic. The Teutonic is to be subdivided into an English, German, and Scandinavian section; the Romanic into a Southern (Provençal and Italian), a Northern (French), and possibly a third section, comprising Spanish and Portuguese. These are, as yet, *pia vota*[5] only; but I have that faith in young Oxford that, with certain modifications, and possibly after some hesitation, some such scheme as Professor Napier is advocating will be carried.

I have thus, I believe, answered all your questions. But I cannot conclude this letter without expressing my opinion that the University, before anything else is done, ought to make proper provision for the ancient Chair of Anglo-Saxon. That Chair has been filled for years by a most excellent and hard-working scholar.[6] He may belong to the 'Vieille Garde' – so do I; but he belongs to the 'Vieille Garde qui ne se rend pas.'[7] His lectures, as I know from personal experience, have been most vigorous and useful, and I cannot understand why, when the endowment of every other Chair has been raised in some way or other, the Chair of Anglo-Saxon alone should have remained to the present day miserably underpaid. If the present holder of that Chair has not spoken for himself, it becomes all the more the duty of others who have known and honoured him for years to speak out.

As to log-rolling, you know my opinion from former correspondence. I am afraid it is a pest which cannot easily be stamped out.

Walter Pater (1839–1894) was educated at Queen's College, Oxford, graduating in classics in 1862. In 1864 he was elected a Fellow of Brasenose College and was a tutor there. He became interested in philosophy and in art, and was closely associated with the Pre-Raphaelite Brotherhood. He wrote essays for a number of periodicals, in particular the *Westminster Review* and the *Fortnightly Review*. He wrote the philosophical novel, *Marius the Epicurean* (1885) and *Plato and Platonism*(1893).

Pater shows himself enthusiastic about English literature as a subject of study for young men. He is careful to stress that he will not support anything which tends to a diminution of classical study, but he shares Collins's belief that modern literature might help to revitalize Classics. His chief fears lie in the area of examinations: examinations in English might ruin what is currently a delightful study; on the other hand, students might choose English in the belief that the examinations could be crammed for and would be easy. Pater is not willing to commit himself wholeheartedly until he has more details of a proposed scheme.

Letter to PMG

You have asked me to express an opinion on a proposal to establish here a School of English Literature. I have long had an interest in the teaching of young men at Oxford, and in the study of English literature; and proposals similar to this have from time to time occurred to me. The university has done little for English literature by way of direct teaching. Its indirect encouragement of what is best in English literature has, I think, been immense, as regards both the appreciation of what is old, and the initiation of what is new. The university has been enabled to exercise this influence mainly as a consequence of its abundant and disinterested devotion, in the face of much opposition, to Greek and Latin literature – to the study of those literary productions wherein lie the sources of all our most salutary literary traditions, and which must always remain typical standards in literature, of a stirring interest in the matter together with absolute correctness in the form. I should, therefore, be no advocate for any plan of introducing English literature into the course of university studies which seemed likely to throw into the background that study of classical literature which has proved so effective for the maintenance of what is excellent in our own. On the other hand, much probably might be done for the expansion and enlivening of classical study itself by a larger infusion into it of those literary interests which modern literature, in particular, has developed; and a closer connection of it, if this be practicable, with the study of great modern works (classical literature and the literature of modern Europe having, in truth, an organic unity); above all, by the maintenance, at its highest possible level, of the purely literary character of those literary exercises in which the classical examination mainly consists.

An examination seems to run the risk of two opposite defects. Many of those who most truly enjoy this or that special study are jealous of examinations in it. The 'fine flower' of English poetry, or Latin oratory, or Greek art, might fade for them, in the long, pedantic, mechanical discipline (perhaps the 'cram') which is the necessary accompaniment of a system of examination; indispensable as that may nevertheless be for certain purposes. Intelligent Englishmen resort naturally for a liberal pleasure to their own literature. Why transform into a difficult exercise what is natural virtue in them? On the other hand, there are those who might give the preference to these studies for their fancied easiness, and welcome such a change in the interest of that desire to facilitate things, at any cost, the tendency of which is to suppress every kind of excellence born of strenuous labour, and, in literature especially, to promote what is lax and slipshod alike in thought and expression. That is the last thing we require from the university, in an age already overloaded with the heavy, incondite 'brute matter' of knowledge, and too bustling in its habits to think of that just management of its material which is precisely what we admire in the Greek and Latin writers. Much, then, will depend upon the details of the proposed scheme; that scheme itself possessing, perhaps, a more general interest than usually belongs to matters of the kind. Certainly it would show a poor sense of responsibility towards the interests of literature if one judged such a proposal as this on any other ground than its own intrinsic reasonableness.

G.W. Kitchin (1827–1912) was educated at Christ Church, Oxford, graduating with Firsts in both classics and mathematics in 1850. In 1852 he was ordained and became a tutor in his college. After a period as a preparatory-school headmaster, he returned to Christ Church in 1861 as 'censor,' but left again in 1863 when he married. He remained in Oxford, lecturing on history in several colleges and working for the university press. He was Secretary to the Schoolbooks Committee, and in this role organized the first Clarendon Press editions of English classics, much used in schools. In 1883 he left Oxford to become Dean of Winchester, then in 1894 Dean of Durham. In 1908 he took on the Chancellorship of Durham University.

Kitchin is enthusiastic about English literature in education, but his experience of the India Civil Service examinations has taught him the dangers of cramming associated with examinations in English. His wish would be to find ways of encouraging Oxford students to read and enjoy English literature without creating an Honours School, for an Honours School of English would constantly tend to become something other than a school of letters. In order to avoid the tag of an 'easy' school, it would focus on language or history, on anything rather than literary qualities.

Letter to **PMG**

The university, in consequence of its very reforms, has moved too far in the direction of examination; so that examination controls the course of education instead of being subsidiary to it. Now, English literature fares very badly in the excitement of the examination school, and is singularly ill adapted for such tests as we are wont to apply. It is safe to say that if we can make our examinations stimulate real study they will have fulfilled their chief end. I am afraid it must be confessed that this result has not followed in the case of literature. I can speak here with some little experience. The way in which the candidates for the Indian Civil Service used to 'get up' English literature, simply because they could score so many marks by it, degraded the study of the subject to the lowest level. Here and there a really clever fellow, who would have done justice to any subject, used to answer his papers as if he had read the books he offered, and had entered into the spirit of them; but the great bulk of candidates reproduced monotonously the terrible cram that had been poured into them by their tutors. Once, by the way of an easy opening to a *viva voce* examination, I asked a candidate, 'How does Bacon begin his famous essay on Marriage?' And the man, with a scared look, replied, 'Might I ask you to erase that book from my list of authors offered?' 'Well,' I said, 'it is a very unusual request. Why do you make it?' 'Oh!' he rejoined, 'I have unluckily lost my notebook to it.' In other words, he had taken down from his tutor's dictation the recognized 'tips' from Bacon, and these, had he not mislaid his book, he would have learned by heart, prepared to impose on his examiner. As to looking into the author himself, that he had never dreamed of doing; his tutor no doubt told him he could save him all that trouble and 'waste of time.' I have also often examined the ladies who attend the literature lectures given under the London Society for the Extension of University Teaching, and they, on the whole, decidedly confirm the view I take. Theirs is a stronger case; they attend the lectures solely to improve themselves, the examination is not compulsory, and, so far as I have seen, does its best to discourage cramming. Yet, with some very honourable exceptions, the results show that here also there is a great risk of the student's mistaking the teacher's dicta or the facts given in some text book for a real knowledge of the literary masterpieces to which her attention has been called. It is often hard to see whether the student has read the works on which she has, in name at least, been engaged.

In the old Oxford days a 'School' meant, as it should, a place where men were taught some subject; now 'the Schools' are nothing but a gigantic building full of examination rooms, and a man reads 'for his School' instead of 'in his School.' If we were to subject English literature to this system and make it into 'a School' I fear the knowledge so enforced on the men would be far worse than the ignorance they now enjoy. Still, every one will grant that the absence of all attempt to encourage the study of the English classics is a very serious blot on our university system. I say this, not because I hold with the mistaken view that a university should be a place of universal teaching and learning, but because our literature is so splendid that the neglect of it is a great crime against our country. There is something quite touching in the way in which young Englishmen, inheritors of one of the finest literatures in the world, and called on to use a language which, take it altogether, has a power and flexibility worthy of its high destiny, go through their lives unconscious of their great literary privileges. In no country are so many books bought, and in none is authorship so well rewarded; for all that, how rare it is to find a man who has any familiarity with, any friendship for, our English masterpieces! And yet I am sure that were we to establish a school of English literature, side by side with our classics and philosophy, mathematics, history, &c., we should be more likely to ruin what present study there is than to bring it into fuller recognition.

Classical scholarship has undergone this very degadation that I dread. Last century it was a thing of good taste, accurate grammar, intelligent study of masterpieces of thought and form, skilful power of rendering in prose or verse from one tongue to another. Now, the appreciation of the chief classical authors, for the sake of their grace and literary beauty, seems to be almost lost. Though we know that scholar-like style, with good taste and skill in rendering and in answering, give a special charm to the work of the few who form the élite of every First Class, there is little or nothing of it visible in the papers of the remainder who find their places in the class lists; the alliance of the study with linguistic and other subjects is too much for the literature as such. English letters treated similarly would suffer in the same way; a constant endeavour would be made to harden the subject, so as to enable it to compete on something like equal terms with the older 'schools': for an easy honour school is fatal. This would force students to pay attention chiefly to the developments of language, or the historical subject matter, or the philosophical theories to be found in each author; and so here, too, the school would gradually cease to be one of letters; the English masterpieces would become mere vehicles for instruction in this or that branch of learning; the aim of the new school would be missed, and an inferior treatment of other studies substituted instead. How, then, can our problem – the discovery of the best way of encouraging the knowledge by Englishmen of English literature – be solved?

I am not inclined to underrate the value of an efficient Professorship; no doubt the results are often disappointing, yet I cannot help thinking that if we were to strengthen the Anglo-Saxon Professorship so as to include the intelligent study and teaching of all our earlier literature, and the Professorship of Poetry for the drama and both prose and poetical masterpieces, we should have taken a step in the right direction. I should like, in spite of the times, to go a little further, and to pray that no examination system should be attached to this study. There might be prizes, not too many, for composition or for essays on English subjects, and colleges might more often than is their present use encourage the knowledge of our home literature in their scholarship examinations. If it could be kept within bounds, men might be taught to reproduce on this stage from time to time, so far as is compatible with more serious studies, some of the best of our English plays. And if it also seems well to recognize our literature in the class schools, it might be done, as has been suggested, by introducing carefully selected works to be studied for 'Moderations' side by side with the Greek and Latin classics, and (as is already partially done) English writers on historical or philosophical subjects in the final schools. Such an extension of 'Moderations,' at any rate, would tend to bring back the word 'philology' to a more wholesome use, and to strengthen the education which aims at cultivation as distinct from that which seeks only to store the mind with linguistic knowledge. The study of English masterpieces, undertaken in an intelligent and appreciative spirit, might still save that admirable product of Oxford, the cultured and well-educated Englishman. After all said, I think that the hope chiefly lies in the natural taste and intelligence of the choicer spirits in the university; in the better direction of private reading, as distinct from the great effort of preparing for the Honour schools; in the best work done for and at the Union and other debating societies; in the encouragement of those literary coteries, such as the Dante Club, or the Browning Society, which show at any rate that Oxford has not altogether lost her taste for literature, even though our great authors are still excluded from that gigantic examination system to which the university is now unhappily, though, it must be confessed inevitably, committed.

F.W.H. Myers (1843–1901) was educated at Trinity College, Cambridge, going on to become a Fellow and classical lecturer. In 1869 he left Cambridge, and in 1871 joined the Schools Inspectorate, retaining this post until shortly before his death. Myers was also a published poet and author of a number of literary essays.

Myers's view is that, although English literature has qualities to commend it as a subject of study, there are a number of other subjects which are superior to it in terms of their capacity to stretch the student. English literature is simply not difficult enough to form the basis of a university education.

Letter to PMG

Your invitation to me to say something on the question of the teaching of English literature at the universities enables me to suggest an aspect of the question which has, I think, been somewhat overlooked. For brevity's sake, I shall put the point in its simplest form, and omit obvious and important qualifications. In order to deserve a permanent place in academical training a subject should fulfil one or more of the requirements which follow:-

A. It should call forth thought, sagacity, perseverance, acumen, by offering a number of problems for solution which can be so graduated as to exact the learner's utmost effort at each stage of his career.
B. The actual facts learned should be interesting and important.

C. The student's taste and imagination should be stimulated and elevated.

Of these requisites B and C are the easiest to fulfil, but A is surely the most important. We want to make the man *think*, to teach him to concentrate his attention; we desire to evoke reason and invention rather than memory. If he has never gone through a training of this kind he may be tasteful and well-informed, but he is not *educated* in the true sense of the word.

How, then, do our ordinary subjects of study answer to these requirements? (1) Mathematics and (2) physical science satisfy A completely, but do not attempt C. Physical science and the higher mathematics satisfy B; but it is an objection to the earlier parts of mathematics that to many minds they lack interest and attraction. (3) Greek and Latin scholarship satisfy B adequately and C perfectly, and they used to satisfy A perfectly also. But, setting aside composition, the problems which the Greek and Latin classics present are limited in number, and the solutions are becoming too complete and accessible. Nothing could be better than to puzzle out a passage, say, of Sophocles or of Lucretius, with no help but a dictionary. But good texts, notes, and translations make a 'royal road.' Lucretius has exhausted much of his educative power in the act of educating Lachmann and Munro.[8] Sophocles is gradually depositing his invaluable obscurities as he filters through the brain of Professor Jebb.[9] (4) Philosophy, and (5) history, satisfy B completely and C in great measure; but many of the problems of philosophy and moral science are too indeterminate, many of the problems of history too lengthy and complex, to train the students to arrive at definite results from limited data. History may teach accuracy, but it seldom demands concentration. (6) How, then, will the study of English literature satisfy the above requirements? It may teach things important and interesting to know; it may elevate the imagination; but as a subject affording a graduated series of definite problems it surely falls below any of those above-mentioned. There is matter for critical discussion; there is matter for exact research; but there are few points where the student's mind must grapple with a close train of unfamiliar reasoning to reach a definite goal. And even as a field of accurate acquirement, English literature, taken alone, does not possess the range which is usually covered by an examination for honours. In the recently established Mediaeval and Modern Languages Tripos the University of Cambridge has attempted, by blending other linguistic studies with that of English, to give (so to say) to this latter the requisite volume and difficulty. Persons interested in this subject might, I should think, consult with advantage the carefully considered regulations of this new Tripos. This

Tripos, doubtless, is not intended to direct the student's attention to absolutely modern books. But should anything so easy and so agreeable as the reading, say, of Burke or Macaulay, be classed as serious work at all? It may be as useful in one way to read Macaulay as to read Thucydides. But the educationally important point – the stress of mind required – is in the two cases entirely different. A man may be excused for thinking it a labour to read Thucydides, but if he does not read Macaulay as a pleasure he does not deserve to read him at all. It is indeed, most desirable that the universities should try to give their students as many chances as possible of actually hearing eminent men discourse on their favouite studies. Poetry and *belles-lettres* are among the best themes for these inspiring orations. But though the undergraduate who has heard, say, Professor Ruskin or Mr Matthew Arnold lecture, may feel that he has received a quickening impulse which will live long within him, he should not, I think, be encouraged to count this stimulating enjoyment among the serious and strenuous hours during which his own effort, not the brilliancy of others, must upbuild his intellectual being.

Edward Dowden (1843–1913) was educated at Queen's College, Cork and Trinity College, Dublin. He graduated in 1863, and in 1867 was appointed to the newly founded Chair of English Literature, a post which he retained until his death. He wrote widely on English literature, his best-known work being *Shakespeare: His Mind and Art* (1875).

Dowden is mainly concerned in his letter to urge something more substantial for English studies than *belles lettres*. English should not be concerned with taste, but rather with a history of the nation's thought and feeling.

Letter to PMG

Mr F.W.H. Myers has said much that I should have tried to say had I not his letter, as printed in your columns, in my hands. For my own part I would remark that while the study of literature may have something to fear, on the one hand, from the science of philology, which threatens to usurp its place and name, it views with alarm, on the other hand, what I may name the *belles-lettres* heresy. The study of literature – English or other – is not a study solely of what is graceful, attractive, and pleasure-giving in books; it attempts to understand the great thoughts of the great thinkers. To know Greek literature we must know Aristotle; to know French literature, we must know Descartes. In English literature of the eighteenth century Berkeley and Butler and Hume are greater names than Gray and Collins. The object – hardly indeed attainable – of the student should be to follow the total development of thought and feeling during the successive periods of a nation's life. In order that such a comprehensive study of letters should be something better than a series of 'views,' in order that it should be a reality, much time would be needed, and a careful selection from the characteristic writings of the greatest writers. I should like students to spend four years in the school, which might be named the 'School of Philosophy and Letters.'

J.M. Wilson (1836–1931) attended St John's College, Cambridge, being Senior Wrangler in Mathematics in 1859; he was made a Fellow of his college in 1860. In 1859 he was appointed to teach mathematics at Rugby, and he remained at Rugby until 1879, when as well as being ordained he was also made Headmaster of Clifton. While at Clifton he still found time to teach classics to the Sixth Form. In 1890 he left schools to become Archdeacon of Manchester, then finally in 1905 Canon of Worcester.

Wilson here concerns himself more with the question of English in schools than with English at Oxford. He argues that it is best kept for the ablest boys and needs to be taught by very able teachers. Otherwise, English becomes mere cramming with facts, whether philological, historical or whatever. At university level there may be some scope for further encouraging the study of English literature, but an honours school of literature would be going too far.

Letter to **PMG**

I have lived through one educational reform which has much in common with the reform now under discussion. I mean the introduction of experimental science into our public schools and universities. It might be a valuable contribution to educational science if the results of that reform were carefully estimated and compared with the anticipations of the reformers. This I cannot attempt. But my judgment on the present question is influenced by the unformulated estimate and comparison of these results which I have been compelled to make. Literature at schools is perhaps of all subjects the most stimulating and valuable when it is taught by a man of genius to boys of over average ability and at the right moment of their development. Rugbeians and Marlburians of an older generation do not forget the lessons of De Tocqueville and Guizot, nor do recent Cliftonians who have passed through the Upper Fifth forget their Burke, or the discourses we have all listened to by the author of *Fo'c'sle Yarns*.[10] But these are exceptions. The conditions of school life, the want of leisure, the incessant interruption, the masses of detail, the constant association with young minds, all quite inseparable from the existence of an active and good schoolmaster, are not the atmosphere in which the ideal teacher of literature can in general thrive. The teacher of literature must himself have something of the creative faculty – he must be the essayist and the poet; he must be fired with an enthusiasm so strong and sturdy that years of school life, with its *crambe repetita*,[11] shall not kill it. But such men are rare, very rare in any class of society, under any conditions. Hence school teaching of literature will in general be either the getting up of little annotated text books, with their scraps of philology and ready made criticism and antiquarianism, all to be got up for examination, very often at the expense of neglecting the text; or the mere compulsory reading of English books in the same slight way that nineteen people out of twenty read them. The results are not valueless at the time, but I think it may be doubted whether this sort of study attracts boys to literature, and does not rather repel them. A study that is begun too soon is rarely loved. It is spoilt as a pleasure, and if literature is not a pleasure it is not read. If *Marmion* or *Ivanhoe* is set even as a holiday task, Scott is *ipso facto* reduced to a school book, or, in other words, he becomes not a book at all. I doubt whether the present generation who have passed through our schools during the last fifteen years care at all more for literature than we of thirty years ago cared. Indeed, my belief is that they care less, and that we should have cared less if we had had masters prescribing to us what to read and interfering with our own growing tastes. Very bad some of those tastes doubtless were. I remember swearing by Alexander Smith as a poet. But then they were our own, and the correction came when we were ripe for it.

I suppose the truth is that literature and criticism appeal, like science, to few among the young; language and mathematics can be studied with interest and advantage by the many. And therefore, in my judgment, the universities will do well to recognize in their scholarship examinations, and thus encourage, the literary and critical faculties of the abler boys, and of them only. They do this already at Oxford to a considerable extent. In fact the reform seems to me to be already taking place, and proceeding downward from the universities in the right way. I hope Professor Huxley, who is severe on the English of head masters, will not object to this expression, 'proceeding downward.' If so, I shall remind him that it is his own. More than twenty years ago I had the honour of serving with Huxley[12] and Tyndall[13] and Farrar[14] on a British Association Committee on the Teaching of Science at Schools; and in the draft that I prepared for our first meeting I used the expression that 'reform in education must begin from above.' Huxley gravely objected; he feared that the phrase might be held to commit him to theological views which he was not prepared to accept. As regards the universities themselves, I should like to see them feeling their way towards the recognition of English literature as an alternative in honour examinations, and allowing men, after passing their first public examination, to choose as their 'special subject' for an ordinary degree some branch or some period of English literature. But I should be very sorry to see an honour school. Honour men will read all they want without the stimulus or the burden of an impending examination.

F.W. Farrar (1831–1903) was educated at King's College, London, where he came under the influence of F.D. Maurice, and Trinity College, Cambridge. In 1854 he was appointed to a mastership at Marlborough, but stayed there for only one year before transferring to Harrow, where he remained for fifteen years. In 1871 he returned to Marlborough as Headmaster. In 1875 he left the world of schools to become a Canon of Westminster and Rector of St Margaret's. In 1883 he was appointed Archdeacon of Westminster, and in 1895 moved to his last job as Dean of Canterbury. Farrar was very much associated with the Broad Church, and in 1877 provoked a storm of protest over five sermons he preached in Westminster Abbey in which he questioned the doctrine of eternal punishment. He did not lose his job, though, as F.D. Maurice had in 1853. Farrar was the author of work on philology, grammar and theology, as well as a work of fiction, and was the editor of the influential *Essays on a Liberal Education*, containing the essays by J.W. Hales and Henry Sidgwick which are included in this volume.

Farrar considers that the teaching of English literature is often too philological and that this leads to cramming. He would like to see 'fine taste' stimulated, and believes that a chair of literature might help in this regard. However, it is clear that he does not have in mind anything too parochially English in scope.

Letter to PMG

Though I have no claim to be heard on the subject, yet, in answer to your request, I will venture to express my opinion that the teaching of English literature has long tended to become too exclusively philological. For this reason the notes to many plays and poems written to 'cram' students for examinations are more likely to repel than to allure them. On the other hand, I have seen reason to believe that a prize for the knowledge of English literature, *purely as literature*, which has been founded for many years in my name by my Marlborough pupils, has produced very valuable results.

If a Chair of Literature at either university would occasionally en-sure the publication of books like H.N. Coleridge's *Classic Poets*, or Nisard's *Poètes Latins de la Décadence*, and Villemain's *Tableau de l'Eloquence Chrétienne du IV Siècle*, I think that such lessons in the art of criticism would be widely useful in stimulating a fine taste. We have among us such men as Mr Ruskin, Mr Matthew Arnold, and Mr Lowell; and professors who taught in their spirit would soon spread a just, genial, and catholic appreciation for every form of literary ex-cellence.

John Percival (1834–1918) was educated at Queen's College, Ox-ford, taking a double First in classics and mathematics, and being elected a Fellow. In 1860 he was appointed to a mastership at Rugby, and in 1862, at a very young age, became Headmaster of Clifton College. In 1879 he moved back to Oxford as President of Trinity College, using this position to work hard for the higher education of women and for the University Extension movement. In 1886 Percival returned to schools as Headmaster of Rugby, where he stayed until becoming Bishop of Hereford in 1895.

Percival subdivides into two the question of whether Oxford should embrace English: should it be admitted into one or another existing school, and should there be a separate School of English Literature? However, he sees no reason to oppose either, recom-mending a collective getting down from 'the classical high horse.'

Letter to PMG

Your inquiry, as I understand it, is twofold, referring first to the introduction of English literature into one or other of our existing schools, and secondly to the establishment of a separate school of English literature. On the first point there is, I imagine, a growing feeling in Oxford that such a change would be of real advantage to the university, and not difficult to bring about. I will venture, therefore, to assume the desirability of such a change in the abstract, and will merely indicate how it might be made without any dislocation of present arrangements. In the first public examination[15] it would be easy, and I hope it might not be considered altogether inappropriate, to allow candidates who do not offer Latin verse, or Greek verse, or Greek prose composition to substitute for each of these some specified portion of English literature. Such candidates are already at liberty to substitute some other subjects for these, so that the introduction of English literature would involve no radical change.

Again, in the Final Honours School of Literae Humaniores candidates are allowed to offer a special subject from a list arranged under the heads of Greek and Latin Language, Ancient History, Philosophy. It could hardly be argued that there would be anything inappropriate in adding English literature to this list; if we may be permitted to think of a study of the Elizabethan age of our literature as being no less germane to Literae Humaniores than 'the languages of ancient Italy other than Latin,' or 'Political Economy,' or 'Assyrian and Babylonian History with the Fragments of Berosus,' which are all open to the choice of candidates as things are at present arranged.

The other part of your question will doubtless elicit differences of opinion. Many persons, when asked if it is desirable to establish a School of English Literature not immediately connected with any one of our Classical Schools, may be expected to give deprecatory answers based on their feeling as to the continuity of literature, and the impossibility of understanding our own literature without first understanding the literature of Greece, and so forth. Such views, reiterated as they are from many influential quarters, naturally impose upon our imagination; but when we get down from what I would venture to call the classical high horse, and turn to Shakspeare and his contemporaries, or even consider the matter in the light of actual facts and experience, we begin to have a suspicion that there is something unreal in this way of looking at the question, and that we have, in fact, been slipping into a conventional misapplication of those well-deserved praises of the classics which we have inherited from our fathers.

Let us see what a proposal to establish a Final Honours School of

English Literature would really mean if carried into effect. At present we have in Oxford, besides the School of Literae Humaniores, which is the peculiar pride and glory of Oxford education, Honour Schools of mathematics, natural science, theology, jurisprudence, and modern history; and every student when he has passed the first public examination, which is supposed, rightly or wrongly, to testify to his having a gentleman's equipment in classical languages and literature, can freely make his choice between these various schools. Now the question which I would venture to put is this, Whether any one can seriously maintain that any detriment would accrue to scholarship or learning or to the reputation of the university as a home of the higher education if our undergraduates were at liberty, after passing their first public examination, to choose, instead of natural science, mathematics, theology, law, or modern history, the literature of our own country? I hope I am not unreasonably bold in thinking that the answer to this question may safely be left to the verdict of common sense.

Edward Thring (1821–1887) was educated at Eton and King's College, Cambridge, being elected a Fellow at King's in 1844. After two curacies and two years spent as a private tutor, he was appointed Headmaster of Uppingham in 1853, a post which he held until his death. At Uppingham he organized a varied curriculum which went well beyond the usual classics, and which included English as well as classical composition. Thring was the founder of the Headmasters' Conference.

In this letter, Thring is very negative about proposals for English Literature at Oxford. 'Cram and indigestion' are the only results which he considers might be expected. This conclusion is all the more notable in that it comes from someone who owns that a scheme for English is his 'dream of right.' Unfortunately, he has nothing to say about what might make the dream practicable. Thring's contribution to the debate provides striking evidence of the damage done to the cause of English by its association with philology and cramming.

Letter to PMG

The idea of a school for English Literature at Oxford, whether an honour school, or in any other form, is very fascinating, but the longer I think over it the more impossible does it appear to me to put the idea into working shape. There is such an utter want of fixity in the whole matter, such flabbiness of opinions on literature, such rivalries of pet idolatries, such an entire absence of any principles to decide what literature is, and still more what ought to be attempted, that I cannot see my way to move in it. I fear, from the knowledge I have of modern omniscience and its ways, that the only result would be an increase of cram and indigestion. Alas! there are no hot springs to cure the dyspeptic of literature and take the gout out of his head. The stomach has a clear advantage in this. I am an ardent advocate of a thorough English education, and have the stongest convictions that the whole foundation of teaching should be English, that English and mastery of English should be the aim of the classical work, that all things should work from English, and all things work back to English. But then it must be possible to carry this out. In my judgment it is impossible; my experience makes me know that there are no men to teach it, and at present no one is willing to be taught. It will all end in scraps of philology and lumps of cram. I am afraid, therefore, that I cannot write to support what is my dream of right and ought to be my cause in practice. On the other hand, I cannot write in opposition, lest I be thought to be opposing literature, when I am only opposing literary folly, and to be resisting worship while rejecting idolatry.

Edward Charles Wickham (1834–1910) was educated at Winchester and New College, Oxford, where he was elected to a Fellowship. He taught for two years at Winchester before returning to New College as a tutor. In 1873 he became Headmaster of Wellington, retaining the post until 1893. In 1894 he was appointed Dean of Lincoln.

Wickham would favour finding a place for English within the existing schools at Oxford, but does not believe there should be a School of English Literature. He reiterates the common fear that it would be either an 'easy school' or a philological school dealing with Early English.

Letter to PMG

I should be very sorry to see a 'School' of English Literature started at Oxford. It would be a mistake, I think, both on theoretical grounds and on practical ones. I do not see, in practice, how it would steer between the two dangers of becoming the 'easy school' of which the Professor of Modern History[16] speaks with such just horror, and of becoming a philological school given up to 'Early English.' In theory, an academical study should be of principles and foundations. It is difficult to imagine in what sense the great English writers can be 'studied' if you exclude from view the ancient literatures, which, both in form and substance, they constantly presuppose. I should be glad on many grounds to see some recognition given in university examinations to English literature, not as a rival, but as (to an Englishman) the natural interpretation and completion of the study of the classics. It would act favourably on that study itself, saving it from pedantry, and also lessening the prevailing disposition to subordinate too completely its literary to its philosophical and historical interest.

Edward White Benson (1829–1896), Archbishop of Canterbury, was educated at King Edward's School, Birmingham and Trinity College, Cambridge, where he became a Fellow. From 1852 to 1859 he was a master at Rugby, moving on to become the first Headmaster of Wellington College, which he established as one of the top-rank public schools. In 1872 he became Chancellor of Lincoln, setting up a theological college there, and also involving himself in the organization of University Extension classes in Lincoln. In 1877 he was appointed first Bishop of Truro, then in 1882 Archbishop of Canterbury.

Benson supports the Collins agenda, including the necessity of linking the study of English literature to classics. He agrees with Collins's argument that the already existing Extension classes in English literature mean that the universities must take responsibility for ensuring that the Extension lecturers are properly trained for their task.

The *Pall Mall Gazette* text is not in the form of a letter, but rather an authorized statement.

Statement to PMG

We are authorized to state that the Archbishop of Canterbury is in favour of the universities providing for the adequate study of English literature, especially as the universities undertake to provide instruction in English literature through their Extension Lecturers and through the teachers in schools and professors in the various colleges and institutes which the modern side of education is every year multiplying both in Great Britain and in the Colonies. But he is of opinion that the study of English literature should be closely associated with the study of the Greek and Roman literatures, not simply on account of their intimate historical connection, but because sound and adequate literary culture must be based on the study of its sources. He would deplore any attempt to establish a school either for the independent study of our national literature, or for a study of it in connection only with modern literatures. He agrees with those who think that its proper place as an instrument of education, and as a branch of study, is with the literatures of Greece and Rome.

Henry Edward Manning (1808–1892), Cardinal Archbishop of Westminster, was educated at Harrow and Balliol College, Oxford, graduating with a First in Classics. Manning then worked briefly in the Colonial Office before returning to Oxford and being elected to a Fellowship at Merton College in 1832. Also in 1832 he was ordained in the Church of England, going on to become Archdeacon of Chichester in 1840 and Select Preacher at Oxford in 1842. In 1851 he was received into the Roman Catholic Church and re-ordained. He then studied in Rome for three years. He became Archbishop of Westminster in 1865 and Cardinal in 1875.

Manning skilfully avoids tackling the question of what precisely Oxford should do, although this does not stop him remarking that most of the changes at Oxford since he left there seem to have been for the worse. He believes that English literature, as distinct from philology, should be taught, and in close connection with the classics, which have already lost too much ground. Nevertheless, he also welcomes increased attention to Early English and to English grammar.

Letter to PMG

Before I attempt to answer the questions you have put I must say that for the last thirty-five years I have only watched the changes at Oxford – for of Cambridge I cannot speak – from a distance and without the duty of any minute inquiry. I may, however, say at once that, so far as I can judge, the changes in Oxford, both in studies and collegiate discipline, are not in my judgment for the better. I shall be thought, no doubt, a 'laudator temporis acti;'[17] but I believe the system of study and examination, as I knew it more than fifty years ago, was a severer tax upon the student willing to study; and if it did not multiply a diversity of subjects tested by early and isolated examinations, had nevertheless a permanent effect in training men for the studies and works of after life. I have been confirmed in this belief by finding many young men who have come to me possessed of various but partial knowledge, but comparatively wanting in the knowledge of Greek and Latin.

1. I will now endeavour to answer the three questions in your letter. I fully agree with you that in the curriculum of university study, literature as distinct from philology ought to be cultivated. Philology is as necessary to literature as analysis to chemistry; but it is subordinate and cannot supply its place. By literature I understand the intellectual product of cultivated nations. Inasmuch as the Latin language and literature sprung so largely from the language and literature of Greece, and inasmuch as our own language and literature are to so great an extent pervaded by the language and literature of the Greek and Roman world, I do not see how it is possible to have an intelligent knowledge of our own language and literature without the Greek and Roman classics.

2. In this full sense it is evident that English literature ought to form a part of university studies, and I have seen with satisfaction such works as those of Morris and Skeat on Early English,[18] and the volumes of selections printed at the Clarendon Press, and the knowledge of English which is exacted by the London University. I think I am correct in saying that few Englishmen have ever learnt English grammar. They master their mother-tongue unconsciously, and they learn its grammatical rules from the Latin grammar. This defect, however, I believe, is being at this time carefully supplied.

3. From what I have already said you will know that I believe the office of a university is not so much to fill men's minds with information, howsoever valuable it may be, as to educate the man himself, and I believe that the two great traditions of classical literature in the Greek and Roman world form an intellectual system in the order of nature, essential to the development and cultivation of the faculties and powers of the mind. I say in the natural order, because I am not speaking of the higher cultivation by the tradition of revealed truth. The Greek is the oldest language, and has outlived all others. It is at this day as fresh as in its origin. For subtlety, flexibility, precision, and fertility it has no equal, and I have always believed that between the Greek and the English languages there is a wonderful analogy and affinity.

I look, therefore, with dismay upon the tendency of these days to exclude the Greek and the Latin world from the education of Englishmen and to substitute the modern languages which are in demand in our commercial and utilitarian days.

John Bright (1811–1889) was a Liberal politician and a famous orator. He was born into a Quaker family in Rochdale, Lancashire, the son of a cotton-mill owner. He attended several different Quaker schools in Lancashire and Yorkshire, learning very little Latin and no Greek. He had no higher education, instead entering the family business. He became involved in the Anti-Corn-Law League, and worked tirelessly for free trade.

He first entered the House of Commons as MP for Durham in 1843, and was subsequently elected for Manchester and then Birmingham. Bright and his friend, Richard Cobden, were leading representatives of the manufacturing class in English politics following the 1832 Reform Act. He went on to espouse the cause of further reform, and led the agitation which finally led to a huge extension of the franchise in the Reform Act of 1867.

Bright was commonly seen as a leader of the middle classes, a point made by Henry James when he met him in 1880, at a time when Bright was already an old man. James described his air of 'sturdy, honest, vigorous, English middle-class liberalism, accompanied by a certain infusion of genius, which helps one to understand how his name has become the great rallying-point of that sentiment.'[19]

In this letter, Bright is replying, not to the standard *Pall Mall Gazette* questions, but to the question 'whether this great master of "classical" English had not after all been somewhat of a classical scholar.' He revels in his own relative lack of classical education and the fact that this lack has not prevented him from achieving success in English. The Authorized Version and Milton are more than adequate literary models for English youth. Study of the classics is damned as being a 'luxury,' a pleasant diversion for a 'limited' class.

Letter to **PMG**

Your letter has caused me some surprise and has afforded me some amusement. You pay me a great compliment in asking my opinion on the question you put to me, which is one with which I do not feel myself competent to deal. As you know, I have not had the advantage of what is termed a classical education. My limited school time scarcely allowed me to think of Greek, and I should now make but slow steps in Latin, even with the help of a dictionary. From this it will be clear that my knowledge of, or any success I may have attained in, my own language owes nothing to instruction derived from the great authors of antiquity. I have read some of their works in English translations; only recently I have read Mr Jowett's translation of the *Dialogues* of Plato, and have been more astonished at the wonderful capacity and industry of the Master of Balliol than at the wisdom of the great Philosopher of Greece.

I suppose the youth of ancient Greece read the best authors of their own country, and the Roman youth the best authors of Rome. To have read Greek among the Romans would not have done so much to create and continue a classic Latin as to read and study the best books of Roman writers. So now, and with us, what can Greece and Rome do for English students more than can be done for them by the best writers of their own tongue? Is there anything in the writings of the ancients that can compare in value for the youth of England with our translation of the Bible, especially of many of the Psalms and some of the Prophets, or with the unsurpassable grandeur and beauty of Milton? If all existing Greek and Latin books were destroyed, is there not in our English classics sufficient material whereon to build a future of which our successors need not be ashamed? The learned men who were recently employed to revise the translation of the New Testament[20] were, I presume, especially learned in the tongue of ancient Greece. No one has complained of their ignorance of Greek, but many have been surprised at and have complained of their failure in regard to English. They may have been profound in their knowledge of the ancient classics, but in English equal to the translation they were engaged to revise, they seem to me to have shown more of feebleness than of strength.

You ask me if I believe that the classics of the modern world are an equivalent, from an educational point of view, for the Greek and Roman classics? I answer that, as probably all the facts of history, or of biography, or of science, and all the reasoning to be found in ancient books, are to be found in modern translations, it follows that the study of the ancient languages is not now essential to education so far as the acquisition of knowlege is concerned; and that as the study of the best writers of English must be more effective in creating and sustaining what we may term classic English than the study of any foreign or dead language can be, it seems to follow that the classics of the modern world are, from an educational point of view, an equivalent for the Greek and

Roman classics. The knowledge of the ancient languages is mainly a luxury. It is useful from the fact that science has enlisted it in its service, and it is pleasant to possess, and because it is pleasant it is a possession of value, with those who wander among ancient books, and whose association is chiefly with the limited class who are enabled by leisure and temperament to give themselves up to studies which are not open to the multitude.

I have written what has occurred to me after reading your letter. I do not feel competent fully to discuss the questions submitted. I am one of the unlearned, having derived little or no nourishment from the fountain from which you have drunk so abundantly. If my answer to your questions disappoints you, or seems to you shallow and unworthy, I am afraid it will add to the proofs you have of the insufficiency of an education in which classical learning has not been included.

Henry Howard Herbert, Earl of Carnarvon (1831–1890) was educated at Eton and Christ Church, Oxford. He was active as a Conservative in the House of Lords, and for a number of years held the post of Colonial Secretary.

The Earl of Carnarvon is very doubtful about whether English literature should be sanctioned at Oxford. He clearly suspects that as a subject it is often 'mere cram' and the authors set are not even read. More seriously, though, it represents a threat to classics.

Letter to **PMG**

A proposal to add the study of English literature – which I understand to include a period ranging from Chaucer to the nineteenth century – to the Oxford curriculum is naturally attractive. My fear is that such an addition cannot be made without the sacrifice of something still more valuable.

The study of the classics – the most useless if inaccurate – is, if exact, the best instrument for forming the mind; it has stood the test of 'infinite time,' and it has been immemorially honoured in the university. Further, it is not too much to say that a real understanding of English literature is impossible without a knowledge of at least Latin. For these reasons it seems to me that a further reduction of classical instruction in the supposed interests of English literature would be only a melancholy delusion, and a fresh and mischievous tribute to the 'smattering' tendencies of modern education. On the other hand, the study of English literature – if it is not to be a mere cram, or a shallow and pretentious acquaintance with authors not read or wholly undigested – comes far better at a rather later period of life, when the foundations of knowledge have been laid, and taste is more formed.

Briefly, therefore, I would say, if it is certain that without prejudice to the classics English literature can be introduced into the university curriculum, no reasonable objection can be offered; but if, as I fear is more likely, its introduction tends to disturb or weaken the existing classical system, then I would unhesitatingly refuse the specious but perilous gift.

Matthew Arnold (1822–1888). For brief biographical details see pp. 182–3.

Letter to **PMG**

I have no difficulty in saying that I should like to see standard English authors joined to the standard authors of Greek and Latin literature who have to be taken up for a pass, or for honours, at the universities. I should be sorry to see a separate school, with degrees and honours, for the modern languages as such, although it is desirable that the professors and teachers of those languages should give certificates of fitness to teach them. I would add no literature except that of our own country to the classical literature taken up for the degree, whether with or without honours in Arts. These seem to me to be elementary propositions, when one is laying down what is desirable in respect to the university degree in Arts. The omission of the mother tongue and its literature in school and university instruction is peculiar, so far as I know, to England. You do a good work in urging us to repair that omission.

But I will not conceal from you that I have no confidence in those who at the universities regulate studies, degrees, and honours. To regulate these matters great experience of the world, steadiness, simplicity, breadth of view, are desirable. I do not see how those who actually regulate them can well have these qualifications; I am sure that in what they have done in the last forty years they have not shown them. Restlessness, a disposition to try experiments and multiply studies and schools, are what they have shown, and what they will probably continue to show; and this though personally many of them may be very able and distinguished men. I fear, therefore, that while you are seeking an object altogether good – the completing of the old and great degree in arts – you may obtain something which will not only not be that, but will be a positive hindrance to it.

W.J. Courthope (1842–1917) was educated at Harrow, then Corpus Christi and New College, Oxford. At New College he was a pupil of E.C. Wickham. After Oxford he became a civil servant, first as an examiner in the Education Office, then as a Civil Service Commissioner from 1892 to 1907. In addition to this Civil Service career, however, he edited a number of volumes of Pope's works, wrote a life of Pope and a life of Addison, and also a six-volume *History of English Poetry*. In 1895 he became Professor of Poetry at Oxford.

Courthope wishes to include English literature as part of Literae Humaniores, rather than to establish a separate school. In this way, the study of English literature and of classics can have a fruitful influence on each other: the study of English can become careful and accurate; the study of classics can become something more than mere language study.

Letter to **PMG**

The paper in the *Quarterly* shows very conclusively two things – first, the absence from our university course of any provision for the sound and accurate study of English literature; and, secondly, that the training of the universities in respect of classical scholarship is too exclusively philological. What is wanted, therefore, is to provide that the works of the great English writers shall be studied in the same accurate manner as those of the great Latin and Greek authors, and to enlarge the scope of the Classical schools so as to allow the ancient authors to be read for the sake of their spirit and genius, not simply for the sake of their language. I cannot conceive that the establishment of 'a Modern Literature School' *per se* would effect what is required. It would cover too large a surface, and the number of students who would care to master all modern literatures thoroughly would be probably small. I think a better proposal would be to read the ancient classics and the English classics together, so that the one might illustrate the other. This, it seems to me, would be practical and definite, and if the scheme were thoroughly worked out it could not fail to elevate the character of university teaching. Englishmen are naturally ready to study the literature of their own country if the opportunity be given them, and for the study of English literature I have little doubt that if a separate school were instituted, or if the scope of 'Moderations' were enlarged so as to make the examination one of taste as well as philology, scholarship would be generally benefited. I have not studied the *pros* and *cons* of the matter, but my own instincts would prompt me if possible rather to *enlarge* the present system by regarding English literature as part of the *literae humaniores*, than to start a separate school for English literature. The English philosophers are studied for the final schools. Why should not the English poets and orators be studied for 'Moderations'? If, on the other hand, a separate school for English literature seemed preferable, I presume that all scholars examined in it would be required to give proof of their acquaintance with the Greek and Roman classics.

Henry Craik (1846–1927) was educated at Glasgow University, then Balliol College, Oxford. After Oxford he became a civil servant, as an examiner in the Education Department. In 1885 he became secretary to a committee of the Privy Council controlling Scottish education. He was also a writer, who contributed numerous articles to the *Quarterly Review* and other periodicals, as well as writing *The Life of Swift* (1882) and *The State and Education* (1883). In 1906 he became a Conservative MP, representing the Universities of Glasgow and Aberdeen until his death.

Craik argues that English can be a respectable subject only if linked inseparably with classics and sharing in the thoroughness associated with the study of classics. He believes the evidence already exists of just what a superficial subject English literature can be.

Letter to PMG

I have doubts as to the success which would attend the introduction of a School of English Literature into Oxford. Such a school might easily offer opportunities for specious and superficial instead of sound and accurate work; and the difficulty which lies before any one who has made good use of the opportunities already open at the university, in gaining for himself a knowledge of English literature at least as sound as that which any courses of lectures could give him, seems to me to be usually much exaggerated. I can understand, however, that a fair case may be made out for the proposal now that Oxford provides from her graduates many who enter at once upon the duties of Literature Chairs elsewhere. But I have no hesitation whatever in agreeing with the opinion – which is confirmed in my own case by very considerable opportunities of testing, in different ways, the educational value of the subject – that if this study is to be carried on with that thoroughness which is alone worthy of the university, it must be connected inseparably with that classical training which can alone open up the foundations upon which all that is most valuable in our literature rests. We have not to look far at present for symptoms of the harm that may be done by a study of English literature apart from such a connection, and if it is not secured in any curriculum adopted by Oxford, I trust that Oxford, for her own sake and that of literature, will leave English literature alone.

James Anthony Froude (1818–1894), the historian, was educated at Oriel College, Oxford, subsequently being elected a Fellow of Exeter College. He was ordained a deacon in 1844, but he gradually broke with orthodox Christian faith, was never ordained a priest, and later divested himself of his deacon's orders. Froude wrote a number of articles for the *Westminster Review* and *Fraser's Magazine*, and in 1860 became editor of *Fraser's*, a post which he held for fourteen years. He was best known for some weighty works of history, the multi-volume *A History of England in the Sixteenth Century* and *The English in Ireland in the Eighteenth Century*, and for a life of Carlyle. In 1892, just two years before his death, he returned to Oxford, succeeding E.A. Freeman as Regius Professor of Modern History.

Froude expresses no strong views about what Oxford should do. He wishes to retain classics, but since the system seems to be changing to one in which students can choose their branch of study, English could be such a branch. He does not go along with Collins's thesis that classics and English literature have to be studied together.

Letter to PMG

I will answer your questions as briefly as I can.
1. Should English literature be included in the university curriculum? This depends on what universities undertake to do. In my time there was one special curriculum (or two, including mathematics) which was

insisted on for all. It did not include English literature, nor could it have done so in my opinion without impairing the excellence of the teaching which it actually gave. If, on the other hand, the English Universities are to revert to their original character as places where all learning is taught, and the students are to select their special branches, then I think that English literature certainly ought to form one of those branches.

2. I hesitate to say that an understanding of English literature is impossible without a knowledge of Greek and Latin literature. Many of our very best writers knew little or no Greek and Latin. Shakspeare had 'small Latin and less Greek.' Pope translated Homer, but was a poor scholar. Defoe, Bunyan, Burns, Byron, Carlyle, Cobbett, Charles Lamb – these and many other names occur to me which disprove the position, as it concerns writers; and I think you might find very good students of English literature also equally ignorant. The Scandinavian literature, not the classical, was the cradle of our own. At the same time I regard the Greek and Latin literature as the best in the world, as superior to the modern as Greek sculpture is superior to the schools of England and France; and no one can be a finished scholar and critic (I do not say writer) who is ignorant of it. Our national taste and the tone of the national intellect will suffer a serious decline if it ceases to be studied among us. The most essential of all things, however, is not to overload our curriculum. A little, closely and accurately learned, is better than a superficial acquaintance with much, and therefore I regret the operation of the examination system as it is now carried on.

F.J. Furnivall (1825–1910) was educated at Trinity Hall, Cambridge. He was called to the Bar in 1849, but never made a career as a lawyer. He was drawn into the Christian Socialist movement, but soon became an agnostic. Nevertheless, he joined F.D. Maurice in helping to set up the first Working Men's College in Red Lion Square in 1854, and taught there both English grammar and English poetry. He also persuaded his friend, John Ruskin, to teach there. In 1847 he joined the Philological Society, which had originated at University College, and he maintained his involvement with this society until his death, serving for many years as secretary. His philological interests led him into what became his major work, as an editor. In 1861 he was appointed editor of what became the *New English Dictionary*, and he contributed to the work of this dictionary for the rest of his life. He also edited many Anglo-Saxon and Middle English texts, and founded the Early English

Text Society to ensure that as many such texts as possible were edited and published. Furnivall was a great founder of societies, also bringing into being the Chaucer Society, the Ballad Society, the New Shakspere Society, the Wyclif Society, the Browning Society and the Shelley Society.

Furnivall welcomes unreservedly plans for English at Oxford. He is content to see it linked with classics, at least to start with, if that will make it possible for Oxford to accept the new subject. In the long term, though, relations with Romance and Teutonic literatures need to be traced, too, and will sometimes prove more important.

Letter to PMG

Such good news is it that Oxford thinks of promoting the study of English Literature by recognizing it in its Tripos, that I do not care to look the gift-horse in the mouth. Though for all early English literature, I think the study of Romance and Teutonic books more important than Classical ones, yet I am sure that the joint study of Classic and English literature, will greatly advantage both. Both are far too much studied now as if they were mere collections of words with roots, and sentences with syntax; but when once a man has got touch of Shakspere's mind, he'll never be content till he's got hold of Virgil's, Horace's, Aeschylus's, and Homer's too. And having once done this, when he gets back (or comes on) to Chaucer's day, and finds that Homer was lookt on as a disreputable old fellow who 'loudly lied' on the side of the Greeks against those Fathers of History and Truth, Dares, Phrygius and Dictys Cretensis, he will not fail to follow his classical writers into their latest stage, and thus enter into the literature of that mediaeval Italy which fired the minds of Chaucer and Shakspere too. Nothing but good can come from Oxford recognizing English literature in its Examinations. That the University should first think of uniting the new subject with its old one of Classics which has made Oxford so famous, is but natural. By all means let this be done. Only, when the new English or Modern Literature or Language Tripos comes to be established – as it soon will be, I hope – don't let the Classical men refuse to allow English Literature to be studied and examined in from the Romance and Teutonic side too. We want all the light on it that we can get. No narrow inheritance is ours. And some of us at least are not afraid that any writer of other lands will 'stain' our Shakspere.

T.H. Huxley (1825–1895) was a famous biologist and education-alist. He spent most of his working life at the School of Mines in London, but also held posts as Fullerian Professor at the Royal Institution, Hunterian Professor at the Royal College of Surgeons, and Honorary Principal of the South London Working Men's College from 1868 to 1880. In 1870 he was elected to the School Board in Marylebone, and was very active in setting up a system of schools under the Education Act of that year.

In his inaugural address at the Working Men's College in 1868, entitled 'A Liberal Education; And Where to Find It,' he had already poured scorn on the neglect of science, modern geography, modern history and modern literature as well as the English language in middle-class schools. Now he joined in the controversy surrounding English at Oxford sparked off by the appointment of Arthur Napier to the Merton Chair, though he was embarrassed when his letter was construed by Professor Max Müller as an attack on Napier. Huxley asserted that his letter was concerned with general principles.

As a scientist, Huxley's support for English had a very different basis from that which underlay Collins's crusade. Huxley was concerned to introduce 'modern' subjects at all levels of education, and English was a natural part of a balanced modern curriculum. Collins and many others, on the other hand, saw English literature as a natural ally of classics against the threat posed by scientific education. English was espoused by both parties, but with different aims.

Letter to **PMG**

I fully agree with you that the relation of our universities to the study of English literature is a matter of great public importance; and I have more than once taken occasion to express my conviction, firstly, that the works of our great English writers are pre-eminently worthy of being systematically studied in our schools and universities, as literature; and secondly, that the establishment of professorial chairs of philology, under the name of literature, may be a profit to science, but is really a fraud practised upon letters.[21]

That a young Englishman may be turned out of one of our universities 'epopt and perfect' so far as their system takes him, and yet ignorant of the noble literature which has grown up in these islands during the last three centuries, no less than of the development of the philosophical and political ideas which have most profoundly influenced modern civilization, is a fact in the history of the nineteenth century which the twentieth will find hard to believe; though, perhaps, it is not more incredible than our current superstition that whoso wishes to write and speak English well should mould his style after the models furnished by Classical antiquity. For my part, I venture to doubt the wisdom of attempting to mould one's style by any other process than that of striving after the clear and forcible expression of definite conceptions; in which process the Glassian precept, 'first catch your definite conceptions,'[22] is probably the most difficult to obey. But, still, I mark among distinguished contemporary speakers and writers of English, saturated with antiquity, not a few to whom, it seems to me, that the study of Hobbes might possibly have taught dignity; of Swift, concision and clearness; of Goldsmith and Defoe, simplicity.

Well, among a hundred young men whose university career is finished is there one whose attention has ever been directed by his literary instructors to a page of Hobbes, or Swift, or Goldsmith, or Defoe? In my boyhood we were familiar with *Robinson Crusoe*, *The Vicar of Wakefield*, and *Gulliver's Travels*; and though the mysteries of 'Middle English' were hidden from us, my impression is we ran less chance of learning to write and speak the 'middling English' of popular orators and head masters than if we had been perfect in such mysteries and ignorant of those three masterpieces. It has been the fashion to decry the eighteenth century, as young fops laugh at their fathers. But we were there in germ; and a 'Professor of Eighteenth Century History and Literature' who knew his business might tell young Englishmen more of that which it is profoundly important that they should know, but which at present remains hidden from them, than any other instructor; and, incidentally, they would learn to know good English when they see or hear it – perhaps even to discriminate between slipshod copiousness and true eloquence, and that alone would be a great gain.

Anna Swanwick (1813–1899) received most of her education at home, and since formal higher education was at this time difficult for women to obtain in England, she went to Berlin to study at the university in 1839. There she studied German and Greek, and when she returned to England in 1843 she began translating the work of German dramatists, including Goethe and Schiller, into English. She later used her expertise in Greek to translate Aeschylus. Anna Swanwick took a great interest in both working-class education and women's education. Her dedication to the latter is borne out by her involvement with the establishment of Queen's College, London, Bedford College, Girton and Somerville.

Anna Swanwick, perhaps influenced by her experience of women's higher education, believes that English is now assured a place in university curricula. Although she proposes an organic model of European literature, likening it to a tree whose parts are all related and whose roots are classics, she does not agree with Collins that English as a subject must be tied to classics. It is too important for that. Her ideal would be to include English literature in all the five honours schools then existing at Oxford; all these schools, not only classics, would gain from the humanizing influence of English literature. Here, applied to university education, is a forerunner of the idea propounded in the Newbolt Report (1921) of English for all as the keystone of education.

Letter to PMG

That English literature should be included in the university curriculum is, I believe, a settled question; whether it should or should not be studied in connection with the literature of Greece and Rome is still open for discussion. Upon this question I have been invited to express my opinion, and I do so with the greatest diffidence. The value of classical study, as an instrument for developing and cultivating the intellectual powers, is universally recognized, as is also the exquisite beauty and flexibility of the language of Hellas, and the richness and variety of her literature. It is also a recognized fact that modern European literature has its roots in classical antiquity; hence the various literatures of Europe, that of England included, may be studied with most profit and advantage when regarded, not as isolated growths, but as members of a living organism – branches, in fact, of a magnificent and ever-growing tree, vitally connected, not only with their common root, but also with their sister branches. The charm and interest of literature would doubtless be greatly enhanced were it studied in this comprehensive method. When, however, it is broadly asserted that a knowledge of the classics is indispensable for the enjoyment and appreciation of English literature, the statement appears to me to be exaggerated, and may, I think, be refuted by a reference to a few of our great master-singers. Chaucer, for example, as is well known, was conversant with Italian literature, and also with the poems of the Trouvères and the Troubadores, and had consequently, through them, had some remote connection with classical antiquity. His inspiration was, however, drawn from the national life by which he was surrounded, and if we would appreciate his wonderful portraiture, we must acquaint ourselves, not with the classics of Greece and Rome, but with the contemporary history of England. The same may be said of the Elizabethan age, with its marvellous outbursts of dramatic song, culminating in Shakspeare, 'the miracle of Stratford.' It is true that the classical scholars of the period, headed by Sir Philip Sidney, strove with might and main to force the national genius to embody itself in forms consecrated by classical antiquity. Their efforts, though fortunately unavailing, were not without effect upon the dramatists of the day, especially upon Marlowe, and through him upon Shakspeare; these facts, though interesting, as illustrating the development of the English drama, are not essential for the enjoyment and appreciation of our immortal bard.

It seems incredible that a native literature so rich in works of transcendent genius should hitherto have been almost practically ignored by our universities, and it is a subject for congratulation that this state of things is drawing to a close. The great master works of our literature might, in my judgment, be employed as educational instruments of the very highest value, and to determine how they may be introduced into our university system, with the greatest possible advantage, appears to me to be a question of paramount importance. In the present day, when the field of knowledge is so vastly extended, it is practically admitted by the university authorities that the study of the classics can no longer hold its former exceptional position in their curriculum. Thus, after passing his first public examination, the student is at liberty to choose between the Honour schools of natural science, mathematics, theology, jurisprudence, and modern history. It appears to me that all these studies, three more especially – namely, natural science, mathematics, and jurisprudence – require to be supplemented by a thorough knowledge of English and, to a certain extent, of European literature.

The ever narrowing area of research to which in the present day the man of science finds it absolutely essential to devote himself has a tendency to beget a certain one-sidedness of mind which is opposed to all true catholicity of culture. In the study of literature, especially of poetry, appealing as it does to the more spiritual side of our nature, to the imagination, the love of beauty, the affections, and the moral sentiments, will be found, I venture to think, the best safeguard against this danger, while at the same time a fountain will be opened to the student of never failing refreshments and delights. It is, I believe, generally recognized that the study of the classics would gain by being carried on

271

simultaneously with that of English literature. The same is true of theology and modern history, as well as of natural science, mathematics, and jurisprudence.

Hence, it would seem desirable, if possible, that the study of English literature should form an essential element in all university teaching, and enter into the examinations of the various honour schools. Our youth would thus leave the university with some knowledge of our noble literature, which will, I believe, be found the best nurse of patriotism, and a living source of pure enthusiasm and lofty aspirations. Should this scheme prove impracticable, I should prefer a separate honour school of English literature, in order that it may be accessible to all students, and not to those only who are able to devote themselves to the study of the ancient classics.

Grant Allen (1848–1899) was born in Canada. He was educated in Canada, USA, France and England. In 1867 he entered Merton College, Oxford, where he studied in the Classical School. After Oxford he worked for three years as a schoolmaster, then in 1873 was appointed Professor of Mental and Moral Philosophy in a black college in Spanish Town, Jamaica. The college was not a success, however, and on its closure in 1876 Allen returned to England, where he began a writing career. He wrote many popular scientific articles in the reviews and was for a time on the staff of the *Daily News*. He turned to fiction to try to make money, first producing short stories, then novels. In the last years of his life he wrote guide books to a number of European cities.

Allen loves English literature, and for that reason does not wish it to be studied as an academic subject. He wishes it to remain a delightful private study, rather than become the province of the crammer.

Letter to PMG

It appears to me that nothing could be more prejudicial to the interests of culture in England than the establishment of a real school of English Literature at the universities. If you wish to kill a study, make it the subject of academical teaching. At the present day, most educated Englishmen know and love the literature of their own country. Many of them also know and love the literatures of Germany, France, and modern Italy. But by far the larger part of them cordially hate and dislike the literature of ancient Greece and Rome; and the reason is clear; because it was made to them in childhood and youth a symbol of drudgery and an instrument of torture in the horrid form of licensed vivisection known as public examinations. If I may venture to obtrude, by way of illustration, a personal experience, I would say briefly that I was a classical man at Oxford myself; took my classical scholarship and honours in due course; and imbibed enough Greek and Latin verse by the way to be made composition master for some years to the sixth form at two or three big public schools. But from the day when fate first happily released me from that intolerable servitude to a false system of so-called education to the present moment, I have never dreamt of glancing at Plato or Aeschylus, at Tacitus or Virgil, except for a purely historical or scientific purpose. The bare idea of taking them down and reading them for amusement or culture, as we read Shakspeare and Victor Hugo and Goethe, or as we read true poetry of the present day, like Andrew Lang's or Gosse's or Austin Dobson's (you see, I have the courage of my opinions), would scarcely even so much as occur to the mind of the average classically educated Englishman. He regards all these things as mere 'scholarship;' something that he got over, like chicken-pox and measles, once for all, early in life, and need never again trouble his head with. If a school of English literature were established at Oxford the men who 'took it up for Finals' would come to look upon Keats's 'Nightingale' as a straight tip for examination; they would discuss the text of Shelley's 'Skylark' from the point of view of Mr Forman's[23] conjectural emendations; they would canvass with great deliberation the nice question why Richard Feveril did not return to Lucy; and they would appraise the place of *The Earthly Paradise*[24] by a comparison of the critical opinions held by Mr Stopford Brooke and by the author of the selected literature cram book. Dr Craik[25] and Professor Henry Morley[26] would gain thousands; and English education would lose the one vivifying element it still possesses outside science – the personal study, for pure love, of our great poets, romance writers, essayists, and thinkers. May we never live to see examination papers set in the High on Wordsworth's 'Ode on the Intimations of Immortality,' or frightened undergaduates heckled in *viva voce* over the precise signification of the fourth line in the eighth stanza of the 'Grammarian's Funeral.'[27]

William Morris (1834–1896) was educated at Marlborough, then Exeter College, Oxford. Having abandoned the idea of ordination, Morris started to train as an architect when he left Oxford, but never completed this training. In 1861 he established with some friends the firm of Morris, Marshall, Faulkner and Company (later Morris and Company) which produced a wide range of artistic goods, including fabrics, wallpapers, stained glass and furniture. Morris did much of the designing himself, as well as mastering production techniques. He built the firm into a very successful commercial undertaking, which also had an important influence on nineteenth-century design. Nevertheless, Morris was active and influential in a number of other areas, too. He was a well-known poet, famous particularly for *The Earthly Paradise*; he also wrote a number of prose romances, including *News from Nowhere*. Appalled by the nineteenth-century vogue for 'restoring' medieval buildings, he set up the Society for the Protection of Ancient Buildings, in order to try to save them from the restorers. He was also active politically, using his wealth to support first the Social Democratic Federation, then the Socialist League, and lecturing for the Socialist cause all over Britain.

Morris's letter is one of those most opposed to the whole idea of English literature at Oxford. Very forthrightly he suggests a number of reasons for opposition, but the main one is that what is planned is a Chair of Criticism, with all which that suggests to Morris of vague talk and literary polemics. He identifies proponents of 'culture' as the main force behind the campaign for English, and uses this as evidence against the proposed subject.

Letter to PMG

I expect I shall be in a minority among those who answer your letter as to the proposed Professorship of English Literature, for I think the universities had better let it alone. Those disasters the Slade Professorships of Art ought to warn them off establishing chairs whose occupiers would have necessarily to deal vaguely with great subjects; and this all the more as the Slade Professors chosen have been the best that offered, one a man of genius, and the rest men of talent. Need I mention that queer absurdity the Oxford Chair of Poetry as a further warning? As to the Merton Professorship, which you mention in your note, I think the university did all it could in the matter, because philology can be taught, but 'English literature' cannot. Neither can I admit that there is any analogy between the proposed study of English literature and the way that the universities have dealt with the classics: their study implies that of the language and history of civilized antiquity; they are not taught as literature, not criticized as literature, at any rate. If the function of the proposed chair were to be, or could be, the historical evolution of English literature, including, of course, the English language, it might be well enough; but I do not think that this is intended, judging by the outcry raised about the filling of the Merton Professorship. I fear that most professors would begin English literature with Shakspeare, not with *Beowulf*. What *is* intended seems to me a Chair of *Criticism*; and against the establishment of such a Chair I protest emphatically. For the result would be merely vague talk about literature, which would teach nothing. Each succeeding professor would strive to outdo his predecessor in 'originality' on subjects whereon nothing original remains to be said. Hyper-refinement and paradox would be the order of the day, and the younger students would be confused by the literary polemics which would be sure to flourish round such a Chair; and all this would have the seal of authority set upon it, and probably would not seldom be illustrated by some personal squabble like the one which your note mentions. Pray, Sir, change your mind, and do your best to deliver us from two (or more) Professors of Criticism.

I might suggest as a compromise, however, that the Professor of Poetry might have his position made a thought less ridiculous by his subject being extended so as to embrace the whole of English literature – but I'm not sure. Or, if a new professorship is wanted, might not a humble one of mediaeval archaeology be established, with the definite object of teaching the dons the value of the buildings of which they ought to be the guardians? In the thirty years during which I have known Oxford more damage has been done to art (and therefore to literature) by Oxford 'culture' than centuries of professors could repair – for, indeed, it is irreparable. These coarse brutalities of 'light and leading'[28] make education stink in the nostrils of thoughtful persons, and (*pace* Dr Lombroso)[29] are more likely than is Socialism to drive some of us mad. But I must not end with a joke; so, as a last word, I say that to attempt to teach literature with one hand while it destroys history with the other, is a bewildering proceeding on the part of 'culture.'

Notes

1. John Churton Collins, *The Study of English Literature* (1891), p.98.
2. Frederick Archer (1857–1886), a jockey, who won the Two thousand Guineas, the Oaks, the Derby, the St Leger and the Grand Prix in 1885.
3. # [See letter from T.H. Huxley, pp. 268–9]. But Professor Huxley subsequently wrote to the *Pall Mall Gazette* (28 October, 1886) with reference to the above statement as follows:- 'When I said, in a former note to you, that "the establishment of professorial chairs of philology under the name of

literature" was "a fraud upon letters," I enunciated a general proposition which I conceived to be indisputable. The possibility that my words could be construed into an attack upon Professor Napier, who does not subordinate literature to philology, did not enter my imagination. No one can regret more than I do any annoyance which may have been caused to Professor Napier by the indiscreet and unwarrantable application of my truism to him; but I must disclaim all responsibility for a proceeding which is justified by no act or thought of mine.'

4. William Stubbs (1825–1901). Before becoming Bishop of Chester in 1884, Stubbs was Regius Professor of History at Oxford from 1866 to 1884.
5. pious wishes.
6. John Earle (1824–1903). Earle was Professor of Anglo-Saxon from 1849 to 1854 and again from 1876.
7. 'The Old Guard which does not surrender' (a saying attributed to Pierre-Jacques, Baron de Cambronne).
8. Carl Lachmann produced a number of editions of *De Rerum Natura*. H.A.J. Munro was also an editor and translator of this work.
9. Sir Richard Jebb, a well-known editor and translator.
10. G.E. Brown, *Fo'c'sle Yarns* (1881).
11. stale repetitions (Juvenal, *Satires*, vii.154).
12. See also Huxley's letter to the *Pall Mall Gazette*, included in this volume, pp. 268–9.
13. John Tyndall (1820–1893) was a physicist.
14. See also Farrar's letter to the *Pall Mall Gazette*, included in this volume, pp. 251–2.
15. i.e. Moderations.
16. i.e. Edward Freeman. See also his article, 'Literature and Language,' included in this volume, Chapter 18.
17. someone who praises the way things used to be (Horace, *Ars Poetica*, 173).
18. Richard Morris and Walter Skeat, both editors of many Early English texts.
19. Quoted in Leon Edel, *Henry James: the Conquest of London, 1870–1883* (1962), pp. 363–364.
20. The *Revised Version* of the Bible.
21. See also Friedrich Max Müller's letter to the *Pall Mall Gazette*, included in this volume, pp. 238–41.
22. Hannah Glasse was a cookery writer, to whom the phrase, 'First catch your hare' is attributed.
23. Harry Buxton Forman.
24. *The Earthly Paradise* (1868–1870) by William Morris.
25. Henry Craik. See also his letter to the *Pall Mall Gazette*, included in this volume, pp. 264–5
26. See also the report of the committee at University College which appointed him to his professorship, included in this volume, Chapter 8.
27. 'A Grammarian's Funeral,' by Robert Browning.
28. The phrase is Edmund Burke's, from *Reflections on the Revolution in France* (1790).
29. Cesare Lombroso (1836–1909) had made a study of Anarchists. There was an article in the *Pall Mall Gazette*, 25 October 1886, entitled 'Are Socialists Lunatics?', which dealt with Lombroso's theories.

CHAPTER EIGHTEEN

Edward Freeman

Edward Freeman (1823–1892) was a historian and a prolific writer of books and periodical articles. He entered Trinity College, Oxford in 1841 and graduated in 1845. He took a continuing interest in matters concerning the University of Oxford, writing many articles about Oxford issues and developments, as well as applying for jobs there. In 1858, he applied for the post of Regius Professor of Modern History; in 1861 he tried for the Camden Chair of Ancient History and the Chichele Chair of Modern History. It was not until 1884 that he was finally appointed Regius Professor of Modern History, after almost forty years of working independently as a historian without an academic job, and then the long-sought-after post did not bring him the happiness which might have been anticipated. For one thing, he thoroughly disliked many of the changes which had been effected at Oxford since his time there as an undergraduate. The prospect of a School of Literature at Oxford, as urged by Collins and his supporters, represented yet another change too many for Freeman.

The article from which extracts are printed here, 'Literature and Language,' was published in the *Contemporary Review* in 1887, at the point in the debate where Collins and his allies were vigorously opposing the proposed School of Modern Languages on the grounds that it was a School of Literature which was now needed. Freeman writes as one of the electors responsible for the appointment to the Merton Chair in 1885, and also as one of those involved in considering the current proposal for a School of Modern Languages. He argues that the vociferous demands for literature ignore the fact that language and literature have always been studied together, certainly in the traditional approach to Classics.

Freeman attempts to borrow Collins's clothes when he goes on to urge the necessity of solid scholarship, but for Freeman this means study of the beginnings of the English language and comparison with the early forms of other related languages, precisely the philology which Collins castigated. Universities should exist merely to serve scholarship, and therefore should not concern themselves with preparing students for any profession or calling. Freeman makes this point in his discussion of the teaching of modern foreign languages, but it is very relevant to the question of English studies, since its proponents, Collins in particular, commonly argued that the universities must teach English in order to train the teachers who would go out into the world to preach the literary gospel. The business of universities is scholarship is Freeman's retort.

One of the main planks of Freeman's case is that the proponents of literature are really asking for the teaching of 'taste,' a word which had had a high level of prominence in the old subject of rhetoric, but which had been mocked by Wordsworth, as well as by such important figures in the history of English studies as Maurice and Kingsley. For a degree, Freeman believes, a university must have subjects in which it is possible to examine. Since it is not possible to examine in taste, the temptation will be to import facts into the subject, facts which will often be little more than gossip and scandal about very modern writers. It was Freeman who had created the phrase 'chatter about Shelley' in one of the debates in Congregation, and he repeats it here with an example of precisely the sort of chatter he had in mind. This phrase became a useful expression of derision employed by those opposed to English studies. The importation of examinable facts into the subject will, furthermore, Freeman believes, lead to an industry producing literature about literature, and 'cramming' will come into its own. Then, since the subject will be susceptible to the work of the crammer, English literature will come to be considered an 'easy' school, a designation which is sure to be fatal to its standing.

'Literature and Language'

There has lately been no small stir in many quarters about the relations between 'language' and 'literature' and the supposed opposition between them. To say that there has been a dispute on the subject would perhaps be going too far. For the question may be raised, 'Si rixa est, ubi tu pulsas, ego vapulo tantum.'[1]

A great deal has been said on one side and very little on the other. The side which has had most said against it has said very little against the other side. And it has said little against the other side, because it was slow in understanding that there were two sides. Men who were doing their own work and following their own studies without meddling with the work and studies of others were a little amazed to be suddenly told that they were the enemies of this pursuit and that, that they had committed a 'fraud' – that has been the favourite formula – upon this subject and that. The odd thing was that the subjects which they were charged with treating in this unfair way were subjects towards which they were not conscious of bearing any ill will, subjects to which some of them at least certainly believed that their own lives were largely devoted. Certain electors in the University of Oxford were called on to make an election to a certain professorship, and they made it according to the best of their skill and understanding. Such elections do not commonly turn the world upside down. There may be a few remarks in the newspapers at the time, a few words of approval or disapproval, and that is all. It is certainly not usual for such an election, not only to be made the subject of endless false rumours before and after, but to be branded at the time as either 'a joke or a job,' and to be made the occasion, months and years after, of an abiding charge of 'fraud' against the electors. Some while after the election, the immediate *venue* was changed from Oxford to Cambridge. The demerits, real or alleged, of a certain professor there were made the handle for a fierce attack, not only upon him but upon both Universities,[2] in which the story of the election to the Oxford professorship was of course not forgotten. A little later, the Hebdomadal Council at Oxford proposed a statute to Congregation,[3] a very common event, and one which, as a rule, does not greatly stir the public mind. But the heading of this statute contained the word 'languages;' some of its clauses contained the word 'literature.' The words seemed harmless words; they were certainly used with very harmless meanings; but the words 'language' and 'literature' seem to be to some minds what the red rag is in one proverbial saying and the trailed coat in another. The hubbub began again; in truth it had never stopped. The statute was strongly opposed in Oxford and fiercely denounced out of it, and the favourite formula of 'fraud' did not fail to be brought in.

Now I suppose there are some to whom all this seems right and natural, and to whom these charges of 'fraud' and the like must at least have a meaning. But there are also some to whom the whole thing seems very wonderful. Their difficulty is to understand how 'language' and 'literature' came to be looked at as distinct and even hostile subjects. They had lived all their lives in the belief that 'language' and 'literature' were, perhaps not exactly the same thing, but that they were at least things which could not be kept asunder, things which, if not the same thing, were different sides of the same thing. How, they would have asked, if the question had come into their heads, can language stand without literature or literature without language? Each, they would have said, implied the other. The study of literature might be supposed to be the study of books, and to study books implied a knowledge of the language in which they are written. And, in such study of any language as might be looked for in an University, knowledge of the language would be held to imply, not the mere power of reading and talking it, but a knowledge of the language itself, its history and character and relations to other languages. Such knowledge might not get beyond the level of elegant scholarship or it might rise to that of the higher philology; in either case it would be what the time and place concerned accepted as thorough knowledge of the language. A mere empirical command of a language, the mere power of speaking it, was not the kind of knowledge with which an University would be satisfied. The academical knowledge of a language surely implied both some knowledge of the language itself, of the facts about it, and also some knowledge of the books written in that language. Neither could be conceived apart. One man might give more attention to one side and another to the other; but no man could afford altogether to neglect either. For some ages Greek and Latin were the only languages which formed part of any academic course. In the way in which they were studied there were some manifest faults; but there was certainly no divorce between 'literature' and 'language,' as those words were understood then.

*
* *

If the experience of one man is worth saying anything about, I may say that the fact that there could be any opposition between 'language' and 'literature' came upon me as a new light at the time of the election to the Merton professorship. We who had to elect were beset by cries on both sides. The title of the professorship was certainly an awkward one. Its holder is 'Professor of English Language and Literature.' Something perhaps of an article, something perhaps of an adjective, is needed to make this title suit the rules either of 'language' or of 'literature.' Some people made themselves very merry over this title, and they had a right to do so if they chose; only they seemed to think that their merriment told in some way against the electors. Yet the electors had nothing to do with the title; they, like the rest of the University, had simply to take it as they found it at the hands of the Commissioners.[4] But anyhow the words 'Language' and 'Literature' were both in the title, and if there was any doubt as to what was meant by 'literature,' there was at least no doubt as to what was meant by 'language.' That that word was to be taken in the old scholarly sense was plain from a suggestion made by the Commissioners that the new professorship should be united with the professorship of 'Anglo-Saxon.' It was odd, and it has proved very unlucky, that the Commissioners only suggested when they might have ordained; but at any rate the object of the new chair was to unite the study of 'language' in the fullest and deepest sense with the study of 'literature'in some sense. And to me at least the union seemed perfectly reasonable. For I was still in that state of antiquated darkness which conceived that language implied literature and that literature implied language, and which never thought of any opposition between the two. I had thought in my simplicity that our business was to choose some one who got at the language through the literature and at the literature through the language. From this dream I was awakened, and I dare say others were awakened also, by 'barbarian war-cries on every side.' Many votaries of literature were shouting that literature could have nothing to do with language, and at least one votary of language was shouting no less loudly that language could have nothing to do with literature. The truth gradually dawned upon me as I listened to the shouts and as I did my duty as an elector by studying the testimonials and other credentials of the candidates. I had conceived that a mastery of English literature meant a study of the great masterpieces written in the language, a study grounded on a true historical knowledge of the language, in which knowledge a mastery of its minuter philology was at least a counsel of perfection. It did not occur to me that to have written an article or two on some very modern subject was of itself a qualification for a professor of 'English Language and Literature.' The gift of writing such articles well is a gift by no means to be despised; but I should have called it by some other name, possibly by some less lofty name. I might have thought that 'literature' of such a kind, if 'literature' it is to be, was all very well in its own way, perhaps amusing, perhaps even instructive, but that it was not quite of that solid character which we were used to look for in any branch of an University course. Gradually I learned that there were many people of quite another way of thinking. I found that there was something which claimed the name of 'literature' which certainly had nothing to do with solid scholarship of any kind. Something, it might be that was all very well in its way, something that there might be no occasion for us to go out of our way to say a word against, but still something which we did not wish to have thrust upon us as a subject for University professorships and examinations. In short, I and those who thought with me found out that by 'literature' we meant one thing, and that some other people meant another thing. To us a 'Professor of English Language and Literature,' provided his title was duly strengthened with articles and adjectives, seemed a perfectly reasonable kind of person. He was to be a master of the Language and Literature of England in the same sense in which any really competent professor or reader of Greek or Latin is a master of those languages and their literature. He was to be master of the language, and also master of the books written in that language. He was to begin at the beginning, but he was not to draw in at any arbitrary point, but to go on whithersoever his studies should naturally lead him. Starting from the beginning, he would naturally in course of time come to the end, so far as a thing which was going on could be said to have an end. But we found that the main objection to our notions was that they took in the beginning. The chief position of all was that the beginning ought to have no place in the whole affair. The end was to be reached, but by some other road than starting from the beginning. It was to be English 'literature' in some sense which did not require a knowledge of the earliest forms of the English language or a comparison of those forms with those of kindred languages; nay more, it was absolutely to shut such studies out. Through the whole dispute we have had to strive, not with a mere passive neglect or ignorance of Teutonic studies, but with a positive dislike to them. Whatever English 'literature' was, it was to be something which did not call for any fellowship with the older English, or with Gothic, Scandinavian, or Old High-German. It was to be more than something that did not call for them; it was to be something which distinctively refused to have anything to do with them. The cry from many voices was that a professor of 'literature' ought to have nothing to do with 'language;' the cry from at least one very vigorous voice was that a professor of 'language' ought to have nothing to do with 'literature.'

It is worthy of no small notice that, as has just been hinted, the outcry reached its loudest in the case of our own language. Greek was strangely left out altogether; it might have been curious to see what the objectors would have said to a statute which implied that the Greek tongue was still living, that Homer and Rhêgas, Herodotus and Trikoupês, formed parts of one unbroken series. The Romance tongues and their parent were treated with some respect; for men were not called on to accept the hard saying that Latin is still alive, but only, what the boldest can hardly dispute, that it has still living children. The 'Letto-Slavic group' was looked at as simply something funny, as everything may be looked at as funny by those who think it the mark of a wit and a superior person to mock at whatever he does not understand. The evident dislike to Teutonic studies, above all to English studies, lies deeper. It was plain that, while 'Letto-Slavic' was simply jeered at, Gothic and 'Anglo-Saxon' were seriously dreaded. This is nothing else than another form of the Englishman's wonderful fancy for turning his back on himself and wishing to make himself out to be anything rather than himself. And with this might seem to be mingled an uneasy feeling that the claims of English 'literature,' as a pleasant and easy study, may be seriously threatened, if it be once established that, in English, as well as in other tongues, any scholarly study of the later forms requires a scholarly knowledge of the earlier. Our dificulties as to Greek and our difficulties as to English are of an exactly opposite kind. With Greek it is hard to persuade people to go on to the end; with English it is hard to persuade people to start from the beginning. To many it seems passing strange to be told that Greek literature is still a living thing; but no one who has ever heard of Greek literature denies that Homer is part of it. That *Beowulf* is part of English literature is still a strange saying to many. With some the strangeness is that of pure ignorance; the result of meaningless distinctions and a confusing nomenclature. With others there is a fear, a fear from their point of view well-grounded, that the acknowledgement of *Beowulf* as part of English literature would make the study of English literature another and a graver business than what they wish it to be.

Amid the first echoes of these cries the election to the Merton professorship was made; they became louder and more distinct after the election. Truly the electors, when they made their choice, had little thought of the storm which they were about to draw down upon their heads. And yet perhaps they should have been warned by the number and strangeness of the rumours which went about, even before any action had been taken on which a rumour could be founded. It would not do to say that the tales which went about proved that the 'mythopoeic' faculty had not died out among mankind. For in that which is mythical, that which is *sagenhaft*, we look for some relation to truth; we look for some kernel of truth, in fact or in idea, round which the mythical elements may grow. But the rumours which went abroad about this election had not even this approach to truth. They lacked perhaps all literary skill, they certainly lacked all dramatic probability. Some of the most independent of mankind, some of the men least likely to 'say ditto' to anybody, were painted as all of them humbly following the lead of one of their fellows, and that one whose wishes in the matter were in the end not successful. Some of the legends were not only false, but impossible. Before the electors met, before they could have met, before they had, as a body, any being at all, the world was told in print that the professorship had been offered to a very distinguished man of letters, and had been refused by him. Here was pure fiction. The thing not only never happened, it could not have happened. After the election a like rumour went about that the professorship had been offered to another very distinguished man of letters. This too was pure fiction: the thing might have happened, but it had not. Yet the strength of falsehood was so strong that, when the fiction was officially denied, it was again repeated in the shape that, if the professorship was not offered to that eminent writer, he was at least 'sounded' about it. 'Sounded' is a vague word, and a denial that A or B was 'sounded' might be met by the choice of some other word. But surely all fictions may be shut out by the statement that the electors never offered the professorship to anybody, and that no communication, direct or indirect, about the professorship was made by them to anybody, except in due form to the Vice-Chancellor to announce the result of the election. That that election took many by surprise I do not wonder, for I was myself among the number. Among so many untrue sayings, one true did once get into print in one corner. One account of the election, otherwise very wild, did contain the true statement that I personally had done all that one man among several could do to bring about the election of a most eminent scholar, who was not elected, but who, I still hold, ought to have been.

I should not have said a word about this election, if the rumours about it, however false, had died out within any reasonable time. But they still live and flourish; they are brought up again, in some shape or other, whenever the general subject is discussed. The great 'fraud on literature' committed in choosing a master of language to a professorship of language seems not likely to be forgotten. The discussion of the present statute for establishing a school of 'Modern Languages' has of course stirred it up again. In that statute I regret several things. I regret the name, and the implied separation between 'modern' languages and others. I regret the strange omission of Greek among the languages taken into the scheme. The Romance languages are there, and their connexion with Latin is recognized; but Greek is left out altogether. I regret also a most ill-advised provision for making the examination include a 'colloquial' use of the languages taken up. I regret still more the reason which was given for such a course, namely that it would be useful for candidates who meant to enter the diplomatic service. So it is very likely to be and to plenty of people besides. Whether the diplomatic service is worthy of any particular zeal on its behalf may possibly be doubted; but the point is that the University has nothing to do with the diplomatic service or with any service; it has, at the stage marked by its arts examination, nothing to do with any profession or calling of any kind. Some stop should be put to this lowering of the University by adapting its system to suit this or that calling, instead of cleaving to the sound rule of giving an education which should be good for a man whatever may be his calling. The gift of talking this or that language is a most valuable one; but it is not one which comes within the scope of an University; it is no part of the scientific study of the language. Yet I believe that I could have voted for the clause, if it had gone on to take in the intelligible speaking of Greek. Some consistency might be sacrificed to save us from the hideous sounds which are still flogged into boys by the schoolmasters, and which men at the Universities still quietly accept.

The objections to the Modern Language statute were essentially the outcries against the election to the Merton professorship, put, within the University itself, into a more regular shape. Outside the University the shapes that they took were wilder than ever. We had indeed strange disputants to argue against when a correspondent of *The Times*, signing himself an 'University Extension Lecturer,'[5] showed that he believed that the University contained a 'Professor of Middle English,' and that its various branches of study were managed by 'Boards of Directors.' To drag in this formula of 'Middle English,' which had never been used in the whole matter and which had nothing to do with it, seems to have been thought specially funny. What if some term in natural science should seem equally funny to those who do not understand it? Only it would be thought disrespectful to laugh at a term of natural science, while at terms of philology any one may laugh. The main objection, so far as it could be understood, was the old one. It was proposed to establish a school of 'Languages' – 'Literature' was not mentioned in the title, though it was in several clauses of the statute. This was pronounced to be a 'fraud on literature.' Whether the 'fraud' consisted in making a language statute at all, or in using the word 'literature' in a language statute, was not explained.

I regretted that the word 'literature' was used, as being a word which, latterly at least, has become of doubtful meaning. I assume that the authors of the statute used it in one meaning; some of its supporters certainly did; the objectors use it in another. By 'literature' some of us certainly meant such a study of books in English, French, or any of the languages concerned, as we were used to in the case of Greek and Latin books in the old school of *Literae Humaniores*. That is, we meant a study of the books written in any language in connexion with the history and philology of that language. It soon became plain that the objectors mean by 'literature' something which had nothing to do with historical or philological study. Now it should be clearly understood that nobody has a single word to say against 'literature,' even in the sense in which the word is used by the objectors. The only approach to an unkindly feeling which any one can have towards 'literature' in any sense is one akin to that which some of us feel towards some aspects of natural science. No one has a word to say against natural science as such; no one wishes to discourage its pursuit, no one wishes to refuse it its place alongside of other branches of knowledge. But some of us do feel our backs set up when some of the followers of natural science brag of their own pursuit as if all other pursuits were contemptible, as if their branch of 'science' or knowledge was alone to be called 'science' or knowledge; above all we feel them set up when natural science gets all the money and other branches of 'science' none. Something of the same kind may happen in the case of 'literature' also. No one wishes to discourage any form of the study of 'literature,' even the form which the objectors contend for. But human nature may be tempted to turn against it, if we are ceaselessly told that we are acting fraudulently, simply because we wish to encourage another form of study. Moreover we must know for certain what the study of 'literature' means on the lips of those who talk most loudly about it. They mean by the word, if we rightly understand them, the reading of books, the criticism of books, the finding out everything about the writers of the books, what they did, what they thought, anything that can better make one understand the books and the writers; but all essentially as a matter of taste. I am not sure that the word 'taste' quite expresses all that is wanted, but I know of no one word that will come nearer to expressing it. To talk of 'elegant scholarship' would imply something rather different, something which need not imply any minute philology, but which certainly implies attention to language as language. But, without attempting any very rigid definition, one can guess at the kind of thing that is meant. It is something graceful and elegant, something that cultivates the taste, something which may even imply a good deal of work of its own kind, only work of a different kind from that either of the comparative philologer or of the historical student of language. As far as we can make out from the teaching of the busiest champion of 'literature,' it is something which stands in a close and friendly relation to a certain form of Greek and Latin scholarship. Such scholarship may not be compulsory on all votaries of 'literature,' but it is at least a counsel of perfection, as the minuter philology is with us. The only things that may not be coupled with it are, strangely as it seems to some of us, the historical study of the language in which the books taken in hand are written, the comparative study of the languages which are akin to it, and the study of the earliest specimens of the literature of the language itself. To think of joining these on is a 'fraud;' it is bringing in 'language,' where there ought to be only 'literature.' *Beowulf* and Caedmon are, it seems, not 'literature.' To find out a little more fully where we are, one might ask a question. Milton's *Paradise Lost* is confessedly 'literature;' to study it is a 'literary' business. It would seem to be ruled that, if we bring in any reference to Caedmon, the whole business ceases to be 'literary;' it becomes the forbidden study of 'language.' But how if, instead of 'Anglo-Saxon' Caedmon, we should bring in Latin Avitus? If Avitus is not an 'Anglo-Saxon,' he is something worse. If he is a Latin writer, he is a Latin writer of that class towards whom the feeling of some who think themselves Latin scholars is simply that it is well to sound a trumpet before them to announce to the world that they know nothing about them. Virgil of course would do; he is 'classical': but Avitus is as a mere bishop of the iron age, not fostered on Augustan elegance, but fed on controversial theology at the court of a barbarian king. We are not sure that the mere fact of having read Avitus or heard of Avitus would not at once take away a man's claim to be 'literary.' Now it is quite certain that a really deep and scholarly mastery of Milton would imply a considerable mastery of Virgil and of other 'classical' writers as well. And we believe that even the 'literary' study of Milton would not shut them out. Yet the mere fact that they are 'classical,' that is to say pagan, hinders them from throwing the same kind of light on Milton, from being in the same way forerunners of Milton as either 'Anglo-Saxon' Caedmon or Latin Avitus. For the matter of certain poems of Avitus, of Caedmon, and of Milton has much in common. A thorough comparison of the three and of their relations to one another, would be, one might think, a 'literary' study of the highest kind. One might take it to be a study of 'literature' in the sense of that word which is intended in the Oxford statute. Only such a study could not be made without some attention to 'language,' and even to its most dreaded shape, to the oldest form of the English language. Still it is about Avitus that one specially wishes to know. Some stages of English are clearly ruled to be too old to be 'literary;' at what age does Latin become too new?

Now be it again remembered that no one has a word to say against 'literature' or 'literary' studies, even in the narrowest sense. No one wishes that every one who reads Milton should be constrained to read Caedmon and Avitus as well. A man may read Milton very profitably for many purposes who never heard of either Caedmon or Avitus. All that is said is that there is another way of reading Milton which will naturally take in some reference to Avitus, and even to Caedmon, and that some of us do not understand why this way of reading him should be called a 'fraud' on the other. The two may surely stand side by side; each may be followed by different people with different objects. Only some of us, and among them seemingly the authors of the statute, hold that that way of studying Milton which naturally takes in Caedmon and Avitus, and not the way which shuts them out, is the way of studying Milton which is fit to take its place in an University course. Here doubtless is the rub; but still where is the 'fraud'? All is straightforward and above board; a Language statute is a Language statute; that is the whole grievance. Here in truth comes in a question which goes to the very root of things with regard to University studies and examinations. Many people seem to think that any kind of study for which anything can be said, any study which is found pleasing or profitable for anybody, should at once find its place in the University system, and should be made at least an alternative subject for the BA examination. Some of us, on the other hand, hold that there are many studies which nobody wishes to disparage, studies which some men do well to pursue and which they may very well make the work of their lives, but which may still be quite unsuited to be subjects for the BA examination. I speak this cautiously, because there surely are subjects which are not at all fit to be part of the BA examination, but which are most fit for University study at a later stage, or which at least would be fit for it, if all study higher than that needed for the BA degree had not been made penal by the last Commission. It is surely allowable to hold that some studies are undesirable because they are not solid enough, and others because they are in a certain sense too solid, that is because they are too purely technical. As subjects for the examination for the first degree, we do not want professional subjects – professional subjects, when fit for the University course at all, ought to come after – and we do not want, we will not say frivolous subjects, but subjects which are merely light, elegant, interesting. As subjects for examination we must have subjects in which it is possible to examine. Now I believe that I am right in saying that all the subjects of examination now in use in Oxford, from any survivals that may still abide of the old *Literae Humaniores* to the last and most 'specialized' thing in natural science, agree in this, that all deal with facts, that in all it is possible to say of two answers to a question that one is right and the other is wrong. As long as this can be done, the subject is a possible one for examination. It may or may not be a fit subject; but it is a possible one. And English literature, or any literature, may be so treated as to be a possible subject for examination in this sense. Some forms of literature, we may believe, besides Greek and Latin, may be treated so as to be fit subjects. Moreover the study of facts, the examination in facts, does not shut out differences of opinion. That is, two scholars may, from the same facts, make different inferences, without either having any right to say that the other is wrong. And the knowledge of such differences of opinion about the facts should be part of the student's knowledge of the facts themselves. It is another thing when it comes to mere questions of taste, and surely such a study of literature as we are charged with treating fraudulently is largely a matter of taste. For instance, I delight in the writings of Lord Macaulay, prose and verse; I believe it is now thought more 'literary' to call them 'pinchbeck' or some such uncivil name. But I claim no right to pluck the man who calls them 'pinchbeck,' and I deny that he has any right to pluck me. My taste leads me to prefer verse which I can scan and of which I can follow the sense; it is, I know, more 'literary' to delight in verse of which the metre and the meaning are, to say the least, carefully hidden. My taste in prose leads me to prefer plain English, pure English, straightforward English, rhythmical English, English of which the meaning of every word is clear, English in which, if a thought tending to merriment comes of itself, it is gladly welcomed, but in which it is not thought the first of duties to thrust in a joke in every line, whether there is any material for joking or not. It is, I know, more 'literary' to prefer the modern 'brilliant' style, the forced liveliness, the out-of-the-way allusions, the scraps of foreign tongues, the pet phrases prescribed by momentary fashion, all in short that distinguishes the style of the man who has to say something from the style of the man who has something to say. I must confess that, if I were Examiner in Literature, I should feel strongly tempted to put a man down a class or two who either wrote his papers 'brilliantly' or expressed admiration for the 'brilliant' style in others. And I have no doubt that a master of brilliancy would have just the same feeling towards me and towards the writers in whom I see models of English speech. Now such a temptation on either side ought to be withstood to the uttermost; a class-list drawn up under the influence of such temptations either way would be thoroughly unfair; if the examined knows the facts of the matter in hand, it ought not to make the difference of a line either way whether his mere taste, his mere opinion, agrees with that of the Examiner or not. Only in other subjects of examination the temptation to go by mere taste or opinion is but slight; in some subjects it cannot come in at all. But in an examination in 'literature' only, that is, I conceive, in questions of mere writing, of mere style, of mere fancy, altogether cut off from the facts of language, the temptation to examine in this unfair fashion would be almost irresistible among imperfect beings. An examination in contemporary politics, in which the Home Ruler should be set to examine the Unionist and the Unionist to examine the Home Ruler, would be an easy business by the side of it.

This difficulty seems to me – and I do not think that I stand alone – enough of itself to stamp 'literature,' in the sense of the word intended, 'literature' apart from 'language,' as an unfit subject for University examination. An examination should be in facts, not in taste. At the same time it is not to be denied that the kind of study of literature with which we seem to be threatened, is by no means barren in facts, though the taste in them may sometimes be questioned. A saying which fell from myself in one of the debates in Congregation on the Modern Language Statute has been quoted in several places, and some seem to have been pleased and others displeased with the phrase of 'chatter about Shelley.' But I doubt whether any one has quoted the illustration which I gave of the kind of 'chatter' with which we are threatened. I mentioned that I had lately read a review of a book about Shelley in which the critic, in the gravest way in the world, praised or blamed the author – I forget which, and it does not matter – for his 'treatment of the Harriet problem.' I added that I thought we in Oxford hardly needed to add the 'Harriet problem' to our studies, that we had enough to do with the problems of Helen, Theodora, and Mary Stewart, without going on to the problem of a Harriet in our own century. I think the example is instructive. It was plain that to the critic whom I had been reading, 'the Harriet problem' was something of the deepest importance, something quite on a level with the gravest questions in any branch of knowledge. Now surely this is a fair specimen of a kind of thing which is not necessarily involved in the kind of study of 'literature' which is proposed, but which that kind of study is almost certain to bring with it as its shadow. A great deal of 'literary' talk nowadays seems hardly to rise above personal gossip, sometimes personal scandal, about very modern personages indeed. Now this is a case in which distance of time does make a difference. We are all delighted if we can light on a new fact, however small, in the life of Aeschylus or in the life of Dante. In the case of Dante indeed some minds are so anxious for new facts that, when they cannot be found in any record, they have an ingenious way of dreaming them for themselves. The charm lies partly in the distance of time, partly in the rarity of such scraps of knowledge. They have the charm of relics or curiosities, and they do really add to our knowledge of the age as well as of the man. When we come to times nearer to our own and where personal details can be got at more plentifully, the case is rather different. What in the one case is antiquarian curiosity, harmless at least if not praiseworthy, becomes in the other mere gossip, sometimes rather unhealthy gossip. All this seems to be a tendency of the time. There is an odd kind of relic-worship, or more than relic-worship, about, in which writers of our own time seem to have taken the place of heathen gods or mediaeval saints. Such a strange importance is attached to the very smallest matters, and such queer names are bestowed on all who do not care to be initiated in the new mysteries. They are 'vandals' or 'philistines,' or any other nation whose supposed crimes have brought them down to the dishonour of a small letter. The 'bohemians' are perhaps to be excepted: they are more likely to be found within the new pantheon itself than in the ranks of the unbelievers. Indeed there is so much talk about the writers of books that one is sometimes tempted to ask whether their own writings are not sometimes overshadowed by the witings of their biographers and commentators. It does seem just possible that writers are sometimes largely talked about without having been very deeply read. There is one sense of the word 'Literature' which is a little ominous, the 'Litteratur' with which German scholars do sometimes overshadow and overwhelm an ancient author and his subject. One has sometimes thought that, to understand either Homer or the Old Testament, the best beginning might be to burn all the commentators. And really something like this does seem to threaten our great English writers also. There is so much written about them that it does now and then seem to threaten our great English writers also. There is so much written about them that it does now and then come into a 'vandal' or 'philistine' head to ask whether the 'literature' which is to be studied means the great writings themselves or the little writings about the great writings. The bulk of the literature about 'literature' does now and then seem a little alarming.

Now, as soon as 'literature' becomes a subject of University examination, or of any kind of examination, this danger is at once increased. Examination is held to imply teaching, and teaching has a way of growing into cramming. Some of us, to be sure, are old-fashioned enough to have our doubts whether, as there is a good deal too much examining, there is not also a good deal too much teaching. The thought will thrust itself in whether, amidst so much examining, so much teaching, there is any time left for learning. Amidst the ceaseless grind of the 'tutorial profession,' is there ever a stray hour left for either teacher or taught to do a little quiet reading and thinking for himself? In the elder days, before the 'tutorial profession' was heard of, when it was enough for a man to do the duty of his office, there was time for both. But, bad enough as the overteaching of our times is in other subjects, it would be worse than all, if such a subject as literature without language should ever become a subject of examination. One might perhaps think that this of all subjects might dispense with any kind of teaching, that in matters of pure taste each man might be his own tutor, his own professor. It is said to be a shame that a man should leave the University and not be a master of English literature. So it may be a shame, or at least a pity, that he should leave the University and not be a crowd of other things which he would be the better for being. If every BA were an Admirable Crichton all round, the world would doubtless be the better. But unhappily the Universities and their members are imperfect, like other human beings and human institutions. We cannot do everything that somebody thinks might better be done. All things cannot be taught; facts may be taught; but surely the delicacies and elegances of literature cannot be driven into any man: he must learn to appreciate them for himself. If the poet cannot be made, surely the student and critic of the poet can hardly be made either. Yet once make his work a matter of examination, and those are sure to arise who will undertake to make him. Wherever the examiner goes before, the teacher in some shape or another will follow after. And, in subjects of this kind, which seem so incapable of being taught at all, the teaching is more likely than in other subjects to be of the kind which one would least wish to encourage. Because 'literature,' such as we are asked to take into our University course, is of all subjects that which should be kept most free from the touch of the crammer, it is sure to be the very one which will fall most hopelessly into his hands.

We can guess the kinds of students and the kind of teachers in a school which is sure to be set down as calling for the least work of all. If 'modern history' is an 'easy' school, surely 'modern literature' will be easier still. Once let the crammer touch it, and what will it be like? Does any one suppose that there will be a rush of devoted students of English literature, disinterested admirers of great poets and great orators, with their whole works at their fingers' ends? Because literature, in any worthy sense, cannot be taught, some substitute will be taught instead. The crammer cannot teach taste; he cannot hammer into a man so much as an ear for metre and rhythm; still less can he hammer into him the thousand minute gifts, the endless delicate powers of appreciation, which go to make the literary student in any sense worthy of the name. Those must be born with the man and grow with his intellectual growth. The crammer can but teach facts; the crammer in literature will have to fall back on the facts of literature; and those facts are, in practice, sure to be very largely nothing better than the gossip, the chatter, about literature which is largely taking the place of literature. The art of the crammer has taken many wonderful forms already; it will be surely its lowest – or highest – form of all, if to the endless forms of 'tips' on all matters, new and old, we add the last device of all in the shape of 'tips' on 'the Harriet problem.'

The proposed statute is not perfect; no statute which in any sort parts off 'modern' languages from 'ancient' can be accepted as more than an imperfect provision for the present distress. And the astounding omission of Greek among the spoken languages of Europe makes the provision yet more imperfect than it need have been. Still something like the present statute is the only means available at the moment for asserting the truth that others of the languages of Europe are no less capable, no less worthy, of scholarlike treatment, than the two languages, or rather the two arbitrarily chosen periods of two languages, which have hitherto had the field to themselves. It is really hard that those who have sought this object could not be allowed quietly to carry it out, that they must needs be made the victims of a popular outcry, the defendants on a charge of 'fraud,' simply because they went about to compass their own object and did not labour for another object which, if possible at all, is quite distinct. It does not even follow that all those who simply ask to be allowed to set up their school of language in peace would refuse to set up a school of literature such as is asked for alongside of it. Some of us may have strong doubts about such a course; I for one have the strongest doubts and something more. But it does not at all follow that every one who goes with me on the positive question would go with me on the negative question also. There is no reason why the thing should not be tried, so far at least as to have the literature statute sketched out, that we may see what it would be like. Only we do ask not to be called names, and such very ugly names, simply because we wish to go on in our own way and to do our own work, without the slightest wish to meddle with the goings and doings of any other people.

Notes

1. 'If that be deemed a quarrel, where heaven knows,
   You only give, and I receive, the blows.' (Juvenal, *Satires*, iii. 289.)
2. A reference to the Gosse fracas. See the introductory note on John Churton Collins and the extract included in this volume, pp. 192–217, from Collins's review of *From Shakespeare to Pope*.
3. A statute for a School of Modern Languages. The petition to the Hebdomadal Council had been for a School of Modern Literature. The wording had now changed to 'Modern Languages'. Collins opposed the proposal in either form of words.
4. The question of an English Chair at Oxford was discussed by the University of Oxford Commission as early as 1877. The Commissioners attempted to reach a compromise between the views of philologists and the supporters of more literary studies.
5. The 'University Extension Lecturer' was Collins, in a letter to *The Times* on 1 June 1887.

CHAPTER NINETEEN

The Teaching of English in England

The Teaching of English in England (1921) was the report of a committee appointed by the President of the Board of Education in 1919, just a matter of a few months after the end of the First World War, to inquire into the position of English in the educational system of England. It is often referred to as the Newbolt Report, after its chairman, the patriotic poet and President of the English Association, Sir Henry Newbolt. English was not the only subject to be inquired into at this time; three other committees were appointed, investigating the teaching of science, classics and modern languages.

The terms of reference given to this committee on English stated that regard should be had to '(1) the requirements of a liberal education; (2) the needs of business, the professions, and public services; and (3) the relation of English to other studies.' The committee, which numbered among its members such important figures in the world of university English studies as Caroline Spurgeon, John Dover Wilson and Sir Arthur Quiller-Couch, made the most of the opportunity to promote English as potentially the most important subject in the curriculum.

The extract printed here is the introduction to the report, which includes the well-known image of rebuilding the arch of education in England, using English as the keystone. The committee took very seriously its brief to report on English in the whole education system of England, so that all sorts of schools, as well as colleges and universities, were included. The great merit of English, the committee believed, was that it could provide a source of unity in an education system often fragmented along class lines. It might not be possible to educate rich and poor side by side in the same schools, but this made it only more imperative to find a source of unity in a subject. English could be the way in which Arnoldian culture (it is Arnold who is quoted) manifested itself and united the nation. There were now to be no exceptions; all would study English, which would be the starting point from which all culture would spring. Classics should not be an alternative culture for a particular social class, while at the other end of the social scale, there should be no class beyond the reach of English's cultivating power.

It is recommended that several elements should be contained within the scope of English, but the main stress falls upon literature, as a source of delight and experience and a means of understanding life. Wordsworth is praised for his criticism in *The Prelude* of the way classics was taught in his day, and for his view of poetry in education as something which can foster true feelings and knowledge of human nature, provided the teaching is 'practical' and 'real' rather than 'pedantic' and 'unreal.' English is thus not to be part of 'book learning' at all, but something much greater, an opening up to the self-expression of great natures and to a record of spiritual experiences.

Introduction to the Report

1. We are instructed by the terms of our reference to consider and report upon the position of English in the educational system of the country, that is to say, the position of a part in relation to the whole in which it is included. If the instruction had gone no further, it might have been reasonable to suppose that the present educational system of the country was to be accepted as a fixed framework and that our concern with English was limited to the manner in which it is fitted, or should be fitted, into its place in that framework. But the terms of reference continue as follows:- 'regard being had to the requirements of a liberal education, the needs of business, the professions, and public services, and the relation of English to other studies.' Not only are these words significant in themselves, as giving a wide scope to our consideration of English, but we have found almost from the outset that they have imposed upon us a task at once more extensive and more complex than we had foreseen. As we considered the growing mass of evidence before us, it became more and more impossible to take a narrow view of the inquiry, to regard it as concerned only with one subordinate part of an already existing structure. A declaration that in our present system English holds but an unsatisfactory position would have been, we saw, valueless; for however elaborately set forth it would not have taken account of the most significant part of the facts and judgments laid before us. The inadequate conception of the teaching of English in this country is not a separate defect which can be separately remedied. It is due to a more far-reaching failure – the failure to conceive the full meaning and possibilities of national education as a whole, and that failure again is due to a misunderstanding of the educational values to be found in the different regions of mental activity, and especially to an

underestimate of the importance of the English language and literature. It is not required of us that we should propose in detail a complete scheme of national education, but we are compelled to indicate certain principles which must form the basis of any such scheme; because the recognition of these principles is an indispensable condition of success in providing for the best use of English as a means of intercourse and of education. Our position may be compared to that of an architect called in to advise upon what can be done with a stone which the builders have hitherto rejected. We find that the stone is invaluable; but also that the arch is too faulty to admit it. We propose to meet not one but two imperative needs by rebuilding the arch and using our stone as keystone of the whole – the use for which it, and no other, is available.

2. Before we go further we must give a brief indication of the converging lines of thought along which we have been forced to this conclusion. First, we have been struck by the fact that, although much labour and thought have been expended and many changes made, almost all in the right direction, it is still true that in this country we have no general or national scheme of education. It is understood to be the duty of the State to see that every child shall, during a certain number of years, receive an education, but the meaning of this is not generally understood. Neither by tradition nor by effective instruction has the general body of citizens any clear idea of the benefit to be conferred. To some the word education means reading, writing, and arithmetic; to others, almost any kind of information. Of those who understand it to imply instruction by skilled teachers, the great majority still identify it with the imparting of information, though some consider this largely useless, while others value it as a possible means to obtaining increased wages or some other vocational advantage. In general, it may not unfairly be said that education is regarded as a suitable occupation for the years of childhood, with the further object of equipping the young in some vague and little understood way for the struggle of adult existence in a world of material interests. The existence of other ideals does not diminish the confusion. Sections of the community, for social and intellectual reasons, have persisted in maintaining schools and universities for the special treatment of their own sons and daughters. The education which they have thus provided has, in general, been superior to that provided by the State, but it has been the privilege of a minority only, and has widened the mental distance between classes in England. Matthew Arnold, using the word in its true sense, claimed that 'Culture unites classes.'[1] He might have added that a system of education which disunites classes cannot be held worthy of the name of a national culture. In this respect we have even fallen away from an earlier and better tradition. Many of our great Public Schools, as the

Natural Science Committee have pointed out,[2] though founded originally in the interest of poor scholars, are not open to poor scholars today because the scholarships and exhibitions which they offer are not, as a matter of fact, within the reach of boys from the elementary schools. The age at which they are competed for, and the subjects which they require, make them available only for those who have recieved an expensive special preparation. We may recognise that it is at present more difficult than it was some centuries ago to educate the children of rich and poor side by side in the same schools, but this makes it only the more to be regretted that there is no source of unity to be found in the teaching provided by the different types of school. If there were any common fundamental idea of education, any great common divisions of the curriculum, which would stand out in such a way as to obliterate, or even to soften, the lines of separation between the young of different classes, we might hope to find more easily the way to bridge the social chasms which divide us. For this purpose it must be remembered that classical studies are not available; however effective they may have proved in one type of school, they cannot be made use of universally. Actually, by an unfortunate irony of circumstance, they have been regarded as the possession of a privileged class, and not as a pathway open to all possessed of literary ability or scholarship.

3. A second fact which has impressed us is this. Though there has been a common failure in this country to realise the true nature and effect of education, there has been at the same time a common instinctive perception of one aspect of our ill success. The English are a nation with a genius for practical life, and the chief criticism directed, whether by parents or pupils, against our present system, is a practical one; it amounts, when coherently stated, to a charge that our education has for a long time past been too remote from life. We have come to the conclusion that this charge is supported by the evidence. However men may differ as to the relative importance of different objects in life, the majority are right in feeling that education should directly bear upon life, that no part of the process should be without a purpose intelligible to everyone concerned. At a later stage we shall endeavour to trace the historical process by which the present divorce between education and reality has come about; in the meantime we note the results. A quasi-scientific theory has long been accepted that the process of education is the performance of compulsory hard labour, a 'grind' or 'stiffening process,' a 'gritting of the teeth' upon hard substances with the primary object not of acquiring a particular form of skill or knowledge but of giving the mind a general training and strengthening. This theory has now been critically examined and declared to be of less wide application than was thought. Its abandonment would do much to smooth the

road of education, it would make it possible to secure for the child a living interest and a sense of purpose in his work, and it would replace the old wasteful system of compulsion and mere obedience by a community of interest between pupil and teacher.

4. This community of interest would be felt instinctively and immediately by the pupil, but it is very necessary that it should be consciously understood by all those responsible for the education of the young. It must be realised that education is not the same thing as information, nor does it deal with human knowledge as divided into so-called subjects. It is not the storing of compartments in the mind, but the development and training of faculties already existing. It proceeds, not by the presentation of lifeless facts, but by teaching the student to follow the different lines on which life may be explored and proficiency in living may be obtained. It is, in a word, guidance in the acquiring of experience. Under this general term are included experiences of different kinds; those which are obtained, for example, by manual work, or by the orderly investigation of matter and its qualities. The most valuable for all purposes are those experiences of human relations which are gained by contact with human beings. This contact may take place in the intercourse of the classroom, the playground, the home, and the outer world, or solely in the inner world of thought and feeling, through the personal records of action and experience known to us under the form of literature. The intercourse of the classroom should be for the student, especially in the earlier stages of development, the most valuable of all, since it is there that he will come under the influence of not one but two personal forces, namely, the creative power of the author whose record he is studying, and the appreciative judgment of the teacher who is introducing him to the intimacy of a greater intellect.

5. Not only must the true nature of education be clearly understood, but it will be a matter of equal importance that the teacher, at any rate, and the student, as soon as may be, should have clear and well founded ideas about morals, science and art. They must feel and, as far as possible, understand the direct interest of these as bearing upon practical life and the equipment for it. It has long been accepted, and at the present day it has been reiterated with great force by such teachers as the Dean of St. Paul's[3] and Mr Clutton Brock,[4] that the three main motives which actuate the human spirit are the love of goodness, the love of truth and the love of beauty. It is certainly under heads corresponding to these that education must be divided into the training of the will (morals), the training of the intellect (science) and the training of the emotions (expression or creative art). In school, therefore, science must be, for teacher and for student, the methodical pursuit of truth and the conquest of the physical world by human intelligence and skill. Literature,

the form of art most readily available, must be handled from the first as the most direct and lasting communication of experience by man to men. It must never be thought of or represented as an ornament, an excrescence, a mere pastime or an accomplishment; above all, it must never be treated as a field of mental exercise remote from ordinary life. The sphere of morals in school life is limited by practical considerations with which we cannot here deal, but it is evident that if science and literature can be ably and enthusiastically taught, the child's natural love of goodness will be strongly encouraged and great progress may be made in the strengthening of the will. The vast importance to a nation of moral training would alone make it imperative that education shall be regarded as experience and shall be kept in the closest contact with life and personal relations.

6. The facts and needs of the situation as briefly outlined above did not form the starting point of our inquiry, but they forced themselves irresistibly upon our attention from the moment when we first began to consider the present position of English in the educational system of the country. From the evidence laid before us it became speedily clear that in many schools of all kinds and grades that part of the teaching which dealt directly with English was often regarded as being inferior in importance, hardly worthy of any substantial place in the curriculum, and a suitable matter to be entrusted to any member of the staff who had some free time at his disposal. It would be natural to suppose that there must be some good reason for this neglect, but on the other hand one of the most obvious facts of which we have to take account is that education in English is, for all Englishmen, a matter of the most vital concern, and one which must, by its very nature, take precedence of all other branches of learning. It is self-evident that until a child has acquired a certain command of the native language, no other educational development is even possible. If progress is not made at one time in the region of arithmetic or history or geography, the child merely remains backward in that respect, and the deficiency can be made up later. But a lack of language is a lack of the means of communication and of thought itself. Moreover, among the vast mass of the population, it is certain that if a child is not learning good English he is learning bad English, and probably bad habits of thought; and some of the mischief done may never afterwards be undone. Merely from this point of view English is plainly no matter of inferior importance, nor even one among the other branches of education, but the one indispensable preliminary and foundation of all the rest.

7. It is probable that no one would be found to dissent from this proposition, in which the meaning of the word English is limited to the language itself as a means of communication. The word, however, in our

present inquiry has other and wider meanings, and these must now be brought into consideration. Even as a means of communication a language may be treated in two ways, as practical speech and as a scientific study. With regard to the first of these, the position is clear. With regard to the second, it can be made clear at once. It has been the custom in the past to attempt the teaching of the Classics from two points of view simultaneously. The student has been required during one and the same lesson to treat the work of a classical author from the point of view of science and of art; in a passage of the *Aeneid*, for example, to study simultaneously the structure and idiom of the Latin language and the personal expression of Virgil's mind in his poetry. This made the task a severe and distracting one for both teacher and pupil; success was only achieved in a small minority of cases. In the rest failure was made almost inevitable by the fact that the scientific study of the language, though to the student far less interesting than the poetical narrative, appears to the teacher in general to be an easier task, involving less personal effort on his own part. To give out information and insist on its being accurately registered is an almost mechanical matter; to convey anything of the feeling and thought which are the life of literature the teacher must have been touched by them himself and be moved afresh by the act of communicating the touch to others. Thus not only are two different studies confused, but the less important receives the more attention. No doubt the connection between language and thought is a very intimate one, but we are strongly of opinion that in dealing with literature the voyage of the mind should be broken as little as possible by the examination of obstacles and the analysis of the element on which the explorer is floating. This last is a purely scientific study and can be to a great extent separated from the study of the literary art, as the chemical analysis of water can be separated from the observation of the sounds and colours conveyed by it. It would be a grave misfortune if a defect of method which has proved so injurious in the case of Latin and Greek were to appear also in the teaching of English literature. We believe, therefore, that formal grammar and philology should be recognised as scientific studies and kept apart (so far as that is possible) from the lessons in which English is treated as an art, a means of creative expression, a record of human experience.

8. We have now set apart the preliminary training of the child in the language which is to be his means of communication for all the common purposes of life, and the scientific study of language, which has a value of its own and should hold a high place among the other sciences. It remains for us to consider the actual and the possible position of English in the highest sense, that is as the channel of formative culture for all English people, and the medium of the creative art by which

all English writers of distinction, whether poets, historians, philosophers or men of science, have secured for us the power of realising some part of their own experience of life. Education of the kind here implied has, for some time past, been one of the objects held in view by the Board of Education; and we have found with pleasure that there are now a number of elementary schools in which a considerable degree of success is being obtained on these lines. We must repeat, however, that in this region, as in others, there is not at present in existence any national plan. It is not the absence of a universal curriculum, an educational drill or uniform, that we are here regretting; it is the lack of a general appreciation of the true value of education and the best means of obtaining it. Even in secondary schools we find this lack of understanding evident, and it is widely spread among parents of all classes. The idea of a liberal education is either altogether ignored or struggles feebly for the right of existence; and even where it still lives, there is a singular depreciation of the value of English literature for such a purpose. By the tradition of the public schools the Latin and Greek classics are far more highly estimated. This tradition, however, dates from a time very different in many ways from our own, a time when Latin was the common language of the educated and official world, and Greek the main source of history, philosophy and natural science; when, moreover, the literatures of Greece and Rome were beyond all comparison the greatest available for study. The modern world has a much wider outlook and more numerous and more direct roads by which to explore life, whether on the material or the spiritual side. In one respect Classics do retain their importance for the world. A knowledge of Latin civilisation is still indispensable for the full understanding of the languages, law and society of a great part of Europe, including the British Isles: and Greek literature is still the most life-giving and abundant source to which we trace our highest poetical and philosophical ideas and our feeling for artistic form. The classics then remain, and will always remain, among the best of our inherited possessions, and for all truly civilised people they will always be not only a possession but a vital and enduring influence. Nevertheless, it is now, and will probably be for as long a time as we can foresee, impossible to make use of the Classics as a fundamental part of a national system of education. They are a great watershed of humanistic culture, but one to which the general mass of any modern nation can, at present, have no direct access. We are driven, then, in our search for the experience to be found in great art, to inquire whether there is available any similar and sufficient channel of supply which is within the reach of all without distinction. We feel that, for an Englishman, to ask this question is at the same time to answer it. To every child in this country, there is one language

301

with which he must necessarily be familiar and by that, and by that alone, he has the power of drawing directly from one of the great literatures of the world. Moreover, if we explore the course of English literature, if we consider from what sources its stream has sprung, by what tributaries it has been fed, and with how rich and full a current it has come down to us, we shall see that it has other advantages not to be found elsewhere. There are mingled in it, as only in the greatest of rivers there could be mingled, the fertilising influences flowing down from many countries and from many ages of history. Yet all these have been subdued to form a stream native to our own soil. The flood of diverse human experience which it brings down to our own life and time is in no sense or degree foreign to us, but has become the native experience of men of our own race and culture.

9. We have now come to the point where the evidence forces our lines of thought to converge. On the one hand, our national education needs to be perfected by being scientifically refounded as a universal, reasonable and liberal process of development; on the other hand, we find coincidentally that for this purpose, of all the means available, there is only one which fulfils all the conditions of our problem. Education is complete in proportion as it includes within its scope a measure of knowledge in the principal sciences and a measure of skill in literature, the drama, music, song and the plastic arts; but not all of these are equally useful for the training of the young. We recognise fully, on the one side, the moral, practical, educational value of natural science, on the other side the moral, practical, educational value of the arts and of all great literatures ancient or modern. But what we are looking for now is not merely a means of education, one chamber in the structure which we are hoping to rebuild, but the true starting-point and foundation from which all the rest must spring. For this special purpose there is but one material. We make no comparison, we state what appears to us to be an incontrovertible primary fact, that for English children no form of knowledge can take precedence of a knowledge of English, no form of literature can take precedence of English literature; and that the two are so inextricably connected as to form the only basis possible for a national education.

10. It will be clearly seen that by this statement we have declared the necessity of what must be, in however elementary a form, a liberal education for all English children whatever their position or occupation in life. We are glad to record not only our own strong conviction that such a scheme is, from every point of view, just, reasonable and for the national advantage, but also the fact that in the mass of opinions submitted to us we nowhere find any evidence to the contrary. The judgments and experience laid before us by those

who have a large experience and every right to express a judgment, support us in our belief that an education of this kind is the greatest benefit which could be conferred upon any citizen of a great state, and that the common right to it, the common discipline and enjoyment of it, the common possession of the tastes and associations connected with it, would form a new element of national unity, linking together the mental life of all classes by experiences which have hitherto been the privilege of a limited section. From the same evidence and opinions, we have derived the further belief that to initiate all English children into such a fellowship, to set the feet of all upon that road of endless and unlimited advance, is an undertaking in no way impossible or visionary. The difficulties are undoubtedly great, the means available are at present very inadequate, but the difficulties and the inadequacy are largely those which are already troubling us, and would hamper any conceivable scheme of education at the present moment. On the other hand, we have the advantages given us by the necessity of a new departure among rapidly changing conditions, and by the opportunity of avoiding some causes of past failure.

11. We have already spoken of some of these causes of past failure, but there is one of them upon which we must lay stress again. We believe that in English literature we have a means of education not less valuable than the Classics and decidedly more suited to the necessities of a general or national education, but we see also that in the future, as in the past, success or failure will depend upon our perception of the true purpose of the instrument and the right method of handling it. If we use English literature as a means of contact with great minds, a channel by which to draw upon their experience with profit and delight, and a bond of sympathy between the members of a human society, we shall succeed, as the best teachers of the Classics have often succeeded in their more limited field. If, on the contrary, we cannot obtain a competent body of teachers, if we have to commit the guidance of youth to teachers who, in default of the necessary insight and enthusiasm, will fall back upon conventional appreciations, historical details and the minute examination of words and phrases, we shall repeat the failure of the past upon a wider and more ruinous scale. For a clear view of what we must avoid we may cite the evidence of a very eminent witness. Wordsworth's criticism of the method of dealing with the Classics prevalent in his own time, and still a danger in our own, is set out in a long and remarkable passage in *The Prelude*.[5] It may be summarised as follows:-

He thought that the Classics, as taught in his time, were worthless for education: that books in general came under the same condemnation, because they did not record or foster true feelings or knowledge

303

of human nature; that human nature could be best studied in the largest and least sophisticated masses of men; that the lessons to be learned from it could best be gathered in and delivered to the young by poets and romancers; that the poet especially has this gift because he can create by the power of words, a 'great Nature,' a new world in which things are presented as objects recognised, but in flashes and with a significance or glory not otherwise seen to be their own. Lastly, it is noteworthy that the poets whom he had in mind were not ancient poets but modern ones; even, it would appear, poets of the same age and country as those whom they are to teach.

It will be seen that this is not in reality a destructive, but a constructive criticism. Wordsworth is not bent on differentiating between one literature and another. He is differentiating between two different methods of using literature in education, the practical and the pedantic, the real and the unreal. He advocates the transmission, not of book learning, but of the influence of personality and the experience of human life. The distinction here made between book learning and true education is of the first importance. Books are not things in themselves, they are merely the instruments through which we hear the voices of those who have known life better than ourselves. Wordsworth had perceived what has since been repeatedly demonstrated by great men of science, that the common, unaided senses of man are not equal to the realisation of the world. Just as the physicist or the mathematician show us deeper aspects of matter or of space, which in the life of every day we should never have discovered for ourselves, so poets, philosophers, and historians have the power of revealing new values, relations of thought, feeling, and act, by which the dull and superficial sight of the multitude is illuminated and helped to penetrate in the direction of reality. It is here that Wordsworth and the literature he loves are on the side of life against book learning. The antithesis has been more recently expressed in its simplest and most extreme form by Mr P.B. Clayton, Chaplain at Poperinghe during the late war.[6] He is speaking with very sympathetic appreciation of the ordinary soldiers in the line. 'The only trouble is that their standard of general education is so low. Put the product of the old elementary schools side by side with the man from overseas, and his mental equipment is pitiful.... The overseas man, with his freedom from tradition, his wide outlook on life, his intolerance of vested interests and his contempt for distinction based on birth rather than on worth, has stirred in the minds of many a comparison between the son of the bondwoman and the son of the free.'[7] Some of the values here may be disputable, but the round sums will be accepted. Among the best things which education can give are certainly freedom and independence of thought, a wide outlook on life, and a strong sense of the difference between convention and reality. A less trammelled life has given these in some degree to our men overseas. Literature, which is still more untrammelled, as well as wider and more penetrating, will give them to the children of this country in a still greater degree and from an earlier age. But if it is to do this the teacher must keep it close to life: in no case must the real or practical bearing of the experience be neglected or avoided. And, as Wordsworth saw, though all great literatures will present deep and universal truths, in education that will be the more intelligible and powerful which presents the student with experience of time and circumstances more nearly related to his own.

12. In citing this opinion, which we accept and put forward with entire conviction, we are aware that we are opposing ourselves to those for whom the idea of a liberal education is inseparable from a knowledge of the Classics, and we desire to clear the ground of possible misunderstandings. In the course of our inquiry we have not found either among ourselves or the witnesses whom we have heard, any trace of hostility to the Classics. We recognise that for some minds the study of man's life and thought in a setting so far removed from modern conditions as was the ancient world may have special advantages. We recognise, also, that since many of our great writers have been influenced directly or indirectly by classical studies, the reader who approaches them with the same equipment will, in some ways, find it easier to understand them intimately and without loss of time. Further, we do not despair of the Classics or regard them as having no future in this country. We see in them sources, which can never be forgotten, of our own language, our own art, our own experience, and we hold that no student of English will have completed his exploration, or gained all its advantages, until he has ascended the stream of literature and discovered these perennial sources for himself. Nevertheless, we are convinced, both by necessity and by reason, that we must look elsewhere for our present purpose. The time is past for holding, as the Renaissance teachers held, that the Classics alone can furnish a liberal education. We do not believe that those who have not studied the Classics or any foreign literature must necessarily fail to win from their native English a full measure of culture and humane training. To hold such an opinion seems to us to involve an obstinate belittling of our national inheritance.

13. In any case, and whatever studies may be added to it, English, we are convinced, must form the essential basis of a liberal education for all English people, and in the earlier stages of education it should be the principal function of all schools of whatever type to provide this basis.

Of this provision the component parts will be, first, systematic train-ing in the sounded speeech of standard English, to secure correct pro-nunciation and clear articulation; second, systematic training in the use of standard English, to secure clearness and correctness both in oral expression and in writing; third, training in reading. Under this last head will be included reading aloud with feeling and expression, the use of books as sources of information and means of study, and finally, the use of literature as we have already described it, that is, as a posses-sion and a source of delight, a personal intimacy and the gaining of personal experience, an end in itself and, at the same time, an equip-ment for the understanding of life.

14. Here, again, it may be well to deal at once with possible criticisms. It may be objected that while English is indeed a necessary condition of our education, it is one which may be taken for granted, like the air we breathe or the land on which we live. We do not need, it may be said, to be taught English; to write and read, in Dogberry's opinion, comes by nature. This view is, perhaps, not likely to be now so crudely stated, but it has long been acted upon by many who are engaged in education, and is acquiesced in by many who control it. We must, therefore, state clearly that in our judgment it is an entirely unpractical view. It is repudiated not merely by literary experts but by the numerous practical men of busi-ness whom we have consulted. It is an instance of that divorce of educa-tion from reality which we have already found to be a main cause of failure in the past. English may come by nature up to a certain point; but that point is soon reached, and thenceforward the possibility of mental development, in whatever direction, is seriously diminished for those who have not achieved some mastery of their mother tongue. What a man cannot clearly state he does not perfectly know, and, conversely, the inability to put his thought into words sets a boundary to his thought. Impressions may anticipate words, but unless expression seizes and rec-reates them they soon fade away, or remain but vague and indefinite to the mind which received them, and incommunicable to others. 'A hazi-ness of intellectual vision,' said Cardinal Newman, 'is the malady of all classes of men by nature ... of all who have not had a really good educa-tion.'[8] It is a common experience that to find fit language for our impres-sions not only renders them clear and definite to ourselves and to others, but in the process leads to deeper insight and fresh discoveries, at once explaining and extending our knowledge. English is not merely the me-dium of our thought, it is the very stuff and process of it. It is itself the English mind, the element in which we live and work. In its full sense it connotes not merely acquaintance with a certain number of terms, or the power of spelling these terms correctly and arranging them without gross mistakes. It connotes the discovery of the world by the first and most

direct way open to us, and the discovery of ourselves in our native environment. And as our discoveries become successively wider, deeper, and subtler, so should our control of the instrument which shapes our thought become more complete and exquisite, up to the limit of artistic skill. For the writing of English is essentially an art, and the effect of English literature in education is the effect of an art upon the development of human character.

Here again we desire to guard against any possible misunderstanding. We find that the nature of art and its relation to human life and welfare is not sufficiently understood or appreciated in this country. The prevalence of a low view of art, and especially of the art of literature, has been a main cause of our defective conception of national education. Hitherto literature has, even more than science, suffered in the public mind both misunderstanding and degradation. Science has too often been regarded as a kind of skilled labour, a mere handling of materials for profit. Literature has first been confused with the science of language, and then valued for its commercial uses, from the writing of business letters up to the production of saleable books. The word art has been reserved for the more highly coloured or the less seriously valued examples of the latter. We must repeat that a much higher view may be taken of both science and art, and that this higher view is the only one consistent with a true theory of education. Commercial enterprise may have a legitimate and desirable object in view, but that object cannot claim to be the satisfaction of any of the three great natural affections of the human spirit – the love of truth, the love of beauty, and the love of righteousness. Man loves all these by nature and for their own sake only. Taken altogeher, they are, in the highest sense, his life, and no system of education can claim to be adequate if it does not help him to develop these natural and disinterested loves. But if it is to do this effectively we must discard or unlearn all mean views of art, and especially of the art of literature. We must treat literature, not as language merely, not as an ingenious set of symbols, a superficial and superfluous kind of decoration, or a graceful set of traditional gestures, but as the self-expression of great natures, the record and rekindling of spiritual experiences, and in daily life for every one of us the means by which we may, if we will, realise our own impressions and communicate them to our fellows. We reiterate, then, the two points which we desire to build upon; first, the fundamental necessity of English for the full development of the mind and character of English children, and second, the fundamental truth that the use of English does not come to all by nature, but is a fine art, and must be taught as a fine art.

15. We believe that such an education based upon the English language and literature would have important social, as well as personal,

results; it would have a unifying tendency. Two causes, both accidental and conventional rather than national, at present distinguish and divide one class from another in England. The first of these is a marked difference in their modes of speech. If the teaching of the language were properly and universally provided for, the difference between educated and uneducated speech,[9] which at present causes so much prejudice and difficulty of intercourse on both sides, would gradually disappear. Good speech and great literature would not be regarded as too fine for use by the majority, nor, on the other hand, would natural gifts for self-expression be rendered ineffective by embarrassing faults of diction or composition. The second cause of division amongst us is the undue narrowness of the ground on which we meet for the true purposes of social life. The associations of sport and games are widely shared by all classes in England, but with mental pleasures and mental exercises the case is very different. The old education was not similar for all, but diverse. It went far to make of us not one nation, but two, neither of which shared the associations or tastes of the other. An education fundamentally English would, we believe, at any rate bridge, if not close, this chasm of separation. The English people might learn as a whole to regard their own language, first with respect, and then with a genuine feeling of pride and affection. More than any mere symbol it is actually a part of England; to maltreat it or deliberately to debase it would be seen to be an outrage; to become sensible of its significance and splendour would be to step upon a higher level. In France, we are told, this pride in the national language is strong and universal; the French artisan will often use his right to object that an expression 'is not French.' Such a feeling for our own native language would be a bond of union between classes, and would beget the right kind of national pride. Even more certainly should pride and joy in the national literature serve as such a bond. This feeling, if fostered in all our schools without exception, would disclose itself far more often and furnish a common meeting ground for great numbers of men and women who might otherwise never come into touch with one another. We know from the evidence of those who are familiar with schools of every type that the love of fine style and the appreciation of what is great in human thought and feeling is already no monopoly of a single class in England, that it is a natural and not an exceptional gift, and that though easily discouraged by unfavourable circumstances it can also, by sympathetic treatment, be easily drawn out and developed. Within the school itself all scholars, though specialising perhaps on different lines, will be able to find a common interest in the literature class and the debating or dramatic society. And this common interest will be likely to persist when other less vital things have been abandoned. The purely technical or aesthetic appeal of any art will, perhaps, always be limited to a smaller number but, as experience of life, literature will influence all who are capable of finding recreation in something beyond mere sensation. These it will unite by a common interest in life at its best, and by the perpetual reminder that through all social differences human nature and its strongest affections are fundamentally the same.

16. Our inquiry cannot end here. When we have decided upon the nature and method of the education to be recommended we have still to consider as a necessary corollary the provision of an adequate teaching staff. This is a matter of great moment, for whatever kind of education is recommended, its success or failure will depend chiefly upon the intelligence and sympathy with which it is conducted. This will be even more true of an education in English than of any other; for two reasons. In the first place the teaching of English as the instrument of thought and the means of communication will necessarily affect the teaching of every other subject. Whatever view is taken of specialisation in schools, it is evidently desirable that the general education of every teacher shall be sufficiently good to ensure unceasing instruction in the English language. The teachers of all special subjects must be responsible for the quality of the English spoken or written during their lessons. In every department of school work confused and slovenly English must be regarded as the result of a failure on the part of the teacher. Secondly, since the literature lesson is no mechanical matter and is to consist not in the imparting of information but in the introduction of the student to great minds and new forms of experience, it is evidently necessary that the teacher should himself be already in touch with such minds and such experience. In other words, he must himself have received an education of the kind towards which he is to lead his class. It is no doubt true, as the Board of Education have pointed out in a circular on the teaching of English,[10] that the real teachers of Literature are the great writers themselves – the greater the work the more clearly it speaks for itself; but this only leads to the conclusion that for teachers we must have those who will not come between their pupils and the author they are reading, but will stand by them sympathetically, directing or moderating the impact of the new experience upon their minds.

17. We desire to express our strong conviction that for the purposes of such an education as we have outlined no teacher can, in his own grade, be too highly gifted or too highly trained, and that this is at least as true in the earlier as in the later stages. It is sometimes assumed that a first-rate teacher is wasted in an elementary school. This is, in our judgment, a complete misunderstanding. If any stage in education is to be considered more important than another, it must be that early stage in which

the child at an elementary or preparatory school is first introduced to the great influences which are to invigorate and direct his mental life. For these schools, no teaching can be too good, and we have to consider, in the very first place, what means are available for the provision of a competent staff. Our difficulty would be infinitely lessened if the general population of this country had already for years past been receiving such an education as we now advocate, but in the natural order of things, this could never be; the teacher must exist before the pupil. He is our lever, and we must first apply our whole force to him if we are to raise the mass. This has not been sufficiently recognised hitherto. Teachers have not only been inadequately paid, but care has not been taken to see that they are sufficiently supplied with the libraries and other intellectual opportunities which alone can keep them in the mental health and strength necessary for their task. A still more serious defect has been the inadequacy of their training. They have neither been grounded nor confirmed in the ideal of a liberal education. They are a class for whom a university course is most desirable and yet, for the greater number, such a course is still beyond reach. In our judgment, it is a vital necessity for the nation that in its universities adequate room should always be available for those who are to be engaged in the work of education. In the meantime, until the changes necessary for this purpose can be effected, we believe that something might be done to help the existing staff of teachers by voluntary effort on the part of men and women who have themselves received a university education and have time to spare for lecturing in schools or training colleges. The enrolment of a fraternity of itinerant preachers on English Literature – a panel of men and women who are recognised authorities on their own subjects and are willing to lecture upon them occasionally – would be a step in accord with other movements of the time and with our national tradition of unpaid public service. It would not only reinforce the regular army of teachers but would have an important social effect by counteracting the influences which tend to bitterness and disintegration. Many of the differences between the lot of one class and another are of little importance; but the present advantage of rich over poor in our schools – the difficulty of the attempt to pass up the intellectual ladder and to attain the spiritual freedom conferred by a real education – is keenly and rightly felt as an unnecessary and unjust inequality. Nothing would, in our belief, conduce more to the unity and harmony of the nation than a public policy directed to the provision of equal intellectual opportunities for all, and service to this end would be doubly effective if it came voluntarily as from those who have already received their inheritance, and desire to share with the rest of their countrymen that in which their life and freedom most truly consist.

Notes

1. In *Culture and Anarchy*, Arnold wrote that culture 'seeks to do away with classes.'
2. # Report of the Prime Minister's Committee on the Teaching of Natural Science [the Thomson Committee, 1918], section 23.
3. W.R. Inge (1860–1954).
4. Arthur Clutton Brock (1868–1924).
5. # xiii.160–169; and see v.402–534; 594–607.
6. 'Tubby' Clayton (1885–1972), founder of Toc H.
7. P.B. Clayton, *Tales of Talbot House* (1919).
8. J.H. Newman, 'Elementary Studies' in *Lectures and Essays on University Subjects* (1859), later included in *The Idea of a University* (1873).
9. # This does not refer to dialect, for which see sections 69, 144.
10. #*The Teaching of English in Secondary Schools* (1910), section 21.

Sources of Texts

Abbott, E.A. 'The Teaching of English.' *Macmillan's Magazine*, 18 (1868), 33–9.

Anon. 'On the Teaching of English Language and Literature.' Parts I, II and III. *Museum and English Journal of Education*, 4 (1867), 1–5; 46–50; 81–6.

—— 'The Study of English Classics.' *Museum and English Journal of Education*, 3 (1867), 441–5.

Arnold, Matthew. General Reports for 1852, 1860, 1871, 1872, 1876, 1880; this text from *Reports on Elementary Schools, 1852–1882, by Matthew Arnold*. Ed. Francis Sandford. London, 1889.

Blair, Hugh. *Lectures on Rhetoric and Belles Lettres*. 1783; this text from later edition: London, 1817.

Bradley, G.G. Minutes of Evidence to the Schools Inquiry Commission. *Report of the Schools Inquiry Commission*. London, 1868. Minutes 4022–4170.

Campbell, Thomas. 'Suggestions respecting the Plan of a College in London.' *New Monthly Magazine and Literary Journal*, 13 (1825), 404–19; 14 (1825), 1–11.

[Collins, John Churton]. Review of *From Shakespeare to Pope*, by Edmund Gosse. *Quarterly Review*, 163 (1886), 289–329.

—— Review of Petition addressed to the Hebdomadal Council for the Foundation of a School of Modern Literature at Oxford. *Quarterly Review*, 164 (1887), 241–69.

[Copleston, Edward]. Review of Letter to Mr Brougham on the subject of a London University, together with 'Suggestions respecting the Plan of a College in London,' by Thomas Campbell. *Quarterly Review*, 33 (1825).

Dale, Thomas. *An Introductory Lecture delivered in the University of London on Friday, October 24, 1828*. London, 1828.

Freeman, Edward. 'Literature and Language.' *Contemporary Review*, 52 (1887), 549–67.

Hales, J.W. 'The Teaching of English.' *Essays on a Liberal Education*. ed. F.W. Farrar. London, 1867, pp.293–312.

Kingsley, Charles. 'On English Composition' and 'On English Literature.' *Introductory Lectures delivered at Queen's College, London*. London, 1849, 28–66.

[Macaulay, Thomas Babington]. 'Thoughts on the Advancement of

Academical Education in England.' *Edinburgh Review*, 43 (1826), 315–41.

Maurice, F.D. *Has the Church or the State the Power to Educate the Nation?* London, 1839.

—— 'Introductory Lecture by the Professor of English Literature and Modern History at King's College, London, delivered Tuesday, October 13.' *Educational Magazine*, NS 2 (1840), 273–88.

—— *Learning and Working*. Cambridge, 1855.

Pall Mall Gazette. Letters to the Editor, 1886–1887; these texts from *English Literature and How to Study It* (*Pall Mall Gazette* Extra No. 32). London, 1887.

Ryder, Dudley, Earl of Harrowby. Minutes of Evidence to the Schools Inquiry Commission. *Report of the Schools Inquiry Commission*. London, 1868. Minutes 14056–14128.

Seeley, John. 'English in Schools.' *Macmillan's Magazine*, 17 (1868), 75–86.

Sidgwick, Henry. 'The Theory of Classical Education.' *Essays on a Liberal Education*. Ed. F.W. Farrar. London, 1867, pp.81–143.

The Teaching of English in England: Being the Report of the Departmental Committee Appointed to Inquire into the Position of English in the Educational System of England, London, 1921.

University College, London. Report of a Committee of the Senate on the Candidates for the Chair of English Language and Literature, November 1865. University College London Library. MS. College Correspondence AM105.

Works Cited in the Introduction

Anon. 'Mr Dale's Introductory Lecture.' *Athenaeum*, No. 54 (5 November 1828), 858.

Bacon, Alan. 'Attempts to Introduce a School of English Literature at Oxford: the National Debate of 1886 and 1887.' *History of Education*, 9 (1980), 303–13.

—— 'The Changing Fashions in English Studies at University College, London.' *Durham University Journal*, 85 (1993), 45–66.

—— 'English Literature Becomes a University Subject: King's College, London as Pioneer.' *Victorian Studies*, 29 (1986), 591–612.

De Quincey, Thomas. 'Rhetoric.' *Collected Writings*. Ed. David Masson. Edinburgh, 1890. X, 81–133.

Doyle, Brian. 'The Hidden History of English Studies.' *Re-Reading English*. Ed. Peter Widdowson. London, 1982, pp.17–31.

Maurice, F.D. 'Female Education.' *Metropolitan Quarterly Magazine*, 2 (1826), 265–82.

Maurice, Frederick. *The Life of Frederick Denison Maurice.* London, 1884.

McKerrow, R.B. *A Note on the Teaching of English Language and Literature.* English Association Pamphlet No. 49. London, 1921.

Rose, Hugh James. *Eight Sermons Preached before the University of Cambridge.* London and Cambridge, 1833.

Select Bibliography of Other Works Cited

Angus, Joseph. *A Handbook of the English Tongue.* London, 1862.

Arnold, Matthew. *The Popular Education of France.* London, 1861.

Ascham, Roger. *The Schoolmaster.* London, 1570.

Astle, Thomas. *The Origin and Progress of Writing.* London, 1784.

[Badham, Charles]. 'French Education.' *Quarterly Review,* 117 (1865), 396–418.

Barnes, William. *Se Gefylsta – the Helper: an Anglo-Saxon Delectus.* London, 1849.

Biber, George Edward. *Henry Pestalozzi and his Plan of Education.* London, 1831.

Brinsley, John. *Ludus Literarius: or The Grammar School.* London, 1612.

Campbell, George. *The Philosophy of Rhetoric.* Edinburgh, 1776.

Chambers's Etymological Dictionary of the English Language. Ed. James Donald. London and Edinburgh, 1867.

[Cheney, R.H.]. 'Public Schools.' *Quarterly Review,* 116 (1864), 176–211.

Collins, John Churton. *The Study of English Literature.* London, 1891.

Crombie, Alexander. *The Etymology and Syntax of the English Language.* London, 1802.

Dalgleish, Walter Scott. *Grammatical Analysis.* London and Edinburgh, 1865.

——— *Outlines of English Grammar and Analysis for Elementary Schools.* London and Edinburgh, 1867.

Donaldson, John. *The New Cratylus, or Contributions towards a More Accurate Knowledge of the Greek Language.* Cambridge, 1839.

Edel, Leon. *Henry James: the Conquest of London, 1870–1883.* London, 1962.

Farrar, F.W. *Chapters on Language.* London, 1865.

Furnivall, F.J. *Education in Early England.* London, 1867.

Gosse, Edmund, *From Shakespeare to Pope: an Inquiry into the Causes and Phenomena of the Rise of Classical Poetry in England.* Cambridge, 1885.

Home, Henry, Lord Kames. *Elements of Criticism.* Edinburgh, 1762.

Jonson, Ben. *The English Grammar.* London, 1640.

Morell, John. *A Grammar of the English Language.* Edinburgh, 1857.

Morley, Henry. *English Writers.* 11 vols. London, 1864–1895.

Morris, Richard. (ed.) *Specimens of Early English, selected from the Chief English Authors, AD 1250 to AD 1400.* Oxford, 1867.

Mulcaster, Richard, *Elementarie*. London, 1582.

Newman, J.H. *The Idea of a University*. London, 1873.

Palgrave, Sir Francis, *History of the Anglo-Saxons*. London, 1831.

Rask, Rasmus. *A Grammar of the Anglo-Saxon Tongue*. Translated by Benjamin Thorpe. Copenhagen, 1830.

Rénan, Ernest. *De l'Origine du Langage*. Paris, 1848.

Robinson, Hugh G. *The Literary Reader*. London and Edinburgh, 1867.

Trench, Richard Chenevix, *English Past and Present*. London, 1855.

—— *On the Study of Words*. London, 1851.

Vernon, Edward. *A Guide to the Anglo-Saxon Tongue*. London, 1846.

Wallis, John. *Grammatica Linguae Anglicanae*. Oxford, 1653.

Wilson, Thomas. *The Arte of Rhetorique*. London, 1553.

Index

Italicized page references indicate material collected in this volume.

09-27-99